What's New In Nine: Visual FoxPro's Latest Hits

Tamar E. Granor
Doug Hennig
Rick Schummer
Toni M. Feltman
Jim Slater

Hentzenwerke Publishing

Published by:
Hentzenwerke Publishing
980 East Circle Drive
Whitefish Bay WI 53217 USA

Hentzenwerke Publishing books are available through booksellers and directly from the
publisher. Contact Hentzenwerke Publishing at:
414.332.9876
414.332.9463 (fax)
www.hentzenwerke.com
books@hentzenwerke.com

What's New In Nine: Visual FoxPro's Latest Hits
    By   Tamar E. Granor, Doug Hennig, Rick Schummer, Toni F. Feltman, and Jim Slater
    Technical Editor: Jim Slater
    Copy Editor: Nicole McNeish
    Cover Art: "Premiere" by Todd Gnacinski, Milwaukee, WI

ISBN: 1-930919-64-6

Manufactured in the United States of America.

Our Contract with You, The Reader

In which we, the folks who make up Hentzenwerke Publishing, describe what you, the reader, can expect from this book and from us.

Hi there!

I've been writing professionally (in other words, eventually getting a paycheck for my scribbles) since 1974, and writing about software development since 1992. As an author, I've worked with a half-dozen different publishers and corresponded with thousands of readers over the years. As a software developer and all-around geek, I've also acquired a library of more than 100 computer and software-related books.

Thus, when I donned the publisher's cap eight years ago to produce the *1997 Developer's Guide,* I had some pretty good ideas of what I liked (and didn't like) from publishers, what readers liked and didn't like, and what I, as a reader, liked and didn't like.

Now, with our new titles for 2005, we're entering our eighth season. (For those who are keeping track, the '97 DevGuide was our first, albeit abbreviated, season, the batch of six "Essentials" for Visual FoxPro 6.0 in 1999 was our second, and 2000 through 2004 comprised our third through seventh seasons.)

John Wooden, the famed UCLA basketball coach, posited that teams aren't consistent; they're always getting better—or worse. We'd like to get better...

One of my goals for this season is to build a closer relationship with you, the reader. In order for us to do this, you've got to know what you should expect from us.

- You have the right to expect that your order will be processed quickly and correctly, and that your book will be delivered to you in new condition.

- You have the right to expect that the content of your book is technically accurate and up-to-date, that the explanations are clear, and that the layout is easy to read and follow without a lot of fluff or nonsense.

- You have the right to expect access to source code, errata, FAQs, and other information that's relevant to the book via our Web site.

- You have the right to expect an electronic version of your printed book to be available via our Web site.

- You have the right to expect that, if you report errors to us, your report will be responded to promptly, and that the appropriate notice will be included in the errata and/or FAQs for the book.

Naturally, there are some limits we bump up against. There are humans involved, and they make mistakes. A book of 500 pages contains, on average, 150,000 words and several megabytes of source code. It's not possible to edit and re-edit multiple times to catch every last misspelling and typo, nor is it possible to test the source code on every permutation of development environment and operating system—and still price the book affordably.

Once printed, bindings break, ink gets smeared, signatures get missed during binding. On the delivery side, Web sites go down, packages get lost in the mail.

Nonetheless, we'll make our best effort to correct these problems—once you let us know about them.

In return, when you have a question or run into a problem, we ask that you first consult the errata and/or FAQs for your book on our Web site. If you don't find the answer there, please e-mail us at books@hentzenwerke.com with as much information and detail as possible, including 1) the steps to reproduce the problem, 2) what happened, and 3) what you expected to happen, together with 4) any other relevant information.

I'd like to stress that we need you to communicate questions and problems clearly. For example…

- "Your downloads don't work" isn't enough information for us to help you. "I get a 404 error when I click on the **Download Source Code** link on **www.hentzenwerke.com/book/downloads.html**" is something we can help you with.

- "The code in Chapter 10 caused an error" again isn't enough information. "I performed the following steps to run the source code program DisplayTest.PRG in Chapter 10, and I received an error that said 'Variable m.liCounter not found'" is something we can help you with.

We'll do our best to get back to you within a couple of days, either with an answer or at least an acknowledgment that we've received your inquiry and that we're working on it.

On behalf of the authors, technical editors, copy editors, layout artists, graphical artists, indexers, and all the other folks who worked to put this book in your hands, I'd like to thank you for purchasing this book, and I hope it will prove to be a valuable addition to your technical library. Please let us know what you think about this book—we're looking forward to hearing from you.

As Groucho Marx once observed, "Outside of a dog, a book is a man's best friend. Inside of a dog, it's too dark to read."

Whil Hentzen
Hentzenwerke Publishing
January 2005

List of Chapters

Table of Contents

Chapter 14: Language Improvements   299

Acknowledgements

As always, a book like this doesn't get written without contributions from a lot of people whose names aren't on the cover.

This book was written by the five of us, but it would never have been finished nor would it be as good as we hope it is without the contributions of many others. First and foremost is our friend and publisher, Whil Hentzen, who agreed to publish yet another Visual FoxPro book after telling the world he wasn't going to do that any more. His willingness to take a risk, along with a clever plan for making this book available as it was being written, gave us the chance to dive in.

Thanks as always to our copy editor, Nicole McNeish, who comes along when we're done writing and makes sure that what you get to read is clear and concise.

We tried something new this time and asked our technical editor, Jim Slater, not only to make sure we got it all right, but to write a chapter of his very own. Our thanks to him for taking on a double challenge.

The Visual FoxPro team at Microsoft is a very special group. They keep giving us better and better versions of this wonderful product. They also put up with us when we ask for help understanding how something works or why it's there. We offer deep gratitude to the whole team and particular thanks to Trevor Hancock, Jim Saunders, Aleksey Tsingauz, Randy Brown, Richard Stanton, Lisa Slater Nicholls, and Colin Nicholls.

We learn as much from the other VFP beta testers as we do from the documentation. That's not because the documentation is poor, but because the group of people who test Visual FoxPro are brilliant, hardworking, and generous. We won't single out individuals, but instead thank everyone who helped us in our quest to "get it."

My husband, Marshal, and our sons, Solomon and Nathaniel, are the best part of my life. My deepest appreciation to them for everything they do and for giving me the time and space to do work I love.

Tamar

Thank you to my lifetime programming partner and husband Mike for not being angry when I agreed to work on this book without discussing it with him first. See, writing few chapters was not so bad after all. I also greatly appreciate your help in trying to figure out why things work the way they do. I am truly blessed to have a live-in geek.

Also thank you to my wonderful son Mickey, who always understands when it's not a good time to bug Mommy. Thank you for making me smile when I really wanted to pull my hair out.

Finally, thank you to Doug and Rick for asking me to help out on this project. It was actually pretty fun.

Toni

This book is dedicated my parents (Carole and Phil) and my in-laws (Bob and Marie). Thanks to each of you for teaching me the value of hard work, the importance of honesty and integrity, the significance of helping others by giving back, and providing me the building blocks to be a good husband and father.

Thanks to my wife, Therese, for her unlimited patience and understanding. This time I really, really promise (no fingers crossed) not to take on another book before the list of home projects is reduced. Therese allowed me to break this promise less than four weeks after I told her I would not work on another book when I finished *Deploying Visual FoxPro Solutions* in May. Yes, two books in one year is crazy. Thanks to Tamar and Doug for asking me to be a part of this book, it was a great ride.

Rick

My thanks once again go to the loves of my life, my wife Peggy and son Nicholas. They left me alone on Saturdays and Sundays throughout the summer so I could wrestle with the new features and write about them. Thanks also to my long-time friend Mike White, who showed unbelievable optimism, strength, and courage, and even cheered *me* up, while fighting the big "c."

Doug

Thanks to Dan for his patience when editing took priority over our other work. Thanks to Tom, Karen, Ira, and Sally for listening to my complaints. Thanks to my cat Jack for making sure none of the pages blew away. And thanks to Tamar and Doug for inviting me along once again.

Jim

About the Authors

Tamar E. Granor

Tamar E. Granor, Ph.D., is the owner of Tomorrow's Solutions, LLC. She has developed and enhanced numerous FoxPro and Visual FoxPro applications for businesses and other organizations. She currently focuses on working with other developers through consulting and subcontracting. Tamar served as Editor of FoxPro Advisor magazine from 1994 to 2000. She is the magazine's Technical Editor and co-author of the popular Advisor Answers column.

Tamar is author or co-author of the award winning *Hacker's Guide to Visual FoxPro* and *Microsoft Office Automation with Visual FoxPro* and the previous *What's New in Visual FoxPro* books. Her most recent book is *OOoSwitch: 501 Things You Wanted to Know about Switching to OpenOffice.org from Microsoft Office.*

Tamar is a Microsoft Certified Professional and a Microsoft Support Most Valuable Professional. Tamar speaks frequently about Visual FoxPro at conferences and user groups in North America and Europe, including every FoxPro DevCon since 1993. She is a Lecturer in the School of Engineering and Applied Sciences at the University of Pennsylvania. She served as Technical Content Manager for the 1997-1999 Visual FoxPro DevCons and was part of the coordination team for the Visual FoxPro Excellence Awards.

Tamar earned her doctorate in Computer and Information Science at the University of Pennsylvania, where her research focused on implementation of user interfaces. Tamar lives in suburban Philadelphia with her husband and two sons.
Email: **tamar@tomorrowssolutionsllc.com**

Doug Hennig

Doug Hennig is a partner with Stonefield Software Inc. He is the author of the award-winning Stonefield Database Toolkit (SDT), the award-winning Stonefield Query, and the MemberData Editor, Anchor Editor, New Property/Method Dialog, and CursorAdapter and DataEnvironment builders that come with Microsoft Visual FoxPro.

Doug is co-author of the *What's New in Visual FoxPro* series and *The Hacker's Guide to Visual FoxPro 7.0*. He was the technical editor of *The Hacker's Guide to Visual FoxPro 6.0* and *The Fundamentals*. All of these books are from Hentzenwerke Publishing. Doug writes the monthly "Reusable Tools" column in FoxTalk. He has spoken at every Microsoft FoxPro Developers Conference (DevCon) since 1997 and at user groups and developer conferences all over North America. He is a Microsoft Most Valuable Professional (MVP).
Web: **www.stonefield.com** and **www.stonefieldquery.com**, Email: **dhennig@stonefield.com**

Rick Schummer

Rick Schummer is the president and lead geek at his company White Light Computing, Inc., which is headquartered in southeast Michigan, USA. He prides himself in guiding his customers' Information Technology investment toward success. He enjoys working with top-notch developers; has a passion for developing software using best practices, and for surpassing customer expectations, not just meeting them. After hours he writes developer tools that improve productivity and occasionally pens articles for FoxTalk, FoxPro Advisor, and several user group newsletters.

Rick co-authored Hentzenwerke Publishing's *Deploying Visual FoxPro Solutions* with Rick Borup and Jacci Adams, *MegaFox: 1002 Things You Wanted To Know About Extending Visual FoxPro,* and the award-winning *1001 Things You Wanted To Know About Visual FoxPro (KiloFox)* with Marcia Akins and Andy Kramek.

Rick is a Microsoft Most Valuable Professional (VFP) and a Microsoft Certified Professional. He is founding member and Secretary of the Detroit Area Fox User Group (DAFUG), and he presents at user groups across North America, and at the GLGDW 2000-2003, EssentialFox 2002-2004, Southwest Fox 2004, and VFE DevCon 2K2 conferences.

He spends his free time with his family, cheers the kids as they play soccer and compete in robotics competitions, has a volunteer role with the Boy Scouts, and loves spending time camping, cycling, coin collecting, reading, and cooking breakfast on Sunday mornings. You can reach Rick at **raschummer@whitelightcomputing.com** and **rick@rickschummer.com**. His company Web site is **http://whitelightcomputing.com** and his personal Web site is **http://rickschummer.com**.

Toni M. Feltman

Toni M. Feltman is a partner in F1 Technologies, located in Toledo, OH, and one of the principal developers of the FoxExpress product line. She also wrote the public domain tool ProjectHookX and is a contributor to DBCX which is a public domain data dictionary tool.

Toni has spoken at many technical conferences various user groups throughout the world. She was a judge of the 1998 and 1999 Visual FoxPro Excellence Awards. Prior to F1 Technologies, Toni worked for Fox Software, the company that originated FoxPro. Toni is also an instructor at the University of Toledo where she teaches a wide variety of computer related courses, primarily in the areas of database and Internet development. Toni can be reached via e-mail at **tfeltman@f1tech.com** or on the web at **www.f1tech.com**.

Jim Slater

Jim Slater is an independent developer specializing in VFP client/server applications and .Net web and Windows Forms applications. He has extensive experience with every version of Foxbase, FoxPro and Visual FoxPro, as well as with SQL Server and Sybase databases.

Jim is a Microsoft Certified Professional and past Microsoft MVP. His articles and tips have appeared in several publications including FoxPro Advisor, and he was the technical editor of *What's New in Visual FoxPro 8.0.* He is vice president of the Rocky Mountain FoxPro User Group and a frequent presenter at user group meetings.

Jim lives in Denver, CO and enjoys hiking, fly fishing and snowshoeing in those rare moments away from the computer. Email: **jims@jslater.com**.

How to Download the Files

Hentzenwerke Publishing generally provides two sets of files to accompany its books. The first is the source code referenced throughout the text. Note that some books do not have source code; in those cases, a placeholder file is provided in lieu of the source code in order to alert you of the fact. The second is the e-book version (or versions) of the book. Depending on the book, we provide e-books in either the compiled HTML Help (.CHM) format, Adobe Acrobat (.PDF) format, or both. Here's how to get them.

Both the source code and e-book file(s) are available for download from the Hentzenwerke Web site. In order to obtain them, follow these instructions:

1. Point your Web browser to **www.hentzenwerke.com**.

2. Look for the link that says "Download"

3. A page describing the download process will appear. This page has two sections:

- **Section 1:** If you were issued a username/password directly from Hentzenwerke Publishing, you can enter them into this page.

- **Section 2:** If you did not receive a username/password from Hentzenwerke Publishing, don't worry! Just enter your e-mail alias and look for the question about your book. Note that you'll need your physical book when you answer the question.

4. A page that lists the hyperlinks for the appropriate downloads will appear.

Note that the e-book file(s) are covered by the same copyright laws as the printed book. Reproduction and/or distribution of these files is against the law.

If you have questions or problems, the fastest way to get a response is to e-mail us at **books@hentzenwerke.com**.

Introduction

Like its predecessors, the goal of this book is to bring you up to speed with a new version of Visual FoxPro as quickly as possible.

Writing a book about a new version of Visual FoxPro is a lot of fun, except when it isn't. The product is a moving target and the chapter we wrote last week is wrong this week. On the other hand, writing about the new features of VFP pushes us not only to test them, but to truly understand them so we can explain them to you.

While the VFP documentation is good and gets better with each new version, figuring out what changed and what you can do with it is hard. That's where this book comes in. We took all the new additions and changes and organized them by topic. Throughout the book, we try to show you not just how it works, but why and where you'd use it.

Organization

This book has four major divisions. The first section, comprising chapters 1 to 4, looks at the tools you use to create applications. The changes here range from simple ones, like more control over fonts, to a brand new tool, the Data Explorer.

The second section, chapters 5 through 7, covers the crowning glory of VFP 9, the Report Designer. After almost no changes to this tool in a decade, VFP 9 finally tackles the beast and offers astonishing new functionality.

The third section, chapters 8 through 12, looks at VFP's core expertise, data. We cover the new data types, a new type of index, a host of changes related to working with remote data, and more.

Finally, the last section, chapters 13 to 15, considers everything else. It includes changes to the object model, new and modified commands and functions, and changes related to runtime and deployment.

Picture that

We use two icons throughout this book to help you find some things quickly:

 This image means there's something particularly noteworthy or a behavior to be especially aware of.

This image indicates there's related material available for download. See page xix for details. The code for each chapter is contained in a separate zip file and should include everything you need.

Put it to work

We hope this book provides everything you need to easily make the transition from VFP 8 to VFP 9. We're excited about this new version and believe you will be too.

Chapter 1
Project Manager Improvements

The Project Manager is the key tool for building executables and the primary tool Visual FoxPro developers use to modify the source code in applications they create. Any change the Fox Team can work into the product increasing productivity or making it a better experience has a high impact on Visual FoxPro developers.

The Project Manager has been tweaked over the last few releases to make day-to-day development a little easier. We think you will find the tweaks in this version a big help when you develop your applications. This chapter covers the changes to the Project Manager and the projecthook object, which you can use to respond to the interaction you have with the Project Manager. We also discuss some of the enhancements with respect to building your application using the Project Manager and the BUILD command. If you are looking for information on creating setups and deploying applications check out Chapter 15, "Setup and Deployment."

Generating message logs during project build

Prior to Visual FoxPro 9, the build process (whether you used the Build button in the Project Manager, the BUILD command, or the project object's Build method) did not write out the error log until it was done. This meant if the build failed (stopped by Visual FoxPro or by the developer canceling), the error log was not written, and was not available to be reviewed. Typically you cancel the build when the build process presents an error or a missing file and you realize what the error is and how you want to correct it. The problem is, by the time you open the source code, you forget the details and have no way to get the details without rebuilding. In Visual FoxPro 9, the build process generates the log when the process starts and adds to it as errors and warnings are encountered.

This is a big deal if you have large projects and you hit an error you know you need to fix before testing the build. At the time the error displays, you can cancel the build process and review the error log to gather the details, make the fix in the source, and start the long build process again.

This enhancement gets even better. If the Debug Output window is open (see **Figure 1**), the same error messages are output to this window along with a complete log of the build process. An entry is output to the Debug Output window as each file/module/method compiles. Additional entries are made as the files/modules/methods are analyzed for dependencies (see **Listing 1** for an example of one class library's log output).

The error log file starts fresh each time a build is started. If no errors are recorded during the build process, the error log file is deleted; otherwise, the process would leave an empty error log.

The Debug Output window is not cleared before each build; the new information is appended to the Debug Output window. This allows you to review, compare, and contrast one build with the next. You can also save the logged output in the Debug Output windows to a file using the Save As option in the Debug Output window's shortcut menu. (Save As is not a new feature, just a hint of how you can leverage this logged information.)

Listing 1. *This is a partial listing of the content in the Debug Output window after a project build is complete.*

```
Build Project: Visual Class Library wlcutils
    Module:    cplatform_access
    Module:    cfullosname_access
    Module:    cosversion_access
    Module:    cservicepack_access
    Module:    cshortservicepack_access
    Module:    ccompleteosinformation_access
    Module:    cbasicosinformation_access
    Module:    release
    Module:    getappversion
    Module:    getappfileinformation
    Module:    cappnametosearch_assign
    Module:    cappdirectory_assign
    Module:    init
    Module:    release
Analyzing:
    Module: CPLATFORM_ACCESS
    Module: CFULLOSNAME_ACCESS
    Module: COSVERSION_ACCESS
    Module: CSERVICEPACK_ACCESS
    Module: CSHORTSERVICEPACK_ACCESS
    Module: CCOMPLETEOSINFORMATION_ACCESS
    Module: CBASICOSINFORMATION_ACCESS
    Module: RELEASE
Analyzing:
    Module: GETAPPVERSION
    Module: GETAPPFILEINFORMATION
    Module: CAPPNAMETOSEARCH_ASSIGN
    Module: CAPPDIRECTORY_ASSIGN
    Module: INIT
    Module: RELEASE
```

The COMPILE command lists the modules compiled in the Debug Output window the same way Build does.

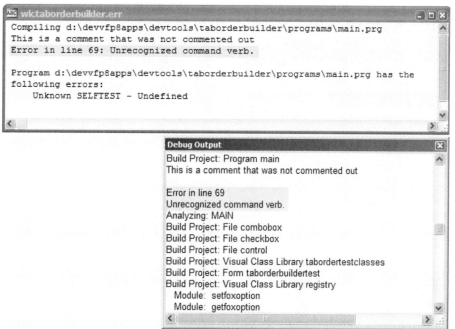

Figure 1. *The build process now records details of the build in the Debug Output window in addition to the normal error log file.*

Change the Project Manager font

The Visual FoxPro Project Manager look and feel has remained virtually unchanged in the last several versions. Visual FoxPro 9 introduces the ability to change the item list (treeview) and file description font (not the page tabs, or any of the command buttons). A change to the font in the Project Manager is hardly a big bang change, but it is our opinion that anything enhancing usability and accessibility is an improvement in productivity for someone visually challenged or for developers running at very high resolutions on smaller monitors.

You can define the default font for all projects by setting the font on the IDE page of the Tools | Options dialog. The process of making the setting is not overly intuitive: first, set the window type to Projects using the Type dropdown list, and then select the font (see **Figure 2**).

Change the Project Manager font for the open project by right-clicking the Project Manager and using the Font... option on the shortcut menu (see **Figure 3**). The Font... menu item is not available if you use the shortcut menu from the Project Manager's item list; you need to right-click outside of the project item list. This feature is not available for a docked project.

If you choose an italic style for the font, the Project Manager displays the file names, categories, and file descriptions in italics, but selecting the bold style has no impact. This is because the main file for the project displays in bold. The font attributes for the project are stored in the FoxUser resource file in a PRJUI record where the Name column contains the project file name (without the extension).

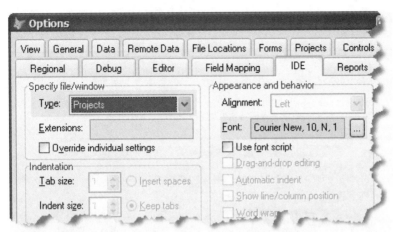

Figure 2. The Options dialog lets you set the default font for all project windows.

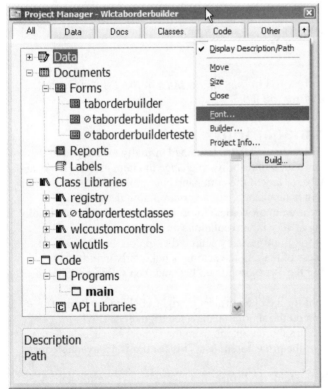

Figure 3. The Project Manager's shortcut menu lets you change the item list font for the open project.

Additional Project Manager shortcut menu items

There are a number of changes to the Project Manager shortcut menus. You see three different shortcut menus. The first when the Project Manager is docked, the second in the item list of undocked/collapsed dropdown tabs (and in tear-off tabs), and the third when the Project Manager is undocked without being collapsed.

The majority of the changes affect developers who dock their projects to a toolbar. The additional items on the shortcut menu for a docked project (**Figure 4**) include:

- Close: closes the project.

- Add Project to Source Control…: opens the add to source control dialog, and is only included on the menu if the active source control provider is selected on the Tools | Options dialog Projects page.

- Errors…: displays the error log file from the last build, and is only enabled if the last build produced and recorded errors.

- Refresh: updates the list of files in the project, and new classes in class libraries.

- Clean Up Project: packs the deleted records from the project file (PJX).

Figure 4. *The shortcut menu when the Project Manager is docked has many more items in VFP 9 than in VFP 8.*

The captions for some items in the shortcut menu for the collapsed or docked Project Manager item list (found on the dropdown tabs and tear-off tabs) has changed; in addition, Rename File moved to a different position in the list. There is no additional functionality (see **Figure 5**).

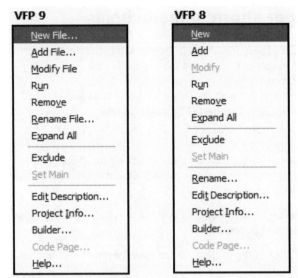

Figure 5. *The shortcut menu for the Project Manager's item list has slightly different (more informative) captions and the Rename File... menu item moved up in the list.*

We already detailed the Font... option in the "Change the Project Manager font" section earlier in this chapter. This option is the only new shortcut menu option added and is only available when the Project Manager is not docked and not collapsed.

Modifying a class library from the Project Manager

You can now double-click a visual class library in the Project Manager item list or click the Modify command button to open the class library in the Class Browser. Prior to Visual FoxPro 9, nothing happened when you double-clicked a class library; the Modify command button was disabled when a class library was selected in the item list.

If you don't like the new behavior, you can prevent it by issuing NODEFAULT in the QueryModifyFile event of projecthook (see **Listing 2**). You can also intercept the QueryModifyFile event and run your own class library tool (see **Listing 3**).

*The Developer Downloads for this chapter, available from **www.hentzenwerke.com**, include two projecthook classes (phkStopClassBrowser and phkRunOldFashionClassHackingTool) in the wn9ProjectHookDemos.vcx.*

Listing 2. *The QueryModifyFile event method can be coded to stop a class library from opening in the Class Browser (example from phkStopClassBrowser class).*

```
LPARAMETERS toFile, tcClassName

* Only for class libraries
IF LOWER(JUSTEXT(toFile.Name)) = "vcx"
   * Only when no class is selected
```

```
      IF EMPTY(tcClassName)
         * Provide behavior found in VFP 8 and earlier
         NODEFAULT
      ENDIF
   ENDIF
ENDIF

RETURN
```

Listing 3. *The QueryModifyFile event method can be coded to open your favorite class hacking tool (example from phkRunOldFashionClassHackingTool class).*

```
LPARAMETERS toFile, tcClassName

#DEFINE IDYES         6        && Yes button pressed
#DEFINE IDNO          7        && No button pressed

* Only for class libraries
IF LOWER(JUSTEXT(toFile.Name)) = "vcx"
   * Only when no class is selected
   IF EMPTY(tcClassName)
      lnAnswer = IDNO

      * Offer choice if this option is enabled
      IF this.lOfferChoiceOfClassBrowser
         lnAnswer = MESSAGEBOX("Would you prefer to open " +  ;
                              toFile.Name + ;
                              " in VFP Class Browser even though" + ;
                              "you have the old-fashioned BROWSE "+ ;
                              "hacking option enabled via " + ;
                              "the projecthook?", ;
                              4+32, ;
                              "Modify Class Library")
      ENDIF

      IF lnAnswer = IDYES
         * No additional functionality, rather "documenting"
         * that the normal behavior is desired in this situation
         RETURN .T.
      ELSE
         * Run your favorite class library tool from
         * White Light Computing
         * DO hackcx4.exe WITH toFile.Name
         IF USED("curHack")
            USE IN (SELECT("curHack"))
         ENDIF

         USE (toFile.Name) IN 0 SHARED ALIAS curHack

         SELECT curHack
         BROWSE LAST FONT "Tahoma", 12 NAME goOldHack NOWAIT
         NODEFAULT
      ENDIF
   ENDIF
ENDIF

RETURN
```

The key to working with the class library functionality of the Project Manager is to check the parameters passed to the QueryModifyFile method. You can determine whether a class library was passed by evaluating the extension of the file parameter, and checking whether the class name parameter is empty. (If it's a VCX and the class name parameter is not empty, you are modifying a specific class of the class library.)

In addition to intercepting, stopping, and altering the behavior of double-clicking the class library, you can allow the Class Browser to open after you alter the normal behavior by returning .T. (also the default return value) from the QueryModifyFile event method. This could be a problem if you open the class library via a USE...EXCLUSIVE in your own tool because the Class Browser expects to open the the class library when it starts. If you want to open the class library in your tool and the Class Browser, make sure to open it via USE...SHARED.

ProjectHook SCCInit and SCCDestroy methods

Since the introduction of ProjectHooks in Visual FoxPro 6, developers have tried to integrate with source code control when opening a project and again when closing a project. According to Microsoft, when a project is opened, the developer wants to check out specific files from source code control, and when a project is closed, some or all the checked-out files should be checked in. You can't use the Init and Destroy methods of the ProjectHook (which fires when project is opened and closed, respectively) because the link to the source code control provider is not established in Init, and is broken in the Destroy. The file object's CheckIn, CheckOut, GetLastestVersion, AddToSCC, RemoveFromSCC, and UndoCheckOut methods only work once the project is opened and displayed in the Project Manager.

In Visual FoxPro 9, Microsoft provides two new projecthook events. The SCCInit event fires after the link to source code control is established, but before the project is activated. The order of projecthook events when opening the project is:

1. Init

2. SCCInit

3. Activate

The SCCDestroy event fires before the link to source code control is broken, and before the projecthook is destroyed. The order of events when closing a project is:

1. Deactivate

2. SCCDestroy

3. Destroy

The following sections explore some of the things you might do with these new events.

Check out files

Microsoft added the new events in response to requests from developers for the ability to check out all the files needed when opening the project. We're not big fans of the integrated source code control functionality and prefer to use the source code control client user interface to check files out as needed. But checking out everything when opening a project sounded interesting and like a potential time saver, so it is the first feature we tried.

 The Developer Downloads for this chapter, available from ***www.hentzenwerke.com***, *include projecthook classes (phkSCCCheckOutAllFiles and phkSCCCheckOutFilesOnce) in the wn9ProjectHookDemos.vcx that demonstrate using the SCCInit event to check out files when opening the project. The sample code provided for this section of the chapter will not work unless you have a source code control application like Visual Source Safe installed and accessible.*

The code in **Listing 4** is found in the CheckOut method of the phkSCCCheckoutAllFiles class. The CheckOut method is called from the SCCInit event method. This follows the best practice of never using an event method to hold the primary code for the desired behavior. In addition, it avoids the problem of losing code if we compile this class in VFP 8 or earlier. Because the SCCInit event is not part of VFP 8, any code in SCCInit disappears during the next compile in that version, and is lost, even if you reopen the class in Visual FoxPro 9. Code in a custom method is not deleted; only the code in the event methods is lost (which is a lot easier to fix if all it does is call the custom method).

Listing 4. *This code programmatically checks out all the files not currently checked out in a project (under source code control).*

```
* phkSCCCheckoutAllFiles::CheckOut()

#DEFINE cnFILECOLUMN          1
#DEFINE cnFILESTATUS          2

* File Object SCCStatus Property (available in FoxPro.h)
#DEFINE SCCFILE_NOTCONTROLLED 0   && Not source controlled
#DEFINE SCCFILE_NOTCHECKEDOUT 1   && Controlled but not checked out to anyone
#DEFINE SCCFILE_CHECKEDOUTCU  2   && Checked out to the current user only
#DEFINE SCCFILE_CHECKEDOUTOU  3   && Checked out to someone else
#DEFINE SCCFILE_MERGECONFLICT 4   && Has a merge conflict
#DEFINE SCCFILE_MERGE         5   && Has been merged without conflict
#DEFINE SCCFILE_CHECKEDOUTMU  6   && Checked out to multiple users

LOCAL loProject, ;
      loFile, ;
      llCheckoutStatus

loProject = _vfp.ActiveProject

IF EMPTY(loProject.SCCProvider)
    * Source Code Control not used for this project
    DEBUGOUT "No source code control provider to check out files"
ELSE
    FOR EACH loFile IN loProject.Files
        IF loFile.SCCStatus = SCCFILE_NOTCHECKEDOUT
            * Attempt to check out file...
            WAIT WINDOW "Checking out file: " + ;
                    TRANSFORM(loFile.Name) + ;
```

```
                    "..." NOWAIT

         llCheckoutStatus = loFile.CheckOut()

         this.nFilesCheckedOut = this.nFilesCheckedOut + 1

         DIMENSION this.aFiles[this.nFilesCheckedOut, 2]
         this.aFiles[this.nFilesCheckedOut, cnFILECOLUMN] = loFile.Name
         this.aFiles[this.nFilesCheckedOut, cnFILESTATUS] = llCheckoutStatus

         DEBUGOUT loFile.Name + ;
                  IIF(llCheckoutStatus, SPACE(0), " not") + ;
                  " checked out - " + ;
                  TRANSFORM(DATETIME())
      ELSE
         * Nothing to do
      ENDIF
   ENDFOR
ENDIF

RETURN
```

The code first checks to see if the project is using integrated source code control. If so, it loops through the Files collection and checks to find files not currently checked out. This is accomplished by evaluating the SCCStatus property for each file. If the file is not checked out, it attempts to check it out by calling the file object's CheckOut method. The CheckOut method returns True if the file was successfully checked out. It logs the process by recording the file name and check out status to an array property called aFiles and displays a message in the Debug Output window.

The drawback of this approach is the Check Out Files dialog (see **Figure 6**) is presented for every file not already checked out when this method runs. The current file is selected for check-out in the dialog, so all you have to do is click the OK button and the checkout process is attempted. Having to click OK or Cancel for each of the files in a project is tedious. You can select all the files you want to check out the first time the dialog is presented. This avoids the dialog being presented for each of the files individually. Still canceling all the files you do not want checked out will reduce your productivity.

If you want to see the Check Out Files dialog once, you can use the code in **Listing 5,** found in the CheckOut method (called from the SCCInit event method) of the phkSCCCheckoutFilesOnce class. The disadvantage of this approach is you lose the individual file logging functionality, so you will not be able to determine if a certain file failed to check out. We think you will find this trade-off well worth it and more productive. If all files are already checked out, you get a message "Project error. There are no files to check out." This is the same message you get when using the Project menu to check out files and no files need to be checked out.

Listing 5. *This code presents the Check Out Files dialog once when opening a project.*

```
LOCAL loProject, ;
      loFile

loProject = _vfp.ActiveProject
```

```
IF EMPTY(loProject.SCCProvider)
   * Source Code Control not used for this project
   DEBUGOUT "No source code control provider to check out files"
ELSE
   loFile = loProject.Files[1]
   loFile.CheckOut()
ENDIF

RETURN
```

The advantage of this approach is you can cancel the Check Out Files dialog and move on to the task of development if you do not want to check any files out. Alternatively, you can select the files when you open the individual source files (the same dialog appears). If you use the check out process when opening a project, you ensure that you have the current versions of the files. Otherwise, one of your teammates could grab a file before you get a chance to edit it.

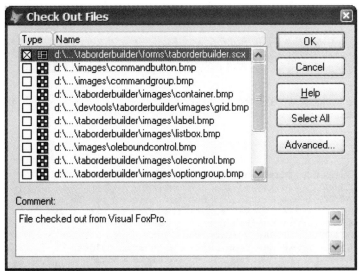

Figure 6. *The Check Out Files dialog appears each time the file object's CheckOut method is called.*

You might ask why we did not write the reverse code to check the files into source code control via the SCCDestroy event method. We feel the check-in process requires a commitment from the developer that the code is solid and tested and ready to be integrated with the rest of the code in the project before it is checked into source control. This is not something we can control programmatically; therefore we did not implement it in our sample classes. We open and close projects frequently and do not want files checked in just because we closed the project.

Get latest version of files

The biggest advantage we saw with the SCCInit event when we first read about it was the ability to get the latest version of the files from source code control. We frequently need to make sure we have the latest version of source code other members of the team might be changing. Automating this when the project is opened could save us the extra step of making the manual request.

 The Developer Downloads for this chapter, available from **www.hentzenwerke.com**, *include projecthook classes (phkSCCGetLatestAllFiles and phkGetLatestFilesOnce in wn9ProjectHookDemos.vcx) that demonstrate how the SCCInit event can help you get the latest version of source code files when opening a project.*

Unfortunately, like the CheckOut example, calling GetLatestVersion leads to dialogs appearing. With this in mind, we created two projecthooks to address the issue the same way we did with the CheckOut process. **Listing 6** shows you how to get the latest version of all files with individual logging, and **Listing 7** shows you how to present the Get Latest Version dialog once, but give up logging.

Listing 6. *This code programmatically gets the latest version of all the files not currently checked out in a project (under source code control), or have a merge conflict status.*

```
* Code to get the latest version of all files that are
* not already checked out.

#DEFINE cnFILECOLUMN         1
#DEFINE cnFILESTATUS         2

* File Object SCCStatus Property (available in FoxPro.h)
#DEFINE SCCFILE_NOTCONTROLLED 0  && Not source controlled
#DEFINE SCCFILE_NOTCHECKEDOUT 1  && Controlled but not checked out to anyone
#DEFINE SCCFILE_CHECKEDOUTCU  2  && Checked out to the current user only
#DEFINE SCCFILE_CHECKEDOUTOU  3  && Checked out to someone else
#DEFINE SCCFILE_MERGECONFLICT 4  && Has a merge conflict
#DEFINE SCCFILE_MERGE         5  && Has been merged without conflict
#DEFINE SCCFILE_CHECKEDOUTMU  6  && Checked out to multiple users

LOCAL loProject, ;
      loFile, ;
      llGetLatestStatus

loProject = _vfp.ActiveProject

IF EMPTY(loProject.SCCProvider)
   * Source Code Control not used for this project
   DEBUGOUT "No source code control provider to get latest version of files"
ELSE
   FOR EACH loFile IN loProject.Files
      IF INLIST(loFile.SCCStatus, SCCFILE_NOTCONTROLLED, ;
                                  SCCFILE_CHECKEDOUTCU, ;
                                  SCCFILE_MERGECONFLICT)
         * Nothing to do, either not in SCC, or already checked out,
         * or there is a merge conflict (highly unlikely with VFP
         * source code and integrated source code control).
      ELSE
```

```
      * Attempt to get the latest version of file...
      WAIT WINDOW "Getting latest version of file: " + ;
                  TRANSFORM(loFile.Name) + ;
                  "..." NOWAIT

      llGetLatestStatus  = loFile.GetLatestVersion()
      this.nFilesUpdated = this.nFilesUpdated + 1

      DIMENSION this.aFiles[this.nFilesUpdated, 2]
      this.aFiles[this.nFilesUpdated, cnFILECOLUMN] = loFile.Name
      this.aFiles[this.nFilesUpdated, cnFILESTATUS] = llGetLatestStatus

      DEBUGOUT loFile.Name + ;
               IIF(llGetLatestStatus, SPACE(0), " not") + ;
               " updated - " + ;
               TRANSFORM(DATETIME())
    ENDIF
  ENDFOR
ENDIF

RETURN
```

Listing 7. *This code presents the Get Latest Version of Files dialog once when opening a project.*

```
LOCAL loProject, ;
      loFile

loProject = _vfp.ActiveProject

IF EMPTY(loProject.SCCProvider)
   * Source Code Control not used for this project
   DEBUGOUT "No source code control provider to update " + ;
            "latest version of files."
ELSE
   loFile = loProject.Files[1]
   loFile.GetLatestVersion()
ENDIF

RETURN
```

The code is very similar to the code used to demonstrate the check out process. The big difference is the checks made to the SCCStatus property to ensure you do not get the latest version of a file you already have checked out and possibly changed. The other difference, of course, is calling the GetLatestVersion method of the file object to tell the source code control provider to copy the latest version to your project folder.

Log source code control state

The final example for the SCCInit and SCCDestroy actually uses both events. In this example, we create a log of the source code control status for each file in the project. This log is sent to a text file, and can later be imported into a DBF given that the output is created as a comma delimited string.

The Developer Downloads for this chapter, available from
***www.hentzenwerke.com**, include a projecthook class (phkSCCListState in
wn9ProjectHookDemos.vcx) that demonstrates how you can list the status to
a log file.*

The ListStatus method (see **Listing 8**) can be found in the phkSCCListStatus class. This
method is called from both the SCCInit and SCCDestroy. The method accepts one parameter
allowing you to determine which of the two methods called it. The method collects details
about each file in the project and outputs them to a text file specified by the
cListStatusFileName property. The text file is always stored in the Visual FoxPro temporary
files folder; if it already exists, ListStatus adds the new information rather than overwriting it.

Listing 8. *This code records the SCCStatus of each file when opening and closing
a project.*

```
LPARAMETERS tcTiming

LOCAL loProject, ;
      lcStatusOutput, ;
      lcFileName

loProject      = _vfp.ActiveProject
lnFiles        = loProject.Files.Count
lcStatusOutput = REPLICATE("=", 60) + ;
                 CHR(13)+CHR(10) + ;
                 tcTiming + " - " + loProject.Name + ;
                 CHR(13)+CHR(10)


lcStatusOutput = lcStatusOutput + ;
                 TRANSFORM(DATETIME()) + ;
                 " - " + ;
                 loProject.SCCProvider + ;
                 REPLICATE(CHR(13)+CHR(10),2)

FOR lnI = 1 TO lnFiles
   lcSCCText      = SPACE(0)

   DO CASE
      CASE loProject.Files[lnI].SCCStatus = 0;
           AND this.lListCheckedOutOnly = .F.
        lcSCCText = "File is not source controlled."

      CASE loProject.Files[lnI].SCCStatus = 1;
           AND this.lListCheckedOutOnly = .F.
        lcSCCText = "File is in source control but is not checked out."

      CASE loProject.Files[lnI].SCCStatus = 2
        lcSCCText = "File is checked out to the current user."

      CASE loProject.Files[lnI].SCCStatus = 3
        lcSCCText = "File is checked out to someone other than " + ;
                    "the current user."
```

```
      CASE loProject.Files[lnI].SCCStatus = 4
         lcSCCText = "File has a merge conflict."

      CASE loProject.Files[lnI].SCCStatus = 5
         lcSCCText = "File has been merged without conflict."

      CASE loProject.Files[lnI].SCCStatus = 6
         lcSCCText = "File is checked out to multiple users."

      OTHERWISE
         IF this.lListCheckedOutOnly = .F.
            lcSCCText = "Invalid SCC Status."
         ENDIF
   ENDCASE

   IF EMPTY(lcSCCText)
      * Skip the output since it is filtered out
   ELSE
      lcStatusOutput = lcStatusOutput + ;
                       loProject.Files[lnI].Name + ;
                       ", " + ;
                       loProject.Files[lnI].Type + ;
                       ", " + ;
                       TRANSFORM(loProject.Files[lnI].SCCStatus) + ;
                       ", " + ;
                       lcSCCText + ;
                       ", " + ;
                       TRANSFORM(loProject.Files[lnI].LastModified) + ;
                       CHR(13)+CHR(10)
   ENDIF
ENDFOR

lcStatusOutput = lcStatusOutput + CHR(13)+CHR(10)
lcFileName     = this.cListStatusFilename

STRTOFILE(lcStatusOutput, lcFileName, .T.)
WAIT WINDOW "SCCStatus saved to:" + lcFileName NOWAIT

RETURN
```

This information collected allows you to review the status of the files over time, almost like an audit file indicating when files were in use by another developer, and changes you made to the state of source code control when you check files in and out.

Naturally this information is easier to analyze if it is in a DBF file. We include a method (called ImportStatus) in the projecthook to create a cursor and populate it with information from the text file. Once the details are loaded, you can write SQL queries to see how often a particular file was checked out by you or another developer, which files were never checked out, and which files in the project are not under source code control.

Summary
The changes to the Project Manager address some long-time enhancement requests (like the shortcut menus for docked projects), correct some usability issues (with the item list fonts and class libraries opening in the Class Browser), and eliminate some shortcomings with the source code control integration. We think you will agree there is a little something for everyone in the changes made with the Project Manager and projecthooks.

Updates and corrections for this chapter can be found on Hentzenwerke's website, **www.hentzenwerke.com**. Click "Catalog" and navigate to the page for this book.

Chapter 2
Controlling the
Properties Window

When creating forms and classes, the Properties Window is a major player. VFP 9 includes many improvements to this tool, from more control over fonts to the ability to add custom editors for properties.

Since its introduction in VFP 3, the Properties Window (known to most VFP developers as the Property Sheet, the term we'll use throughout this chapter) has seen mostly minor changes. Each new version brought a few tweaks. VFP 9 ups the ante significantly. Minor changes include more control over fonts and the addition of icons to the items. More significantly, the Property Sheet now includes a Favorites tab, and provides a mechanism to let you customize its behavior.

Cosmetic changes

No doubt, the first thing you'll notice when you open VFP 9's Property Sheet is that each item now includes an icon to the left of its name. The icons are the same as those used elsewhere in VFP (including IntelliSense's List Members and the Procedure dropdown in the method editor).

The next thing likely to hit your eye is that there are more colors than before. In VFP 8, everything in the Property Sheet is black, except for properties, events, and methods (PEMs) of ActiveX controls, which are blue by default, but can be changed. VFP 9 separates the Property Sheet colors into five groups described in **Table 1**. You can change the color for the first four groups, but the Default color is always black.

Table 1. The Property Sheet now lets you use up to five different colors.

Color group	Includes
ActiveX Color	PEMs of any ActiveX controls.
Non-Default Properties Color	PEMs set at the current level of the class hierarchy.
Custom Properties Color	PEMs added at any level other than the current level of the class hierarchy.
Instance Properties Color	PEMs added at the current level of the class hierarchy
Default	All other PEMs, that is, built-in PEMs not set at this level of the class hierarchy.

To change the color of any group, right-click the Property Sheet and choose the appropriate setting.

To see the Property Sheet's shortcut menu, don't right-click the main body of the Property Sheet (the part where the PEMs are listed). Instead, right-click the border area, the tabs, the object dropdown, or the Property Description section.

The color groups are not mutually exclusive. For example, an instance property or a custom property might also be non-default. The rules are as follows:

- PEMs added at the current level of the class hierarchy use the Instance Properties setting, whether they're changed or not.

- Other PEMs changed at the current level, whether they're inherited or built-in, use the Non-Default Properties setting. This includes PEMs of ActiveX controls.

- Custom PEMs inherited from the parent class and not changed at this level use the Custom Properties setting. This includes PEMs of ActiveX controls.

- PEMs of ActiveX controls not changed at any level of the class hierarchy use the ActiveX color.

- All remaining PEMs are shown in black.

In addition to colors, the VFP 9 Property Sheet gives you control over the font and font size. In VFP 8 and earlier versions, the shortcut menu gives you three choices: Small Font (the default), Medium Font, and Large Font. VFP 9 replaces those choices with a single Font... item; choose it to bring up the Font picker dialog. **Figure 1** shows the Property Sheet after changing the font to 12-point Tahoma bold.

The figure points out one interesting side effect of changing the font. Normally, changed properties are in bold and read-only properties are in italics. It turns out, however, those property attributes actually toggle the specified characteristics. So, in **Figure 1**, where the specified font is bold, the Caption property, which has been assigned at this level, is not bold. Similarly, if you specify an italic font for the Property Sheet, read-only properties are shown as not italic.

Specifying property values

In VFP 8 and earlier versions, the Property Sheet can accept no more than 255 characters for a property value. The introduction of the CursorAdapter class in VFP 8 and the need to specify its CursorSchema property made this limit a significant problem. In VFP 9, the limit has been raised to 8,191 characters.

In addition, earlier versions couldn't handle extended characters, like CHR(13) and CHR(10) (carriage return and line feed, respectively) in the Property Sheet. When you wanted to include them in a property, you had to specify it as an expression, such as "Line 1" + CHR(13) + CHR(10) + "Line 2". VFP 9 accepts these values. (This change was undoubtedly made to accommodate the _MemberData property, discussed in "Customizing the Property Sheet" later in this chapter.)

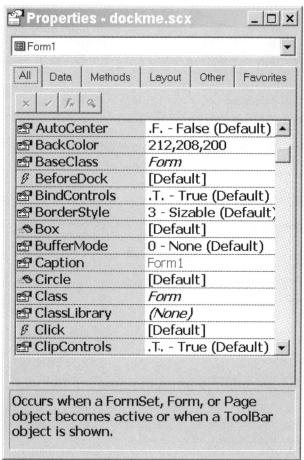

Figure 1. VFP 9 lets you specify the font to use in the Property Sheet.

Despite the new limit, some properties, like Caption and Alias, are limited to 255 characters by their nature. The same properties don't accept extended characters.

To enter long property values or extended characters, you can't just type the value in as usual. You have to use either the Zoom dialog or the Expression Builder. To make the process easier, a Zoom button has been added to the group of buttons above the list of properties. (See **Figure 1**.) In addition, the Zoom dialog is much larger in VFP 9 than in earlier versions.

To store longer property values and extended characters, the technique for parsing classes and forms has changed. As a result, classes and forms that include properties exceeding the limit or using extended characters cannot be opened in earlier versions of VFP. However, forms and classes created in VFP 9 that don't use long property values or extended characters can be opened in earlier versions.

The new format applies to the Properties memo field of the record in the SCX or VCX that represents the object in question. This field stores a list of the properties assigned in the Property Sheet in the form:

```
Property = Value
```

When the value is more than 255 characters or contains any of the extended characters, the format changes. The equal sign is followed by a space, and then 517 instances of CHR(1). After that, the length of the value is stored as an 8-byte character string. The length is followed by the actual value.

Another change makes it easier to get values into the Property Sheet in the first place. In earlier versions, when you add a custom property using the New Property dialog, you have to remember to switch to the Property Sheet and set the initial value for the property. In VFP 9, the New Property dialog (shown in **Figure 2**) includes an editbox to specify the initial value.

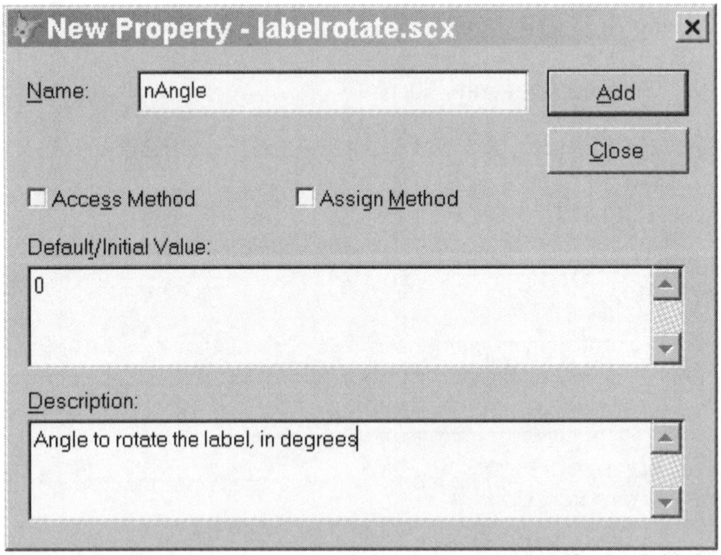

Figure 2. *The New Property dialog lets you specify the initial value of the property you're adding, so you don't have to remember to set it in the Property Sheet.*

Although the caption says "Default/Initial Value," the value you specify is only an initial value. That is, it specifies the property value when the form or class is created, but not the value you get if you choose Reset to Default in the Property Sheet.

Customizing the Property Sheet

The biggest change relating to the Property Sheet in VFP 9 is the ability to customize the contents in a number of ways. All of the customization is tied to a new, optional, property, _MemberData, which contains an XML string. You can set _MemberData manually or use the new MemberData Editor.

What kind of things can you do with _MemberData? First, _MemberData controls the new Favorites tab. For each property, event, or method (PEM) of a class or form, you can indicate whether it should be on the Favorites tab. _MemberData also lets you specify capitalization for custom PEMs. In earlier versions of VFP, once you add a property or method, it appears in lower-case on the Property Sheet and in IntelliSense. With _MemberData, you can specify the way it appears. Finally, for properties, you can specify a "property editor" to use for entering the property's initial value.

Unlike other properties, _MemberData is not included in new forms and classes automatically. You have to add it. (This is actually analogous to the Builder property you can add to a class to specify a custom builder.) However, the MemberData Editor can add it for you automatically.

The structure of _MemberData

_MemberData is an XML string containing VFP data (in the same format created by CursorToXML(), surely no coincidence). Between the <VFPData> and </VFPData> tags, there's one element, called memberdata, for each PEM with customization specified. The element has an attribute for each customization item for that PEM. For example, here's the _MemberData string for a form with a custom property, lFlag, and a custom method, MyMethod, capitalized as shown here, and with the AutoCenter property added to the Favorites page:

```
<VFPData><memberdata name="autocenter" type="property"
favorites="True"/><memberdata name="lflag" type="property"
display="lFlag"/><memberdata name="mymethod" type="method"
display="MyMethod"/></VFPData>
```

The definition for the memberdata element includes six attributes, as shown in **Table 2**. The schema is open, however, so you can add custom attributes and use them at runtime. Note that capitalization is significant in the _MemberData string, both for the attribute names and for True/False values. It appears not to matter for the value of the type attribute.

Table 2. *The memberdata element for each property, event, or method includes a subset of these attributes.*

Attribute	Values	Purpose
name		Contains the name of the PEM. Required.
type	"property" "event" "method"	Contains the type of PEM. Required.
display		Contains the name as it should display in the Property Sheet and with IntelliSense. Must be the same string as the name; only the capitalization can vary. Applies only to custom PEMs.
favorites	"True" "False"	Indicates whether the PEM is included on the Favorites page.
override	"True" "False"	Indicates whether settings unspecified at this level should be inherited from the parent class (False) or draw their values from the default settings for this PEM (True).
script		Contains VFP code to run as a Property Editor. (See "Creating property editors" later in this chapter.)

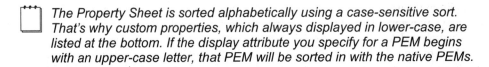

The Property Sheet is sorted alphabetically using a case-sensitive sort. That's why custom properties, which always displayed in lower-case, are listed at the bottom. If the display attribute you specify for a PEM begins with an upper-case letter, that PEM will be sorted in with the native PEMs.

The behavior of the override attribute is somewhat non-intuitive. For attributes specified at the current level, it's irrelevant. They have whatever value you assign at the current level. Override applies only to attributes you don't specify at the current level, and determines where those attributes get their values.

For example, consider a command button class (cmdTopLevel) with two custom properties: cMyFirstProp and cMySecondProp. In the button class, both have display and favorites attributes. The MemberData XML for the class is:

```
<VFPData>
<memberdata name="cmyfirstprop" type="property" display="cMyFirstProp"
favorites="True"/>
<memberdata name="cmysecondprop" type="property" display="cMySecondProp"
favorites="True"/>
</VFPData>
```

With these settings, both properties appear on the Favorites page and they're capitalized as you'd want them.

Now consider a subclass (cmdMiddleLevel). Suppose you set the override attribute for cMySecondProp to True, but also specify the display attribute. The MemberData XML for this class is:

```
<VFPData>
<memberdata name="cmysecondprop" type="property" display="cMySecondProp"
override="True"/>
</VFPData>
```

There's nothing specified for cMyFirstProp, so it draws its behavior from the parent class. That means cMyFirstProp appears on the Favorites page (and the property is capitalized as cMyFirstProp). However, with override set to True, cMySecondProp uses only the settings provided at this level. So, it doesn't appear on the Favorites page, though it's still properly capitalized, because that attribute is specified for this class.

Now consider a subclass of cmdMiddleLevel, called cmdBottomLevel. If you change none of the attributes at this level (that is, specify nothing for _MemberData), cFirst inherits its behavior from cmdTopLevel, so it appears on the Favorites page. cSecond inherits from cmdMiddleLevel and does not appear in Favorites.

*The Developer Downloads for this chapter, available at **www.hentzenwerke.com**, include Chapter2.VCX, a class library that contains the cmdTopLevel, cmdMiddleLevel, and cmdBottomLevel classes described here.*

Setting attributes globally

In addition to customizing a particular PEM in a particular class, you can specify that some customization applies to a PEM in every form or class with that PEM. For example, by default, the Caption and Anchor properties appear on the Favorites page.

Information about global customization is not stored in the _MemberData property of individual forms or classes, but in the IntelliSense table (referenced by the _FoxCode system variable and by default, FoxCode.DBF in the directory indicated by HOME(7)). PEM customization items have "E" in the Type field, the name of the PEM in the Abbrev field, and a MemberData string in the Tip field. For example, the default IntelliSense table contains a record for the Caption property, with the values shown in **Table 3**.

***Table 3**. You can specify custom behavior globally by adding records to the IntelliSense table. Here, the Caption property is added to the Favorites page and a custom property editor is specified.*

Field	Value
Type	E
Abbrev	Caption
Expanded	
Cmd	{CaptionScript}
Tip	\<VFPData>\<memberdata name="caption" type="property" favorites="True" script="DO (_CODESENSE) WITH 'RunPropertyEditor',",'caption'"/>\</VFPData>
Data	

You're not stuck with the global customization for a PEM; to override it in a particular form or class, just change it in the _MemberData string for that PEM in the form or class.

Inheriting _MemberData

_MemberData can be inherited either through the inheritance hierarchy or the containership hierarchy. The rules make sense, but they're different from those for other properties. Here's the order VFP will use to search for a memberdata attribute. Once it finds a value for a particular attribute, VFP stops searching.

- The _MemberData property of the object itself.

- The _MemberData property of classes in the inheritance hierarchy for the object, working upwards in the normal way.

- The _MemberData property of any containers, working upwards through the containership hierarchy.

- Any global memberdata settings, stored in the IntelliSense table.

For a given PEM, each attribute may be found in memberdata at a different point in the list.

Although memberdata can be "inherited" through the containership hierarchy, you can't add the _MemberData property to an object once you put it on a form or class. (That's because you can't ever add a property to a contained object.) However, if a contained object already has a _MemberData property, you can edit it for the instance on the form or class.

The MemberData Editor

Once you understand the structure of MemberData, it's not hard to specify it, but it's tedious enough that you're not likely to do so. That's especially true for global member data, where you have to modify the IntelliSense table.

Fortunately, there's an alternative. VFP 9 includes a new tool called the MemberData Editor, available from the Form or Class menu. The MemberData Editor (**Figure 3**) handles all the heavy lifting involved in adding the _MemberData property and populating it.

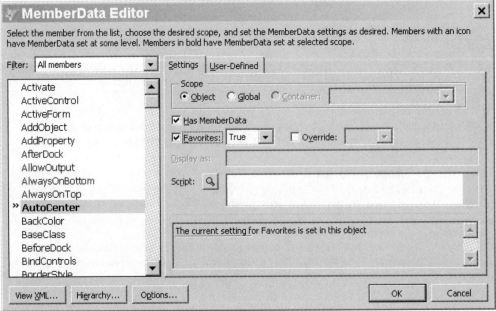

Figure 3. The MemberData Editor makes it easy to customize the Property Sheet.

The MemberData Editor lists all PEMs of the form or class in alphabetical order. PEMs with customization are shown in bold (like AutoCenter in **Figure 3**). You can limit the display in the list using the Filter dropdown. Filters include custom members only, custom members added in this class, native members only, and favorites only.

To customize a PEM, choose it in the list and select the Has MemberData checkbox. Next, specify the attributes you want. **Table 4** shows the relationship between the controls in the MemberData Editor and the _MemberData attributes.

Table 4*. The items in the MemberData Editor map to the attributes of the*
_MemberData string.

Control(s)	Attribute	Notes
Object/Global/Container	None	Determines whether the settings for this PEM are stored in the local _MemberData property (Object), the IntelliSense table (Global), or in the container's _MemberData property (Container).
Has member data	None	Indicates the PEM has member data. Provides a one-click way to remove all customization for a PEM.
Favorites checkbox and dropdown	favorites	Determines whether this PEM appears on the Favorites page. The checkbox indicates whether the memberdata element for this PEM has the favorites attribute. The dropdown specifies the setting for that attribute.
Override checkbox and dropdown	override	Determines whether unspecified settings at this level use the inherited settings or the defaults. The checkbox indicates whether the memberdata element for this PEM has the override attribute. The dropdown specifies the setting for the attribute.
Display as	display	Specifies the capitalization for this PEM.
Script	script	Specifies the code for a property editor for this property. (See "Creating property editors" later in this chapter.)

If a control on a form or class is selected when you open the MemberData Editor, the tool attempts to edit _MemberData for that control. If the control's class doesn't have a _MemberData property, you get a warning, after which the MemberData Editor opens showing the PEMs for the object, but saving any changes you make to the _MemberData property of the containing form or class.

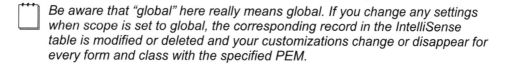
Be aware that "global" here really means global. If you change any settings when scope is set to global, the corresponding record in the IntelliSense table is modified or deleted and your customizations change or disappear for every form and class with the specified PEM.

The Description Pane (the disabled editbox near the bottom) shows you the current settings for the selected PEM. It indicates, for each attribute with memberdata at some level, which setting is in control. **Figure 3** shows the simplest case, with the attribute set at the local level. The listing can also indicate a global setting, a setting drawn from a container (in which the container is named), and a setting inherited from a parent class (in which case, the parent class is named).

Two buttons on the MemberData Editor also help you see exactly what settings apply. Click View XML to see the string that will be stored to the object's _MemberData property if you click OK. Click Hierarchy... for a detailed look at each level in the inheritance and containership hierarchy that affects the currently selected PEM, as well as the result, the settings that will be used for that PEM.

Listing 1 shows the result for the Caption property of the cmdMiddleLevel class in Chapter2.VCX.

Listing 1. When you click Hierarchy... in the MemberData Editor, you see each setting that has an effect on the selected PEM's memberdata.

```
Class - cmdmiddlelevel
<memberdata name="cmysecondprop" type="property" display="cMySecondProp"
override="True"/>
  Class - cmdtoplevel of chapter2.vcx
<memberdata name="cmysecondprop" type="property" display="cMySecondProp"
override="True"/>
Effective settings:
<memberdata name="cmysecondprop" type="property" display="cMySecondProp"
override="True"/>
```

Adding custom attributes

In addition to specifying the standard memberdata attributes, the MemberData Editor lets you define and specify your own attributes. While VFP itself won't use your custom attributes, they give you a place to store information (even code) for a class and have that information always present whatever you do with the class.

The user-defined page of the MemberData Editor (**Figure 4**) lets you add custom attributes. The page is available for a PEM only if **Has MemberData** is checked. Click the Add button to add an attribute—an input box appears for you to specify the name. Once you do that, use the Value textbox to provide the attribute's value.

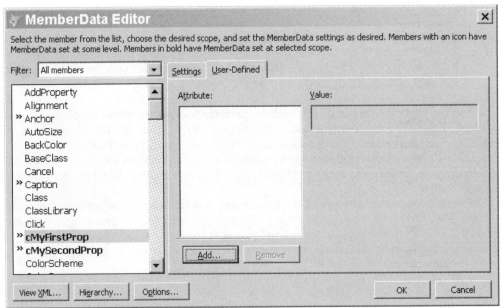

Figure 4. The User-Defined page of the MemberData Editor allows you to add custom attributes, which you can use to ensure information travels with a class.

What can you do with custom attributes? Here's one example. While you can specify a property editor for a custom property (see "Creating Property Editors" later in this chapter), you can't force people to use it. So imagine having an attribute called Valid that contains an expression determining the validity of the property's value. Of course, you need code to look for the attribute and evaluate the expression—you could put such code in a project hook. Here's a simple example of code to do so in the BeforeBuild method:

```
LPARAMETERS cOutputName, nBuildAction, lRebuildAll, lShowErrors, lBuildNewGuids

#DEFINE CRLF CHR(13) + CHR(10)

LOCAL oFile, aObj[1], cMembData, lFileResult, lResult
LOCAL cProblems

lResult = .T.

FOR EACH oFile IN This.oProject.Files
  DO CASE
  CASE INLIST(oFile.Type, "K", "V")
    * Open without running code
    IF oFile.Type="K"
      MODIFY FORM (oFile.Name) NOWAIT
    ELSE
      MODIFY CLASS (oFile.Name) NOWAIT
    ENDIF

    cProbs = "Validity checking " + oFile.Name + CRLF

    * Grab memberdata
    ASELOBJ(aObj, 1)
    IF PEMSTATUS(aObj[1],"__MemberData",5)
      cMembData = aObj[1].__MemberData
      * Convert to cursor
      XMLTOCURSOR(cMembData, "__MembData")
      * Look for Valid specs
      SELECT __MembData
      IF TYPE("__MembData.Valid") <> "U"
        * At least one item has a Valid attribute, so process it.
        lFileResult = .T.
        SCAN
          IF NOT EMPTY(__MembData.Valid)
            cValidExpr = __MembData.Valid
            * Substitute for "This"
            cValidExpr = STRTRAN(cValidExpr, "This", "aObj[1]")
            IF NOT EVALUATE(cValidExpr)
              cProbs = cProbs + "Failed test: " + __MembData.Valid + CRLF
              lFileResult = .F.
            ENDIF

          ENDIF
        ENDSCAN
      ENDIF
    ENDIF

    * Close the form or class
  OTHERWISE
    * Do nothing
  ENDCASE
```

```
   cProbs = cProbs + CRLF
   lResult = lResult AND lFileResult
ENDFOR

IF NOT lResult
  MESSAGEBOX(cProbs)
ENDIF

RETURN lResult
```

This simple version doesn't drill down to check for a Valid attribute at another level of the inheritance or containership hierarchy, but should give you a sense of the possibilities offered by custom attributes.

 The project hook described above is included in Chapter2.VCX in the Developer Downloads for this chapter, available from **www.hentzenwerke.com**

Customizing the MemberData Editor

The Options button on the MemberData Editor lets you control several aspects of its behavior. When you click it, the MemberData Options dialog (**Figure 5**) opens. The settings there are remembered between invocations of the MemberData Editor, and between classes. They're stored in the Resource table (by default, FoxUser.DBF in the directory specified by HOME(7)); the relevant record's ID field contains "MEMBERDATAED" while the Name field is "MemberDataEditor".

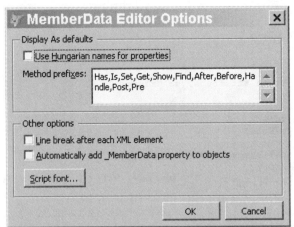

Figure 5. *You can control the behavior of the MemberData Editor using the settings in the Options dialog.*

The Display As defaults section simplifies the task of setting capitalization through the display attribute. When Use Hungarian names for properties is selected and you check Has Member Data for a property, its name is shown in the Display as textbox with the first letter in lowercase and the second letter in uppercase; this is useful for those of us who use the first letter of a property name to specify the type and begin the actual name with the second character.

It's not unusual for many method names to begin with one of just a few words. **Method prefixes** lets you specify a list of strings that should be seen as words at the beginning of a method and capitalized appropriately. That is, when a method name begins with one of the specified strings, the suggested **Display as** value capitalizes the first letter of that string and the first letter following the string. For example, using the default settings (shown in **Figure 5**), the suggested capitalization for a method named isnumeric would be "IsNumeric".

The **Other options** section lets you control appearances. If you select the **Line break after each XML element** checkbox, the XML created for _MemberData puts the memberdata element for each PEM on a separate line in the XML string. For example, with this setting selected, the _MemberData string shown in "The structure of _MemberData" section would appear as:

```
<VFPData>
<memberdata name="lflag" type="property" display="lFlag"/>
<memberdata name="mymethod" type="method" display="MyMethod"/>
</VFPData>
```

Newly created forms and classes don't have a _MemberData property. The MemberData Editor adds it as needed. However, you may prefer for each form or class to have the property; if so, select the **Automatically add _MemberData property to objects** checkbox. When that item is selected, a record is added to your IntelliSense table that automatically adds the _MemberData property to each form or class as you create or open it.

Finally, the **Script font** button lets you set the font used for the Script editbox on the Member Data page. Note that the font you choose isn't used for the window that opens when you click the Zoom button for the script; that's controlled by your setting for PRG files on the IDE tab of the VFP Options dialog.

When you click the **OK** button and at least one PEM has local customization specified, the MemberData Editor checks whether the current form or class has a _MemberData property, adds it if necessary, and generates the appropriate string. At the same time, any global customization specified is handled by adding records to the table specified by _FoxCode.

Replacing the MemberData Editor

Like many other tools in the VFP development environment, the MemberData Editor is written in VFP. (In fact, it was written by Doug Hennig, one of the authors of this book.) That means you can replace it with your own tool if you prefer.

However, the mechanism for replacing the MemberData Editor is different than for other tools written in VFP. Rather than providing a system variable (like _GenMenu or _CodeSense), the MemberData Editor is hooked into the Builder system. The table that drives the built-in Builder system (by default, Builder.DBF in the Wizards directory) contains a record for the MemberData Editor that points to MemberDataEditor.APP in the VFP home directory.

If you prefer to use another MemberData Editor, you have several choices. Once you create or acquire another application to serve this purpose, you can put it in the VFP home directory and name it MemberDataEditor.APP. (Of course, if you choose to name your replacement MemberDataEditor.APP, you should probably save a copy of the version that comes with VFP 9.) Alternatively, you can modify the record in the Builder table to point to the application you want to use. A third choice is to add another record to Builder.DBF for your editor; and then, when you invoke the MemberData Editor, you're prompted to choose between the editor provided and your custom version.

Finally, as with the other VFP tools written in VFP, the source code for the MemberData Editor comes with VFP. (Look in the XSource.ZIP file located in VFP's Tools\XSource directory.) If you just want to make minor changes, your best bet may be to modify the source code and build a custom version of the tool.

Playing favorites

While you can add PEMs to the Favorites tab using the MemberData Editor, there's actually an easier way. Right-click any PEM in the Property Sheet and choose **Add to Favorites**. Doing so automatically generates the appropriate MemberData string, adding the _MemberData property, if necessary.

Removing a PEM from the Favorites page isn't quite as easy; there's no Remove from Favorites item on the shortcut menu. You have to edit the _MemberData string directly or use the MemberData Editor.

Creating property editors

While a Favorites page and displaying the names of custom PEMs as you want them are both useful, the truly exciting feature enabled by _MemberData is the ability to create custom property editors.

A number of VFP's built-in properties provide a mechanism for choosing a value other than simply typing it in. For example, the various color properties (such as BackColor) use the Color Picker, while the Icon and Picture properties use a special version of the Open dialog (the same as the GetPict() function). You invoke these editors by clicking the ellipsis (...) button next to the textbox (called the "Property settings box" in Help) in the Property Sheet. In VFP 9, you can create your own dialogs or call on built-in dialogs for any property.

VFP 9 includes two property editors, both defined globally in FoxCode.DBF for the relevant property. The first uses the InputBox() function to let you specify a Caption. It's designed so you can use it for other properties as well. (See "Using IntelliSense for property editors" later in this chapter.)

The second Property Editor is for the new Anchor property. Anchor requires a numeric value, computed by adding the values of the appropriate settings. The Anchor Editor (AnchorEditor.App in the VFP home directory) lets you choose the settings you want and test them. Details of both the Anchor property and the Anchor Editor are discussed in Chapter 13, "Forms and Controls."

A Property Editor is, essentially, a builder, though it's generally focused on one or a few properties, where a builder addresses many properties of a control. Like a builder, a Property Editor has to do the heavy lifting involved in setting properties at design-time in its code. It receives no parameters and must figure out what object it's addressing and what property it's intended to change. (For global property editors, IntelliSense offers a somewhat smarter alternative; see "Using IntelliSense for property editors" later in this chapter.)

Use the ASELOBJ() function to figure out which object you're working on. There's one complication; if the property belongs to a form or container class rather than a control, ASELOBJ() doesn't find a selected object. In that case, you need to call it again, passing 1 for the optional second parameter, so it can find the form or container. This code finds the selected control, if there is one, and the form or container, if no control is selected. If it can't find either, it gives up:

```
IF ASELOBJ(aControl) = 0
   IF ASELOBJ(aControl, 1) = 0
      RETURN
   ENDIF
ENDIF
```

After executing this code (if it doesn't issue RETURN), aControl[1] contains an object reference to the selected control, form, or container. (In fact, if multiple objects are selected, the array contains references to all of them.)

Unfortunately, there's no generic way to figure out which property called the Property Editor, so you have to hard code the property name. **Listing 2** shows a Property Editor for a custom nEmphasisColor property; it brings up the Color Picker dialog.

Listing 2. *This Property Editor lets you use the Color Picker to choose a value for a custom property called nEmphasisColor.*

```
LOCAL aControl[1], nColor

IF ASELOBJ(aControl) = 0
   IF ASELOBJ(aControl, 1) = 0
      RETURN
   ENDIF
ENDIF

* Grab default value
IF VARTYPE(aControl[1].nEmphasisColor) = "N"
   nColor = aControl[1].nEmphasisColor
ELSE
   nColor = 0
ENDIF

nColor = GETCOLOR(nColor)

aControl[1].nEmphasisColor = nColor

RETURN
```

Clearly, a Property Editor is most useful for items that can't be easily typed in, like RGB color values. Another such item is the second parameter to the MessageBox() function, which specifies the icon and buttons to use. **Figure 6** shows a form that lets you make your choices and computes the value to pass. A Property Editor that calls on this form is shown in **Listing 3**; it's connected to a property called nMessageBoxParam. (Of course, if the parameter form is in a different directory than the form you're creating, the DO FORM command needs to include the appropriate path.)

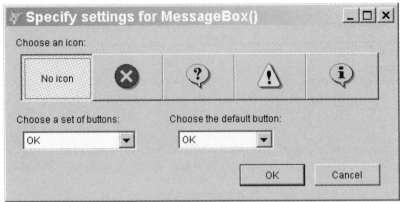

Figure 6. *Calculating the second parameter for MessageBox() is complicated. A Property Editor like this one makes it much easier.*

Listing 3. *Using the form in* ***Figure 6*** *as a Property Editor is simple.*

```
LOCAL aControl[1], nParam

IF ASELOBJ(aControl) = 0
  IF ASELOBJ(aControl, 1) = 0
    RETURN
  ENDIF
ENDIF

DO FORM MessageboxParams WITH aControl[1].nMessageBoxParams TO nParam

aControl[1].nMessageboxParams = nParam
```

 The Developer Downloads for this chapter, available from ***www.hentzenwerke.com****, include MessageBoxParams.SCX (the form in Figure 6) and PropertyEditors.SCX, a form that demonstrates the Color Picker Property Editor and the Property Editor for MessageBox() parameters.*

Using IntelliSense for property editors

Defining a Property Editor every time you need it would get tedious enough that you'd do it only for the most complicated properties. Fortunately, the VFP team included an alternative approach that takes advantage of the existing IntelliSense script system.

In addition to the new "E" record in the FoxCode table to support global _MemberData, the IntelliSense engine was enhanced with a method called RunPropertyEditor; this method lets you execute the code in a script record (type "S") as a Property Editor.

The Property Editor for the Caption property uses this mechanism, so we'll examine it to see how it works. The "E" record for Caption has "{CaptionScript}" in the Cmd field. The Tip field contains:

```
<VFPData><memberdata name="caption" type="property" favorites="True" script="DO
(_CODESENSE) WITH 'RunPropertyEditor','','caption'"/>
</VFPData>
```

The key item there is the script attribute, with the value:

```
DO (_CODESENSE) WITH 'RunPropertyEditor','','caption'
```

This line runs the IntelliSense engine, telling it to execute its RunPropertyEditor method and pass "caption" to that method. RunPropertyEditor finds the type "E" record in FoxCode corresponding to the parameter it receives. If the Cmd field of that record contains the name of a script record, the method locates that script record and executes the contents of the script record's Data field. For the Caption record, therefore, RunPropertyEditor looks for a record in FoxCode with Type = "S" and Abbrev = "CaptionScript". There is such a record; its Data field contains the code in **Listing 4**, which receives the property name as a parameter, finds all selected controls (or the form or container if no control is selected), prompts the user for a new caption, and then assigns the new value to the specified property of each selected object.

Listing 4. *This script (which comes with VFP 9) uses InputBox() to prompt for a new string value.*

```
#DEFINE    IBOX_CAPTION   "Caption Property Editor"
#DEFINE    IBOX_TEXT      "Enter value for property: "
#DEFINE    USER_CANCEL    "__usercancelled__"

LPARAMETERS tcProp
LOCAL ARRAY laObjs[1]
LOCAL lcRetVal, lnCnt, loCtl,lcDefValue, lnSuccess
IF ASELOBJ( laObjs)=0
  IF ASELOBJ( laObjs,1)=0
    RETURN
  ENDIF
ENDIF
lcDefValue=IIF(ALEN( laObjs,1)=1,laObjs[1].&tcProp,"")
lcRetVal=INPUTBOX(IBOX_TEXT + tcProp, IBOX_CAPTION, lcDefValue, 0, ;
               "", USER_CANCEL)
IF lcRetVal==USER_CANCEL
  RETURN
ENDIF
FOR lnCnt = 1 TO ALEN( laObjs,1)
  loCtl = laObjs[lnCnt]
  IF PEMSTATUS( loCtl, tcProp, 5 )
    loCtl.&tcProp = lcRetVal
  ENDIF
ENDFOR
```

This two-record architecture makes it easy to use a single Property Editor (defined in a type "S" record) for many different properties. For example, to use the CaptionScript for the Name property, add a type "E" record for Name with "{CaptionScript}" in the Cmd field and specify this line as the script for Name (using the MemberData Editor):

```
DO ( _CODESENSE) WITH 'RunPropertyEditor','','name'
```

Note that the line of code is identical to the one used for Caption, except for the final parameter.

You can apply the same mechanism to other property editors. For example, you might want to make the MessageBox() parameters Property Editor available as a script. To do so, first add a record to the FoxCode table, with the values in **Table 5**.

Table 5. *To create a new script record for the MessageBox() parameters, add a record to FoxCode with these settings.*

Field	Value
Type	"S"
Abbrev	"MessageScript"
Cmd	"{}"
Data	

```
LPARAMETERS tcProp

LOCAL ARRAY laObjs[1]
LOCAL lnRetVal, lnCnt, loCtl,lnDefValue, lnSuccess
IF ASELOBJ( laObjs)=0
  IF ASELOBJ( laObjs,1)=0
    RETURN
  ENDIF
ENDIF

lnDefValue=IIF(ALEN( laObjs,1)=1,laObjs[1].&tcProp,0)
lnRetVal =0
DO FORM "d:\writing\books\newin9\code\chapter2\MessageBoxParams.SCX" ;
    WITH lnDefValue to lnRetVal

FOR lnCnt = 1 TO ALEN( laObjs,1)
  loCtl = laObjs[lnCnt]
  IF PEMSTATUS( loCtl, tcProp, 5 )
    loCtl.&tcProp = lnRetVal
  ENDIF
ENDFOR
```

> 📝 Debugging IntelliSense scripts is difficult. If a script contains any compile-time errors, it will fail to run without any messages. If you're having trouble getting a script to run, try copying it to a PRG and compiling to find your errors. In addition, tracing may or may not work with property editors; in some cases, issuing SYS(2030,1) prior to running your Property Editor may work.

Once you have the script record set up, add a record to FoxCode for each property name you want to be able to set with this script. **Table 6** shows an example, for a property called nMessageParam. You can set up type "E" records that use the same script for as many properties as you want. Unfortunately, there doesn't appear to be a way to call on a script record without adding a type "E" record; it would handy to be able to create MemberData at the class level (ideally, using the MemberData Editor) that calls RunPropertyEditor to use a property editor defined in the IntelliSense table.

Table 6*. To use the MessageBox() parameters script, add a record like this to FoxCode.*

Field	Value
Type	"E"
Abbrev	nMessageParam
Cmd	{MessageScript}
Tip	

```
<VFPData><memberdata name="nmessageparam" type="property"
display="nMessageParam" script="DO (_CODESENSE) WITH
'RunPropertyEditor','','nmessageparam'
"/>
</VFPData>
```

*The Developer Downloads for this chapter, available at **www.hentzenwerke.com**, include AddMessageScript.PRG, a program that adds the records needed for the MessageBox() parameter Property Editor to the IntelliSense table.*

The bottom line

FoxPro developers spend a lot of their time working in the Property Sheet. With VFP 9, working there is easier and more configurable. We expect the FoxPro community to create and make available a number of property editors that will smooth your way through form and class definition.

Updates and corrections for this chapter can be found on Hentzenwerke's website, **www.hentzenwerke.com**. Click "Catalog" and navigate to the page for this book.

Chapter 3
Writing Code

No matter how good the visual tools, the vast majority of our work as FoxPro developers involves writing code. VFP 9 makes that task easier with a number of enhancements. Perhaps most welcome is the ability to use IntelliSense inside the WITH clause.

Day in and day out, VFP developers write code. We write code in PRG files, in the Command Window, in the method editor, in stored procedures, in memo fields, and many other places. Over the years, more and more tools to support writing code have been added, including such things as color-coded syntax, IntelliSense, Document View, and Code References. While code support isn't a major goal for VFP 9, several new or enhanced features make it easier than ever to work with code.

IntelliSense improvements

The addition of IntelliSense in VFP 7 increased the odds of getting code right in the first place. VFP 9 makes IntelliSense even more useful by offering support for it in the memo editor and inside the WITH and FOR EACH clauses. In addition, VFP 9 saves your IntelliSense settings between sessions, so you can configure it once and keep it that way. Perhaps most intriguing, IntelliSense is now supported at run-time.

Enable IntelliSense in memo fields

It's not unusual to store code in memo fields. In fact, most of the VFP tools themselves have at least one memo field that stores code. In VFP 8 and earlier, IntelliSense doesn't work in the memo field editor. VFP 9 adds support for IntelliSense there, providing it both at design-time and run time. (See "Give your users IntelliSense" later in this chapter for more on IntelliSense at run time.)

To turn on IntelliSense in a memo field, turn on syntax coloring for the field (right-click, Properties, and select Syntax coloring—if Word wrap is selected, you have to unselect it before the Syntax coloring check box is enabled). Once you turn syntax coloring and IntelliSense on for a given memo field, that information is stored in your resource file (by default, FoxUser.DBF) and persists for the specified field. (The syntax coloring requirement applies only in the design-time environment. When you offer IntelliSense at run time, syntax coloring does not have to be on.)

You can make syntax coloring and IntelliSense the default for all memo fields on the IDE page of the Options dialog (**Figure 1**). Choose Memo Fields from the Type dropdown list, and then check Syntax coloring. You can override this setting for individual memo fields by unchecking Syntax coloring in the Properties dialog for the specific field.

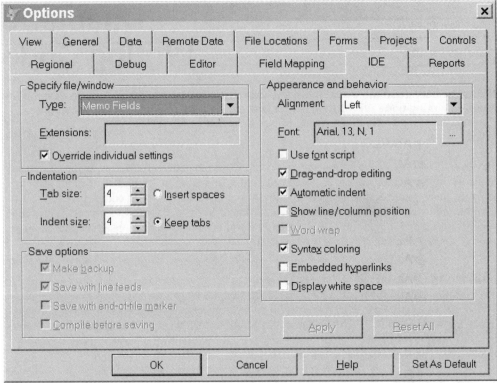

Figure 1. *To make IntelliSense the default for memo fields, use the IDE page of the Options dialog and turn on syntax coloring for memo fields.*

IntelliSense in WITH and FOR EACH commands

The WITH and FOR EACH commands offer shortcuts when writing code that works with objects. In earlier versions of VFP, however, WITH has a weakness; it doesn't support IntelliSense for the object named in the WITH statement. To get IntelliSense for the loop variable of a FOR EACH, you have to declare the variable as the appropriate type ahead of time.

VFP 9 provides a way to turn IntelliSense on inside these constructs. In both cases, the secret is to tell the editor the type of object you're addressing, and the syntax for both commands has been expanded to do so. The new syntax for WITH is:

```
WITH Object [ AS Class [ OF ClassLibrary ] ]
  Commands
ENDWITH
```

For example, if you're in a method of a control on a form based on the VFP form class, you could write:

```
WITH ThisForm AS Form
```

Then, when you hit the period, the list of properties, events, and methods (PEMs) for the form class appears, as in **Figure 2**.

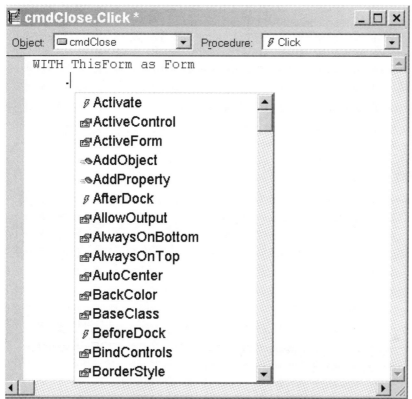

Figure 2. *When you specify the class of the object you're using in WITH, you get IntelliSense inside the WITH command.*

If the object is based on a custom class rather than a base class, you need to specify the class name and class library, like this:

```
WITH This.oRegistry as Registry OF HOME() + "\ffc\registry.vcx"
```

For an Automation object, you need to specify the server and object, such as:

```
WITH oDoc AS Word.Document
```

However, most Automation objects need to be registered with the IntelliSense Manager in order to have IntelliSense for their objects. (Use the Type Libraries button on the Type page of the IntelliSense Manager, available from the Tools menu.)

In addition to allowing you to specify the class of a named object, WITH now understands THIS at design-time, so you get the list of PEMs when you type the period inside:

```
WITH This
```
.

However, WITH does not support THISFORM. So, you can't use WITH THISFORM inside a control and get IntelliSense in the WITH, unless you add the AS clause to specify the form class. Similar syntax is used in the FOR EACH command. You can specify the class and, if necessary, the class library for the variable used to control the loop, and then have IntelliSense available for that variable inside the loop. The same rules used for the WITH apply for specifying the class:

- For VFP base classes, use just the name of the class.

- For VFP subclasses, use the name of the class and the class library, providing an appropriate path.

- For Automation objects, use the server name and class.

In **Figure 3**, the loop is controlled by oDoc, which is defined as Word.Document. Inside the loop, pressing "." after oDoc brings up the list of PEMs for a Word document.

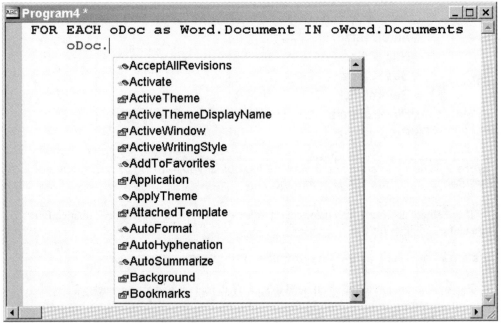

Figure 3. By defining the class of the variable controlling a FOR EACH loop, you enable IntelliSense for that variable inside the loop.

With the FOR EACH command, you can get the same effect by declaring the loop variable to be of the appropriate class prior to the loop.

Saving IntelliSense settings

The VFP IntelliSense Manager and the _VFP.EditorOptions property let you control the behavior of IntelliSense. However, in VFP 8 and earlier, some settings are not remembered from one VFP session to the next.

Most significantly, when you turn off IntelliSense, using either the Enable IntelliSense check box in the IntelliSense Manager or by setting _VFP.EditorOptions to omit the "L" and "Q" options, the setting lasts only until you shut down VFP and restart it. At that point, IntelliSense is turned on again. To turn off IntelliSense permanently (something we do not recommend), you have to set _VFP.EditorOptions in a startup program.

VFP 9 is smarter about this. It assumes that if you turn off IntelliSense or make some settings manual, you mean it.

Give your users IntelliSense

One of the coolest things about VFP's brand of IntelliSense is its extensibility. VFP 9 lets us take advantage of that feature to offer IntelliSense to the people who use our applications.

To include IntelliSense in an application, point the _FoxCode variable to an IntelliSense table in your code. The table can be the one that comes with VFP or a custom table containing shortcuts for your application. (If you use VFP's FoxCode table or any scripting, you should probably also set the _CodeSense system variable to point to FoxCode.App and make sure you distribute FoxCode.App with your application.) You can even provide a tool to allow your users to define their own shortcuts.

Not every type of IntelliSense item is supported at run time. **Table 1** shows the item types supported and what they cover. Script items can't be triggered directly (that's normal for IntelliSense), but are executed when triggered by other items.

Table 1. *Run-time IntelliSense supports only a subset of the items found in an IntelliSense table.*

Item type	Purpose
C	Command items. Expands the command as indicated and shows the tip for the command. Runs any specified script.
F	Function items. Expands the function name, and shows the tip for the function, including moving the highlight as parameters are entered. Runs any specified script.
S	Script items. Runs the script, inserting the result if there is one.
U	User items. Performs the specified substitution, including executing associated scripts.

Run-time IntelliSense applies only to the program editor (MODIFY COMMAND), file editor (MODIFY FILE), and memo windows. Unlike design-time, you do not have to turn on Syntax Coloring to use IntelliSense at runtime. Unfortunately, you can't turn on IntelliSense in edit boxes.

Consider using a custom IntelliSense table to provide shortcuts for phrases your users often need. By making it easy to enter boilerplate text, you increase the chance of users getting it right.

Background compilation

The first time you start typing in VFP 9, you may be baffled to see your code underlined. As you continue to type, the underlines go away...until you start the next line. The underlines are part of a new feature in VFP called *background compilation*. As you type, the VFP compiler checks to see whether what you've typed so far is syntactically valid. Until it is, it uses a special highlight (underlines, by default) to let you know.

You can control the appearance of background compilation in several ways. The Editor page of the Options dialog offers a dropdown (see **Figure 4**) where you can choose how syntactically invalid code is to appear. **Table 2** shows the four options.

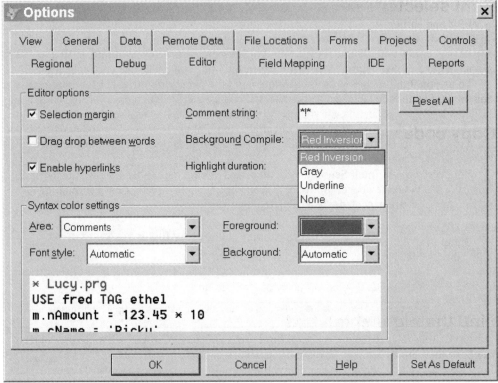

Figure 4. Use the Background Compile dropdown on the Editor page to control the coloring used for code that can't yet compile.

Table 2. You have four options for background compilation, including turning it off.

Option	Effect
Red Inversion	Shows invalid syntax in red, but valid keywords change to pink.
Gray	Shows invalid syntax in gray, including valid keywords.
Underline	Underlines invalid syntax, including valid keywords.
None	Invalid syntax uses the regular syntax coloring settings.

As soon as what you type forms a valid command, the colors change to whatever is specified for Syntax color settings on the same page of the Options dialog.

Background compilation occurs only with syntax coloring on. You control the use of syntax coloring on the IDE page of the Options dialog. It's controlled separately for each type of window. You can also control syntax coloring for an individual window using that window's Properties dialog.

Overall, our view is that, for experienced VFP developers, this feature isn't terribly useful. For newcomers, along with IntelliSense, it probably helps in coming up to speed. We suspect that eventually, all of us will turn background compilation off.

Print selected text

In VFP 8 and earlier, the Selection option button of the Print dialog is disabled. VFP 9 enables it when text is selected. This means you can print just some text from a program, memo field, or method without having to copy and paste the selected text into another window or application.

To use the Print dialog, you need to choose File | Print from the menu. Clicking the printer icon on the Standard toolbar prints the entire file.

Copy code with formatting

VFP 5 introduced syntax coloring. VFP 8 added the ability to print code in color. In VFP 9, you can take your syntax coloring with you when you copy code from VFP to another application.

When you copy from a code editor, including the Command Window, the highlighted text is placed on the clipboard as RTF (rich text format). If you paste into another application capable of dealing with RTF, the font used in the editor and syntax coloring are preserved.

We're of two minds about this behavior. It's great if you're posting code into, say, an online discussion, but for those of us who write about VFP regularly, it's inconvenient. Fortunately, the VFP team understood this distinction and gave us control over the behavior. Include "X" in the EditorOptions property of _VFP to turn off RTF copying.

Find the highlighted text

The last editing-related change is a minor one, but very elegant. If text is highlighted when you open the Find dialog, the first highlighted word is placed in the Look for text box, so you don't have to do a copy and paste. It's highlighted in the text box, so if it's not what you want, it's easy to overwrite it with the right search string. **Figure 5** demonstrates this; note that the highlighted string is trimmed before it's put into the text box.

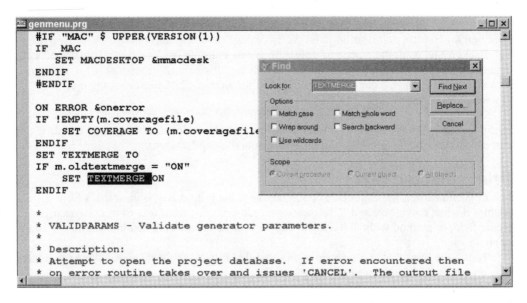

Figure 5. *When you open the Find dialog, highlighted text is automatically inserted as the string to search for.*

Better editing

While none of the changes in editing are revolutionary, all of them simplify the daily task of writing code. Together with the various improvements described in Chapter 1, "Project Manager Improvements," Chapter 2, "Controlling the Property Sheet," and Chapter 4, "Better Tools," they show the VFP team's commitment to making our day-to-day work easier.

Updates and corrections for this chapter can be found on Hentzenwerke's website, **www.hentzenwerke.com**. Click "Catalog" and navigate to the page for this book.

Chapter 4
Better Tools

Visual FoxPro has a long tradition of providing developers with tools that increase productivity so you can bring applications to market quicker. Visual FoxPro 9 continues this tradition in grand style.

The overhaul of the Report Designer seems to be the central focus for most developers in VFP 9. The Report Designer is the tool that garnered the biggest share of resources and definitely has a big impact for developers from a productivity viewpoint, and for end-user applications. However, it is not the only tool in Visual FoxPro that is better than in previous versions. This chapter focuses on the changes to the other IDE components, and shows you some of the changes we think will have a big impact on your productivity and the day-to-day development experience with Visual FoxPro.

Changes to Options dialog

Microsoft adds new settings to the Options dialog in each new version of Visual FoxPro, and Visual FoxPro 9 is no different.

The View page now has the setting to control the IntelliSense dropdown list count (formerly on the Editor page). You can use List display count to increase or decrease this setting from the default of 15 as low as 5 or as high as 200.

The File Locations page has new entries for the Menu Designer, Report Builder, Report Output, and Report Preview. These settings are related to the new _MENUDESIGNER hook for the Menu Designer discussed in detail later in this chapter, and the new Report System features hooked in by the _REPORTBUILDER, _REPORTOUTPUT, and _REPORTPREVIEW system variables (discussed in Chapter 5, "Enhancements in the Reporting System," Chapter 6, "Extending the Reporting System at Design Time," and Chapter 7, "Extending the Reporting System at Run Time").

The IDE page has one simple change, the new option of selecting Project from the Specify file/window dropdown (**Figure 1**). We discuss additional options for setting the Project Manager font in Chapter 1, "Project Manager Improvements."

The Reports page (**Figure 2**) is where Microsoft made the most changes to the Options dialog. All the changes to this page of the dialog reflect the new report system functionality. The Report Engine behavior dropdown allows you to configure the SET REPORTBEHAVIOR command to 80 for report functionality compatible with VFP 8 and earlier, or 90, which uses the object-assisted features included with Visual FoxPro 9. The impact of this new command is discussed in Chapter 7, "Extending the Reporting System at Run Time."

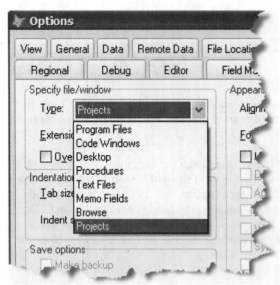

Figure 1. The IDE page of the VFP Options dialog is where you set the font for all projects.

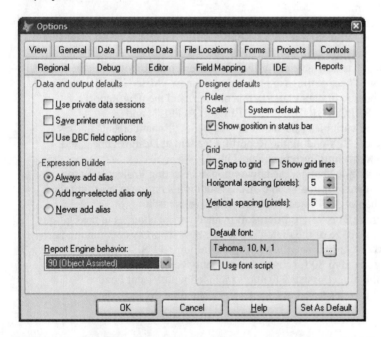

Figure 2. The Reports page of the Options dialog is where Microsoft made the most changes, specifically to support the new Reporting System.

Redirect Options dialog output

One of the little known tricks we often demonstrate to Visual FoxPro developers is the ability to send the Option dialog settings to code. The code is only generated if you hold down the Shift key when you click the OK button on the Options dialog. Prior to Visual FoxPro 9, this output was created in the Command Window. The output is now redirected to the Debug Output window if it is open. If the Debug Output window is not open, the code is not generated. The advantage of this new output location is simply not adding extra code to the Command Window because the code is retained between VFP sessions. Also, it's easy to save the contents of the Debug Output window to a file. The shortcut menu has a "Save As," so you don't have to cut and paste.

View and Query Designers

Microsoft made significant improvements to the View and Query designers in Visual FoxPro 8. The Visual FoxPro 9 upgrade includes one important enhancement and one major change in behavior.

Spaces in table and view names in FROM clause

The one enhancement to the View/Query designer centers on creating SQL Selects with spaces in either the base table or the base view name. Here is an example of a remote view to the SQL Server Northwind database using the "Current Product List" view.

```
SELECT Current_product_list.ProductID, ;
       Current_product_list.ProductName ;
   FROM dbo."Current Product List" Current_product_list ;
   WHERE  Current_product_list.ProductName LIKE ?vp_ProductName ;
   ORDER BY Current_product_list.ProductName
```

You must have an alias for the base table/view and the alias cannot have spaces in the name.

Visual FoxPro 8 allows you to create a local and remote view with spaces in the base table/view name. Error 36, "Command contains unrecognized phrase/keyword", occurs when the view is reopened in the designer and you attempt to save the view again. The View Designer now opens without an error and does not trigger the error when the view is saved again.

Macro expansion based SQL clauses

The behavior change with the View Designer involves views using macro expansion in the SQL Select clauses for local views. Microsoft has changed the way developers need to structure the SQL Select code to include one or more macro expansion variables inside the view. The macro expansion is performed when the view is opened. The design of such views allows developers to use one view for many different conditions (WHERE and HAVING clause for filtering, ORDER BY sorting, GROUP BY aggregation) instead of maintaining one view for every condition on the same set of base tables. It enables developers to create "on-the-fly" queries and still maintain the views in a database container.

> *Microsoft is on record stating views were not designed to support macro substitution for any clause. Developers have tried this and made it work and have implemented applications relying on this behavior. The View Designer behavior change discussed in this section demonstrates that Microsoft is not responsible for undocumented behavior, and your use of it might break code in your applications.*

 The Developer Downloads for this chapter, available from **www.hentzenwerke.com**, *include a database with views that include macro expansion clauses and some programs to create and use the macro expansion views. The database is called ViewDesignerChanges.DBC, and the programs are called CreateMacroSubViews.PRG and TestMacroSubViews.PRG.*

The big change with respect to macro expansion in view clauses is the way you store the macro expansion variable inside the DBC. This technique changed with the release of Visual FoxPro 8 and again with Visual FoxPro 9. Prior to Visual FoxPro 8, you had to ensure the macro variable was **not** declared or in scope when you created the view with code like this:

```
CREATE SQL VIEW AuthorsWithFlexibleClauses2 AS ;
    SELECT Authors.Authors_Pk, ;
           Authors.cLastName, ;
           Authors.cFirstName, ;
           Authors.cCountry;
      FROM viewdesignerchanges!Authors ;
      WHERE &?lcWhere ;
```

Note that the macro expansion variable is prefixed in the code with "&?." In VFP 8, Microsoft changed the rules so developers needed to remove the question mark normally used for view parameters:

```
CREATE SQL VIEW AuthorsWithFlexibleClauses2 AS ;
    SELECT Authors.Authors_Pk, ;
           Authors.cLastName, ;
           Authors.cFirstName, ;
           Authors.cCountry;
      FROM viewdesignerchanges!Authors ;
      WHERE &lcWhere ;
```

In Visual FoxPro 9, the rules change again. Macro expansion has reverted to the same style as Visual FoxPro 7 (both the ampersand and question mark). This means all existing views created or saved in Visual FoxPro 8 need the question mark added back in. If you skipped Visual FoxPro 8, you will not have to change a thing if you implemented macro expansion based views.

No matter how you create the views, the first step in Visual FoxPro 9 is to declare memory variables for each of the macro expansions you plan on including in your view. This is completely different from any previous version of Visual FoxPro. If you are using the View Designer or a third-party view editor, you can create PUBLIC memory variables in the Visual

FoxPro Command Window. If you create the view programmatically, you can declare the memory variables directly in the code. The variable is a character data type and must contain Visual FoxPro syntax that compiles cleanly. The variable or variables must be in scope when the view is saved.

The View Designer does not support the process of saving a view with macro expansion in a straightforward manner. If you use the View Designer you set up the entire view, skipping any of the normal designer pages associated with the macro expansion clause. Once the view is completely defined, switch to the SQL code editor. Add the macro expansion clauses and remain in the SQL code editor. Save the view by clicking the save button on the Visual FoxPro toolbar or File | Save on the menu. When you close the SQL code editor, you are presented with a syntax error. Click the OK button and another message is displayed (**Figure 3**) asking if you want the designer to reload the SQL code editor based on content from the View Designer. At this point the view is saved, so answering yes does not harm anything. Make sure when you close the SQL code editor (**Figure 4**) the second time do not save your changes; otherwise they will overwrite the saved view.

Figure 3. *The View Designer will choke on the macro-substitution any time you try to close the SQL code editor window.*

You might find it easier to create the views programmatically, or use one of the third-party view editors available. **Listing 1** shows how to create the view programmatically, and **Listing 2** shows how you can use the macro-substituted views in your applications.

Listing 1. *You have to ensure the variables substituted in the view are declared and in scope when the view is created. This code is a shortened version of the view generation code found in CreateMacroSubViews.PRG.*

```
CLOSE DATABASES ALL
OPEN DATABASE ViewDesignerChanges

PUBLIC lcWhere
lcWhere = ".T."

PUBLIC lcOrderBy
lcOrderBy = ".T."

CREATE SQL VIEW AuthorsWithFlexibleClauses2 AS ;
    SELECT Authors.Authors_Pk, ;
           Authors.cLastName, ;
           Authors.cFirstName, ;
           Authors.cCountry;
      FROM viewdesignerchanges!Authors ;
```

```
WHERE &?lcWhere ;
ORDER BY &?lcOrderBy
```

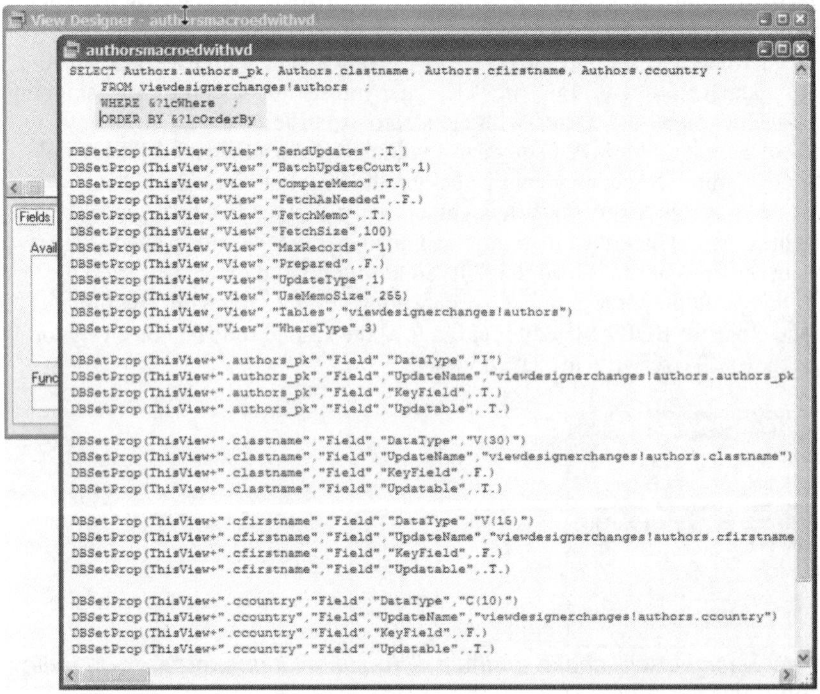

Figure 4. *Add the macro expansion clauses (highlighted) after you set up the rest of the view so you can take advantage of the designer to set all the basic properties.*

Opening views that use macro expansion does not change. Declare the variables used in the macro expansion, assign appropriate values to the variables, and open the view. Also remember the memory variables need to be in scope during any REQUERY().

Listing 2. *This code sample shows how you can use macro-substitution to have a single view retrieve a completely different set of records from the same base table.*

```
LOCAL lcWhere, ;
      lcOrderBy

IF USED("curAuthorsWithSInName")
   USE IN (SELECT("curAuthorsWithSInName"))
ENDIF

IF USED("curUsAuthors")
   USE IN (SELECT("curUsAuthors"))
ENDIF

IF USED("curCanadianAuthors")
   USE IN (SELECT("curCanadianAuthors"))
ENDIF
```

```
lcWhere = "cLastName LIKE [S%]"
lcOrderBy = "Authors.cFirstName"
USE ViewDesignerChanges!AuthorsWithFlexibleClauses IN 0 ALIAS
curAuthorsWithSInName
SELECT curAuthorsWithSInName
BROWSE NORMAL

lcWhere   = "cCountry = [USA]"
lcOrderBy = "Authors.cLastName, Authors.cFirstName"
USE ViewDesignerChanges!AuthorsWithFlexibleClauses IN 0 ALIAS curUsAuthors
SELECT curUsAuthors
BROWSE NORMAL

lcWhere   = "cCountry = [CANADA]"
lcOrderBy = "Authors.cLastName, Authors.cFirstName"
USE ViewDesignerChanges!AuthorsMacroedWithVD IN 0 ALIAS curCanadianAuthors
SELECT curCanadianAuthors
BROWSE NORMAL

USE IN (SELECT("curAuthorsWithSInName"))
USE IN (SELECT("curUsAuthors"))
USE IN (SELECT("curCanadianAuthors"))
USE IN (SELECT("authors"))

RETURN
```

> *One technique recommended by developers who deploy macro expansion based views is to adopt a naming convention and consistently name the clauses with the same memory variable. Then declare the variables as part of your VFP startup program if you have one.*

If you use the View Designer to make changes, a syntax error is displayed when you open the view each time and the view is opened in the SQL code editor. You can make changes and save the changes, but only in the code.

Class Designer and Form Designer changes

The Class and Form Designers might just be the tools most often used by Visual FoxPro developers. Any changes that enhance the usability or increase productivity with these designers usually have a big impact.

Class/Form Designer Tab Order selection

There have been two different ways to change the tab order of controls in the Form and Class Designers since VFP 3.0. Some developers prefer By List, some developers prefer the Interactive method, and some of you prefer to use one under certain circumstances and the other under different circumstances. If you like to change frequently, you might find toggling between the two styles a tedious task. Prior to Visual FoxPro 9, there were two ways to toggle your tab order method; you could either use the Options dialog, or write some code to toggle the Windows Registry entry.

Visual FoxPro 9 extends the Tab Order menu option found on the View pad (**Figure 5**). Your selection in the Visual FoxPro Options dialog no longer toggles the menu option, and you have to select which one you want to use each time you set the tab order.

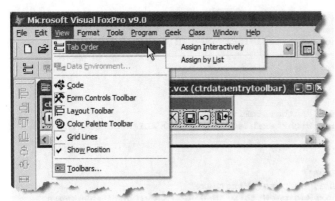

Figure 5. The Form Designer and Class Designer allow you to select which style of Tab Ordering you want from the View Menu.

If you use the Form Designer Toolbar, the button for Tab Order on the toolbar respects the current setting of the Tab Order selected on the Options dialog.

Keyboard shortcuts for adjusting object spacing

Sometimes the simple things in life are the most enjoyable. Visual FoxPro has a number of alignment and object spacing tools included on the Layout toolbar and the Format menu. Specific to Visual FoxPro 9 are some new keystroke combinations (see **Table 1**) to assist with adjusting the space between objects.

Table 1. There are two new keyboard combinations to adjust the space between the objects.

Keystroke	Adjustment
Alt+Arrow Key	Adjusts the space in the direction of the arrow key between the objects by one pixel.
Alt+Ctrl+Arrow Key	Adjusts the space between the selected objects by one grid scale in the direction of the arrow key. This is similar to snap-to-grid movement.

Data Environment changes

One small, but helpful change to the Data Environment Designer is the display of the database container (DBC) and the full path to the database container in the Visual FoxPro status bar (**Figure 6**) when you add a table or view to the data environment. The trick to displaying the database container is to drop down the Database combobox. Obviously you need SET STATUS BAR ON to observe this functionality.

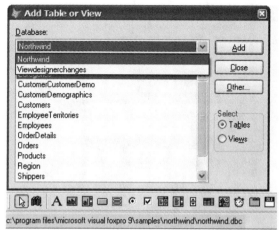

Figure 6. The database container (highlighted) is displayed in the VFP status bar when the Database dropdown is opened.

Enhancements to title bar descriptions

If you have several classes or forms open in the designer and want to add a new property or method, or want to work with the Edit Property/Method, how do you tell what class or form you are working with when you open one of the various dialogs associated with the designer? You hope you can see the front most designer, but often it is hidden under several code windows. Visual FoxPro 9 adds the form file name (if working with a form) or the class library and class name (if working with a class) to the title bar of the dialog box. These four dialogs have this addition:

- New Property

- New Method

- Edit Property/Method

- Class Info

Enhancements to Document View

The Fox Team listened to a common request from developers with respect to the Document View (**Figure 7**). You can now sort the list by name (object name / member name) in addition to the default sort by location. Previously, the Sort By Name was only available when you worked with programs (PRG).

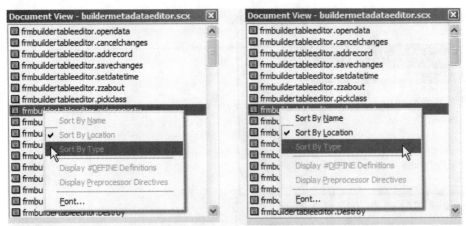

Figure 7. *In VFP 9, more sort options are enabled in Document View (seen on the right).*

Builder behavior changes

Builders registered in the Builder.DBF file and marked deleted respect the current setting of SET DELETED. If you have SET DELETED OFF, the Builder Selection dialog operates like previous versions of VFP (displaying builders deleted in the registration table). The behavior change is more apparent if you have SET DELETED ON. If you have one builder registered for an object type, and it's deleted, no builder runs for that object type; if you have multiple builders registered for the same object type, any builders marked deleted do not show up in the Builder list. This means developers can remove builders without the need to PACK the builder registration table.

Integrate your own menu designer

The Menu Designer has been slightly enhanced over the years to add icons to the menu and let you move menu items from one pad to another, but the basic interface has not changed dramatically. Developers have asked for enhancements to the designer to make it easier to use. Instead of dedicating the resources to overhaul the Menu Designer, Microsoft decided to expose a hook to allow developers to run their own customized designer. We do not anticipate the majority of developers will go out and write a menu designer taking advantage of this functionality, but we know of at least one and expect other third-party developers to create menu designers that do take advantage of this feature.

The hook is centered on a new system variable called _MENUDESIGNER. This system variable should be set to the program, application, or executable you want run instead of the standard Menu Designer. You set this in the Visual FoxPro Options dialog (**Figure 8**) on the File Locations page, or by programmatically setting the _MENUDESIGNER system variable via the Config.FPW, during the execution of your start up program or directly in the Command Window.

```
_MENUDESIGNER = "d:\WLCProjects\DevTools\MenuDesigner\MenuDesigner.exe"
```

The advantage of this implementation is the ability to switch between a custom menu designer and the native designer. If you specify a custom menu designer, none of the native features are available until you reset the system variable to the null string.

```
_MENUDESIGNER = SPACE(0)
```

Obviously you can toggle the setting between your custom menu designer and the native menu designer by setting the _MENUDESIGNER system variable. This way, if your custom designer does not provide all the features of the native designer, it is simple to use the designer with the functionality you need. If several third-party tool providers ship products you literally can use all of them, just one at a time.

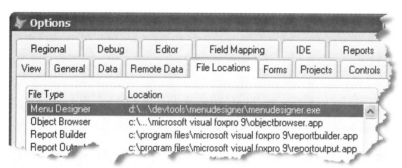

Figure 8. *The _MENUDESIGNER system variable is set on the File Locations page of the Options dialog.*

Once the new system variable is set, you open the customized menu designer the same way you open the native Visual FoxPro Menu Designer:

- MODIFY MENU

- CREATE MENU

- Modify a menu via the Project Manager.

- Create a new menu via the Project Manager.

- Select Menu from the New dialog presented after picking File | New on the menu or clicking the New button on the standard toolbar.

- Use the EDITSOURCE() function to open the source code of a menu.

- Use the Files Object Modify method to edit a menu.

If you use the CREATE MENU ?, MODIFY MENU ?, or MODIFY MENU commands, or click the Add button on the Project Manager, the Open File dialog is presented. If you pick a menu file or provide the file name, you continue to the custom menu designer, just as you would with the native Menu Designer. If you cancel the Open File dialog, the custom menu designer is not called at all.

If you CREATE MENU, click the New button on the Project Manager, or select the File | New menu option or New button on the Standard toolbar, you are presented with the New Menu dialog to select a regular menu or a shortcut menu. Selecting one of the two menu styles starts the designer; canceling indicates to Visual FoxPro the designer should not be started.

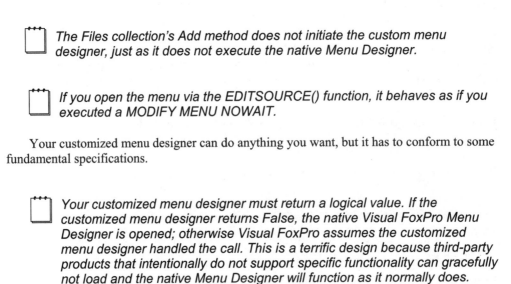

The Files collection's Add method does not initiate the custom menu designer, just as it does not execute the native Menu Designer.

If you open the menu via the EDITSOURCE() function, it behaves as if you executed a MODIFY MENU NOWAIT.

Your customized menu designer can do anything you want, but it has to conform to some fundamental specifications.

Your customized menu designer must return a logical value. If the customized menu designer returns False, the native Visual FoxPro Menu Designer is opened; otherwise Visual FoxPro assumes the customized menu designer handled the call. This is a terrific design because third-party products that intentionally do not support specific functionality can gracefully not load and the native Menu Designer will function as it normally does.

The entry point into the designer code must accept three parameters. The parameters help you determine how the menu designer was called, important items like the menu file name, and the different clauses used in the MODIFY/CREATE MENU commands. The contents of the parameters differ depending on how the menu was called.

The first parameter is the file name. This parameter is a fully qualified path and file name (with MNX extension) when you specify a menu file or pick one via the Open dialog. When you do not provide the file, the file name is a generic file without the path and extension. In this case the parameter is "Menu" followed by an auto-incrementing number.

The second parameter is a numeric value indicating how the menu designer was started. **Table 2** lists the valid parameter values and what they mean.

Table 2. *Valid settings for the second menu designer parameter and the meaning of each of the values.*

nCommandType	Meaning
1	A standard system menu was selected using the New Menu dialog.
2	A shortcut menu was selected using the New Menu dialog.
3	The menu designer was started by MODIFY MENU.

The last parameter is an array with additional information about how the menu designer was called; if there's no additional information to pass in, this parameter receives False. If the menu is new via the Project Manager's New button, the array is has one row and is populated with "PROJECT" in the first column, and the project name with fully qualified path in the second column.

The other scenario causing an array to be passed in for the third parameter is to execute a CREATE MENU or MODIFY MENU command (in code or in the Command Window) with the optional IN, NOWAIT, SAVE, or WINDOW clause. The resulting array has one row for each of the clauses used in the command. If you do not use any of the clauses, there is no array. The clause is in the first column of the array. If you use the NOWAIT or SAVE clause, the second column always contains True. The IN clause has the name of the window or "SCREEN" in the second column. If you use the WINDOW clause, the name of the window is put in the second column of the array.

If neither of the two scenarios applies, the third parameter is passed as False. If you check PCOUNT(), you will see all three parameters are passed, so the third parameter is deliberately passed as .F., and is not just an optional parameter.

So the implementation is as simple as creating a program that accepts three parameters and deals with them appropriately, and assigning this program (with path if necessary) to the _MENUDESIGNER system variable. That is the easy part. If you are going to keep compatibility with the MNX file structure and allow the GenMenu process to run, you need to do a little research on how Visual FoxPro stores the menu source code in the MNX metadata file, and get your head around the GenMenu process. These are not difficult tasks, just something to consider before you start coding.

The menu metadata source code files (MNX/MNT) are documented in the 60Spec.PJX project found in the Tools\Filespec\ under the Visual FoxPro root directory.

So you have the implementation requirements, what are some practical implementation ideas? Here is a short list we considered since we learned about this functionality:

1) Write a menu designer just to edit prompts, results, or address a specific weakness of the native designer so your menu editing is less painful.
2) Write a menu designer that pre-processes the MNX file to add standard security, SKIP FOR logic, set the hot keys, or order the items on the menu pad to your preferences.
3) Write a menu designer that supports custom object menus you created over the years. There is nothing saying you need to conform to or support the MNX structure.
4) Write a menu designer with custom hooks for GenMenuX.
5) Write a complete replacement for the native Menu Designer with complete compatibility with the existing menu infrastructure.

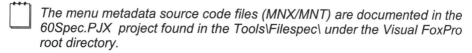

*The Developer Downloads for this chapter, available from **www.hentzenwerke.com**, include a test program called TestMenuDesignerParameters.PRG to demonstrate the parameters passed and the values assigned. Assign this program to the _MENUDESIGNER system variable and interact with the various menu designer calls to see what is passed to your custom menu designer.*

While it would be great to supply you with a complete replacement for the Menu Designer, we do not have a couple hundred spare hours to do so and finish writing this chapter. Instead, we implement a quick menu designer sample to address the prompt editing and execution code (commands and procedures), Skip For, Message, and Comment properties because we think the native designer does not have enough space on the user interface to be very workable.

 The Developer Downloads for this chapter, available from www.hentzenwerke.com, include a form (RasSimpleMenuDesigner.SCX) and a program (RasSimpleMenuDesignerMain.PRG) that collaborate and demonstrate how to write a very simple and functional custom menu designer.

The example provided is not very robust and was created for demonstration purposes only. We recommend you make backups of the menus you want to work with in case something bad happens. The Save button is enabled, but does not actually save any changes. If you want to take the time to make sure the robustness you need is added to this sample code, you can uncomment the TABLEUPDATE command in the form's Save method.

The main program (see **Listing 3**) accepts the three parameters passed by Visual FoxPro, checks to see if the menu exists, and calls the form presented as the "Simple Menu Designer." If the menu file does not exist, which is the case if a new menu is created via the Project Manager New button or a CREATE MENU command, the native Menu Designer is called.

Listing 3. The main program for a simple menu designer.

```
* Simple Menu Designer - meant to serve as an example, not production solid
LPARAMETERS tcFileName, tnCommandType, taDetail

LOCAL loParameter AS Line, ;
      loForm AS Form, ;
      llReturnVal AS Logical

* Consider it default custom designer handled
* the request so native designer does not start
llReturnVal = .T.

IF VARTYPE(tcFileName) = "C"
   IF FILE(tcFileName)
      * Good, we have an existing menu, continue
      * Create an object the form can use to pass along parameters
      * which are used before the form Init() fires.
      loParameter = CREATEOBJECT("line")
      loParameter.AddProperty("cFileName", tcFileName)
      _screen.AddProperty("__oRASSimpleMenuParameter", loParameter)

      * Start user interface in modal mode
      DO FORM RASSimpleMenuDesigner NAME loForm LINKED NOSHOW
      loForm.Show(1)

      _screen.__oRASSimpleMenuParameter = .NULL.
```

```
    ELSE
        * Let the native designer fire up and handle request.
        llReturnVal = .F.
    ENDIF
ELSE
    MESSAGEBOX("You need to pass parameters to this program and the file name
parameter is not valid", ;
                0 + 16, ;
                "Simple Menu Designer")
ENDIF

RETURN llReturnVal
```

The Simple Menu Designer (see **Figure 9**) example form reads the property _screen. _oRASSimpleMenuParameter.cFileName, opens the MNX file, filters out records without prompts, and displays the menu information. You can navigate to other menu items using the grid. The command and procedure code displays when you navigate to a menu item with command or procedure code. The Prompt, Skip For, Message, and Comment can be edited for any menu item. The Object Code combobox (display only) tells you what type of menu item is currently available for editing. Take a look at this combobox in the Form Designer so you can see how you can translate the underlying "codes" to something more understandable in your custom designer. There are several items in the menu metadata you will want to translate on your designer.

As we noted earlier in this section, we do not expect every developer to jump on this new feature and create their own menu designer, but we do expect developer tool vendors to take a shot. We know there is a lot of room for improvement over the native Menu Designer. If you do consider creating your own, make sure to consider all the functionality you want to provide and understand that you do not need to write a complete replacement for the native designer. Design and create something that services the pain you feel the most with the native designer and start with this functionality. Think outside of the box and know you can break the mold and even skip the native MNX metadata source code and the GenMenu process of creating the MPR source code. As with other parts of Visual FoxPro 9, Microsoft has removed limitations and in this case has blown the lid off and exposed hooks so you can completely replace the native functionality.

Debugger

Microsoft did not place the Debugger high on the Visual FoxPro 9 priority list, but there are some very handy enhancements that should make it easier to figure out why your code does not work as you expect it to.

Constant support in Trace Window

Prior to Visual FoxPro 9, when stepping through code in the Trace window, there was no way to determine the value of a constant other than opening the source code containing the #DEFINE. In Visual FoxPro 9, hover the mouse over the constant and a tooltip appears showing the value, similar to memory variables.

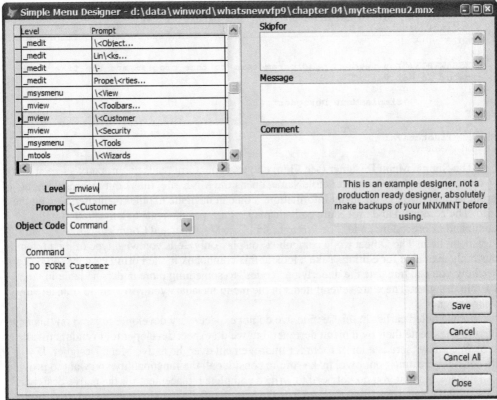

Figure 9. *The Simple Menu Designer is an example of how you can use the new _MENUDESIGNER hook to create your own menu designer replacement.*

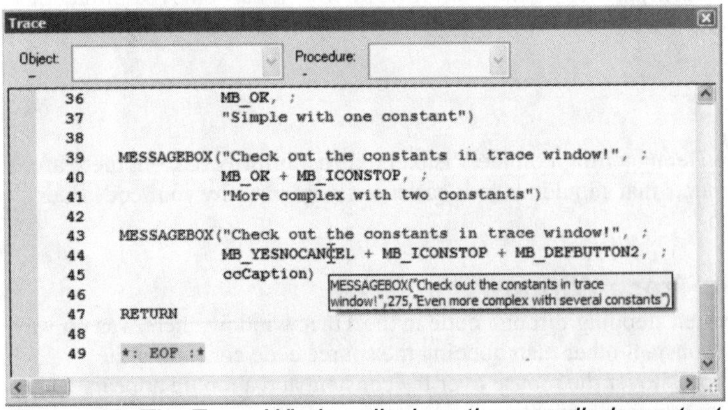

Figure 10. *The Trace Window displays the compiled constant values in a tooltip.*

There is one issue you need to be aware of with this new debugging feature. The tooltip shows the compiled line as the Visual FoxPro p-code interpreter sees it. If you use several constants together in a calculation, you only see the resulting value. We demonstrate this in

Figure 10 with the MESSAGEBOX() function. The dialog box type parameter typically has two or more constants to determine the icon and buttons displayed with the message. Visual FoxPro compiles these together and the Trace Window displays the results.

Watch Window errors

The Watch window literally accepts anything you type into the watch expression textbox and tries to evaluate the expression. If errors occur prior to Visual FoxPro 9, you had no way of knowing it. In VFP 9 the errors display in the Debug Output (**Figure 11**) window. One example is typing THIS. in the expression and seeing the resulting error message in the Debug Output window.

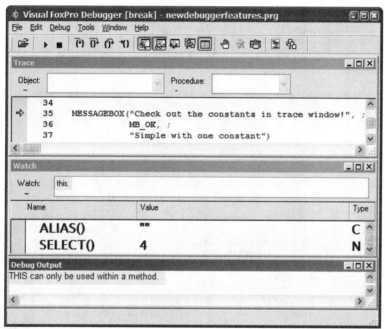

Figure 11. *The Watch window allows you to include almost anything, including code that triggers errors. VFP errors triggered in the Watch window now display in the Debug Output window.*

Debug output window is mouse wheel enabled

One debugger oversight the Fox Team fixed in Visual FoxPro 9 is the ability to use the mouse scroll wheel in the Output Window. This is not an earth-shattering fix, but if you are accustomed to using the mouse wheel, it is a nice addition.

Reports can be debugged

Reports have never interacted with the Visual FoxPro debugger prior to Visual FoxPro 9. This presents a problem for developers who have reports with user-defined functions (UDFs) called in report expressions.

Visual FoxPro 8 throws Error 1651, "CANCEL or SUSPEND is not allowed," if you execute SET STEP ON in a procedure or function called from a report. One of the alternatives you have to debug code is to simulate the call after setting up the data via the Command Window or a program. Alternatively, developers who stage the data using SQL Selects before calling the report call the UDFs in the SQL Select where the debugger is available rather than calling the UDF in the report expression.

The changes to the Report Designer (especially, the new ReportListener object) required the Fox Team to integrate debugging capabilities into reports. The integration is not limited to the ReportListener. You can debug your own UDF code as well, as shown in **Figure 12**.

 The Developer Downloads for this chapter, available from **www.hentzenwerke.com**, *include a report and a procedure file used to demonstrate how to call the debugger when previewing or printing a report. The report is called AuthorDebugging.FRX, and the program is called AuthorInitials.PRG.*

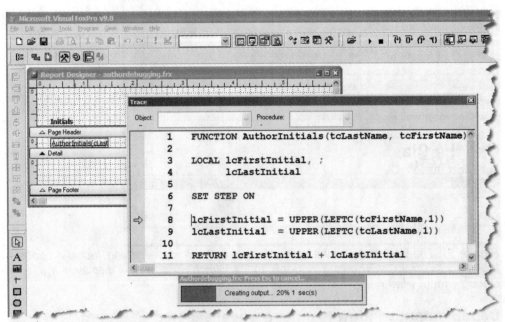

Figure 12. The debugger now works with reports so you can step through code called from a report expression or triggered through a ReportListener.

This enhancement is critical for developers who are writing ReportListener extensions, otherwise you would not have any way to debug your code as the report was executing. See Chapter 7, "Extending the Reporting System at Run Time," for more details on the ReportListener object. The debugger is called in the same manner with SET STEP ON (or your favorite style of calling the debugger) in your code. The debugger does not interact with report expressions unless they trigger custom code in a ReportListener object, or call code in an object you created (different from a ReportListener), or run a user-defined function in program code.

The example we ship in the downloads is very easy to follow. First we create a report and in one of the report expressions call the AuthorInitials function. The AuthorInitials function takes the first and last name and assembles the initials from the name. In the function we add SET STEP ON. To simplify running the report we add the SET PROCEDURE TO code in the report data environment's BeforeOpenTables method. The Trace window displays when the report is previewed or printed to a printer using the IDE toolbar buttons or the REPORT FORM command.

The Fox Team also wrote a special ReportListener subclass to help with debugging object assisted reports. This class, DebugListener, is found in the ReportListener.VCX class library in the FFC subdirectory of the VFP home directory. It is very easy to work with. First you instantiate the DebugListener class, and then you pass it to the REPORT FORM command:

```
loDebugListener = NEWOBJECT("debuglistener", HOME()+"ffc\_reportlistener.vcx")
REPORT FORM AuthorDebugging PREVIEW OBJECT loDebugListener
```

The DebugListener class records details about how the report is executed and how the various objects are rendered. Along the way it records various property settings during the different stages of report execution. This class will be extremely handy in determining why a report is not functioning as expected. The report isn't displayed or printed when the DebugListener is the ReportListener hooked into the report. The report is processed, the different properties are recored, and stored in a text file. This text file (see **Figure 13**) is displayed after the report is finished. You can review the contents of this report to determine how the report was processed from a ReportListener perspective.

Use the Class Browser for PRG-based classes

The Class Browser has always been able to open VCX files, but many developers prefer to write at least some of their classes in program code (PRG). One of the disadvantages of taking the PRG route was the inability to use the Class Browser to maintain the classes and get a visual representation of the class hierarchy. Visual FoxPro 9 removes this limitation.

The base functionality of the Class Browser (see **Figure 14**) is available for PRG-based classes, although there are a few differences when working with them. The first is the descriptions for the class library (the program in this case) and the descriptions for the individual classes are not available in the description pane (lower left corner). The second is the member descriptions (normally maintained in the lower right pane) cannot be added or edited. The third difference is you cannot filter out empty members in the member pane (upper right pane).

Figure 13. *The DebugListener class records numerous property settings and rendering processes as a report is executed. The findings are saved in a text file and displayed when the report is done.*

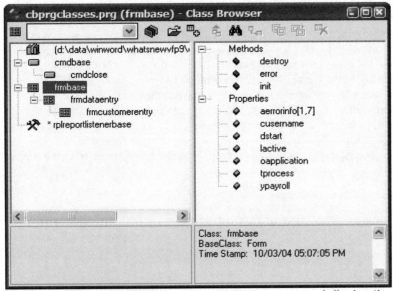

Figure 14. *The Class Browser can open a program and display the classes just like it does for VCX class libraries.*

Class Browser is dockable

The Class Browser does not dock by default, but because it is a VFP form and VFP forms are dockable, you can write code to dock the Class Browser. This is accomplished by running an add-in for the Activate event.

 The Developer Downloads for this chapter, available from ***www.hentzenwerke.com****, include a program called CBMakeDockableAddin.PRG, which demonstrates how you can create an add-in to dock the Class Browser.*

Listing 4*. Code that runs to dock the form when the Class Browser is started.*

```
LPARAMETERS toBrowser

LOCAL lcName                          && Name of the Add-in
LOCAL lcComment                       && Comment for the Add-in

* Self registration if not called form the Class Browser
IF TYPE("toBrowser")= "L"
   lcName    = "Rick Schummer's Make Class Browser Dockable"
   lcComment = "Developed by RAS for online forum discussion and example"

   IF TYPE("_oBrowser")= "O"
      * If Class Browser is running, use Addin() method
      _oBrowser.Addin(lcName, STRTRAN(SYS(16),".FXP",".PRG"), "ACTIVATE", ;
                  , , lcComment)
   ELSE
      * Use the low level access of the Browser registration table
      IF FILE(HOME() + "BROWSER.DBF")
         lcOldSelect = SELECT()

         USE (HOME() + "BROWSER") IN 0 AGAIN SHARED ;
            ALIAS curRASClassBrowserAddinReg
         SELECT curRASClassBrowserAddinReg
         LOCATE FOR Type = "ADDIN" AND Name = lcName

         IF EOF()
           APPEND BLANK
         ENDIF

         * Always replace with the latest information
         REPLACE Platform WITH "WINDOWS", ;
                 Type     WITH "ADDIN", ;
                 Id       WITH "METHOD", ;
                 Name     WITH lcName, ;
                 Method   WITH "ACTIVATE", ;
                 Program  WITH LOWER( STRTRAN( SYS(16), ".FXP", ".PRG")), ;
                 Comment  WITH lcComment
      USE

      SELECT (lcOldSelect)
```

```
      ELSE
         MESSAGEBOX("Could not find the table " + HOME() + ;
                    "BROWSER.DBF" + ", please make sure it exists.", ;
                    0 + 48, ;
                    _screen.Caption)
      ENDIF
   ENDIF

   RETURN
ELSE
   * Check to see if we really got called from the Class Browser
   * and it is valid for VFP 9 and higher.
   IF NOT PEMSTATUS(toBrowser, "Dockable", 5)
      RETURN .F.
   ELSE
      toBrowser.Dockable = 1
      toBrowser.Dock(1)
      toBrowser.Refresh()
   ENDIF
ENDIF

RETURN
```

The first three-quarters of the program register the program in Browser.DBF (the Class Browser Registration table). The docking code first confirms the developer is running in a version of Visual FoxPro supporting docking forms, docks the form to the left-side, and refreshes the Class Browser. See Chapter 13, "Forms and Controls," for more details on how form docking is implemented.

Code References changes

Code References was introduced in Visual FoxPro 8 and has some nice usability enhancements added in Visual FoxPro 9.

The biggest benefit of using the updated Code References tool is the ability to have separate columns for the class, method, and line number instead of one column in the results grid. This simple enhancement allows developers to easily sort the results by method name. You can still retain the single column with the information concatenated together if you like. In fact, the tool defaults to the older style. You make the change to individual columns by selecting the **Show separate columns for class, method, and line** option in the Code References Option dialog (**Figure 15**).

The result set sort menu (**Figure 16**) is a little tricky to find. You have to select a cell in the grid, and then right-click the cell. The new option on this menu is the Sort By | Method. This option is available whether you show the Class/Method column or the individual class/method/line number columns.

The last set of additions is to the results treeview shortcut menu. There are three new options. The Expand All option expands all the nodes on the tree. The treeview is optimized to load the results as the nodes are expanded, therefore, expanding all could take some time depending on your existing results. The Collapse All option does the reverse and collapses all the nodes on the tree. The Sort by Most Recent First toggles the order of the search treeview. When it's selected, the newest searches are at the top of the list; when it's not selected, the searches are shown in the order they were done (oldest to newest).

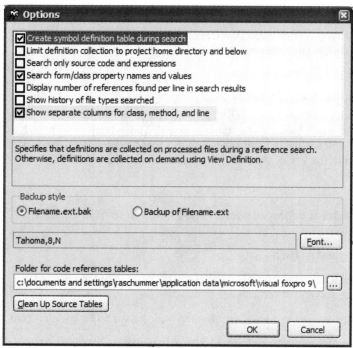

Figure 15. *The Code References tool now allows developers to choose between one column for the class/method/line or three separate columns. The Code References Options dialog is where you make this choice.*

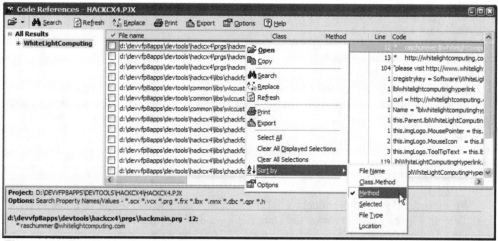

Figure 16. *The Code References tool has a Sort By option on the result set shortcut menu. One of the new options is to sort by Method.*

Task Pane Manager

The Task Pane has a completely new pane called the Data Explorer and the Environment Manager pane has a couple of nice enhancements.

The Data Explorer

The Data Explorer lets you examine data and components in Visual FoxPro databases, SQL Server databases, VFP free tables, or any other ODBC or OLE DB compliant database via an ADO connection. It can run as a task pane or as a standalone tool. Those familiar with SQL Server's Enterprise Manager will see many similarities, but this tool works with all kinds of data, is completely integrated in the Visual FoxPro IDE, and is extensible in true VFP tradition.

This tool offers:

- A way to view schema information for VFP, SQL Server, or ADO-connected data sources.

- Quick access to the data itself.

- Centralized maintenance of multiple databases without the need to change to different folders, servers, or projects.

- The ability to run queries in a similar fashion to SQL Server's Query Analyzer.

- Functionality similar to the Visual Studio Server Explorer.

To use the Data Explorer, you set up a connection for each database you want to explore. The key to using the tool efficiently is understanding the features available for the type of connection you establish.

While you can run the Data Explorer through the Task Pane Manager, you can also run it as a standalone tool like this:

```
DO HOME()+"dataexplorer.app"
```

In this case, the Data Explorer runs as a regular form and creates a public memory variable called _oDataExplorer. You can use this memory variable to manipulate the look and feel of the Data Explorer window including docking the form. The code needed to dock this form is:

```
_oDataExplorer.Dockable = 1
_oDataExplorer.Dock(1)
```

We show the Data Explorer docked to the left side of the Visual FoxPro IDE and in the Task Pane in **Figure 17**. If you want the Data Explorer docked each time you start it, you have to run the docking code each time you start the tool. You can write a wrapper program you call from the Command Window or add a custom menu item.

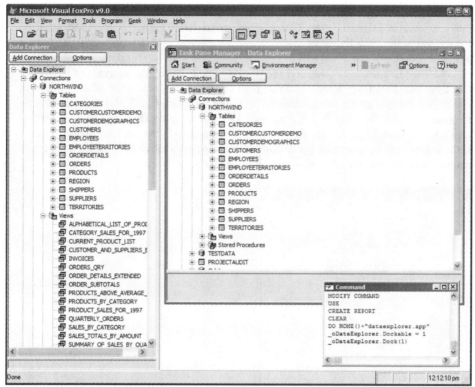

Figure 17. *The Data Explorer is available in the Task Pane Manager; it can be run standalone without the Task Pane Manager, in which case, it's dockable.*

There are no options available for this pane via the Task Pane Options window. However, the Data Explorer has a separate Options dialog accessed from the Options button. The Data Explorer Options dialog provides you with the ability to change the font, determine whether the description pane and column schema information is displayed, plus manage add-ins, shortcut menus, and drag and drop operations. If you change things and then want to restore the default options, a button on this dialog lets you do so.

Connections
Connections are links pointing to the data you want to access via the Data Explorer. Connections aren't needed to work with SQL Server data. Each of the SQL Server instances available on your machine or the network are loaded under the SQL Servers node when you expand that node.

You have several options when you define a connection. The connection types shipping with Visual FoxPro 9 include FoxPro databases, a FoxPro directory, a FoxPro table (free or contained), SQL Server, SQL database, and an ADO connection. Each of these connection types have different properties to set up. You modify the list by adding or removing "S" records in the DataExplorer.DBF file.

If you are working with native Visual FoxPro data or remote data that is not SQL Server, you need to add a connection. All connection information is stored in the DataExplorer.DBF file (discussed in the "DataExplorer.DBF" section later in this chapter) so it is available the next time you start the Data Explorer. To add a new connection, click the **Add Connection** button at the top of the Data Explorer.

Adding a connection for a Visual FoxPro database or a SQL Server database places the database under the Connections node and provides direct access to the internals of the database. You need to specify which database the connection refers to. You select the Visual FoxPro database by navigating to a folder and selecting the DBC file. SQL Server database selection is performed using the SQL Connection Properties dialog (**Figure 18**). SQL Server database connection requires you specify security information. Other connection attributes include the connection timeout and query timeout parameters, and if you want the column information displayed and the objects sorted alphabetically.

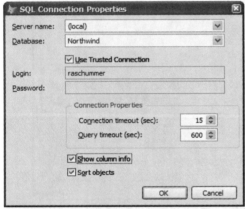

Figure 18. *The SQL Connections Properties dialog lets you specify the server and database when adding a new connection.*

A FoxPro Table connection is to a specific table (free or contained); all you do to set up this connection is pick a table via the Open dialog. You can use this connection type to save time drilling down through a database container connection if you regularly work with a particular table. For example, you might use it for an error log table you're evaluating as you test a particular bug.

The FoxPro Directory connection lets you pick a folder once for the connection. This type of connection provides access to all the database containers in the specified folder. If you add or remove a database container from this folder, the connection reflects the change.

The FoxPro Directory connection has a distinct productivity advantage for developers who segregate data into several VFP databases (such as a database for tables, another for views to maintain tables, and another for views used in reporting), provided you keep all the databases in one folder. Now all the databases are available without the need to change to the folder, open all the databases, and switch between them to access the views and stored procedures.

SQL Server connection allows you to put a SQL Server on the connections node. You pick the SQL Server you want using the same dialog as the SQL Connection Properties dialog (Figure 18). The only difference is you don't specify a database.

If you are working with a specific SQL Server database, we have found it quicker to add a connection to the SQL Server database rather than traversing through the SQL Server node. The reason it is faster is the SQL Server node initiates a search for all SQL Servers on the network the first time it is expanded for each Data Explorer session. Making a connection provides direct access without the search each time you use the Data Explorer.

ADO connections are perfect for databases you access via an OLE DB provider. You can base the connection on a DataSource Name (DSN) or specify a connection string. There is a Build... button available to assist you with the construction of the connection string, including the ability to test the connection. Operations available with ADO connections depend on the OLE DB provider.

After you establish a connection you may want to change properties of the connection. This is done via the shortcut menu for the connection and selecting the Property item. Each of the different connections have a different property dialog. The FoxPro databases, tables, and directories property dialog presents two properties: show column info and sort objects. You need to decide if these are turned on or off. The SQL Connection Properties dialog (Figure 18) previously discussed is displayed for SQL database connections. A variation of the SQL Connetion Properties dialog is displayed for SQL Servers. The dialog only allows you to set the default security, connection and query timeout parameters, and the show columns / sort properties for SQL Server connections. You can change the ADO DSN or connection string, the connection and query timeout parameters, and the show column info on the ADO Connection Properties.

The interface has a bit of a quirk for ADO connections. Once you add the ADO connection database it does not change the name on the treeview node if you pick another database via a connection string or DSN. You need to right-click the connection and select the Rename Connection menu option.

Shortcut menus

The Data Explorer has shortcut menus defined throughout the treeview interface. If you do not take time to right-click items in the Data Explorer, you will miss a lot of the built-in functionality. Some of the menu options are common, while some of them are specific to the data object you are clicking.

The Run Query menu item is common to all the nodes in the Data Explorer. This menu item starts the Run Query dialog (**Figure 19**), which provides a user interface to build queries and view the results in a read-only grid. You can save the query to a file, load a query from a file to the edit area, toggle the format between VFP SQL syntax and SQL Server syntax, and copy the query to the clipboard in two formats (as a literal assigned to a variable, or using the TEXT/ENDTEXT syntax). The clipboard code can be pasted into your programs. This allows you to work on the query, get it the way you want,and then dump the code into your applications. If you are running queries against SQL Server data, the Messages page shows you the message results of the query. This is very similar to the SQL Server Query Analyzer.

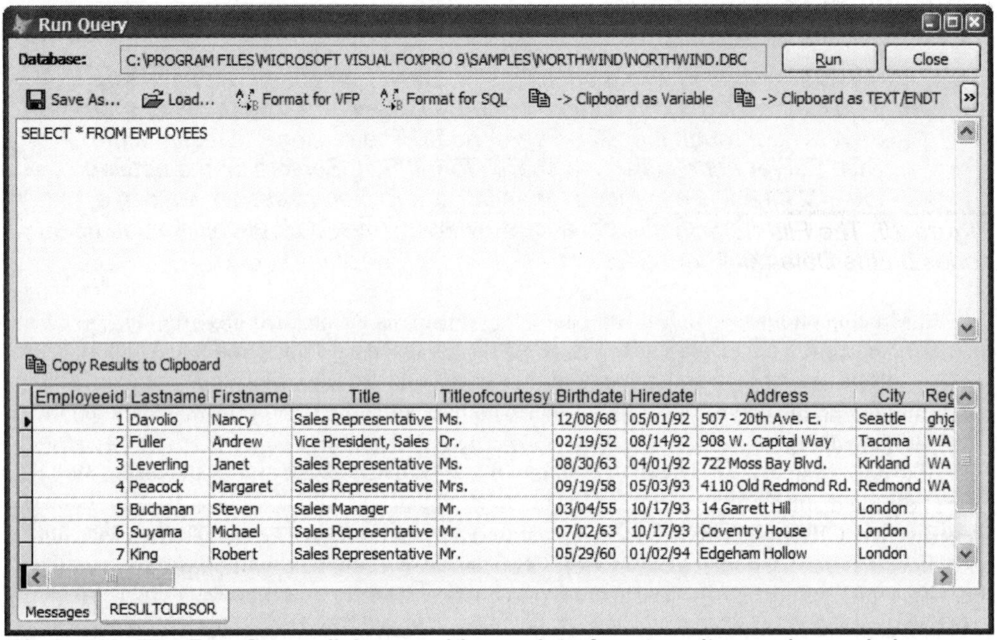

***Figure 19.** The Run Query dialog provides an interface to write queries and view result sets.*

The Copy Results to Clipboard button performs a _VFP.DataToClip() with the result set of the query copied to the clipboard with space delimiters.

Refresh is the second most common shortcut menu item. Selecting Refresh from the shortcut menu reloads the Data Explorer with updated information. This is handy if you or someone on your team is making changes to the database and want them reflected in the Data Explorer.

The Filter menu item opens the Filter dialog (**Figure 20**), which allows developers to reduce the number of items shown on a node in the Data Explorer. This comes in handy when you have a lot of tables, columns in a table, stored procedures, or other elements, and you want to reduce the number of items to be displayed. You might be asking, how is this useful? If you are using a naming convention and want to filter out just the related tables that start with a string, or you just cannot see the table in the long list, you can use it to find this single table.

When you are working with tables or views, there is a Browse menu item. It opens the table or queries the view and displays the records in a window with a grid. This grid is read-only for SQL Server tables and views, but is editable for VFP data. With VFP views, you can change the data in the grid, but the data is never committed to the underlying tables.

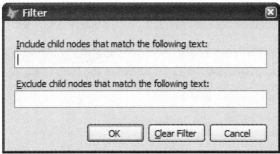

Figure 20. The Filter dialog gives developers the option to include or exclude certain nodes on the Data Explorer treeview based on the text of the node.

The Design menu item is available for VFP tables and views. By default, the Design option opens the Visual FoxPro Table Designer or View Designer, letting you change the structure of table, add triggers and rules (both column and table level), add comments, and create and maintain indexes. Views by default are opened in the View Designer.

The View Definition option is available for local and remote views and stored procedures. The view definition code or stored procedure code displays in a separate window (see **Figure 21**). The code displayed for local views is the SQL Select, selecting a remote view displays CREATE VIEW code, and a stored procedure shows the actual program code (for both VFP and remote databases). You can copy the code (by highlighting and pressing CTRL+C) from the View Definition window in case you want to run it or put it into a program.

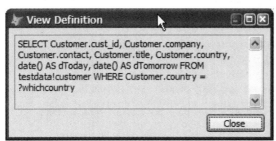

Figure 21. The View Definition dialog displays the SQL Select code for the view (both VFP local and remote views).

The shortcut menu for stored procedures includes a number of items not on any other shortcut menus. For remote data, you can run, edit, delete, and create new stored procedures from the Data Explorer. The remote data stored procedures are updated by running queries that alter, delete, and insert new stored procedures via SQL language scripts. Template code is provided for you when you select these options. You can also edit stored procedures for a local Visual FoxPro database. Doing so opens the native editor allowing procedures to be edited, added, or deleted.

Rename Connection and Remove Connection are only on the shortcut menu when you have a connection selected. They allow you to work with the connections after you add them. The rename option allows you to change the text in the connection treeview node. The remove option lets you remove this connection from the Data Explorer. Note that it only removes the reference; it doesn't delete the database, server, or the FoxPro table.

Dragging and dropping

The drag and drop options are not very obvious, but are documented in the Help file in the Data Explorer Task Pane topic. You can select a node in the Data Explorer treeview, and drop it into a program editor or onto the Form/Class Designer. Each of the node types in the Data Explorer has different results, documented in **Table 3**.

The code generated in the program editors is well commented. These comments are important as they tell you what needs to be changed to make things work. Important details like adding a user name and password to the connection string, telling you objects that go out of scope are not available (all object reference memory variables are declared LOCAL), where to add error checking, and where your custom code to process the data should reside.

Table 3 documents the results delivered with Visual FoxPro, but drag and drop behavior is customizible. It's driven by scripts written in VFP and the scripts can be edited via the Data Explorer Options dialog (**Figure 22**). Click the Manage Drag/Drop button on this dialog.

Table 3. The drag and drop functionality from the Data Explorer differs depending on whether you drop on a program editor or the Form/Class designer.

Object	Code Editor (program, method, stored procedure)	Form/Class Designer surface
Databases	For a SQL Server or ADO connection, code is pasted into the editor to establish a connection, create an ADO recordset, and set up a CursorAdapter to access the data. For a VFP database, it just pastes the database name.	Nothing
Tables/Views	For VFP Tables and Views, a SQL Select statement including all the columns is pasted into the editor. For SQL Server and ADO connections, code is pasted into the editor to establish a connection, create an ADO recordset, and set up a CursorAdapter to access the data. The table name is included in in the query in the CursorAdapter.SelectCmd property.	A grid is added to the form or class; the grid class used is based on the current Field Mapping settings. You still need to set the RecordSource to the table, and add a way to connect to data. Your class must be a class that can contain other objects, otherwise a message is displayed indicating the need for a container class.
Columns	For VFP tables/view columns, a SQL Select statement is pasted into the editor: SELECT <ColumnName> FROM <table or view name>. For SQL Server and ADO connections, code is pasted into the editor to establish a connection, create an ADO recordset, and set up a CursorAdapter to access the data. The column and the table/view name are included in the query in the CursorAdapter.SelectCmd property.	A textbox is added to the form or class; the textbox class is based on Field Mapping settings. The ControlSource is bound to the column, but you need to add a way to connect to data. Your class must be a class that can contain other objects, otherwise a message is displayed indicating the need for a container class.

Object	Code Editor (program, method, stored procedure)	Form/Class Designer surface
Stored Procedures	For SQL Server and ADO connections, code is pasted into the editor to connect to the data and execute the stored procedure. The stored procedure name is included in the EXEC call, and stored in the CursorAdapter.SelectCmd property. Parameters are included if the stored procedure has parameters. VFP Stored Procedures are SQL Select statements instead of a procedure call. This is a bug in the initial release and hope it will be fixed in the future.	Nothing
Stored Procedure Parameters	There is a bug with SQL Server and ADO connections creating a SQL Select statements where the FROM clause is the parameter, We expect this to be corrected in the future.	Nothing
Functions	For SQL Server and ADO connections, code is pasted into the editor to connect to the data and execute the function. The function name is included in the EXEC call, and stored in the CursorAdapter.SelectCmd property.	Nothing

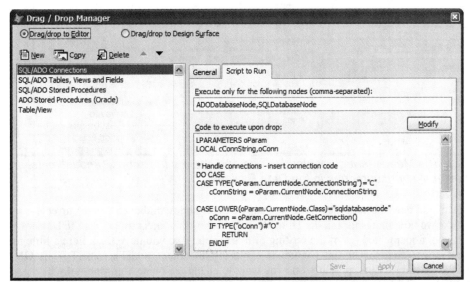

Figure 22. *The Drag/Drop Manager is used to add/change the scripts, and ultimately the behavior of drag and drop operations in the Data Explorer.*

Each of the operations can have a different script (and behavior) when items are dropped on a program editor or the Form/Class design surface. The script is Visual FoxPro code. The code can be changed directly in the editbox, but you can get colorization and IntelliSense when editing the script code via the **Modify** button. Documentation for the Data Explorer object model was not available at the time this material was written, but we hope Microsoft will release a white paper on the object model so developers can write powerful scripts. Some information on the object model can be understood by placing SET STEP ON in the existing scripts and exploring the code as it is executed, or by reviewing the Data Explorer source code available in the XSource folder.

Changing menu shortcut behavior

Just as drag and drop functionality can be customized (see "Dragging and Dropping" earlier in this chapter), so can shortcut menu behavior. Click the **Manage Menus** button in the Data Explorer Options dialog to open the Menu Manager dialog (**Figure 23**).

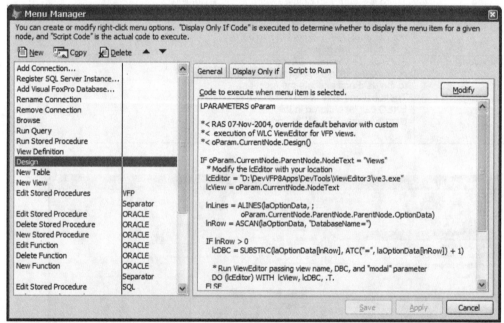

Figure 23. *The Menu Manager is used to add and change the scripts, and ultimately the behavior of shortcut menus in the Data Explorer.*

You can add new shortcut menu options, copy existing ones, and even delete current behavior. As we note in discussing the Drag/Drop Manager, the object model for the Data Explorer is not documented (as of the writing of this chapter), so you have to explore a little to understand how to code this script. The key to exploring the object model is to SET STEP ON in one of the existing scripts, possibly one you want to change. You need to find out what properties are available to determine whether the node is a view, what the view name is, and what database contains the view.

For our example, we selected a real developer requirement. Developers who use third-party tools instead of the View Designer might want their favorite third-party tool to run instead of the View Designer when they design a VFP view. The same shortcut script is called to design both tables and views. The normal behavior is to call the Design method for the currently selected node. Because you only want to change the behavior for views, you need to check what node is selected and what type of node it is, as in the code in Figure 23.

In the case of the ViewEditor (a free tool originally developed by Steve Sawyer, and a professional version currently sold by White Light Computing, both available at **www.whitelightcomputing.com**), three parameters must be passed to start with the view selected. The first is the view name, the second is the name of the DBC, and the third is a logical value that determines whether the tool runs in a modal state or not.

The view name is easy to find because the current node in the treeview has a property called NodeText. This property contains the name of the selected database object. You can use the current node's parent node to determine whether the NodeText for the parent node is "Views." If so, you are designing a view; otherwise you perform the native behavior for tables. The tricky part is determining the database name. We searched for a while and found the current node's grandparent node (parent's parent node) has a property called OptionData, which is a multi-line text field storing property name and property value pairs. One of the properties is DatabaseName. The code parses out this information, and you can pass the three parameters to the ViewEditor as required. The complete code to override the Design script is included in **Listing 5**.

 The Developer Downloads for this chapter, available from **www.hentzenwerke.com**, *include a script to change the way the Data Explorer's Design shortcut menu option behaves (opens up the ViewEditor instead of the native VFP View Designer). The script is found in DataExplorerDesignMenuScript.prg.*

Listing 5. *This code is intended for use in the Manage Menu section of the Data Explorer options. Specify this code as the Script to Run for the Design menu option and when you select this shortcut menu option, White Light Computing's ViewEditor (free or commercial version) will run.*

```
LPARAMETERS oParam

*< RAS 07-Nov-2004, override default behavior with custom
*<  execution of WLC ViewEditor for VFP views.
*< oParam.CurrentNode.Design()

IF oParam.CurrentNode.ParentNode.NodeText = "Views"
   * Modify the lcEditor with your location
   lcEditor = "D:\DevVFP8Apps\DevTools\ViewEditor3\ve3.exe"
   lcView = oParam.CurrentNode.NodeText

   lnLines = ALINES(laOptionData, ;
                  oParam.CurrentNode.ParentNode.ParentNode.OptionData)
   lnRow = ASCAN(laOptionData, "DatabaseName=")

   IF lnRow > 0
      lcDBC = SUBSTRC(laOptionData[lnRow], ATC("=", laOptionData[lnRow]) + 1)

      * Run ViewEditor passing view name, DBC, and "modal" parameter
      DO (lcEditor) WITH  lcView, lcDBC, .T.
```

```
   ELSE
      * Problem, could not find database for view, use native
      * Data Explorer call as default
      oParam.CurrentNode.Design()
   ENDIF
ELSE
   oParam.CurrentNode.Design()
ENDIF
```

You need to change the folder in the sample code to match the location of the ViewEditor on your machine (see the assignment of lcEditor). If you want, you can make this code even more dynamic to search the registry for the key that indicates where the ViewEditor is installed. We did not include it in this sample code because the key is different for different versions.

Add-in Manager
The Add-in Manager allows you to extend the Data Explorer query and data results providing functionality not yet considered or implemented by Microsoft. The Add-in Manager is accessed through the Data Explorer Options dialog using the Manage Add-ins button. You can add new and delete existing add-ins, and adjust the sequence the add-ins are listed on the menu. All add-ins are stored in the Data Explorer.DBF file. Like all the other extensibility features of the Data Explorer, the add-in is driven by VFP script program code. There is no documentation as of this writing on how you can use this functionality, so the only way to understand the extensions is to review the code delivered with VFP 9.

DataExplorer.DBF
The DataExplorer.DBF free table resides in your HOME(7) folder and stores metadata about the connections and data sources you have defined, queries defined for later use, the extensibility data for treeview nodes, add-ins, and shortcut menus. This table is automatically maintained when you add connections, define queries, alter the menus and other extensibility features, or register add-ins. If this information is important to you, add the HOME(7) directory to your backup scheme.

Environment Manager - field mappings and form templates
The Environment Manager was introduced with the Task Pane Manager in Visual FoxPro 8, but has been improved in Visual FoxPro 9. It now reduces the struggle developers have setting Field Mapping for the IntelliDrop functionality used when you drag and drop fields from a cursor in the data environment onto a form. In addition, you can specify the form and formset template classes for a specific environment, and associate a FoxPro resource file with an environment set.

Developers who gravitated to the IntelliDrop capabilities introduced in Visual FoxPro 5 quickly became frustrated with the built-in Field Mapping dialog found in the Options dialog. It is tedious to use. If you have more than one set of base classes because you work on more than one project or use more than one framework, and have to reset the Field Mapping settings often, you probably find this dialog too time consuming to deal with and gave up. Several developers wrote utilities to manage the settings and with the projecthook class introduced in Visual FoxPro 6, integrated their utilities to work with the Project Manager. The Field Mapping functionality in the Environment Manager finally provides developers a built-in capability to define the base classes for the various data types and have the IntelliDrop settings defined to a specific environment so you can quickly change them as needed.

Use the Field Mapping page in the Environment Manager (**Figure 24**) to specify the settings.

> *You can get to the Environment Manager two ways. Start the Task Pane Manager and navigate to the Environment Manager pane or execute the Environment Manager as a standalone application inside of the IDE from the Command Window.*

```
DO HOME()+"envmgr.app"
```

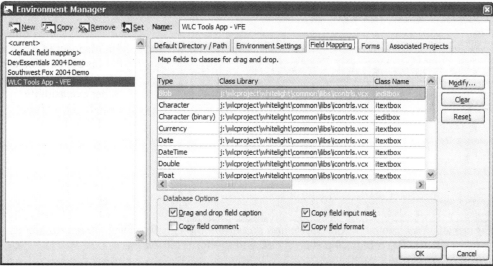

Figure 24. *The Task Pane Environment Manager tool has a new Field Mapping page where you configure the IntelliDrop settings for the environment.*

> *If you are running multiple instances of Visual FoxPro and set Field Mapping using the Environment Manager, the Options dialog, or programmatically via a project hook, the other instance of Visual FoxPro will use the changed Field Mapping settings. This is not a new behavior introduced in Visual FoxPro 9, but a gotcha you need to be aware of.*

Setting each of the data types through the dialog is as tedious in the Environment Manager as it is in the Options dialog. You need to select the data type, click the Modify button, navigate to the class library, and pick the class. Repeat this for each data type in your application. To eliminate a setting, pick the data type and click the Clear button. This clears the class and class library for only one data type. Use the Reset button to clear the settings for all the data types.

One way to work around this manual process is to hack the table where the settings are saved. The table is called EnvMgr.DBF and is located in the HOME(7) folder. The Field Mapping settings are saved in the SetValues column. In our opinion, editing this memo field is faster than using the user interface as it currently stands. Each data type is represented by a line in the field (**Figure 25**). The line begins with an asterisk, followed by the data type, an equal sign, and the class name. The class library immediately follows the class name; it's delimited by the less than (<) and greater than (>) signs, and includes the full path.

Figure 25. *You can hack the SetValues column in the EnvMgr.DBF file to edit the settings for the Field Mapping data types and the form templates.*

The <default field mapping> environment allows you to specify which classes are assigned to the data types automatically when you create a new environment. This is useful for developers who use one set of base classes for many different projects. It is not going to help developers with different sets of base classes for different projects, different clients, or different frameworks. The default mappings are initially set to the field mappings set in the Options dialog and saved in the Registry.

Like the field mapping capability, the Environment Manager can now reset the current Form and Formset Template for each defined environment. These are the same templates set on the Forms page of the Visual FoxPro Options dialog. The new Forms page on the Environment Manager allows you to pick the class you want used as the superclass for any new forms or formsets created. These settings work the same way as the settings on the Forms page of the Options dialog. First, indicate you want to use one or both of the templates by selecting the checkbox, and then pick the class using the ellipsis button next to the textbox displaying the class and classlibrary.

If you are running multiple instances of Visual FoxPro and set the Form or FormSet Template using the Environment Manager, the other instance of Visual FoxPro will not use the changed template settings. This behavior is different from the Field Mapping behavior. If you want the second instance to use the new setting, open the Visual FoxPro Options dialog and click the Set As Default button to save the settings to the Windows Registry.

The last change to the Environment Manager is support for specifying a FoxUser resource file on the Environment Settings page. This allows you to have a specific resource file for each environment. If the resource file does not exist when you switch to a particular environment, you will be asked whether you want to have the Environment Manager create a new, completely empty one.

Replacing VFP native menu behavior

IntelliSense was introduced in Visual FoxPro 7. VFP's version is still considered one of the most extensible implementations of the IntelliSense technology. When you first saw the properties, events, and methods (both intrinsic and custom) show up in the dropdown as you typed in an editor or the Command Window, many of you recognized the potential for increased productivity. But in your wildest imagination, did you ever think the IntelliSense engine could be used to hook into the VFP menu system? Beginning in VFP 9, when you make a selection from the menu, Visual FoxPro looks for a record in the IntelliSense table and determines whether there is custom code to run in response to your selection, instead of the native behavior. This means you can replace the native functionality with your own functionality.

You must have IntelliSense turned on to take advantage of the menu hit capability.

So how does this work? Visual FoxPro's IntelliSense engine does the following when you make a menu selection from any of the system menus or native shortcut menus, if you have IntelliSense enabled:

1. Searches in the IntelliSense table for a MENUHIT record (described in detail later in this section). If it does not find one, the native behavior is performed.

2. Executes the script contained in the Data memo field of the MENUHIT record. A single object parameter is passed to this script.

3. Examines the return value of the script. If the script returns False or the ValueType property is not set to "V" or "L", the native behavior is performed.

> *All menus built into Visual FoxPro are hooked into the MENUHIT script capability. This includes menu items dynamically added to the system menu (like those on the Table pad), and all the native shortcut menus.*

The first thing you need to do is add the single MENUHIT record to the IntelliSense table. You do this with a simple browse or write a program to create the record. There's also a Solution Sample that can do it for you (see Foxcode menu scripts). The record needs data in three columns with specific information. See **Table 4** for the values required to turn on this functionality.

Table 4. Set up the MENUHIT record in the IntelliSense table for the three columns specified. The Data column does not have a fixed value; it contains the script code you write to call your menu hit handler code.

Column	Value	Description
Type	S	Indicates the record is a Script type.
Abbrev	MENUHIT	Indicates the record is a menu hit script record.
Data		Visual FoxPro code with your customized behavior (presents a custom dialog or runs some code to gain the desired result).

The Data column contains script code (VFP program code) to execute a menu hit handler. You might think you need a separate MENUHIT record for each menu item you want to change. Visual FoxPro only supports one MENUHIT record so the script code needs to be generic to handle all the various menu calls you want to change. If you have multiple MENUHIT records in the IntelliSense table, Visual FoxPro uses the first record it finds.

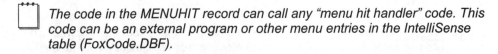

> *The code in the MENUHIT record can call any "menu hit handler" code. This code can be an external program or other menu entries in the IntelliSense table (FoxCode.DBF).*

There are many approaches to deal with this, but the script in this record needs to call other code and pass along the parameter passed into the MENUHIT script. The two most common are a call to an external program, and a scheme to look up other records in the IntelliSense table. The sample MENUHIT scripts shown in **Listing 6** is the script inserted from the Solution Sample. This script blends the both techniques into one.

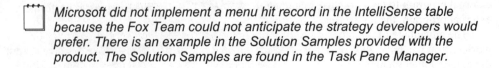

> *Microsoft did not implement a menu hit record in the IntelliSense table because the Fox Team could not anticipate the strategy developers would prefer. There is an example in the Solution Samples provided with the product. The Solution Samples are found in the Task Pane Manager.*

Listing 6. This sample script code for the MENUHIT record uses the IntelliSense table to define behavior for individual menu items. If there is no IntelliSense defined behavior records, then an external menu handler program is called.

```
LPARAMETERS toParameter

LOCAL lnSelect, lcCode, llReturn, lScriptHandled

TRY
   * First try FoxCode lookup for Type="M" records
   lnSelect = SELECT()
   SELECT 0
   USE (_FOXCODE) AGAIN SHARE ORDER 1
   IF SEEK('M' + PADR(UPPER(toParameter.MenuItem), LEN(ABBREV)))
     lcCode = DATA
   ENDIF
   USE
   SELECT (lnSelect)
   IF NOT EMPTY(lcCode)
      llReturn = EXECSCRIPT(lcCode, toParameter)
      lScriptHandled=.T.
   ENDIF

   * Handle by passing to external routine as specified in Tip field
   IF !lScriptHandled
      lcProgram = ALLTRIM(toParameter.Tip)
      IF FILE(lcProgram)
         DO (lcProgram) WITH toParameter,llReturn
      ENDIF
   ENDIF

   * Custom script successful so let's disable native behavior
   IF llReturn
      toParameter.ValueType = 'V'
   ENDIF
CATCH
ENDTRY

RETURN llReturn
```

This example implements MENUHIT functionality by first looking up individual "M" (menu) records in the IntelliSense table for menu items you want to handle. If a menu record is found, the script for the specific menu item runs. The menu item script code can still return False so the native behavior runs, but normally, it will return True so the replacement behavior you added runs instead of the native behavior. If no record is found, and there is a program in the Tip property (implemented by adding a program to the Tip column of the MENUHIT record), the program is called to handle the menu item. If there are no menu records, no external program to call, or if False is returned from both the menu record script and the external program, the native behavior runs.

The advantage of the menu hit Solution Sample approach is you get the best of both worlds. You can have all the script code encapsulated in the IntelliSense table, or have it all in the external menu handler program, or a mix of the two. The encapsulation in the IntelliSense table allows team environments to avoid the pathing issues associated with the location of a external menu hit handler program. The disadvantage of the menu records is debugging is harder than using a menu hit handler program. If you want easier debugging you can call the external program with a big DO CASE statement. Using this scheme you can implement menu hit examples created by developers in the Fox Community no matter which technique they adopt.

Now that you have established the menu hit record in the IntelliSense table, you need to put this feature to work with a specific menu hit. The key to the menu hit handler code is to determine what menu item was selected from the menu. This information is stored in a property called MenuItem of the object passed as a parameter to the MENUHIT script. The prompt for the pad is stored in a property called UserTyped. This is why it is important to pass this parameter from the menu hit script to the menu hit handler code. The properties of the parameter object are detailed in **Table 5**.

Table 5. *The parameter object passed into the MENUHIT script has a number of parameters, this table only details the parameters used for MENUHIT.*

Parameter	Description
MenuItem	The prompt of the menu item selected.
UserTyped	The prompt of the system menu pad from which the menu item was selected. If it was a shortcut menu, this is an empty string.
ValueType	This is a return value to Visual FoxPro. Set it to "V" or "L" (both have the same results) to prevent the default behavior, and leave it blank if you want the native menu behavior to be performed.

The implementation details of the menu hit handler code depend on your approach to the MENUHIT record in the IntelliSense table. Regardless, it needs to receive a parameter for the menu hit parameter object so you can use the various properties detailed in Table 5. The code should evaluate the situation and either process the altered behavior or do something to tell the menu hit script to run the native behavior.

The example demonstrated is for a replacement of the File | New… menu option discussed in the next section of this chapter. The code is based on adding a record to the IntelliSense table for each menu hit handled. The record in the IntelliSense table is found in **Table 6**.

If the "M" record is found, the frmNewDialog is instantiated and displayed, and True is returned, indicating the menu hit was intercepted and handled.

> *The prompts passed in with the parameter are localized. If you plan to distribute your menu hit code to developers using a different language, your code must take this into account.*

The implementation of menu hits provides a completely new way to customize your Visual FoxPro IDE in ways we never thought possible. The next two sections provide concrete examples of implementations we think provide some added productivity and inspiration to create additional menu hit behavior.

Table 6. The details necessary to implement a replacement for the New dialog. You need to change the directory in the Data column to match where you install the APP.

Column	Value
Type	M
Abbrev	NEW...
Expanded	
Cmd	
Tip	
Data	```LPARAMETERS toParameter
LOCAL llReturn

TRY
    RELEASE _oNewDialog
    PUBLIC _oNewDialog
    _oNewDialog = NEWOBJECT('frmNewDialog', 'WlcNewDialog.vcx', ;
            'd:\devvfp9apps\devtools\newdialog\wlcnewdialog.app')
    _oNewDialog.Show()
    llReturn = .T.
CATCH
ENDTRY

RETURN llReturn``` |
Case	
Save	
Timestamp	10/16/2004 11:11:11 PM
Source	
Uniqueid	_1CU1DP395
User	

New Property / New Method replacement

Doug Hennig took the lead in exploring this technology during the beta and quickly developed a replacement for the New Property and New Method dialogs in Visual FoxPro. This replacement dialog (see **Figure 26**) addresses some shortcomings and extends the native behavior to integrate with some of the new MemberData features. Specifically, Doug wanted to address the following issues:

1. The native dialog does nothing to integrate with the Display and Favorites attributes of the new _MemberData property. (See Chapter 2, "Customizing the Property Sheet.")

2. The native dialog is modal, which means you have to close it before you can do anything else. The custom dialog is not modal.

3. While the VFP 9 New Property dialog allows you to set the initial value for new properties, the default value is still False. In the custom dialog, default values are automatically set based on the Hungarian object naming convention. So if you name a property nBalance, the dialog assumes you are defining a numeric property and sets the initial value to zero.

4. The native dialog doesn't tell you a member name is invalid until you press the Add button. The custom dialog disallows invalid member names as you are entering them. The Add and Add & Close buttons are only enabled if you enter a valid member name.

5. The native dialog requires you to first add the property, and then close the dialog. Closing the native dialog before adding means you lose the member. The custom dialog includes an Add & Close button so you can add the member and close the dialog in one step.

6. The custom dialog is dockable, resizable, and saves its position and size attributes to the FoxUser resource file so it shows up in the same place the next time it is opened. You can not only dock the dialog to one of the sides, you can also tab-dock it with other IDE forms like the Property Sheet, or any of the user dockable forms and tools (such as the Class Browser and Data Explorer discussed earlier in this chapter).

The NewPropertyDialog.APP is available as a Solution Sample. The Foxcode menu scripts Solution Sample installs the needed records in the IntelliSense table.

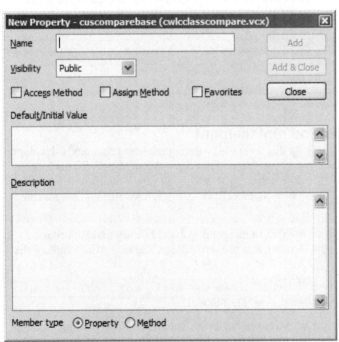

Figure 26. *A replacement for the native Visual FoxPro New Property Dialog, it is modeless and handles the new _MemberData feature automatically.*

The NewPropertyDialog application registers itself in the IntelliSense file by adding three records. The first record is the generic MENUHIT record. The implementation technique used is the one discussed earlier in this chapter (see section "Replacing VFP native menu behavior") where individual menu item records are added to the IntelliSense table. The other two records added are for the New Property,,, and New Method,,, menu items. You can inspect the entries to see how it works.

Once you register the dialog, when you edit a form or class and choose to add a new property or method, the replacement dialog displays. If you want to revert to the native dialogs, remove the menu item records using the the Solution Sample or delete the records manually in the IntelliSense table. You can use the replacement dialogs even with classes compiled in VFP 8 and earlier, just keep the properties and methods in lower case and don't turn on the Favorites. If you follow this procedure no member data will be written. You do not need to remove the generic MENUHIT record unless you want to use a different style of implementation.

New Dialog replacement

The second menu behavior replacement we want to demonstrate is the ability to replace the File | New... dialog. The replacement new dialog (**Figure 27**) addresses several things:

1. It has one click access to create a new file. You create a new file by clicking the hyperlink label or the associated command button. The native VFP dialog forces a selection of the file type, followed by the selection of New or Wizard.

2. It has one click access to the appropriate Visual FoxPro wizard by right-clicking the hyperlink label or the command button. Alternatively, select the Run Wizard checkbox, and then click on the file type (hyperlink or button).

3. The dialog is not modal; you can create as many files as you want before closing the dialog. (The native VFP dialog is modal and closes when the file is created.)

4. The file types are organized in order of expected use (based on the developers preference of course).

There are some design decisions made with this version because of the way the various create commands work. For instance, the new class prompts you for the class name because the CREATE CLASS <class name> NOWAIT command cannot be executed with the NOWAIT unless the class name is provided. We wanted the code to continue processing after the class is created; otherwise clicking off the class prompts you to save it, making the dialog modal like. The same situation applies to CREATE FILE, CREATE FORM, CREATE LABEL, CREATE REPORT, CREATE PROGRAM, and CREATE PROJECT. We did leave some of the other objects with the modal like feel so you understand the design decision.

The Developer Downloads for this chapter, available from ***www.hentzenwerke.com***, *include the source code for the New Dialog replacement dialog. The project file is called WlcNewDialog.PJX and the application is WlcNewDialog.APP.*

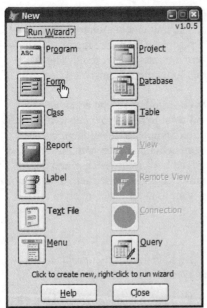

Figure 27. *This modeless New Dialog is a replacement for the native Visual FoxPro New Dialog.*

Again, there is not enough room in this chapter to detail the source code for this tool, but using it is simple. First change to the directory where you installed the WlcNewDialog.APP and execute it:

```
DO WlcNewDialog.app
```

The application registers itself in the IntelliSense file by adding two records. The first record is the generic MENUHIT record (the same one used by the New Property / New Method menu hit and Solution Sample), which is only added if it isn't already there. Like the New Property/Method dialog, this replacement adds individual menu item records to the IntelliSense table. The other record added is for the New... menu items. You can inspect the entries to evaluate the implementation. A text file displays with Help when you click the Help button.

Replacing native VFP shortcut menus

The MENUCONTEXT script in the IntelliSense table allows you to replace native shortcut menus in the Visual FoxPro IDE. The MENUCONTEXT script works like the MENUHIT scripts. Unfortunately, recreating an entire shortcut menu and its functionality is not a trivial task in most cases. We wish the implementation allowed developers to add items to a shortcut menu without replacing the entire shortcut menu.

This implementation is limited, as follows:

- You cannot replace or remove individual shortcut menu items. The script code can only stop the menu from displaying; you have to replace the entire menu.

- The script executes when the shortcut menu is invoked via the right-click or shortcut menu keyboard, not when the menu item is selected from the system menu.

- The internal menus are referenced by number and these numbers are not documented. You have to discover the internal menu identifiers using a technique described later in this section.

- The parameter object passed from IntelliSense provides a list of shortcut menu prompts, but no access to the result, SKIP FOR, MESSAGE, hot keys, or other menu clauses helpful in creating a custom shortcut menu.

- Creating a replacement for each item on a shortcut menu is not always possible because the IDE does not expose all the native functionality.

The first thing you need to do is add the single MENUCONTEXT record to the IntelliSense table. You do this with a simple browse or write a program to create the record. The record needs a minimum of three columns with the information indicated in **Table 7**.

Table 7. *Set up the MENUCONTEXT record in the IntelliSense table for the three columns specified. The Data column does not have a fixed value; it contains script code you write to call your shortcut menu code.*

Column	Value	Description
Type	S	Indicates the record is a Script type.
Abbrev	MENUCONTEXT	Indicates the record is a shortcut menu script record.
Data		Visual FoxPro code with your customized behavior (presents a custom shortcut menu or is some proxy code that runs other code to generate the shortcut menu).

The MENUCONTEXT script must accept a single parameter, the same type of object passed into the MENUHIT script.

One of the tricky parts is determining the menu ID for each of the shortcuts you want to implement. Fortunately there is a straightforward way you can determine them. The menu ID is stored in the parameter object's MenuItem property. **Listing 7** provides some code to discover details about the parameter object passed to the MENUCONTEXT script. **Listing 8** shows the results of this script when you invoke the Command Window's context menu.

Listing 7. *Insert this code into the Data field of the MENUCONTEXT record in the IntelliSense table to discover the details about the MENUCONTEXT parameter object properties.*

```
LPARAMETERS toParameter

LOCAL lnI, llReturn

DEBUGOUT toParameter.MenuItem
DEBUGOUT toParameter.UserTyped
DEBUGOUT toParameter.ValueType

FOR lnI = 1 TO ALEN(toParameter.Items, 1)
   DEBUGOUT lnI, "=", toParameter.Items[lnI]
ENDFOR

DEBUGOUT "---------"

RETURN llReturn
```

Listing 8. *The results of running the MENUCONTEXT script in Listing 7 when the Command Window shortcut menu is invoked.*

```
24446

.F.
            1 = Cut
            2 = Copy
            3 = Paste
            4 =
            5 = Build Expression...
            6 = Execute Selection
            7 =
            8 = Clear
            9 =
           10 = Properties...
```

You need the menu ID to determine which menu was called so you can write code to respond to this menu invocation. These menu IDs will be part of a DO CASE statement in the shortcut menu hit handler program or used to identify records you might add to the IntelliSense table using the same technique implemented for the menu hit implementation.

The parameter object has an array property called Items containing each of the menu items on the shortcut menu. As we noted at the beginning of this section, this is the only information about the shortcut menu we can gather. We cannot determine, for each item, what the SKIP FOR clause is, what the menu hot keys are, or what the status bar message includes.

Replacement menus should use the DEFINE POPUP...SHORTCUT menu syntax. You can generate them using the Visual FoxPro Menu Designer or create the menus on-the-fly using Visual FoxPro code.

Because of all the limitations, we chose not to provide a sample of this technology. In summary, the MENUCONTEXT scripts are a disappointment, but still hold potential if you have the inspiration to replace an entire shortcut menu with better functionality. We suspect MENUCONTEXT scripts will be used sparingly.

GenDBC changes

GenDBC is a utility program included with Visual FoxPro since VFP 3.0. This tool generates a program to recreate a specified database and its associated tables, views, relations, connections, stored procedures, and so forth. GenDBC has been enhanced to support the new Varchar, Varbinary, and Blob data types for fields. One bug fix is included—GENDBC now generates the code for the AllowSimultaneousFetch, RuleExpression, and RuleText properties for views. The AllowSimultaneousFetch property was added to views in Visual FoxPro 8. The RuleExpression and RuleText properties for views have been around since Visual FoxPro 3.

New Solution Samples

The Visual FoxPro Solution Samples are a gold mine of interesting techniques that demonstrate various features of the product. If you are not familiar with the Solution Samples, you are missing an opportunity to learn new concepts and see how you can leverage new features of Visual FoxPro. The Solution Samples can be viewed two ways. The Task Pane Manager includes a Solution Samples pane. You can run the sample solutions application standalone as well:

```
CD HOME(2) + "Solution"
DO solution.app
```

Many of the new samples for Visual FoxPro 9 focus on the Report Designer and the new features introduced in this version. The rest show some of the new functionality, including some features that can seriously impact your end user applications.

We are not going into great detail for the new Solution Samples. It is up to you to review them, look at the code to see how they are done, and take advantage of this opportunity to learn. Here is a list of the new Solution Samples:

- The typical multiple detail band report

- A multiple detail band report used for calculations

- Control preview window for your report

- Add a custom report previewer in your form

- Dynamic formatting using ReportListeners

- Report to several outputs simultaneously using a ReportListener

- HTML and XML output with ReportListeners

- Create column chart reports using GDI+

- Anchors Away

- BINTOC and CTOBIN binary conversion

- Binding to Windows Message events

- Control button caption and image placement

- Coverage Profiler Performance Add-In

- Dockable Image Viewer

- Fox Media Player

- Foxcode menu scripts

- Fun with polygons

- Utility to scan for Memo corruption

 The Developer Downloads for this chapter, available from **www.hentzenwerke.com**, *include Chapter 4 Bonus, "Solution Samples" with more details on the new Solution Samples.*

Summary

It is obvious from the length of this chapter that the Fox Team focused on improving the development experience in several of the tools and designers. While much of the focus and attention has been given to the Report Designer changes, we think the changes to the other IDE tools will improve your development experience significantly.

Updates and corrections for this chapter can be found on Hentzenwerke's website, **www.hentzenwerke.com**. Click "Catalog" and navigate to the page for this book.

Chapter 5
Enhancements in the
Reporting System

A major focus of VFP 9 was improving the reporting system. The list of new and improved features is enormous: multiple detail bands, protection of objects in the Report Designer, design-time events, ability to position objects absolutely, more zoom levels, better menus, and a lot more. This chapter explores these enhancements in detail, demonstrates some types of reports you couldn't do in earlier versions of VFP, and introduces the "Extending the Reporting System" chapters.

One of the biggest changes in VFP 9 is the incredible improvement made in the reporting system. Three aspects of this are an enhanced Report Designer and other design-time improvements, enhanced run-time capabilities including output to HTML and XML, and new engine capabilities such as support for multiple detail bands. We look at each of these areas in this chapter.

Enhanced Report Designer

Microsoft had several goals in mind when working on the Report Designer:

- Protecting developers' investment in existing reports.

- Using an open architecture so it would be highly customizable.

- Improving the user interface.

- Providing new features: protection, design-time captions, absolute positioning, DataEnvironment handling, and others.

For the first point, the VFP team worked very hard to ensure existing reports would work exactly the same in VFP 9 as they did in earlier versions. In addition, the FRX structure didn't change (although some previously unused fields are now used in VFP 9 and there's now support for user-defined fields and user-defined records).

The keys to a more open architecture are a new system variable called _REPORTBUILDER and report events. The Report Designer can now call a VFP application when events occur at design time, such as adding a field or invoking a dialog. This application is specified in _REPORTBUILDER, which by default points to ReportBuilder.APP in the VFP home directory. You can use your own application if you wish by setting _REPORTBUILDER to point to a different application. This topic is discussed in detail in Chapter 6, "Extending the Reporting System at Design Time."

Let's discuss the remaining two points.

Improved user interface

One of the first things you notice in the VFP 9 Report Designer is the greatly improved dialogs. In VFP 8 and earlier, there were many dialogs related to reporting: properties dialogs for each type of object and band, a Page Setup dialog for the report, Data Grouping and Variables dialogs, and so forth. Some of them had rather unusual interfaces, and some spawned yet other dialogs. You can see an example of the clunky interface when you double-click a field object (see **Figure 1**): that action opens a properties dialog for the field, but the dialog doesn't allow you to change all properties of the field (font and color are missing, for example) and you have to click buttons to open other modal dialogs to change some properties.

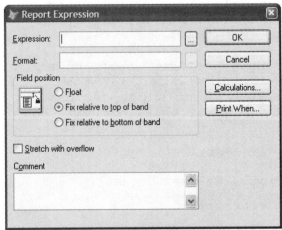

Figure 1. The Report Expression dialog is an example of the Report Designer's clunky interface in earlier versions of VFP.

In VFP 9, there are only a few dialogs because all the properties for an object are now in one place. The Properties dialog for all object types uses a tabbed interface, so you can edit all possible properties for the object in one dialog without launching additional modal dialogs. **Figure 2** shows the Properties dialog for a field.

The new Report Properties dialog, shown in **Figure 3**, combines the features of the Page Setup, Title/Summary, Data Grouping, Variables, and Set Grid Scale dialogs from earlier versions, plus adds new features as well.

These dialogs aren't actually part of the product, but are provided by ReportBuilder.APP. That's right, they're VFP forms! The source code for ReportBuilder.APP comes with VFP (unzip XSource.ZIP in the Tools\XSource subdirectory of the VFP home directory, and then look in the ReportBuilder folder), so you can customize or subclass the various dialogs and behaviors to suit your needs. If your application provides access to the Report Designer at run-time, be sure to distribute ReportBuilder.APP (or your replacement for it) with the other files you ship.

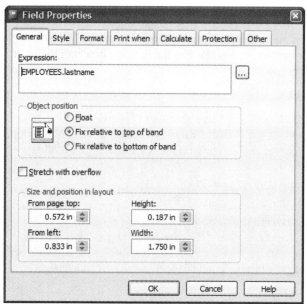

Figure 2. *The Properties dialog in VFP 9 uses a tabbed interface to make all properties for an object available in a single dialog.*

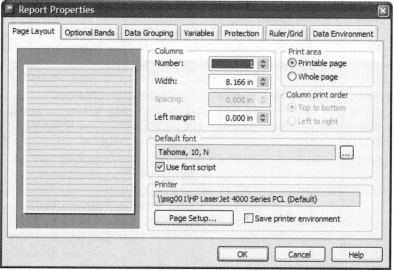

Figure 3. *The new Report Properties dialog combines the features of several former dialogs and adds some new features.*

Other UI improvements are:

- The Report menu and the shortcut menu for a report are reorganized and have additional items (including Properties, which invokes the Report Properties dialog) to make it easier to work with reports.

- The mouse cursor now changes to provide a visual cue when an object is resizable.

- The Report Designer toolbar includes Page Setup and Font Properties buttons. Also, the View menu includes an item for the Report Designer toolbar. Previously, you had to choose Toolbars from the View menu and turn on the Report Designer toolbar in the resulting dialog.

- The Reports tab of the Tools | Options dialog is reorganized and has three new options: how the Expression Builder should deal with aliases for fields, whether the default run-time behavior is backward-compatible (the equivalent of using the new SET REPORTBEHAVIOR 80 command; see "New reporting syntax" later in this chapter) or object-assisted (the same as SET REPORTBEHAVIOR 90), and whether to use the script for a font (see the "International support" section of this chapter).

Protection

If you allow users to modify reports in the Report Designer in your run-time applications, you may have wished for a way to protect them from themselves. The Report Designer has many features that can get an unsuspecting user in trouble, such as the data environment. If you only want the user to make simple changes, such as moving fields around or adding a company logo, exposing all the features available in the Report Designer is overkill.

VFP 9 has a new keyword for the MODIFY/CREATE REPORT/LABEL commands: PROTECTED. When this keyword is used, you can prevent certain operations. You control which actions a user can take at the object, band, and report levels using the Protection tab of the properties dialogs. For obvious reasons, this tab isn't available in protected mode.

You can control whether an object can be moved, resized, edited (that is, whether the Properties dialog can be invoked), or deleted. You can even control whether the object can be selected, or if it appears or not. **Figure 4** shows the settings available for fields.

Figure 4. *The Protection tab of the properties dialogs allows you to control what capabilities the user has in the Report Designer when using the PROTECTED keyword.*

As you see in **Figure 5**, you can control whether bands can be edited or resized.

Figure 5. *You can control the editing or resizing of bands when protection is used.*

At the report level, you can control which tabs of the Report Properties dialog and which menu items are available (see **Figure 6**).

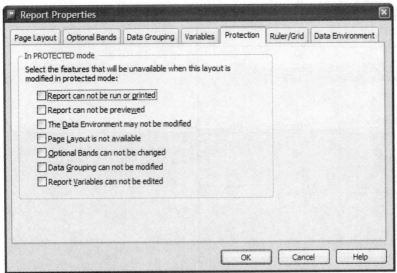

Figure 6. *The Protection page of the Report Properties dialog allows you to specify which tabs and menu items are available to the user.*

Figure 7 shows what the Report Properties dialog looks like when MODIFY REPORT ... PROTECTED is used for a report with the Optional Bands, Data Grouping, and Data Environment tabs turned off.

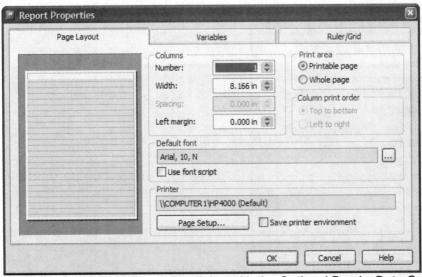

Figure 7. *The Report Properties dialog with the Optional Bands, Data Grouping, and Data Environment tabs turned off.*

Design-time captions

You may have noticed the Protection tab for a field object has an additional setting: design-time caption. This allows you to indicate what appears in place of the field expression when a report is modified in protected mode.

For example, compare the two Report Designer sessions shown in **Figure 8** and **Figure 9**. Figure 8 used MODIFY REPORT without the PROTECTED keyword.

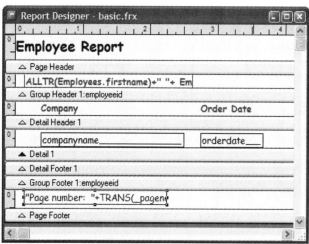

Figure 8. *The expression used to output the page number displays as an expression when PROTECTED isn't used.*

Figure 9 used the PROTECTED keyword. Notice the fields show descriptive names such as Employee Name rather than the actual expression such as ALLTR(Employees.firstname)+" "+ Employees.lastname. This lets you shield your users from seeing the real expressions used for fields and display meaningful descriptive names instead. Note if they bring up the Properties dialog, they will see the real expression because that's the value they would edit rather than the descriptive name.

Design-time tooltips

In addition to design-time captions, you can also specify design-time tooltips for report objects (all object types, not just fields). Set the desired tooltip text in the Tooltip setting on the Other page of the properties dialog for an object. **Figure 10** shows the tooltip for the COMPANYNAME field.

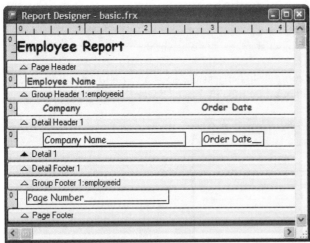

Figure 9. *Design-time captions display in place of expressions in protected mode.*

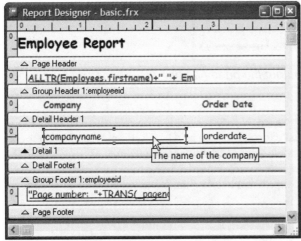

Figure 10. *The Tooltip setting in the Other page of an object's properties dialog allows you to specify the tooltip for the object.*

Absolute positioning

One thing VFP developers have wanted for a long time is the ability to specify the exact size and position of an object by typing the top, left, height, and width values rather than having to carefully move or resize it one pixel at a time to get it to the correct place and shape. As you can see in Figure 2, the General tab of the object properties dialog now allows you to do just that. However, note that while the size and position values are shown to 1/1000th of an inch, the Report Designer measures things to 1/960th of an inch, so if you enter a value like 0.575, you may find the actual value is 0.572, the closest possible value to what you specified.

Trim mode for character expressions

In earlier versions of VFP, unless you turn on the Stretch with overflow setting, the value of a character expression is truncated if it's too long for the field. In VFP 9, you can specify how the value should appear. The Trim mode for character expressions setting on the Format page of the Field Properties dialog controls this. The choices are:

- Default trimming: an ellipsis is added to the end of the text indicating there's more data that can't be seen. Notice in **Figure 11** that several company names have an ellipsis at the end.

Figure 11. One choice in the Trim mode for character expressions setting displays an ellipsis to indicate a value is truncated.

- Trim to nearest character: this cuts off the text at the last character that fits.

- Trim to nearest word: this cuts off the text at the last whole word, similar to the truncation used in earlier versions of VFP.

- Trim to nearest character, append ellipsis: like Trim to nearest character, but adds an ellipsis.

- Trim to nearest word, append ellipsis: same as Default trimming.

- Filespec, show inner path as ellipsis: this has the same effect as the DISPLAYPATH() function; characters at the start and end of the expression appear but middle characters are replaced by an ellipsis.

Note that these settings are ignored unless you run the report in object-assisted mode; see "New reporting syntax" later in this chapter for information on that mode.

Data grouping enhancements

There are three improvements in data grouping in VFP 9.

The first is where VFP places group headers when the report has multiple columns printed left to right rather than top to bottom. **Figure 12** shows that in earlier versions, the report engine places a group header in line with the detail band; it takes up the first column and the detail starts in the second column. This first position is reserved for the group header band even if you size the height of the band to zero; in that case, the first column is blank. It's also a fixed height—that of the detail band—so group header objects may overlap the second row of detail objects if the group header band is taller than the detail band.

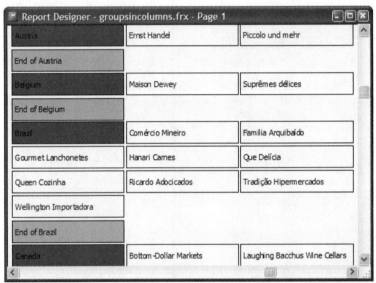

Figure 12. *The group header band is placed in line with the detail band in earlier versions of VFP.*

As you can see in **Figure 13**, VFP 9 places group header objects on their own row. This row is the height of the group header band, not the detail band, so group header objects don't overlap detail objects nor is any space taken up if the group header is sized to zero.

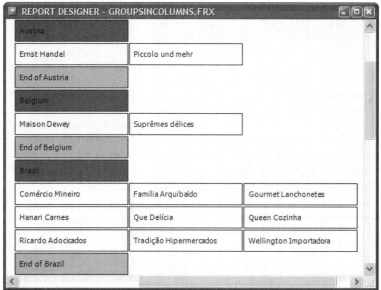

Figure 13. *The group header band prints on its own row in VFP 9.*

(The authors wish to thank Cathy Pountney for providing this example.)

The second enhancement also pertains to reports with multiple columns printed left to right. Although the design surface only appears to be as wide as a column in the Report Designer, you can actually place objects in group header and footer bands across the page so they span multiple columns. **Figure 14** shows what the GroupsInColumns2 report looks like in the Report Designer and **Figure 15** shows its appearance when previewed.

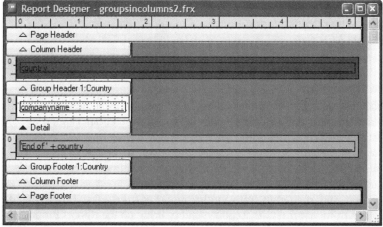

Figure 14. *Although it looks odd in the Report Designer, you can put objects in group header and footer bands across the page when a report has multiple columns printed left to right.*

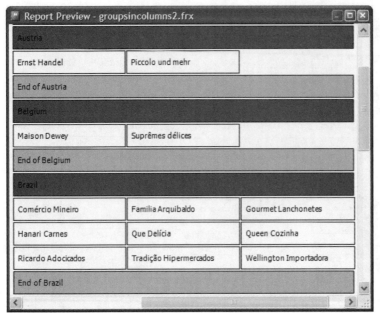

Figure 15. *The objects in the group and footer header bands span all columns of the report.*

The final improvement is that you can now create up to 74 data groups in VFP 9. While the report engine supported that many groups in earlier versions, you were limited to 20 data groups in the Data Grouping dialog.

 *The Developer Download files for this chapter, available at **www.hentzenwerke.com**, include GroupsInColumns.FRX and GroupsInColumns2.FRX.*

DataEnvironment handling

There are two changes dealing with the DataEnvironment of a report: you can now save the DataEnvironment as a class and you can load the DataEnvironment from another report or from a DataEnvironment class.

VFP 8 added the ability to visually subclass a DataEnvironment. In VFP 9, to save the DataEnvironment of a report as a class, open the DataEnvironment window and choose Save As Class from the File menu.

To load the DataEnvironment of a report from another report or from a DataEnvironment class, choose Load Data Environment from the Report menu or bring up the Report Properties dialog and choose the Data Environment page. Copying the DataEnvironment from another report is pretty straightforward; it simply copies the DataEnvironment-related records from the specified FRX to the current one. This means, of course, changes made later in the other report aren't reflected in this report.

Linking the DataEnvironment to a DataEnvironment class, on the other hand, may not do quite what you expect. Unlike a form or form class, an FRX doesn't support referencing a DataEnvironment class. Instead, the various members of the DataEnvironment are loaded into records in the FRX. For example, if there are two cursors and a relation in the DataEnvironment class, records for these objects are added to the FRX. Code in the DataEnvironment class is handled in a very interesting way: code is inserted into various methods of the DataEnvironment, Cursor, and Relation records, and the BeforeOpenTables method has code that instantiates the specified DataEnvironment class and binds events of the DataEnvironment in the report to the appropriate events in the DataEnvironment class. That way, the code in the DataEnvironment class fires as you'd expect. It's just wired up differently than a form or form class.

International support

The Windows Font dialog includes a Script setting that allows a user to select the desired language script. Values include Western, Cyrillic, Japanese, Hebrew, and Arabic. VFP objects support this with their FontCharSet property. Unfortunately, earlier versions of VFP didn't store the selected script in a report, either for report objects or for the default font of the report. In VFP 9, this value is now saved so full support is provided. The Use font script setting in the Style page of the Field Properties and Label Properties dialogs and the Page Layout page of the Report Properties dialog allows you to control this.

In addition, the VFP team ensured that alignment works better than before in both left-to-right and right-to-left languages.

Other new features

The FRX file has had a USER memo field for a long time. This field wasn't used by the VFP Report Designer and was intended to hold user-defined information. (A bug in earlier versions of VFP wiped out the contents of this field whenever a report was saved. This is fixed in VFP 9.) However, this field wasn't exposed in any of the Report Designer's dialogs. In VFP 9, this is now available in the Other page of the properties dialog for objects (see **Figure 16**).

The Other page also provides access to "run-time extensions." This is actually XML stored in the STYLE memo field for objects in the FRX. Here's an example:

```
<VFPData><reportdata name="" type="R" script="" execute="test" execwhen="test2"
class="" classlib="" declass="" declasslib=""/></VFPData>
```

The XML schema is quite open; you can add your own attributes and remove attributes you don't need.

Neither the Report Designer nor the run-time reporting tools that come in the VFP box make any use of this XML, but your own enhancements to these tools certainly could. (See Chapter 6, "Extending the Reporting System at Design Time," and Chapter 7, "Extending the Reporting System at Run Time," for information on enhancements you can make.) Click the Edit Settings button to bring up a dialog for entering some of the information stored in the XML for the current object. This dialog only allows you to edit the execute and execwhen attributes of the first node in the XML. However, you can replace the dialog with your own if you need more functionality; see Chapter 7, "Extending the Reporting System at Run Time," for details.

***Figure 16**. The Other page of the properties dialog for objects allows access to several new features, including the USER memo, design-time tooltips, and run-time extensions.*

The Format page of the Field Properties dialog has what appears to be a new feature: the **Template characters** setting. This option, which is only available for character fields, has **Overlay** and **Interleave** choices. However, this is really not a new feature, but instead determines whether "@R" is added to the picture. The "@R" does not display, but is stored when **Interleave** is selected.

The Expression Builder dialog no longer shows tables from the DataEnvironment, only the cursors currently open. This gives you greater control over what fields the user can select in this dialog.

Multiple detail bands

Crystal Reports is one of the most popular reporting tools in the world. One of the main reasons many VFP developers, who already have a report writer built into the product, use Crystal is because it supports sub-reports. A sub-report is a report that runs within a report. The most common use for a sub-report is to report on multiple children for a parent table.

For example, suppose you have a customers table, an invoices table, and a credit notes table. You may want to show customers, their invoices, and credit notes on a report. The complication here is that the report has three tables it needs to go through, and while invoices and credit notes are related to customers, they aren't related to each other. The way you resolve this in Crystal is to create a report showing customers and their invoices, and then add a sub-report to it showing the credit notes for the current customer.

Unfortunately, until now, there wasn't a good way to do this in VFP. A common workaround is to create a cursor combining invoices and credit notes, with a "record type" field distinguishing which records come from which table. The report includes fields from both types of records in the detail band with Print When expressions on the fields so only certain fields print for each type of record. This makes for a very ugly report to maintain!

Fortunately, VFP 9 solves this problem nicely with a new feature: multiple detail bands.

Record processing

Before looking at multiple detail bands, let's discuss how VFP moves through records in a report. A report has a single "driving" cursor. VFP moves through this cursor in a single pass; that is, the cursor is processed only once. The processing of these records is paused by group breaks; the report engine takes whatever action is specified (for example, printing a group footer for the former group and a group header for the new one), and then continues processing the cursor. The set of records processed without interruption is referred to as a "detail scope." If there are any groups for the report, the detail scope is the records inside the innermost group. If not, it is the entire report scope.

In VFP 9, there can now be multiple detail scopes (up to 20). The records for a particular detail scope can be from related records in child tables or from the driving alias, which means it can be processed multiple times. The Report Designer presents these multiple detail scopes as multiple detail bands. An important thing to note is detail scopes are consecutive, not nested like group breaks.

Calculated fields and report variables can now be scoped to a particular detail band. Interestingly, variables retain their values until the band they're scoped to is processed again. This means you can use these variables in later detail bands if necessary. The Variables page of the Report Properties dialog now uses "reset based on" rather than "reset at" as the prompt for a variable's scope to reinforce this idea.

Creating multiple detail bands

Every report has at least one detail band. To create additional detail bands, choose Optional Bands from the Report menu, the report shortcut menu, or bring up the Report Properties dialog and choose the Optional Bands page (see **Figure 17**). The Add button adds a new detail band and the Remove button removes the selected detail band. You can rearrange the order of the bands in the list.

In the Properties dialog for a detail band, you can specify whether the band has header and footer bands and indicate the target alias expression for the detail scope (see **Figure 18**). Ordinarily, the report engine processes a single record in the driving cursor before moving to the next detail band. However, if you specify a child cursor as the target alias, the report engine will process all child records of the current driving cursor record before moving to the next band. Note: you enter the target alias as an expression; to use a hard-coded name, surround it with quotes. Because this is an expression, you could enter the name of a variable that contains the target alias or even call a user-defined function (UDF). This may lead to some very interesting types of reports!

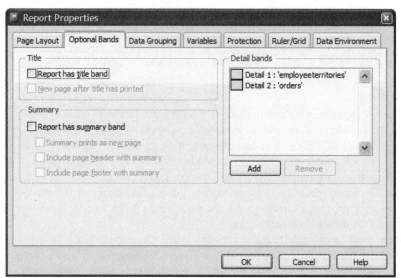

Figure 17. *You can define multiple detail bands in the Optional Bands page of the Report Properties dialog.*

Figure 18. *Use the Detail Band Properties dialog to specify whether the selected band has header and footer bands and provide the target alias.*

The target alias expression can evaluate to one of three values:

- An empty string means use the driving alias.

- The alias of a child table tells the report engine to process all the child records of the current driving cursor record before moving to the next band. This requires a relationship to exist between the driving alias and the child table, either using the

SET RELATION command or by creating a relationship in the DataEnvironment of the report.

- The driving alias, which is valid in the first detail band only, tells the report engine to process all driving alias records until it encounters a group break or the end of the report scope before moving to the next detail band.

Detail bands now also have some of the same options as group bands: starting on a new column or page, resetting the page number to 1 for each detail set, reprinting the detail header on each page, and starting the detail set on a new page when the amount of space remaining on the page is less than a desired value.

Let's look at a couple of examples of multiple detail band reports.

Example 1: Multiple children

The first example, EmployeesMD.FRX, uses the Employees, EmployeeTerritories, and Orders tables from the Northwind sample database that comes with VFP (in the Samples\Northwind subdirectory of the VFP home directory). EmployeeTerritories and Orders are both child tables of Employees, related on the EmployeeID field in each table. We want a report showing each employee, the territories he or she represents, and the orders taken by this employee.

The DataEnvironment for this report is set up as shown in **Figure 19**. The relationships between Employees and its child tables are one-to-many (the OneToMany property for the Relation objects is .T.) so all child records for a given Employees record will process in a detail band. Note this isn't strictly necessary; if you neglect to set OneToMany, the report engine automatically uses SET SKIP to do the same thing.

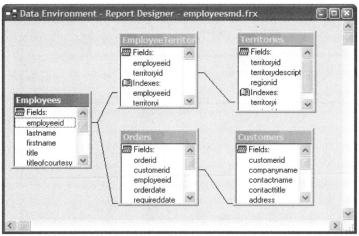

Figure 19. *The DataEnvironment for EmployeesMD.FRX defines EmployeeTerritories and Orders as children of Employees.*

The report has a group expression on Employees.EmployeeID and the desired fields from the Employees table appear in the group header band. There are two detail bands, one with a target alias of EmployeeTerritories and the other with a target alias of Orders; the appropriate fields appear in each band. **Figure 20** shows what the report looks like in the Report Designer. **Figure 21** shows the result when the report is run.

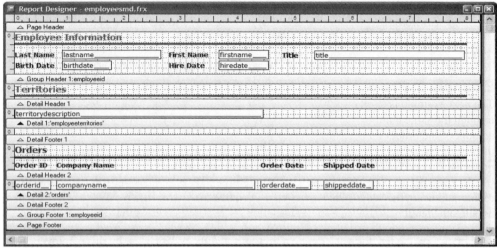

Figure 20. *EmployeesMD.FRX has two detail bands, one for fields of EmployeeTerritories and one for Orders.*

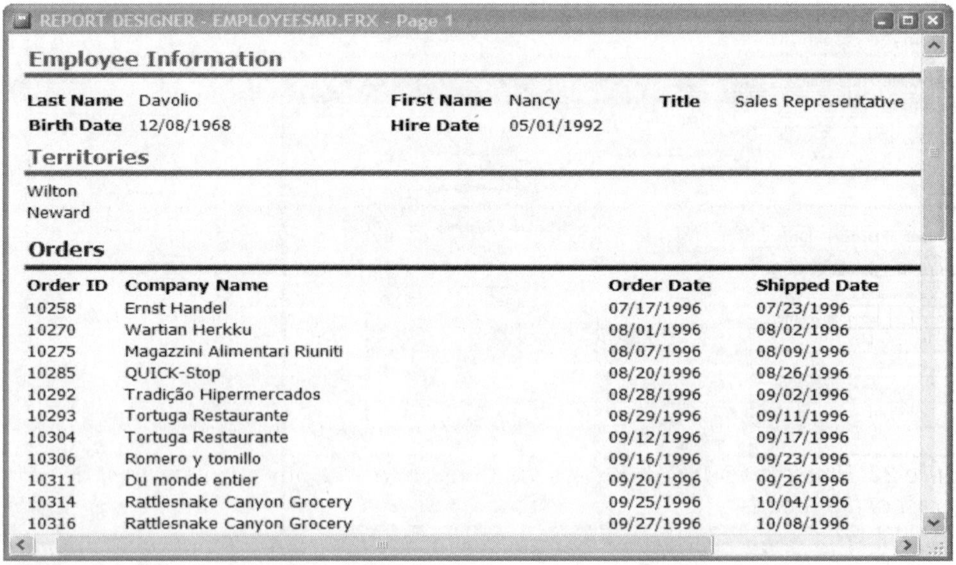

Figure 21. *Running EmployeesMD.FRX shows how a multiple detail band report works.*

The Developer Download files for this chapter, available at ***www.hentzenwerke.com****, include EmployeesMD.FRX. Because of path differences, you will likely have to locate Northwind.DBC (it's in the Samples\Northwind subdirectory of the VFP home directory) when you open this report.*

Example 2: Pre-calculation of totals

The next example is similar to the first one, but doesn't show two child tables; instead, it runs through the same child twice. The idea here is we want to calculate the number and total amount of the orders for each employee, but we want to show these calculations *before* displaying the actual orders. In addition, we want to show the amount of each invoice as a percentage of the total amount, meaning we have to pre-calculate the total.

In previous versions of VFP, this would require doing the calculations prior to running the report, and using the results of those calculations in the report. In VFP 9, this simply means having one detail band performing the calculations and another displaying the results. In the case of this example, EmployeesMD2.FRX, both detail bands have the Orders table as the target alias. **Figure 22** shows what the report looks like in the Report Designer; notice there are no objects in the Detail 1 band.

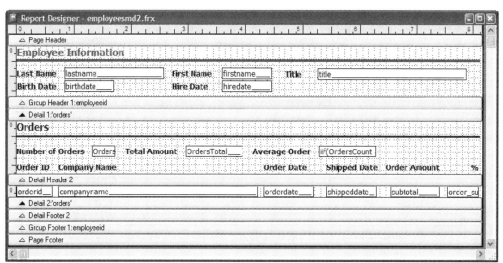

Figure 22. EmployeesMD2.FRX uses the Detail 1 band to pre-calculate totals used in the rest of the report.

The DataEnvironment for this report is set up as shown in **Figure 23**. The relationship between Employees and Orders is one-to-many so all orders for a given employee will process in both detail bands. The Customers table is related to the Orders table so the customer name for an order is included in the report. Order_Subtotals is a view that calculates the subtotal for each order into its Subtotal field. We want Order_Subtotals to be a child table of Orders, but because you can't define indexes or relationships for views in a database, we do it in code in the OpenTables method of the DataEnvironment:

```
local lnSelect
dodefault()
if empty(cdx(1, 'Order_Subtotals'))
  lnSelect = select()
  select Order_Subtotals
  index on OrderID tag OrderID
  select Orders
  set relation to OrderID into Order_Subtotals additive
  select (lnSelect)
endif empty(cdx(1, 'Order_Subtotals'))
nodefault
```

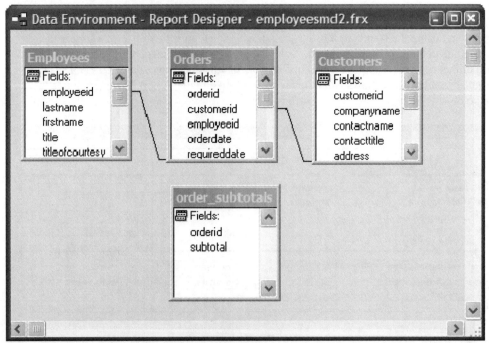

Figure 23. The DataEnvironment for EmployeesMD2.FRX sets up the relationships needed for this report.

There are two variables defined: OrdersCount, which is a "count" variable reset based on Detail 1, and OrdersTotal, which sums Order_Subtotals.Subtotal and is also reset based on Detail 1. So, all the Detail 1 band is used for is to process all order records for the current employee and calculate the proper values for the OrdersCount and OrdersTotal variables. Then, the order records are processed a second time in Detail 2. The number of orders and total amount is shown in the header for Detail 2 and the orders and the percentage each is of the total amount is shown in the detail band.

Figure 24 shows what the report looks like when it's run.

Figure 24. *Showing totals before the details and computing percentages of a total are easy using multiple detail bands.*

 The Developer Download files for this chapter, available at ***www.hentzenwerke.com****, include EmployeesMD2.FRX. Because of path differences, you will likely have to locate Northwind.DBC (it's in the Samples\Northwind subdirectory of the VFP home directory) when you open this report.*

Enhanced run-time capabilities

The VFP development team had several goals in mind when they worked on the run-time improvements, including:

- Handling more types of report output than just printing and previewing.

- Using GDI+ for report output. This provides many significant improvements, such as more accurate rendering, smooth scaling up and down of images and fonts, and additional capabilities such as text rotation.

- Providing a more flexible and extensible reporting system.

Before VFP 9, the report engine was monolithic: it handled everything–data handling, object positioning, rendering, previewing, and printing. Also, with a few exceptions (UDFs in field, grouping, and variable expressions, expressions for OnEntry and OnExit of bands, and so forth), you couldn't interact with it during a report run.

The new reporting engine in VFP 9 splits responsibility for reporting between the report engine, which now just deals with data handling and object positioning, and a new object known as a report listener, which handles rendering and output. Because report listeners are classes, you can interact with the reporting process in ways you could only dream of before.

VFP 9 includes both the old report engine and the new one, so you can run reports under either engine as you see fit. However, once you see the benefits of the new report engine, you won't want to go back to old-style reporting unless it's absolutely necessary.

New reporting syntax

VFP 9 supports running reports using the old report engine; simply use the REPORT command as you did before (although, as you will see in a moment, you can use a new command to override the behavior of REPORT). To get new-style reporting behavior, use the new OBJECT clause of the REPORT command. OBJECT supports two ways of using it: by specifying a report listener and specifying a report type. Microsoft refers to this as "object-assisted" reporting.

A report listener is an object providing new-style reporting behavior. Report listeners are based on a new base class in VFP 9, ReportListener. To tell VFP to use a specific listener for a report, instantiate the listener class, and then specify the object's name in the OBJECT clause of the REPORT command. Here's an example:

```
loListener = createobject('MyReportListener')
report form MyReport object loListener
```

If you'd rather not instantiate a listener manually, you can have VFP do it for you automatically by specifying a report type:

```
report form MyReport object type 1
```

The defined types are 0 for outputting to a printer, 1 for previewing, 4 for XML output, and 5 for HTML output. You can also define your own types.

When you run a report this way, the application specified in the new _REPORTOUTPUT system variable (by default, ReportOutput.APP in the VFP home directory) is called to figure out which listener class to instantiate for the specified type.

You're probably thinking "But I have tons of reports in my application. Do I have to find and modify every REPORT command in the entire application?" Fortunately, there's an easier way: SET REPORTBEHAVIOR 90 turns on object-assisted reporting by default. This means the REPORT command behaves as if you specified OBJECT TYPE 0 when you use the TO PRINT clause or OBJECT TYPE 1 when you use the PREVIEW clause. SET REPORTBEHAVIOR 80 reverts to VFP 8 and earlier behavior. If most or all of the reports in your application work just fine in object-assisted mode, use SET REPORTBEHAVIOR 90 at application startup. Because of rendering differences between new and old-style reporting, you may need to tweak some reports to work properly with new-style reporting, so either tweak them or use SET REPORTBEHAVIOR 80 to run just those reports. See the "Changes in Functionality for the Current Release" topic under the "What's New in Visual FoxPro" heading in the VFP help for details on the differences in rendering between backward-compatible mode and object-assisted mode.

ReportOutput.APP is primarily an object factory; it instantiates the appropriate listener for a report. It also includes some listeners that provide XML and HTML output. However, because it's just a VFP application, you can substitute your own application for it by setting

_REPORTOUTPUT accordingly. Be sure to distribute ReportOutput.APP (or your replacement for it) to your users so your applications use object-assisted reporting.

ReportOutput.APP and report listeners are discussed in detail in Chapter 7, "Extending the Reporting System at Run Time."

Let's take a look at some specifics of the run-time improvements.

New preview window

At first glance, the VFP 9 preview window shown in **Figure 25** may not look much different than it does in earlier versions. However, take a close look at the toolbar.

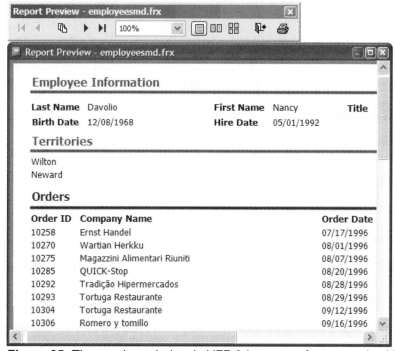

Figure 25. The preview window in VFP 9 has more features, plus it's a VFP form, so you have complete control over its appearance.

Notice there are new buttons allowing you to specify the number of pages displayed at a time. **Figure 26** shows what four pages at a time looks like (you must reduce the scale of the report to 25% to see all four pages at once).

Also notice you can now scale the report above 100%: 200, 300, and 500% are supported. This works in both the new and old preview windows. However, the old preview window will display rather jagged text at higher scales while the new preview window will show smooth text; this illustrates one of the benefits of GDI+ over GDI. Another new feature is a shortcut menu that duplicates the functions in the toolbar, plus allows you to hide or show the toolbar.

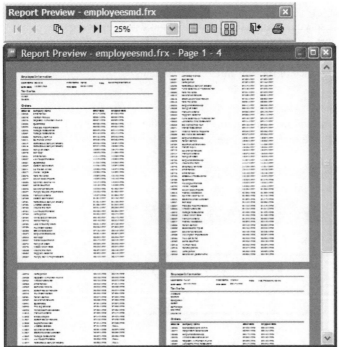

Figure 26. *You can display one, two, or four pages at a time in the preview window.*

Finally, try the following:

```
_screen.Forms[2].Caption = 'This is my report'
```

That's right—the preview window is a VFP form rather than a native window. That means you have full control over its appearance, something painful to do in previous versions. This preview window is used when you run a report in object-assisted mode; otherwise, the same window available in earlier versions of VFP is used.

A new system variable, _REPORTPREVIEW, specifies the name of a VFP application that provides the preview window for reports. By default, this variable points to ReportPreview.APP in the VFP home directory, but you can substitute your own application if you wish to. You can specify the form used for output in other ways as well; however, a discussion of how to do that is beyond the scope of this chapter. As with the other new VFP modules, be sure to distribute ReportPreview.APP or your replacement for it if your applications use the new preview window.

Progress feedback

When a long report runs, you may wish there was some way to show the user that something is happening. The UpdateListener class built into ReportOutput.APP does this; it displays the progress as the report is processed, and also gives the ability to cancel (see **Figure 27**). You can disable this feedback if you want to, or provide your own using a report listener. An example of this is shown in Chapter 7, "Extending the Reporting System at Run Time."

Figure 27. *The UpdateListener class displays the progress of a report and gives the user the ability to cancel.*

HTML and XML output

Although you've been able to output a report to HTML for several versions using GenHTML.PRG, the results, frankly, aren't very good. Fortunately, in VFP 9, you can create high-quality HTML output, as well as XML output, using some listeners built into ReportOutput.APP.

Listener type 5 specifies HTML output and type 4 is for XML output, so you can use the following command to output to HTML:

```
report form MyReport object type 5
```

However, this doesn't give you any control over the name of the file to create or other settings. Instead, call ReportOutput.APP for a reference to the desired listener, set some properties, and then tell the REPORT command to use that listener.

The following code (taken from HTMLOutput.PRG) creates an HTML file called MyReport.HTML from the first six pages of the EmployeesMD report. When you specify type 5, ReportOutput.APP uses its built-in HTMLListener class to provide output.

```
loListener = .NULL.
do (_reportoutput) with 5, loListener
loListener.TargetFileName = 'MyReport.html'
loListener.QuietMode = .T.
report form EmployeesMD object loListener range 1, 6
```

Figure 28 shows what the output looks like.

The following code (taken from XMLOutput.PRG) creates an XML file called MyReport.XML from the first six pages of the EmployeesMD report, containing only the data. In this case, the XMLListener class (type 4) in ReportOutput.APP is used.

```
loListener = .NULL.
do (_reportoutput) with 4, loListener
loListener.TargetFileName = 'MyReport.xml'
loListener.QuietMode = .T.
loListener.XMLMode = 0 && 0 = data only, 1 = layout only, 2 = both
report form EmployeesMD object loListener range 1, 6
```

Figure 29 shows the results.

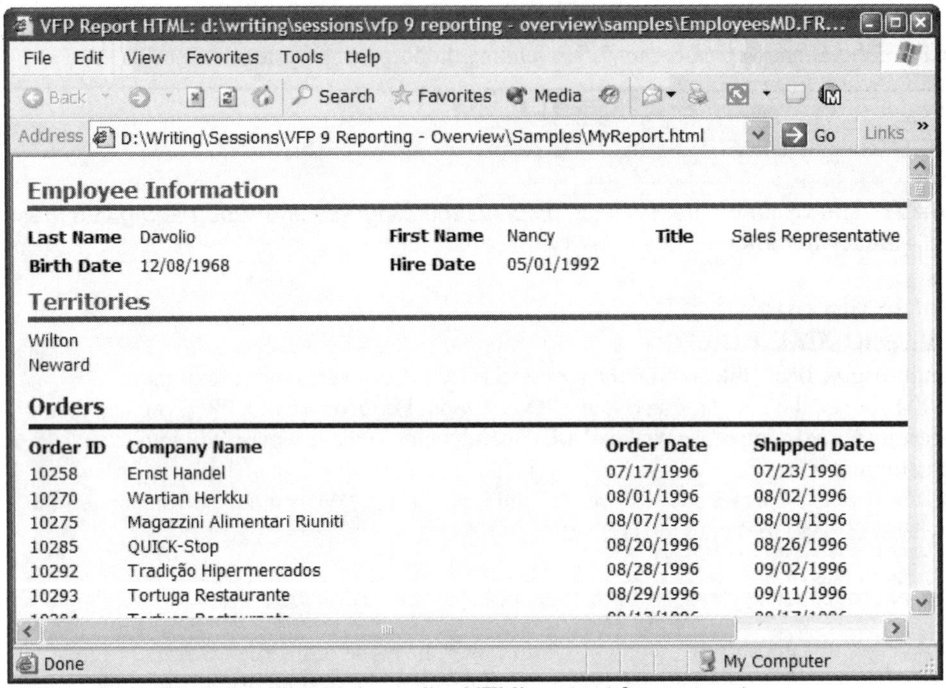

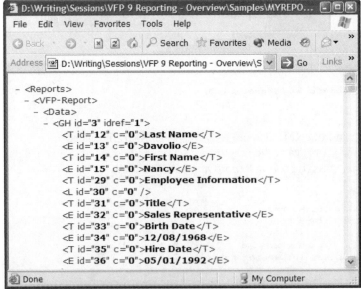

Figure 28. *VFP 9 provides high-quality HTML output from reports.*

Figure 29. *Using the XMLListener class, you can generate XML from a report that includes only the data, only the report layout, or both.*

The Developer Download files for this chapter, available at
www.hentzenwerke.com, *include HTMLOutput.PRG and XMLOutput.PRG.*

HTML output actually uses the XML listener to produce XML, and then uses XSLT to produce the HTML end-result.

Both of these listener classes have additional properties you can use to further control the output. See the VFP documentation for details.

Graphic file output

With a report listener, you can also output to a graphic file. VFP 9 supports EMF, TIFF (single and multi-page), JPG, BMP, PNG, and GIF. Third-party listeners may support other files types as well.

Here's some simple code, taken from GraphicOutput.PRG, that outputs a single page of the EmployeesMD report to a GIF file. **Figure 30** shows the resulting GIF file.

```
loListener = createobject('ReportListener')
loListener.ListenerType = 3
report form EmployeesMD object loListener range 1, 1
loListener.OutputPage(1, 'MyReport.gif', 104) && 104 = GIF
```

Employee Information

Last Name	Davolio	First Name	Nancy	Title	Sales Representative
Birth Date	12/08/1968	Hire Date	05/01/1992		

Territories

Wilton
Neward

Orders

Order ID	Company Name	Order Date	Shipped Date
10258	Ernst Handel	07/17/1996	07/23/1996
10270	Wartian Herkku	08/01/1996	08/02/1996
10275	Magazzini Alimentari Riuniti	08/07/1996	08/09/1996
10285	QUICK-Stop	08/20/1996	08/26/1996
10292	Tradição Hipermercados	08/28/1996	09/02/1996
10293	Tortuga Restaurante	08/29/1996	09/11/1996
10304	Tortuga Restaurante	09/12/1996	09/17/1996
10306	Romero y tomillo	09/16/1996	09/23/1996
10311	Du monde entier	09/20/1996	09/26/1996
10314	Rattlesnake Canyon Grocery	09/25/1996	10/04/1996
10316	Rattlesnake Canyon Grocery	09/27/1996	10/08/1996

Figure 30. *You can output a report to a graphics file, such as this GIF image.*

See Chapter 7, "Extending the Reporting System at Run Time," for details on this topic.

The Developer Download files for this chapter, available at **www.hentzenwerke.com**, *include GraphicOutput.PRG.*

What about PDF?

Of course, the question you're asking now is "What about PDF output?" VFP 9 does not include PDF output in the box. However, there are several ways you can get PDF output from VFP (in both 9 and previous versions):

- Use Adobe Acrobat or another PDF writer such as Print2PDF.

- Use a VFP-specific third-party tool supporting PDF output, such as Mind's Eye Report Engine, XFRX, or FRX2Any. Most of the creators of these tools are working on or have finished VFP 9 versions of their tools.

- Output to a PostScript file by printing to an appropriate driver, and then use the freeware GhostScript utility to convert it to a PDF file.

Other printing enhancements

There are a number of other general printing enhancements in VFP 9.

SYS(1037), which displays the Page Setup dialog, has some new capabilities. First, the dialog looks different (**Figure 31**).

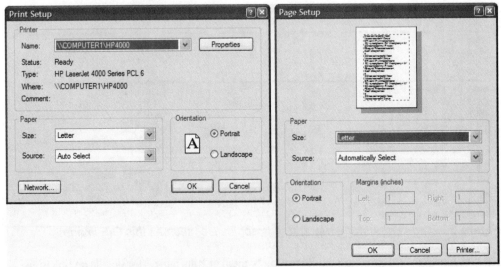

Figure 31. The SYS(1037) dialog in VFP 9 (right image) has a more modern interface than its VFP 8 counterpart (left image).

Second, it now has a return value indicating whether the user pressed OK ("1") or Cancel ("0").

The biggest change, though, is that you can pass it a parameter to tell it what to do. Passing 0 or no parameter displays the default Page Setup dialog. To display and possibly change the Page Setup settings for a particular report, open the report as a table (that is, USE MyReport.FRX), and then call SYS(1037, 1). You can save and restore the current default printer settings using SYS(1037, 2) (which writes the default printer settings to an FRX opened as a table in the current workarea) and SYS(1037, 3) (which sets the default printer settings to those in a FRX open in the current workarea); neither of these displays the Page Setup dialog. This is typically used to push and pop printer settings.

> *SYS1037.PRG, included in the Developer Download files for this chapter (**www.hentzenwerke.com**), demonstrates how SYS(1037, 2) and SYS(1037, 3) can save and restore the default printer settings.*

APRINTERS() can now accept a new optional argument of 1, in which case the resulting array has three new columns showing the driver, comment, and location.

Like the SYS(1037) dialog, the Print dialog displayed when you use the PROMPT keyword in the REPORT command has a more modern appearance (**Figure 32**).

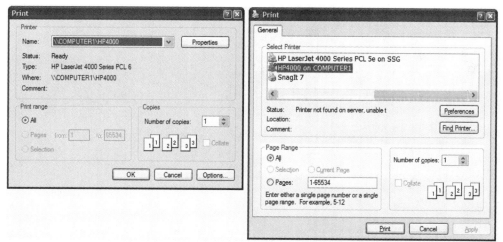

***Figure 32**. The dialog displayed with the PROMPT clause of the REPORT command has a more modern interface in VFP 9 (right image) than in VFP 8 (left image).*

Summary

VFP 9 has an incredible number of changes in the reporting engine. These changes make it easier to work with the Report Designer, make it possible to create types of reports you either couldn't do before or were hard to do, and provide new types of output. In addition, the VFP team provided the hooks necessary to extend the capabilities of the reporting engine in both design-time and run-time environments; we will examine these in detail in the next two chapters. You can expect a lot of new uses for VFP reporting, and many new discoveries about what its capabilities are in the years to come.

Updates and corrections for this chapter can be found on Hentzenwerke's website, **www.hentzenwerke.com**. Click "Catalog" and navigate to the page for this book.

Chapter 6
Extending the Reporting System at Design Time

Among the new and improved features in the reporting system of VFP 9 is the ability to extend the Report Designer to provide easier-to-use, more powerful, and more flexible report writing for your development team and even your end-users. In this chapter, you will learn about the new Report Builder application, how it captures and handles events raised by the Report Designer, and how you can create your own handlers to extend the VFP Report Designer in ways you never thought possible.

Earlier versions of VFP provided very little means of customizing the Report Designer, other than perhaps the appearance of the window it appeared in. One of the design goals for VFP 9 is to provide a mechanism for hooking into the behavior of the Report Designer to customize its appearance and behavior as much as possible. This is implemented by having events in the Report Designer, such as opening a report or adding an object, passed to an Xbase component that can take any action necessary when events occur.

The new system variable _REPORTBUILDER points to an application (referred to in this chapter as "the report builder application") that receives notification about events from the Report Designer. When a design-time report event occurs and _REPORTBUILDER points to an existing application, the Report Designer creates a private data session, opens a copy of the FRX currently being edited in that data session, and then calls the report builder application. By default, _REPORTBUILDER is set to ReportBuilder.APP in the VFP home directory, but you can substitute another application if you wish. If you specify a non-existent application, no error occurs but events are not raised. Any application specified by _REPORTBUILDER must be modal in nature because the Report Designer expects to call it and receive a return value indicating what happened.

The Report Designer passes the parameters shown in **Table 1** to the report builder application when an event occurs.

Table 1. *The parameters passed to the report builder application by the Report Designer.*

Parameter	Type	Description
ReturnFlags	N	Passed by reference with an initial value of -1. Used to return values to the Report Designer.
EventType	N	An integer representing the event that occurred.
CommandClauses	O	An object (based on the Empty baseclass) with properties indicating the clauses used in the CREATE/MODIFY REPORT command.
DesignerSessionID	N	The data session ID of the Report Designer.

ReturnFlags is used to return a value to the Report Designer. The possible return values are bit flags that can be summed. Adding 1 means the event was handled by the report builder application so the Report Designer's normal action is suppressed (sort of like using NODEFAULT). Adding 2 indicates the report builder application made changes in the FRX cursor so the Report Designer should reload the changes into its internal copy of the FRX.

EventType contains a value identifying the event that occurred. **Table 2** shows the possible values, along with the type of event (a report event, an object event, or a band event). The table also indicates whether adding 1 to the ReturnFlags parameter can suppress the event. "Must delete record" means a newly created object's record has already been added to the FRX, so to suppress the creation of an object, you must delete its record in the FRX cursor and set the ReturnFlags parameter to 3 (the event was handled and changes should be reloaded).

Table 2. *The EventType parameter contains one of these values indicating the type of report event.*

Value	Description	Type	Can Suppress
1	A Properties dialog (for the report, a band, or an object) is being invoked.	Report, Object, Band	Yes
2	An object or band is being created.	Object, Band	Yes (must delete record)
3	Reserved for future use.		
4	An object or band is being removed.	Object, Band	Yes
5	One or more objects are being pasted into the report from the clipboard. Each pasted object has the CURPOS field set to .T.	Object	Yes (must delete records)
6	The report has been saved.	Report	No
7	The report has been opened.	Report	No
8	The report is to be closed.	Report	Yes
9	The DataEnvironment is to be opened.	Report	Yes
10	The report is to be previewed.	Report	Yes
11	The Optional Bands dialog is being invoked.	Report	Yes
12	The Data Grouping dialog is being invoked.	Report	Yes
13	The Variables dialog is being invoked.	Report	Yes
14	Ctrl-E was pressed on a label object.	Object	Yes
15	The Grid Scale dialog is being invoked.	Report	Yes
16	One or more objects are being created by a drag-and-drop operation from the DataEnvironment, a DBC, or the Project Manager. This event fires once for each object being created, and if a label is created, once for each label as well.	Object	Yes (must delete record)
17	"Load data environment" was selected from the Report menu.	Report	Yes
18	The report is to be printed.	Report	Yes
19	"Quick Report" was selected from the Report menu.	Report	Yes

CommandClauses has the properties shown in **Table 3**.

Table 3. The properties of the CommandClauses object provide information about how the Report Designer was invoked.

Property	Type	Description
AddTableToDE	L	.T. if the Add Table to DataEnvironment option was turned on in the Quick Report dialog.
Alias	L	.T. if the Add Alias option was turned on in the Quick Report dialog or the ALIAS clause was specified in the CREATE REPORT FROM command.
FieldList	O	A collection of numeric field numbers representing the fields specified in the Quick Report dialog or the FIELDS clause of the CREATE REPORT FROM command.
File	C	The file name of the FRX open in the Report Designer. This file may not actually exist if CREATE REPORT/LABEL was used.
Form	L	.T. if a form layout was chosen in the Quick Report dialog or the FORM clause was specified in the CREATE REPORT FROM command; .F. if a column layout was chosen or COLUMN was specified.
From	C	Contains the table name specified in the CREATE REPORT FROM command.
InScreen	L	.T. if the IN SCREEN clause was specified in the CREATE/MODIFY REPORT/LABEL command.
InWindow	C	The name of the window specified in the IN <window> clause of the CREATE/MODIFY REPORT/LABEL command.
IsCreate	L	.T. if the command was CREATE REPORT/LABEL; .F. if the command was MODIFY REPORT/LABEL.
IsQuickReportFromMenu	L	.T. if the Quick Report function was invoked.
IsReport	L	.T. if the command was CREATE/MODIFY REPORT; .F. if it was CREATE/MODIFY LABEL.
NoEnvironment	L	.T. if the NOENVIRONMENT clause was specified in the MODIFY REPORT/LABEL command.
NoOverwrite	L	.T. if the NOOVERWRITE clause was specified in the CREATE REPORT FROM command.
NoWait	L	.T. if the NOWAIT clause was specified in the CREATE/MODIFY REPORT/LABEL command.
Protected	L	.T. if the PROTECTED clause was specified in the CREATE/MODIFY REPORT/LABEL command.
Save	L	.T. if the SAVE clause was specified in the CREATE/MODIFY REPORT/LABEL command.
Titles	L	.T. if the Titles option was turned on in the Quick Report dialog or the TITLES clause was specified in the CREATE REPORT FROM command.
Width	N	The number of columns specified in the CREATE REPORT FROM command (-1 if this clause was omitted).
Window	C	The window name specified in the WINDOW <name> clause of the CREATE/MODIFY REPORT/LABEL command.

The report builder application runs within a private data session that contains the FRX cursor. The Report Designer passes its own data session ID to the report builder application in case the report builder needs to access the tables open in the DataEnvironment of the Report Designer.

The FRX cursor the Report Designer creates for the report builder application has the alias "FRX." The record pointer is on the record for the object the event occurs for; this is the report header record (the first record in the cursor) if it's a report event rather than an object event. The records for any objects selected in the Report Designer have the CURPOS field set to .T. There's one slight complication with this: because the report header record uses CURPOS to store the value of the Show Position setting, you should ignore this record when looking at records with CURPOS set to .T. For example, to count the number of selected objects, use:

```
count for CURPOS and recno() > 1
```

ReportBuilder.APP

By default, _REPORTBUILDER is set to ReportBuilder.APP in the VFP home directory. This application provides a framework for handling design-time report events, plus it includes a set of more attractive and functional dialogs that replace the native ones used by the Report Designer (as discussed in Chapter 5, "Enhancements in the Reporting System"). You can distribute ReportBuilder.APP with your applications to provide its behavior in a run-time environment; see the "How To: Specify and Distribute ReportBuilder.App" topic in the VFP help for details.

In addition to the Report Designer calling it automatically, you can call ReportBuilder.APP manually to change its behavior for the current VFP session. It doesn't write settings to any external location, such as a table, INI file, or the Windows Registry, so, with one exception you will see in a moment, state isn't preserved from session to session.

- If you call it with no parameters or pass it 1, it displays an options dialog (see **Figure 1**) where you can change its behavior. You can also right-click any of the properties dialogs and choose Options to launch the Options dialog.

- Pass 2 and optionally the name of an FRX file to browse a report. Right-click the properties dialogs and choose Browse FRX to do the same thing for the current report.

- Pass 3 and the name of a DBF file to use that DBF as the handler registry or a blank string to use the internal handler registry table. (The handler registry is discussed later in this chapter.)

- Pass 4 and a numeric value to set the "handle mode." The numeric values match the buttons in the **When handling Report Designer events, the builder will** setting shown in the options dialog. For example, DO (_REPORTBUILDER) WITH 4, 3 tells ReportBuilder to use the event inspector.

- Pass 5 and optionally the name and path of a file to create a copy of the internal handler registry table (if you don't pass the second parameter, you'll be prompted for the table to create).

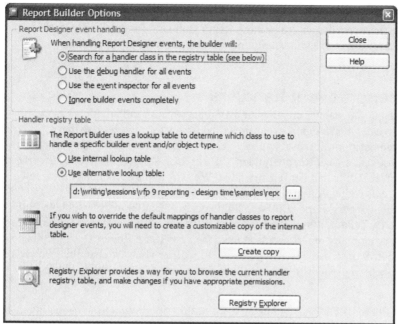

Figure 1. Configure the behavior of ReportBuilder.APP using the Report Builder Options dialog.

The Options dialog has the following features:

- You can define what happens when ReportBuilder.APP receives a report event. The choices are to search for a handler class in the handler registry table (the default behavior), use a "debug" handler for events (displays a dialog showing the FRX in a grid and allows modifications to it and other settings), use an "event inspector" handler (displays information about the event and the FRX in a MESSAGEBOX() window), or ignore report events. You can also display the event inspector window by right-clicking any properties dialog and choosing Event Inspector.

- You can specify what handler registry table to use, or make a copy of the internal one (the handler registry is discussed in "Registering report event handlers," later in this chapter). You can also browse the selected registry table.

Here are some ways you can extend the functionality of the Report Designer.

- Replace ReportBuilder.APP with your own report builder application by changing _REPORTBUILDER.

- Wrap ReportBuilder.APP by changing _REPORTBUILDER to your own application and having your application call back to ReportBuilder.APP. If you used FoxPro 2.x, this may remind you of the GENSCRNX approach.

- Register event-handling objects in ReportBuilder.APP's registry table. This will likely be the most popular choice because ReportBuilder.APP provides a report builder framework and lets you simply focus on handlers for report events.

Registering report event handlers

Two steps are required if you want to create your own report event handlers for ReportBuilder.APP to call when a report event fires. The first is to create a class that implements the desired behavior. It must have an Execute method that accepts an event object as a parameter, because that's what ReportBuilder.APP expects. The second is to register the handler in ReportBuilder.APP's handler registry table. We look at the second task first, and then spend the rest of this chapter discussing the first.

When a report event occurs, ReportBuilder.APP looks in a handler registry table to find a handler for the event. By default, it uses the handler registry table built into the APP file. This table provides handlers for many report events to have the new Xbase Report Designer dialogs used rather than the native ones. However, if you want to register your own handlers, you have to tell ReportBuilder.APP to use a different handler registry table. There are several ways to do this:

- DO (_REPORTBUILDER) and click on the **Create copy** button to write the internal handler registry table to an external one. By default, this copy is named ReportBuilder.DBF. When ReportBuilder.APP starts, it looks for a table called ReportBuilder.DBF in the current directory or VFP path. If it finds such a table, it uses that table rather than the internal one. So, simply creating this copy means ReportBuilder.APP will use it without having to do anything else.

- DO (_REPORTBUILDER) and click the **Choose** button to select the table to use.

- As mentioned earlier, use DO (_REPORTBUILDER) WITH 3, <DBF to use>, to specify the desired handler registry table without any UI.

Once you specify an external handler registry table, you can manually add or edit records in that table or, in the ReportBuilder.APP Options dialog, click the Explore Registry button and edit the records in the resulting dialog.

You can tell ReportBuilder.APP to use the internal handler registry table by selecting **None** in the dialog that appears when you click the **Choose** button or with DO (_REPORTBUILDER) WITH 3, ''. Note this only affects the current session of VFP, since ReportBuilder.APP will use any ReportBuilder.DBF it finds when VFP is restarted.

The handler registry table has the structure shown in **Table 4**.

Table 4. *The structure of the handler registry table.*

Field Name	Type	Values	Description
REC_TYPE	C(1)	E, F, G, H, or X	Specifies the type of record: H: report event handler record F: report event filter record X: exit handler record G: GetExpression wrapper record E: run-time extension editor class
HNDL_CLASS	C(35)		The name of the class to instantiate.
HNDL_LIB	C(50)		The library containing the class. This field is too short for most paths, so the library (either VCX or PRG) should be in the current directory, VFP path, or open with SET CLASSLIB.
NOTES	C(50)		Not used by ReportBuilder.APP.
EVENTTYPE	I	0 - 19 or -1	Report event type ID (-1 means any event). See Table 2 for a list of the values.
OBJTYPE	I	0 - 10, 99, or -1	Report object type. 99 is a special object type meaning multiple selected objects. -1 means any type of object. The rest of the values correspond with those in the OBJTYPE column in an FRX.
OBJCODE	I	0 - 26 or -1	Report object code (-1 for any code). These values correspond with those in the OBJCODE column in an FRX.
DEBUG	L	.T. or .F.	.T. to use the debug handler instead of the class specified in HNDL_CLASS.
NATIVE	L	.T. or .F.	.T. to pass the report event back to the Report Designer for native behavior.
FLTR_ORDR	C(1)	" ", "1", "2", etc.	For filters and exit handlers only, specifies the order to apply them in.

When a report event occurs, ReportBuilder.APP looks for the handler class to instantiate by looking for a record where EVENTTYPE matches the report event ID (or is -1), OBJTYPE matches the OBJTYPE column of the selected FRX record (or is -1), and OBJCODE matches the OBJCODE column of the selected FRX record (or is -1). Because ReportBuilder.APP uses the first handler record it finds that meets its conditions, you may need to delete or disable built-in handlers if you want to implement your own. One way you can disable a handler record without deleting it is to change EVENTTYPE to an invalid value. For example, you can add 100 to EVENTTYPE to disable a record, and then easily re-enable it by subtracting 100.

As you can see in Table 4, REC_TYPE registers different types of records. Here are the different types available:

- The report event handler (REC_TYPE = "H") handles a report event. This is the only type of record where the ReportBuilder.APP checks the EVENTTYPE, OBJTYPE, and OBJCODE columns.

- The report event filter (REC_TYPE = "F") is a class that gets an earlier crack at the report event than a handler does. While only a single handler is instantiated, ReportBuilder.APP instantiates the classes specified in all filter records, in FLTR_ORDER order, and calls their Execute methods. If any filter object's

AllowToContinue property is .F., no further processing happens and ReportBuilder.APP informs the Report Designer that the event was handled.

As you can see from these descriptions, although they can both respond to report events, there's a big difference between event handlers and filters:

- Filters are instantiated on every report event, while a handler is only instantiated for the event it's registered for in the handler registry table.

- All filters are instantiated on an event, while only a single handler is.

This means filters are good for behavior you want to occur on multiple, possibly all, events, while handlers are specific for one type of event.

- The exit handlers (REC_TYPE = "X") are similar to a combination of filters and event handlers. After the other processing finishes, ReportBuilder.APP runs all registered exit handlers by instantiating the appropriate classes in FLTR_ORDER order and calls their Execute methods. These handlers are really just intended to perform any post-event cleanup behavior.

- The GetExpression wrapper (REC_TYPE = "G") provides a wrapper or replacement for the GETEXPR dialog. It's useful in the various places where a user clicks a button with an ellipsis (such as the one beside a field expression). There should only be one record with REC_TYPE = "G."

- The Run-time extension editor (REC_TYPE = "E") replaces the dialog that displays when you click the Edit Settings button for the Run-time Extension property in the Other page of the properties dialog for an object in the Report Designer. There should only be one record with REC_TYPE = "E."

The report event handling process

When ReportBuilder.APP is called because a report event occurred, it does the following:

- Runs any registered filters as described earlier. Processing stops if any of them have AllowToContinue set to .F.

- Tries to find the handler for the event using the following search priority:

REC_TYPE = "H," EVENTTYPE = event type, OBJTYPE = OBJTYPE value for the object, OBJCODE = OBJCODE value for the object

REC_TYPE = "H," EVENTTYPE = event type, OBJTYPE = OBJTYPE value for the object, OBJCODE = -1

REC_TYPE = "H," EVENTTYPE = event type, OBJTYPE = -1, OBJCODE = -1

REC_TYPE = "H," EVENTTYPE = -1, OBJTYPE = -1, OBJCODE = -1

- If a handler is found, ReportBuilder.APP instantiates it and calls its Execute method. If a handler is not found, the event is passed back to the Report Designer and native behavior is used instead.

- If a handler is found, ReportBuilder.APP runs all registered exit handlers as described earlier.

Handler interfaces

Report event filters, event handlers, exit handlers, GetExpression wrappers, and run-time extension editors can be based on any class and have only a single required method. The method signatures are:

- Filters: Execute(toEvent). ReportBuilder.APP passes this method a reference to an event object, which we look at in the next section ("Event object"), with properties containing information about the event. To prevent further processing, set the custom AllowToContinue property to .F. in this method; in that case, you should set the ReturnFlags property of the event object appropriately.

- Event handlers: Execute(toEvent). This method also receives an event object. The return value is not important, but the ReturnFlags property of the event object is.

- Exit handlers: same signature as event handlers.

- GetExpression wrapper: GetExpression(tcDefaultExpr, tcDataType, tcCalledFrom, toEvent). tcDefaultExpr is the default expression for the dialog. tcDataType is the data type of the expression. tcCalledFrom indicates where this method was called: "PrintWhenExpression," "FieldExpression," "OleBoundField," "OleBoundExpression," "BandGroupOnExpression," "VariableValueToStore," or "VariableInitialValue." toEvent is an event object. The return value is the expression.

- Run-time extension editors: same signature as event handlers.

Event object

ReportBuilder.APP passes an event object to the methods of handlers. This object has properties containing the parameters passed by the Report Designer to ReportBuilder.APP, plus some other useful information (see **Table 5**). It has several public methods, however, some are used by ReportBuilder.APP rather than an event handler. **Table 6** shows the ones useful for an event handler.

Table 5. *The properties of the event object that ReportBuilder.APP passes to report event handlers and filters.*

Property	Type	Description
BuilderPath	C	Path of ReportBuilder.APP.
CommandClauses	O	The same CommandClauses object passed to ReportBuilder.APP from the Report Designer.
DefaultRecno	N	The record pointer in the FRX cursor.
DefaultSessionID	N	The data session of the Report Designer (the fourth parameter passed in from the Report Designer).
EventType	N	The event type (the second parameter passed in from the Report Designer).
FRXCursor	O	A helper object containing useful functions for interacting with the FRX cursor (discussed in the section of this chapter, "FRXCursor helper object").
FRXSessionID	N	The data session the FRX cursor is open in (the default session when the event handler is instantiated).
HandleMode	I	Indicates how ReportBuilder.APP handles events: 1 means search for a handler class in the registry table, 2 means use the debug handler, 3 means use the event inspector, and 4 means ignore builder events.
MultiSelect	L	.T. if multiple objects are selected in the Report Designer.
ObjCode	N	The value of the OBJCODE field of the selected record in the FRX cursor.
ObjType	N	The value of the OBJTYPE field of the selected record in the FRX cursor.
Protected	L	.T. if the Report Designer was launched with the PROTECTED keyword.
ReturnFlags	N	The value of this property is returned to the Report Designer in the first parameter passed in from the Report Designer. It's initially set to 0; set it to the same range of values described for the ReturnFlags parameter.
SelectedObjectCount	N	The number of selected objects in the report layout, determined by counting CURPOS = .T. in the FRX cursor (not counting the header record).
SessionData	O	A reference to a Name-Value pair manager object used to store data between ReportBuilder.APP invocations.
UniqueID	C	The value of the UNIQUEID field of the selected record in the FRX cursor.
UnitConverter	O	A reference to an FRX unit converter object (the FRXUnitConverter class in FRXBuilder.VCX built into ReportBuilder.APP). This class has methods to convert between FRU (FoxPro Report Units, 1/10000 inch) and other units.
UsingInternalRegistry	L	.T. if the internal registry table is used.

Table 6. *The methods of the event object that are useful to an event handler.*

Method	Parameters	Returns	Description
GetEventTypeText	[tiEvent]	C	Returns the name of a given event type.
GetExpression	tcDefaultExpr, tcDataType, tcCalledFrom	C	Displays a Get Expression dialog and returns the selected expression.
GetExtensionEditor	None	O	Instantiates and returns a reference to a run-time extension editor class as specified in the handler registry table.
GetTargetTypeText	[tiObjType, tiObjCode]	C	Returns the name of a given object type/object code.
SetHandledByBuilder	tlNoDefault	.T.	Pass .T. to add 1 to ReturnFlags.
SetReloadChanges	tlReload	.T.	Pass .T. to add 2 to ReturnFlags.

FRXCursor helper object

This object, referenced in the FRXCursor property of the event object, provides methods you may find useful when working with an FRX. These methods are shown in **Table 7**. In the Parameters column of the table, "tcFRXAlias" is the alias of the FRX cursor; if it isn't passed, "FRX" is assumed. This object also has a single property, ScreenDPI, that contains 96, because that's the number of dots per inch used by the Report Designer.

Table 7. *The methods of the FRXCursor helper object.*

Method	Parameters	Returns	Description
BinStringToInt	tcBytes	N	Returns the numeric equivalent of the binary data (in least significant byte order) in a string of bytes. For example, BinStringToInt(CHR(55) + CHR(1)) returns 311 because 55 + 1 * 256 = 311.
BinToInt	tcValue	I	Converts a string of binary digits into an integer. For example, BinToInt('10000010') returns 130.
CharsetToLocale	tnCharSet	N	Converts a font Charset value to a locale ID, usually for use with the STRCONV() function.
CreateBandCursor	[tcFRXAlias]	L	Creates a cursor with the alias Bands containing information about the bands in the report.
CreateCalcResetOnCursor	[tcFRXAlias]	L	Creates a cursor with the alias Reset_On containing information for each option in the Calculation Reset combobox.
CreateDefaultPrintEnvCursor	[tcFRXAlias [, tcDestAlias]]	L	Creates a one-record cursor with the alias specified in tcDestAlias ("DefPrnEnv" by default) with the same structure as an FRX, with the default printer environment data loaded into EXPR, TAG, and TAG2.

Method	Parameters	Returns	Description
CreateGroupCursor	[tcFRXAlias]	L	Creates a cursor with the alias Groups containing information about data grouping in the report.
CreateObjCursorRecord	[tcDestAlias, tlRuntime]	-	Called by CreateObjectCursor to do the actual insertion of records in the Objects cursor
CreateObjectCursor	[tcFRXAlias [, tcDestAlias [, tiFilter [, tlRuntime]]]]	L	Creates a cursor with the alias specified in tcDestAlias ("Objects" by default) containing information about the objects in the report. Calls CreateBandCursor() if the Bands cursor isn't open. The values for tiFilter are: 0 (the default): all objects in the FRX with grouped items omitted 1: selected (CURPOS = .T.) records only 2: all objects with grouped items as a single record 3: all objects with grouped items as individual records If tlRuntime is .F., each object's start and end band are determined using the Report Designer's algorithm. Specify .T. to use the reporting engine's algorithm instead (there are some differences in the algorithms). Deleted records are included, so use SET DELETED ON to ignore them.
CreateVariableCursor	[tcFRXAlias]	L	Creates a cursor with the alias Vars containing information about the variables defined in the report.
FRUToPixels	tnFRU	I	Returns the corresponding pixels for a given number of FRU.
GetBandFor	tcUniqueID [, tlStart]	O	Returns an object containing information about the start or end band that surrounds the given report object.
GetFRUTextHeight	tcText, tcTypeFace, tiSize [, tcStyle]	N	Returns the height in FRU of a given text and font spec.
GetFRUTextWidth	tcText, tcTypeFace, tiSize [, tcStyle]	N	Returns the width in FRU of a given text and font spec.
GetFRXTimeStamp	[ttDateTime]	I	Returns a FoxPro time stamp for a given datetime (DATETIME() is used by default).
GetMetaDataDOMDoc	[tcFRXAlias]	O	Returns an MSXML.DOMDocument object loaded with the meta data XML for the current record (stored in the STYLE memo). You can create this XML using the Runtime Extensions editor or by opening the FRX as a cursor and inserting it into STYLE.

Method	Parameters	Returns	Description
GetObjectsInBand	tcBandID [, tlRecnos]	O	Returns a collection of UNIQUEID values or record numbers (depending on the value of the second parameter) for each object contained in the specified band.
GetReportAttribute	tcAttrib [, tiAlternate]	Value	Returns the specified attribute of the report header. The attributes are: Units: returns the units used by the ruler as a numeric value. Specify 1 for tiAlternate to retrieve the ruler units as a string (e.g. "inches"). MultiColumn: returns .T. if the report has more than one column. ColumnCount: returns the number of columns in the report. Protection: returns a binary string with the protection flags for the report. Snaked_Columns: returns .T. if columns are printed horizontally, .F. if printed vertically.
GetSelectedObjectCount	[tcFRXAlias]	I	Returns the number of currently selected objects (CURPOS=.T.) in the FRX cursor.
GetTargetTypeText	tiObjType, tiObjCode	C	Returns the name of a given object type and object code.
GetTimeStampString	tiTimeStamp	C	Converts a FoxPro time stamp into a readable string.
GetUnitValueFromFRU	tnFRUValue, tiUnits	N	Converts a value in FRUs to another specified unit. The choices for tiUnits is 0 or 1 for inches, 2 for metric, or 4 for characters; any other value assumes pixels.
GoRec	tiRec [, tcAlias]	-	Positions the specified alias (the default is the selected alias) to the desired record number with range checking.
HasBand	tiObjCode	L	Returns .T. if the report contains a band of the specified type.
HasDetailHeader	tcDetailBandID	L	Returns .T. if the specified detail band record has a detail header.
HasProtectionFlag	tcBytes, tiFlag	L	Returns .T. if the given binary data (bytes) has a specific protection flag set.
InsertBand	tiObjCode	-	Inserts a band of the specified type into the FRX cursor. The FRX cursor must be selected and positioned to the appropriate record for the insertion.
InsertDataEnvRecord	tiObjType, tcName, tcExpr, tcMethods	-	Inserts a DataEnvironment record into the FRX cursor using the specified values for OBJTYPE, NAME, EXPR, and TAG. The FRX cursor must be selected and positioned to the appropriate record for the insertion.
InsertDetailBand	None	-	Inserts a detail band record into the FRX cursor. The FRX cursor must be selected and positioned to the appropriate record for the insertion.

Method	Parameters	Returns	Description
InsertDetailHeaderFooter	None	-	Inserts detail header and footer records into the FRX cursor. The FRX cursor must be selected and positioned to the appropriate detail band record, and that detail band must not already have header and footer records.
InsertSummaryBand	tlNewPage, tlPageHeader, tlPageFooter	-	Inserts a summary band into the FRX cursor. The FRX cursor must be selected and not already have a summary band.
InsertTitleBand	tlNewPage	-	Inserts a title band into the FRX cursor. The FRX cursor must be selected and not already have a title band.
IntToBin	tiValue	C	The opposite of BinToInit: converts an integer into a string of binary digits.
IntToBinString	tiValue	C	The opposite of BinStringToInit: returns the binary version of an integer as a string of bytes in least significant byte order.
PixelsToFRU	tnPixels	N	Returns the corresponding FRU for a given number of pixels.
PopPrintEnv	None	-	Restores the printer environment from a previously saved cursor (likely created in PushPrintEnvToCursor). The cursor to pop from must be selected.
PushPrintEnvToCursor	tcRegisterAlias	-	Creates the specified cursor and saves the printer environment to it.
SetColumnCount	tiCols	-	Adjust the number of columns in the report to the specified value by adding or removing column, column header, and column footer records as necessary. The FRX cursor must be selected.
StripQuotes	tcValue	C	Strips single and double quotes from the specified string.
SynchObjectPositions	None	-	Resets non-deleted objects in the FRX relative to the start of the band they are in. This is typically used after bands have been resized. The Bands and Objects cursors must have been created and the FRX cursor must be selected. This method moves and doesn't restore the record pointer.

Creating report event handlers

Because most report event handlers have common requirements, for this chapter we created a base class handler called SFReportEventHandler, defined in SFReportBuilder.VCX. It's a subclass of Custom. Its Init method instantiates an SFReportEventUtilities object into the oUtilities property. Like FRXCursor, this object has utility methods for dealing with report objects and events.

The Execute method of SFReportEventHandler saves the passed-in event object to its oEvent property and the oEvent property of the SFReportEventUtilities object, and then calls the OnExecute method, which is abstract in this class. In a subclass, don't override the Execute method, but instead put the appropriate code into the OnExecute method.

```
lparameters toEvent
with This
  .oEvent              = toEvent
  .oUtilities.oEvent = toEvent
  .OnExecute()
  .oEvent              = .NULL.
  .oUtilities.oEvent = .NULL.
endwith
```

To handle a particular report event, create a subclass of SFReportEventHandler and register it in the handler registry table. To make it easy to do the latter, use a program called InstallHandler.PRG. Pass it the class and library for the handler, the event number, and optionally the object type and code. It adds a record to the registry table (expected to be named ReportBuilder.DBF; change the USE and INSERT INTO statements to use a different table name) if it doesn't exist, and disables any other handlers for the same event. Here's the code for InstallHandler.PRG:

```
lparameters tcClass, ;
  tcLibrary, ;
  tnEventType, ;
  tnObjType, ;            .
  tnObjCode
local lcClass, ;
  lnObjType, ;
  lnObjCode

* Open the report builder table (creating it if necessary first).

if not file('reportbuilder.dbf')
  do (_reportbuilder) with 5, 'reportbuilder.dbf'
endif not file('reportbuilder.dbf')
use ReportBuilder

* Use defaults for the object type and code if they weren't passed.

lnObjType = iif(vartype(tnObjType) = 'N', tnObjType, -1)
lnObjCode = iif(vartype(tnObjCode) = 'N', tnObjCode, -1)

* If the specified handler is already there, ensure it's enabled by
* setting EventType to the proper value. Otherwise, add a record for it.

lcClass = padr(upper(tcClass), len(Hndl_Class))
locate for upper(Hndl_Class) == lcClass and (EventType = tnEventType or ;
  EventType = tnEventType + 100) and ObjType = lnObjType and ;
  ObjCode = lnObjCode
if found()
  replace EventType with tnEventType
else
  insert into ReportBuilder ;
      (Rec_Type, ;
      Hndl_Class, ;
      Hndl_Lib, ;
      EventType, ;
      ObjType, ;
      ObjCode) ;
    values ;
      ('H', ;
```

```
        tcClass, ;
        tcLibrary, ;
        tnEventType, ;
        lnObjType, ;
        lnObjCode)
endif found()

* Disable any other handlers for the same event by setting their
* EventType code to an used value.

replace EventType with EventType + 100 for ;
  EventType = tnEventType and ;
  ObjType = lnObjType and ObjCode = lnObjCode and ;
  not upper(Hndl_Class) == lcClass

* Clean up and exit.

use
```

The Developer Download files for this chapter, available at
www.hentzenwerke.com, *include Samples.PJX, SFReportBuilder.VCX,*
InstallHandler.PRG, InstallFilter.PRG, and files used by classes in
SFReportBuilder.VCX. Note that one of the include files, SFReporting.H,
includes \Program Files\Microsoft Visual FoxPro 9\FFC\FoxPro_Reporting.h.
If you install these samples on a different drive than where VFP is installed,
or if VFP is installed in a different directory than \Program Files\Microsoft
Visual FoxPro 9, be sure to change the #INCLUDE statement in
SFReporting.H to point to the correct path, and then rebuild Samples.PJX
with the "Rebuild project" and "Recompile All Files" options checked.

Let's look at some examples of useful report event handlers.

Report templates

When you create a new report, you get a blank report. Wouldn't it be nice if VFP would automatically add certain common elements you want in every report? In other words, a report that's used as the template for all new reports.

FoxPro has actually had this capability (although it's undocumented) since the FoxPro DOS days. If you modify a report called Untitled.FRX, FoxPro will prompt you for a new name when you save it. However, this requires that you modify this report rather than creating a new one and only allows you to have one such template.

Now, with design-time report events, you can have report templates. There isn't an event that fires when a report is created, but there is when one is opened, so simply check if the report is a new one or not (the utility method IsNewReport returns .T. if that's the case). If it's a new report, ZAP existing records in the FRX, APPEND FROM a template FRX file, and set the return flag to indicate the event was handled and the FRX was changed. Here's the code in the OnExecute method of SFNewReportHandlerBasic (contained in SFReportBuilder.VCX):

```
with This
  if .oUtilities.IsNewReport() and not empty(.cTemplateReport)
    zap
    append from (.cTemplateReport)
    .oEvent.SetHandlerByBuilder(.T.)
    .oEvent.SetReloadChanges(.T.)
    go top
  endif .oUtilities.IsNewReport() ...
endwith
```

The custom property cTemplateReport contains the name of the template FRX to use. By default, it contains Template.FRX. To register this class, run InstallNewReportHandlerBasic.PRG.

Now, to get even fancier, how about asking the user which template they want to use? SFNewReportHandlerFancy is a subclass of SFNewReportHandlerBasic with the following code in OnExecute:

```
local loForm
if This.oUtilities.IsNewReport()
  loForm = newobject('SFSelectTemplateForm', 'SFReportBuilder.vcx')
  loForm.Show()
  if vartype(loForm) = 'O'
    This.cTemplateReport = loForm.cTemplate
  endif vartype(loForm) = 'O'
endif This.oUtilities.IsNewReport()
return dodefault()
```

This code uses the SFSelectTemplateForm class to display a list of available templates. This list comes from Templates.DBF that has fields containing the name of the template FRX, a descriptive name for the template, and a memo containing comments about the template. To register this class, run InstallNewReportHandlerFancy.PRG.

Figure 2 shows the Report Designer after running InstallNewReportHandlerBasic.PRG and typing CREATE REPORT MyNewReport in the Command window.

The Developer Download files for this chapter, available at
www.hentzenwerke.com, *include SFReportBuilder.VCX, SFCtrls.VCX, InstallNewReportHandlerBasic.PRG, InstallNewReportHandlerFancy.PRG, Templates.DBF, Template.FRX, ExecTemplate.FRX, and LedgerTemplate.FRX.*

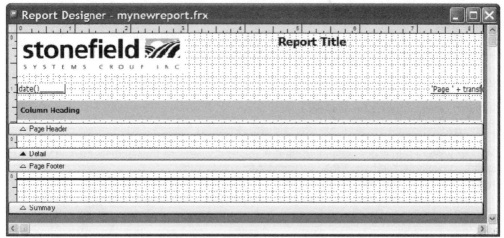

Figure 2. A report event handler that creates a new report from a template makes it easy to create consistent, attractive reports.

Custom dialog for new fields

One thing many VFP developers have wanted to do is replace the dialog that appears when a user adds a new field to a report. They want a dialog that's both simpler (it displays descriptive names for tables and fields) and more powerful (it doesn't require the tables to be in the DataEnvironment or open and it has options for adding a label to go along with the field). Now you can take over the "new field" report event to finally create the dialog you want.

TestNewField.PRG calls several "install" programs to ensure the appropriate handlers are registered. It also creates a meta data object with collections of tables and fields read from a meta data table. We won't look at that object here; feel free to examine it yourself.

When you run TestNewField.PRG, it automatically creates a new report, but nothing else appears different. However, because a class named SFNewTextBoxHandler is now the handler for new fields, when you add a field, you get the dialog shown in **Figure 3** rather than the usual one.

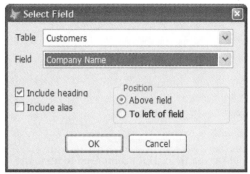

Figure 3. This dialog, which appears when the user adds a new field to a report, makes it easy to select the desired field.

This dialog displays descriptive names for the tables and fields in the SQL Server Northwind database, which, of course, aren't in the DataEnvironment or open in VFP. They don't need to be because this information comes from meta data; the meta data table named REPMETA.DBF contains the name of each table and field, their descriptive names, field data types, sizes, and so forth. This dialog also allows you to indicate whether a label is created or not, and if so, whether it should be placed in the page header band above the field or to the left of the field in the same band as the field.

As with other subclasses of SFReportEventHandler, it's the OnExecute method of SFNewTextBoxHandler that does the work. We won't go over all the code in this method, just the more interesting stuff. First, this method displays the dialog shown above. If the user clicks OK, it retrieves some information about the selected field from the meta data (the data type, size, etc.). It then uses the SFReportEventUtilities object to retrieve the default font, size, and style from the header record in the FRX. It uses the FRXCursor helper object to determine the height and width of the field in FRUs, and updates the field's record in the FRX accordingly.

```
lcFontName  = .oUtilities.GetReportHeaderValue('FONTFACE')
lnFontSize  = .oUtilities.GetReportHeaderValue('FONTSIZE')
lnFontStyle = .oUtilities.GetReportHeaderValue('FONTSTYLE')
lcFontStyle = .oUtilities.GetFontStyle(lnFontStyle)

* Determine the width and height for the textbox.

lnWidth  = .oEvent.FRXCursor.GetFRUTextWidth(lcText,  lcFontName, ;
  lnFontSize, lcFontStyle)
lnHeight = .oEvent.FRXCursor.GetFRUTextHeight(lcText, lcFontName, ;
  lnFontSize, lcFontStyle)

* Update the properties of the new textbox.
```

```
replace EXPR  with lcField, ;
  NAME      with lcName, ;
  WIDTH     with lnWidth, ;
  HEIGHT    with lnHeight ;
  PICTURE   with iif(empty(lcPicture), '', '"' + lcPicture + '"'), ;
  FILLCHAR  with lcType, ;
  FONTFACE  with lcFontName, ;
  FONTSIZE  with lnFontSize, ;
  FONTSTYLE with lnFontStyle, ;
  USER      with 'EXPR=' + lcExpr + ccCRLF ;
  in FRX
```

Next it determines where to put the label object for the field. If it's supposed to go in the page header, OnExecute asks the SFReportEventUtilities object to find a label in the page header band with "*:TEMPLATE" in its USER memo in the FRX cursor (this memo field is accessible on the Other page of the properties dialog). If such an object exists, it's the template for the new label (font, style, vertical position, etc.). If "REMOVE" also appears, the code removes the template object from the report and makes the label the code is about to create the new template.

```
if lnPosition = 1
  loBand      = .oUtilities.GetBandObject(FRX_OBJCOD_PAGEHEADER)
  loTemplate = .oUtilities.FindTemplateObject(loBand, ;
    FRX_OBJTYP_LABEL, '*:TEMPLATE', .T.)
  if vartype(loTemplate) = 'O'
    if '*:TEMPLATE REMOVE' $ upper(loTemplate.User)
      .oUtilities.RemoveReportObject(loTemplate.UniqueID)
      loTemplate.User = strtran(loTemplate.User, ;
        '*:TEMPLATE REMOVE', '*:TEMPLATE')
    endif '*:TEMPLATE REMOVE' $ upper(loTemplate.User)
    loObject = loTemplate
    lnVPos   = loObject.VPos
  else
    lnVPos = loBand.Stop - lnHeight - BAND_SEPARATOR_HEIGHT_FRUS
  endif vartype(loTemplate) = 'O'
```

If the label is supposed to go in the same band as the field, OnExecute asks the SFReportEventUtilities object to find the band the field is in, and then like the previous code, to look in that band for a label with "*:TEMPLATE" in its USER memo and use it as the template.

```
else
  loBand      = .oEvent.FRXCursor.GetBandFor(FRX.UniqueID)
  loTemplate = .oUtilities.FindTemplateObject(loBand, ;
    FRX_OBJTYP_LABEL, '*:TEMPLATE', .T.)
  if vartype(loTemplate) = 'O'
    if '*:TEMPLATE REMOVE' $ upper(loTemplate.User)
      .oUtilities.RemoveReportObject(loTemplate.UniqueID)
      loTemplate.User = strtran(loTemplate.User, ;
        '*:TEMPLATE REMOVE', '*:TEMPLATE')
    endif '*:TEMPLATE REMOVE' $ upper(loTemplate.User)
    loObject = loTemplate
  endif vartype(loTemplate) = 'O'
endif lnPosition = 1
```

Finally, a new label is added to the report.

```
with loObject
  .UniqueID  = sys(2015)
  .TimeStamp = This.oEvent.FRXCursor.GetFRXTimeStamp(datetime())
  .Name      = ''
  .Expr      = '"' + lcCaption + '"'
  .Height    = lnHeight
  .Width     = lnWidth
  .VPos      = lnVPos
  .HPos      = lnHPos
  .ObjType   = FRX_OBJTYP_LABEL
endwith
insert into FRX from name loObject
```

This is the most complicated event handler we've seen because it has to deal with more things in the FRX. Doing this type of work requires a fair bit of knowledge about the structure of an FRX, so be sure to check out the 90FRX report in the Tools\FileSpec subdirectory of the VFP home directory for documentation on the FRX.

By the way, this sample shows another cool new feature in VFP 9: design-time labels, discussed in Chapter 5, "Enhancements in the Reporting System." Notice that when you add a field to the report, it displays the caption rather than the field name in the field object. That's because the OnExecute method fills in the NAME column of the field object in the FRX with the caption for the field. When you use CREATE or MODIFY REPORT with the PROTECTED keyword, the Report Designer displays the contents of the NAME column rather than the EXPR column for field objects. This means you can display nice descriptive names for fields rather than the actual field names. Of course, the user will see the actual field names in the Properties dialog, but at least they see the nice names on the design surface.

 *The Developer Download files for this chapter, available at **www.hentzenwerke.com**, include SFReportBuilder.VCX, InstallNewField.PRG, TestNewField.PRG, and SFMetaData.VCX.*

Generating cursors on the fly

So, now you can create a report from meta data using the SFNewTextBoxHandler handler, what happens when you try to preview the report? It won't work, because the cursors are not open. Ah, but what if you hook into the preview or print events and generate the cursors before the report runs?

InstallPreview.PRG registers SFPreviewHandler as the handler for events 10 (previewing) and 18 (printing). The OnExecute method of SFPreviewHandler is fairly simple: it generates a SQL SELECT statement by looking at the fields in the report (we won't look at the code that does this here), instantiates an object that opens a connection to the SQL Server Northwind database, sends the SQL SELECT statement to SQL Server to create a cursor, and tells the report engine to cancel the preview or print if it failed for some reason.

```
local lcSelect, ;
  loConnection, ;
  llOK

* Create the SQL SELECT statement we need for the report.

wait window 'Retrieving data...' nowait
lcSelect  = This.CreateSQLStatement()

* Create a connection object and try to connect to the SQL Server
* Northwind database. If we succeeded, execute the SQL SELECT statement
* in the report's datasession.

loConnection = newobject('SFConnectionMgr', 'SFConnection.vcx')
loConnection.cConnectString = 'driver=SQL Server;server=(local);' + ;
  'database=Northwind;trusted_connection=yes'
if loConnection.Connect()
  llOK = loConnection.ExecuteStatement(lcSelect, ;
    This.oEvent.DefaultSessionID, sys(2015))
endif loConnection.Connect()

* If we failed to connect or create the cursor, display a warning and
* flag that we've handled the event so the preview stops.

wait clear
if not llOK
  messagebox(loConnection.cErrorMessage)
  This.oEvent.SetHandlerByBuilder(.T.)
endif not llOK
```

If you want to try this code yourself, change the assignment statement for
loConnection.cConnectString to the appropriate values for your Northwind database.

 The Developer Download files for this chapter, available at
www.hentzenwerke.com, include InstallPreview.PRG, SFConnection.VCX,
and SFReportBuilder.VCX.

Summary

The VFP team certainly met their goals in the improvements they made to the reporting
system. The dialogs available in ReportBuilder.APP are more attractive, easier to use, and
more capable than those in earlier versions. The ability to hook into design-time report events
means you can create customized report designers that are more powerful, flexible, and easier
to use, for both your development team and your end users.

The next chapter looks at further extensibility in the reporting system, this time when
running a report.

Updates and corrections for this chapter can be found on Hentzenwerke's website,
www.hentzenwerke.com. Click "Catalog" and navigate to the page for this book.

Chapter 7
Extending the Reporting System at Run Time

In addition to the design-time extensibility of VFP 9's reporting system discussed in Chapter 6, "Extending the Reporting System at Design Time," VFP 9 also provides the ability to extend the behavior of the reporting system when reports are run. In this chapter, you will learn about VFP 9's report listener concept, how it receives events as a report is run, and how you can create your own listeners to provide different types of output besides the traditional print and preview.

As discussed in the "Enhanced run-time capabilities" section of Chapter 5, "Enhancements in the Reporting System," the new reporting engine in VFP 9 splits responsibility for reporting between the report engine, which now just deals with data-handling and object positioning, and a new object known as a report listener, which handles rendering and output. Report listeners are based on a new base class in VFP 9, ReportListener.

During the run of a report, VFP raises events in a report listener as they happen. For example, the LoadReport event of a report listener fires when the report is loaded before being run. When an object is drawn on the report page, the Render method fires. The ReportListener base class has some native behavior, but extensibility really kicks in when you create and use your own subclasses. For example, a subclass of ReportListener could dynamically format a field, so under some conditions it prints with red text and under other conditions it prints in black.

This chapter starts with a discussion of how report listeners work, and then moves on to examining the properties, events, and methods (PEMs) of the ReportListener base class. After that, we discuss some of the subclasses of ReportListener that come with VFP. The rest of the chapter focuses on some cool uses of report listeners to create special effects you can't do in earlier versions of VFP, including drawing charts without using ActiveX controls and creating your own report previewer.

Report listener basics

Report listeners produce output in two ways. "Page-at-a-time" mode renders a page and outputs it, renders the next page and outputs it, and so forth until the report is done. This mode is typically used when printing a report. In "all-pages-at-once" mode, the report listener renders all the pages and caches them in memory. It then outputs these rendered pages on demand, such as when the user clicks on the next page button in the preview window. This mode is typically used when previewing a report.

Report listeners can be used in a couple of ways. One is by specifying the OBJECT clause of the REPORT command. OBJECT supports two ways of using it: by specifying a report listener and by specifying a report type.

To tell VFP to use a specific listener for a report, instantiate the listener class, and then specify the object's name in the OBJECT clause of the REPORT command. Here's an example:

```
loListener = createobject('MyReportListener')
report form MyReport object loListener
```

If you'd rather not instantiate a listener manually, you can have VFP do it for you automatically by specifying a report type:

```
report form MyReport object type 1
```

The defined types are 0 for outputting to a printer, 1 for previewing, 2 for "page-at-a-time" mode without sending the output to a printer, 3 for "all-pages-at-once" mode without invoking the preview window, 4 for XML output, and 5 for HTML output. Other user-defined types can also be used; this is discussed in the "Registering listeners" section of this chapter.

When you run a report this way, the application specified in the new _REPORTOUTPUT system variable (ReportOutput.APP in the VFP home directory by default) is called to figure out which listener class to instantiate for the specified type. ReportOutput.APP looks for the specified listener type in a listener registry table. If it finds the desired class, it instantiates the class and gives the reporting engine a reference to the listener object. ReportOutput.APP is primarily an object factory, but it also includes some listeners that provide XML and HTML output and other utility functions.

Another way to use report listeners is with the new SET REPORTBEHAVIOR 90 command. This command turns on "object-assisted" reporting so the REPORT command behaves as if you specified OBJECT TYPE 0 when you use the TO PRINT clause or OBJECT TYPE 1 when you use the PREVIEW clause.

ReportListener

The next sections in this chapter examine the PEMs of ReportListener to understand its capabilities. One thing to note about ReportListener is that the unit of measure (for example, the values returned by the GetPageWidth method, and the size parameters passed to the Render method) is 960th of an inch.

Properties

Table 1 shows the properties of ReportListener.

Table 1*. The properties of the ReportListener base class.*

Property	Type	Description
AllowModalMessages	L	If .T, allows modal messages showing the progress of the report (the default is .F.).
CommandClauses	O	An object based on the Empty base class with properties indicating the clauses used in the REPORT or LABEL command. See Table 2 for the properties of this object.
CurrentDataSession	N	The data session ID for the report's data.
CurrentPass	N	Indicates the current pass through the report. A report with _PageTotal or TwoPassProcess set to .T. requires two passes; others only require one. 0 indicates the first pass of a two-pass report or that only one pass is required, while 1 indicates the second pass.
DynamicLineHeight	L	.T. (the default) to use GDI+ line spacing, which varies according to font characteristics, or .F. to use old-style fixed line spacing.
FRXDataSession	N	The data session ID for the FRX cursor (a read-only copy of the report file the reporting engine is running opened for a ReportListener's use).
GDIPlusGraphics	N	The handle for the GDI+ graphics object used for rendering. Read-only.
ListenerType	N	The type of report output the listener produces. The default is -1, which specifies no output, so you'll need to change this to a more reasonable value. See the discussion of the OutputPage method for a list of values.
OutputPageCount	N	The number of pages rendered. Read-only.
OutputType	N	The output type as specified in the OBJECT TYPE clause of the REPORT or LABEL command.
PageNo	N	The current page number being rendered. Read-only.
PageTotal	N	The total number of pages in the report. Read-only.
PreviewContainer	O	A reference to the display surface the report will be output to for previewing.
PrintJobName	C	The name of the print job as it appears in the Windows Print Queue dialog.
QuietMode	L	.T. (the default is .F.) to suppress progress information.
SendGDIPlusImage	N	1 or higher (the default is 0) to send a handle to an image for a General field to the Render method. This is numeric rather than logical to allow the possibility for subclasses to treat images differently if desired.
TwoPassProcess	L	Indicates whether two passes will be used for the report. Set this to .T. to force a prepass even if _PageTotal isn't used somewhere in the report.

The CommandClauses property contains a reference to an Empty object with properties representing the various clauses of the REPORT or LABEL command, plus a few other goodies. **Table 2** lists these properties.

Table 2*. The properties of the CommandClauses object.*

Property	Type	Description
ASCII	L	.T. if the ASCII keyword was specified when outputting to a file.
DE_Name	C	The name of the DataEnvironment object for the report. The name specified with the NAME clause or the name of the report if not specified.
Environment	L	.T. if the ENVIRONMENT keyword was specified.
File	C	The name of the report to run.
Heading	C	The heading specified with the HEADING keyword.

Property	Type	Description
InScreen	L	.T. if the IN SCREEN keyword was specified.
InWindow	C	The name of the window specified with the IN WINDOW keyword.
IsDesignerLoaded	L	.T. if the report is run from within the Report Designer.
IsDesignerProtected	L	.T. if the PROTECTED keyword was specified.
IsReport	L	.T. if this is a report or .F. if it's a label.
NoConsole	L	.T. if the NOCONSOLE keyword was specified.
NoDialog	L	.T. if the NODIALOG keyword was specified.
NoEject	L	.T. if the NOEJECT keyword was specified.
NoPageEject	L	.T. if the NOPAGEEJECT keyword was specified.
NoReset	L	.T. if the NORESET keyword was specified.
NoWait	L	.T. if the NOWAIT keyword was specified with the PREVIEW keyword.
Off	L	.T. if the OFF keyword was specified.
OutputTo	N	The type of output specified in the TO clause: 0 = no TO clause was specified, 1 = printer, 2 = file
PDSetup	L	.T. if the PDSETUP keyword was specified.
Plain	L	.T. if the PLAIN keyword was specified.
Preview	L	.T. if the PREVIEW keyword was specified.
PrintPageCurrent	N	Defaults to 0. However, a preview window can set this to the page currently displayed when it calls the listener's OnPreviewClose method. The listener could use this to enable the "Print current page" option in a Print dialog.
PrintRangeFrom	N	Defaults to 1. However, a listener could set it to the starting page number to print from when printing after preview.
PrintRangeTo	N	Defaults to -1. However, a listener could set it to the ending page number to print to when printing after preview.
Prompt	L	.T. if the PROMPT keyword was specified.
RangeFrom	N	The starting page specified in the RANGE clause; 1 if not specified.
RangeTo	N	The ending page specified in the RANGE clause; -1 if not specified.
RecordTotal	N	The total number of records being reported on in the main cursor.
Sample	L	.T. if the SAMPLE keyword was specified with the LABEL command.
StartDataSession	N	The data session that the REPORT or LABEL command was issued from.
Summary	L	.T. if the SUMMARY keyword was specified with the REPORT command.
ToFile	C	The name of the file specified with the TO FILE clause.
ToFileAdditive	L	.T. if the ADDITIVE keyword was specified when outputting to a file.
Window	C	The name of the window specified with the WINDOW keyword.

A special comment about data session handling is in order. Four data sessions are actually involved during a report run. The first is the data session the ReportListener is instantiated in; SET('DATASESSION') will give you the appropriate value when issued in a ReportListener method. The second is the data session the REPORT or LABEL command was issued from; check the StartDataSession property of the CommandClauses object to determine the data session ID. The third is the data session the FRX cursor is open in. The FRXDataSession property contains the data session ID for this cursor, so use SET DATASESSION TO This.FRXDataSession if you need access to the FRX. The fourth is the data session the report's data is in. If the report has a private data session, this will be a unique data session; otherwise, it'll be the data session the REPORT or LABEL command was issued from. The CurrentDataSession property tells you which data session to use, so if a ReportListener needs to access the report's data, you need to SET DATASESSION TO This.CurrentDataSession.

Remember to save the ReportListener's data session and switch back to it after selecting either the report data or FRX data session.

Examine the code in TestDataSessions.PRG and run it to see how these different data sessions work.

 The Developer Download files for this chapter, available at **www.hentzenwerke.com**, *include TestDataSessions.PRG and two reports it uses: PrivateDS.FRX and DefaultDS.FRX.*

Report events

Report events, which fire when something affects the report as a whole, are shown in **Table 3**.

Table 3. Report events of the ReportListener base class.

Event	Parameters	Description
LoadReport	None	Analogous to the Load event of a form in that it's the first event fired and returning .F. prevents the report from running. Because this event fires before the FRX loads and the printer spool opens, this is the one place where you can change the contents of the FRX on disk or change the printer environment before the report runs.
UnloadReport	None	Like the Unload event of a form, UnloadReport fires after the report runs. This is typically used for clean up tasks.
BeforeReport	None	Fires after the FRX loads, but before the report is run.
AfterReport	None	Fires after the report runs.

Band events

Band events fire as a band is processed. These events are shown in **Table 4.**

Table 4. Band events of the ReportListener base class.

Event	Parameters	Description
BeforeBand	nBandObjCode, nFRXRecno	Fires before a band is processed. The first parameter represents the value of the OBJCODE field in the FRX for the specified band, and the second is the record number in the FRX cursor for the band's record.
AfterBand	nBandObjCode, nFRXRecno	Fires after a band is processed. Same parameters as BeforeBand.

Object events

These events fire as a report object is being processed.

EvaluateContents(nFRXRecno, oObjProperties): this event fires for each field (but not label) object just before it's rendered, and gives the listener the opportunity to change the appearance of the field. The first parameter is the FRX record number for the field object being processed and the second is an object containing properties with information about the field object. The properties this object contains are shown in **Table 5**. You can change any of these properties to change the appearance of the field in the report. If you do so, set the Reload property of the object to .T. to notify the report engine that you changed one or more of the other properties. Also, return .T. if other listeners can make more changes to the field.

Table 5. Properties of the object parameter passed to EvaluateContents.

Property	Type	Description
FillAlpha	N	The alpha, or transparency, of the fill color. Allows finer control than simply transparent or opaque. The values range from 0 for transparent to 255 for opaque.
FillBlue	N	The blue portion of an RGB() value for the fill color.
FillGreen	N	The green portion of an RGB() value for the fill color.
FillRed	N	The red portion of an RGB() value for the fill color.
FontName	C	The font name.
FontSize	N	The font size.
FontStyle	N	A value representing the font style. Additive values of 1 (bold), 2 (italics), 4 (underlined), and 128 (strikethrough).
PenAlpha	N	The alpha of the pen color.
PenBlue	N	The blue portion of an RGB() value for the pen color.
PenGreen	N	The green portion of an RGB() value for the pen color.
PenRed	N	The red portion of an RGB() value for the pen color.
Reload	L	Set this to .T. to notify the report engine that you changed one or more of the other properties.
Text	C	The text to be output for the field object.
Value	-	The actual value of the field to output.

AdjustObjectSize(nFRXRecno, oObjProperties): this event fires for each shape or image object just before it's rendered. It gives you the ability to change the object, and is generally used when you want to replace the shape or image with a custom rendered object and need to size the object dynamically. The first parameter is the FRX record number for the object being processed and the second is an object containing properties with information about the shape or image. The properties this object contains are shown in **Table 6**. If you change Height or Width, set the Reload property of the object to .T. to notify the report engine that you changed these properties. Changing the height of an object that spans pages isn't supported; if you change the height of an object so it won't fit on the rest of the current page, the entire object is moved to the next page. The MaxHeightAvailable and Reattempt properties help you determine how much room is left on the current page and whether the object is pushed to the next page.

***Table 6**. Properties of the object parameter passed to AdjustObjectSize.*

Property	Type	Description
Height	N	The height of the object in 960^{ths} of an inch, from 0 to 64000. Increasing this value (decreasing it is ignored) causes other floating objects in the band to be pushed down and the band to stretch.
Left	N	The left position of the object. Read-only.
Top	N	The top position of the object. Read-only.
Width	N	The width of the object in 960^{ths} of an inch, from 0 to 64000.
MaxHeightAvailable	N	The maximum amount of room available on the page for the object. Read-only.
Reattempt	L	.T. if the object has been pushed to the next page because it won't fit on the current page. Read-only.
Reload	L	Set this to .T. to notify the report engine that you changed one or more of the other properties.

Render(nFRXRecno, nLeft, nTop, nWidth, nHeight, nObjectContinuationType, cContentsToBeRendered, GDIPlusImage): this event is the big one. The report engine calls it at least once for each object being rendered (more than once for objects that span bands or pages). As with the other object events, the first parameter is the FRX record number for the object being rendered. The next four parameters represent the position and size of the object. nObjectContinuationType indicates whether a field, shape, or line object spans a band or page; it contains one of four possible values:

- 0: This object is complete; it doesn't continue onto the next band or page.

- 1: The object has been started, but will not finish on the current page.

- 2: The object is in the middle of rendering; it neither started nor finished on the current page.

- 3: The object has been finished on the current page.

cContentsToBeRendered contains the text of a field or the filename of a picture if appropriate. For fields, the contents are provided in Unicode, appropriately translated to the correct locale using the FontCharSet information associated with the FRX record. Use STRCONV() to convert the string if you want to do something with it, such as storing it in a table. GDIPlusImage is used if a picture comes from a General field and the SendGDIPlusImage property is greater than 0; it contains the graphics handle for the image.

You can supply code in this method if you want to render an object differently than it would otherwise be done. Note, however, that pretty much anything you need to do will require calling GDI+ API functions, so this isn't for the faint of heart. See the "_GDIPlus.VCX" topic later in this chapter.

Methods

The methods of ReportListener are shown in **Table 7**.

Table 7. *The methods of the ReportListener base class.*

Event	Parameters	Description
CancelReport	None	Allows VFP code to terminate a report early. Required so the ReportListener can do necessary cleanup such as closing the print spooler.
OnPreviewClose	IPrint	This method should be called from a preview window when the user closes the preview window or prints a report from preview.
OutputPage	nPageNo, eDevice, nDeviceType [, nLeft, nTop, nWidth, nHeight [, nClipLeft, nClipTop, nClipWidth, nClipHeight]]	Outputs the specified rendered page to the specified device. The optional nLeft through nClipHeight parameters allow the listener to specify exactly what area on the target device to use for rendering when the device type is a container. This is discussed in more detail in the text.
IncludePageInOutput	nPageNo	Returns .T. if the specified page is included in the output or not.
SupportsListenerType	nType	Returns .T. if the listener supports the specified type of output.
GetPageHeight	None	Returns the page height during a report run.
GetPageWidth	None	Returns the page width during a report run.
DoStatus	cMessage	Provides modeless feedback during a report run.
UpdateStatus	None	Updates the feedback UI.
ClearStatus	None	Removes the modeless feedback UI.
DoMessage	cMessage [, nParams [, cTitle]]	Provides modal feedback during a report run if AllowModalMessages is .T; otherwise, calls DoStatus. nParams and cTitle are optional parameters; if passed, they are used as the second and third parameters in a call to MESSAGEBOX().

The OutputPage method warrants more discussion. The nDeviceType parameter determines the type of output this method should perform; it also determines the type of parameter expected for eDevice. **Table 8** lists the types of output supported in the base class ReportListener and the values for nDeviceType and eDevice. Subclasses could support other types of output, such as PDF or other custom formats.

Table 8. The types of output supported by OutputPage.

nDeviceType	Description	eDevice
-1	No device	0
0	Printer	Printer handle
1	Graphics device	GDI+ graphic handle
2	VFP preview window	Reference to VFP control to output to
100	EMF file	File name
101	TIFF file	File name
102	JPEG file	File name
103	GIF file	File name
104	PNG file	File name
105	BMP file	File name
201	Multi-page TIFF	File name (the file must already exist)

The ListenerType property affects the value of OutputPage. **Table 9** shows the different values for ListenerType and the effect each has on output.

Table 9. How the different values of ListenerType affect OutputPage.

ListenerType	Output Type	How OutputPage is Affected
0	"Page-at-a-time" mode, sent to printer	The report engine calls OutputPage after each page is rendered in order to output to a printer. The report engine passes 0 (printer) to this method as nDeviceType and the GDI+ handle for the printer as eDevice.
1	"All-page-at-once" mode, previewer automatically invoked	After all rendering is complete, the report engine invokes a preview window, either by calling (_ReportPreview) to create one or using the one in Listener.PreviewContainer. The preview window calls OutputPage to display the specified page. In this case, nDeviceType is 2 and eDevice is a reference to a VFP control used as a placeholder for the output.
2	"Page-at-a-time" mode, not sent to printer	The report engine calls OutputPage after each page is rendered but no output is sent to the printer. The report engine passes -1 as nDeviceType and 0 as eDevice.
3	"All-page-at-once" mode, no automatic preview window	OutputPage must be called manually to output the specified page after all rendering is complete.

By the way, because report listeners use VFP code, it's now possible to trace code during report execution, something that wasn't possible before and was the source of a lot of frustration for those using user-defined functions (UDFs) in their reports.

Registering listeners

Now that you know what a ReportListener looks like, you can create different subclasses that have the behavior you need. Before you do that, though, let's look at how to tell ReportOutput.APP about them.

Like ReportBuilder.APP (see Chapter 6, "Extending the Reporting System at Design Time," for details on ReportBuilder.APP), ReportOutput.APP uses a registry table to keep track of the listeners it knows about. Although this table is built into ReportOutput.APP, you can create a copy of it called OutputConfig.DBF using DO (_ReportOutput) WITH -100. If ReportOutput.APP finds a table with this name in the current directory or VFP path, it uses that table as the source of listeners it looks at when running a report. **Table 10** shows the structure of this table.

Table 10. The structure of the listener registry table used by ReportOutput.APP.

Field Name	Type	Values	Description
OBJTYPE	I	100 for a listener record	Other record types are used as well; see the VFP documentation for details.
OBJCODE	I	Any valid listener type	The listener type (e.g. 1 for preview).
OBJNAME	V(60)		The class to instantiate.
OBJVALUE	V(60)		The class library the class specified in OBJNAME is found in.
OBJINFO	M		The application containing the class library.

You aren't restricted to using the built-in range of listener types (0 through 5); you can assign your own value to the OBJCODE column in a record you add to the registry table, and then specify that value in the OBJECT TYPE clause of a REPORT or LABEL command.

Note that ReportOutput.APP only looks for the first record with OBJTYPE = 100 and OBJCODE set to the desired listener type. So, you need to remove or unregister (set OBJCODE to another value such as by adding 100 to it) other listener records of the same type. Also, note that the registry table contains quite a few records with OBJTYPE set to something other than 100. The listeners built into ReportOutput.APP, especially XMLListener, use these for their own purposes.

You don't need to register a listener to use it; you can simply instantiate it manually and pass a reference to it to the OBJECT clause of the REPORT command. This mechanism is a little more work, but it gives you better control, doesn't require an external copy of ReportOutput.APP's registry table, and allows you to do things such as chain report listeners together. This is the mechanism we recommend and use in the rest of this chapter.

Utilities in the FFC

The FFC (FoxPro Foundation Classes) subdirectory of the VFP home directory includes a few class libraries that assist with reporting issues.

_ReportListener

_ReportListener.VCX contains some subclasses of ReportListener that have more functionality than the base class. The most useful of these is _ReportListener. (_ReportListener.VCX is also contained within ReportOutput.APP.)

One of the most important features of _ReportListener is support for successors. It's possible you will want more than one report listener used when running a report. For example,

if you want to both preview a report and output it to HTML at the same time,
more than one report listener must be involved. As you will see in upcoming sections in
this chapter, listeners can be used for tasks such as dynamically formatting or rotating text, and
it's a better idea to create small listeners that do one thing rather than a monolithic listener that
does everything. A report that needs more than one of these behaviors requires multiple
listeners.

_ReportListener allows chaining of listeners by providing a Successor property that may
contain an object reference to another listener. To support this mechanism, most events call the
same method in the successor object if it exists, using code similar to:

```
if vartype(This.Successor) = 'O'
  This.Successor.ThisMethodName()
endif vartype(This.Successor) = 'O'
```

For example, suppose ListenerA and ListenerB each perform some task and are both
subclasses of _ReportListener, and you want to use both listeners for a certain report. Here's
how to chain these listeners together:

```
loListener = createobject('ListenerA')
loListener.Successor = createobject('ListenerB')
report form MyReport object loListener
```

The report engine only communicates with the listener specified in the REPORT or
LABEL command; this one is the "lead" listener. However, as the report engine raises report
events, the lead listener calls the appropriate methods of its successor, and the successor calls
the appropriate methods of its successor, and so on down the chain. This type of architecture is
known as a "chain of responsibility," because any listener in the chain can decide to take some
action or pass the message on to the next item in the chain.

Because the report engine automatically sets properties of the lead listener, such as
FRXDataSession and CurrentDataSession, _ReportListener sets these properties of successor
listeners as necessary. The SetSuccessorDynamicProperties method, which is called from
many other methods, is responsible for setting the properties that change frequently:
OutputPageCount, PageNo, and PageTotal. Other properties are set as required; for example,
BeforeReport sets the FRXDataSession, CurrentDataSession, CurrentPass, TwoPassProcess,
and CommandClauses properties of the successor to this class' values.

Another interesting capability of _ReportListener is chaining reports. The AddReport
method adds a report to the custom ReportFileNames collection. Pass this method the name of
a report and optionally the report clauses to use (such as the RANGE clause) and a reference
to another listener object. The RemoveReports method removes all reports from the collection.
RunReports runs the reports; pass it .T. for the first parameter to remove reports from the
collection after they run and .T. for the second parameter to ignore any listeners specified in
AddReport. The following code, taken from TestChainedReports.PRG, runs the
TestDynamicFormatting and TestRotate reports as if they were a single report.

```
use _samples + 'Northwind\orders'
loListener = newobject('_ReportListener', home() + 'ffc\_ReportListener.vcx')
loListener.OutputType = 1
loListener.AddReport('TestDynamicFormatting.frx', 'next 20 nopageeject')
```

```
loListener.AddReport('TestRotate.frx', 'next 20')
loListener.RunReports()
```

 *The Developer Download files for this chapter, available at
www.hentzenwerke.com, include TestChainedReports.PRG,
TestDynamicFormatting.FRX, and TestRotate.FRX.*

A number of utility methods exist that make it easier to work with listeners. For example, SetFRXDataSession switches to the data session for the FRX cursor, SetCurrentDataSession switches to the data session for the report's data, and ResetDataSession restore the data session to the one the report listener runs in.

_ReportListener has several custom properties. DrivingAlias contains the name of the main cursor for the report. ReportUsesPrivateDataSession is .T. if, as its name implies, the report uses a private data session. IsRunning is .T. if a report is running, and IsRunningReports is .T. if a collection of reports is being run. IsSuccessor is .T. if this isn't the lead listener. SharedGDIPlusGraphics, SharedPageHeight, and SharedPageWidth contain the value of the GDIPlusGraphics property and the return values of the GetPageHeight and GetPageWidth methods so they can be used in a successor.

UpdateListener

In addition to _ReportListener, _ReportListener.VCX contains UpdateListener, a subclass of _ReportListener that displays feedback information about the report run. It has several properties you can set to customize the appearance of the feedback. InitStatusText contains the message to display before the report is run. PrepassStatusText contains the message to display while the report "prepass" is performed to calculate the value of _PAGETOTAL. RunStatusText contains the message to display while the report is running. ThermFormCaption contains the caption for the feedback form. ThermCaption contains an expression that's evaluated to display the text inside a thermometer. Because it's based on _ReportListener, UpdateListener can be chained together with other listeners.

Here's an example, taken from TestUpdateListener.PRG, that demonstrates how to use this listener:

```
use _samples + 'Northwind\orders'
loListener = newobject('UpdateListener', home() + 'ffc\_ReportListener.vcx')
with loListener
  .InitStatusText   = 'Preparing report...'
  .RunStatusText    = 'Running...'
  .ThermFormCaption = 'Report Progress'
endwith
loListener.ListenerType = 1
report form TestDynamicFormatting.FRX preview object loListener
lnRun = loListener.ReportStopRunDateTime - loListener.ReportStartRunDateTime
wait window 'The report took ' + transform(lnRun) + ' seconds to run'
```

The Developer Download files for this chapter, available at ***www.hentzenwerke.com***, *include TestUpdateListener.PRG.*

_GDIPlus.VCX

As noted when discussing the Render method (the "Object events" section earlier in this chapter), a listener that performs custom rendering will almost certainly have to use GDI+ functions to do so. GDI+ is a set of hundreds of Windows API functions that perform various graphical manipulations and output. For information about GDI+, see **http://msdn.microsoft.com/library/en-us/gdicpp/GDIPlus/GDIPlusReference/FlatGraphics.asp**.

To make it easier to work with GDI+ functions, Microsoft thoughtfully included _GDIPlus.VCX, written by Walter Nicholls, in the FFC directory. _GDIPlus consists of wrapper classes for GDI+ functions, making them both easier to use and object oriented. The "GDI Plus API Wrapper Foundation Classes" topic in the VFP Help lists these classes and provides a little background about them. Interestingly, it recommends you read the documentation for similar .NET framework classes, since the _GDIPlus classes were somewhat modeled on their .NET equivalents.

The most frequently used class is GPGraphics. It provides methods for drawing on a GDI+ canvas as well as other utility functions. It requires a GDI+ handle to work with, so pass its SetHandle method the value of the GDIPlusGraphics property (or SharedGDIPlusGraphics if you're using a subclass of _ReportListener) before calling other methods. You can then call methods such as DrawArc, DrawCurve, DrawLine, and DrawPie to draw shapes on the report page or RotateTransform, ScaleTransform, and TranslateTransform to change the way drawing occurs.

Some of these methods require a reference to another type of GDI+ object, such as a pen, brush, font, or color object. Other classes in _GDIPlus, such as GPPen, GPSolidBrush, GPHatchBrush, GPFont, and GPColor represent these objects. Using these classes is fairly easy: instantiate the desired one, call the Create method to initialize it with the desired attributes such as color, and then pass it to a GPGraphics method.

A couple of examples in this chapter use _GDIPlus classes to perform custom rendering tasks. See the discussion of the SFRotateDirective class in the "Directive handlers" section for an example that rotates text and the "Custom rendering" section for an example that renders column charts.

Creating your own listeners

While the built-in ReportListener class (and even the listeners provided in the FFC) has a lot of functionality, it's almost certain you will eventually want to do more than what comes in the box. Fortunately, you can create your own listeners by subclassing ReportListener or _ReportListener and adding the functionality you need. The rest of this chapter explores some of the possibilities with report listeners.

SFReportListener

While working with _ReportListener, we discovered we needed some additional behavior in our listeners. SFReportListener, defined in SFReportListener.VCX, is a subclass of _ReportListener that handles some things _ReportListener doesn't. It also provides a few utility methods that most listeners require.

One complication with successors that _ReportListener doesn't handle (there are several, actually) is if a successor calls its CancelReport method to cancel the report, the report doesn't actually cancel because only the CancelReport method of the lead listener cancels the report. So, the Assign method of the Successor property uses BINDEVENT() to ensure that when the successor's CancelReport method is called, so is the current listener's. This causes calls to CancelReport to ripple back up the chain to the lead listener.

```
lparameters toSuccessor
dodefault(toSuccessor)
if vartype(toSuccessor) = 'O'
  bindevent(toSuccessor, 'CancelReport', This, 'CancelReport', 1)
endif vartype(toSuccessor) = 'O'
```

There is a new problem now: the behavior of _ReportListener.CancelReport is to call down the chain so all successor listeners have a chance to do something when a report is canceled. When the current listener calls its successor's CancelReport method, its own CancelReport fires again because of event binding. This would result in an endless loop unless something is done about it. SFReportListener.CancelReport handles this by overriding _ReportListener.CancelReport to not call down the successor chain if it was called from a successor via event binding.

```
local laEvents[1], ;
  lnEvents
if not This.IsSuccessor
  ReportListener::CancelReport()
  nodefault
endif not This.IsSuccessor
if not isnull(This.Successor)
  lnEvents = aevents(laEvents, 0)
  if lnEvents = 0 or ;
    not upper(laEvents[1, 1].Name) == upper(This.Successor.Name)
    This.SetSuccessorDynamicProperties()
    This.Successor.CancelReport()
  endif lnEvents = 0 ...
endif not isnull(This.Successor)
```

Rendering is another complication. Rendering requires a GDI+ handle, similar to the way SQL passthrough commands work with a SQL connection handle or low-level file functions work with a file handle. This handle is contained in the GDIPlusGraphics property, which the reporting engine sets to the appropriate value. However, since the reporting engine doesn't know anything about successors, it only sets the property of the lead listener. The first issue you run into, then, is you can't set GDIPlusGraphics of a successor to the proper value because this property is read-only. _ReportListener handles this by setting a custom SharedGDIPlusGraphics property of successors to the proper value. So, a listener subclass can pass the value of SharedGDIPlusGraphics to any GDI+ functions it needs to call. However, a second issue is you can't expect to use DODEFAULT() in the Render method of a successor to get the usual rendering; because the base behavior is to use GDIPlusGraphics as the GDI+ handle and that property contains the wrong value (it defaults to 0) for all but the lead listener, rendering doesn't work. The only object that can successfully use base class rendering behavior is the lead listener.

So, you now have a problem: you want a listener to change the way something is rendered in a report, so you use GDI+ functions to change the GDI+ state to make the appropriate changes (such as rotating some text), but you can't use DODEFAULT() to perform the actual rendering because that doesn't work anywhere but in the lead listener.

Fortunately, there is a workaround: SFReportListener.Render calls custom BeforeRender and AfterRender methods, which in a subclass can do any GDI+ state change before the usual rendering takes place and do any necessary cleanup afterward. Note that this code uses ReportListener::Render rather than DODEFAULT() to get the base behavior because you want to skip the behavior in _ReportListener.Render.

```
lparameters tnFRXRecno, ;
  tnLeft, ;
  tnTop, ;
  tnWidth, ;
  tnHeight, ;
  tnObjectContinuationType, ;
  tcContentsToBeRendered, ;
  tiGDIPlusImage
with This
  if .BeforeRender(tnFRXRecno, tnLeft, tnTop, tnWidth, tnHeight, ;
    tnObjectContinuationType, tcContentsToBeRendered, tiGDIPlusImage)
    ReportListener::Render(tnFRXRecno, tnLeft, tnTop, tnWidth, tnHeight, ;
      tnObjectContinuationType, tcContentsToBeRendered, tiGDIPlusImage)
    .AfterRender()
  endif .BeforeRender(tnFRXRecno ...
  nodefault
endwith
```

BeforeRender and AfterRender support successor listeners. Here's the code for BeforeRender:

```
lparameters tnFRXRecno, ;
  tnLeft, ;
  tnTop, ;
  tnWidth, ;
  tnHeight, ;
  tnObjectContinuationType, ;
  tcContentsToBeRendered, ;
  tiGDIPlusImage
with This
  if vartype(.Successor) = 'O' and pemstatus(.Successor, 'BeforeRender', 5)
    .Successor.BeforeRender(tnFRXRecno, tnLeft, tnTop, tnWidth, ;
      tnHeight, tnObjectContinuationType, tcContentsToBeRendered, ;
      tiGDIPlusImage)
  endif vartype(.Successor) = 'O' ...
endwith
```

To make it clear how this mechanism works, suppose the lead listener for a report is an SFReportListener object and a successor is a subclass called SFRotateDirective that does text rotation. Here's what happens when rendering an object. The report engine calls the Render method of the lead listener that in turn calls the BeforeRender method. That method calls down the successor chain, so BeforeRender of each successor has a chance to do whatever is necessary. SFRotateDirective.BeforeRender calls some GDI+ functions to rotate the object about to be rendered. Once the BeforeRender chain finishes, SFReportListener.Render performs its base behavior and causes the object to be rendered in a rotated manner because of what SFRotateDirective did. Render then calls AfterRender that calls down the successor chain so AfterRender of each successor has a chance to do its job. SFRotateDirective.AfterRender resets the GDI+ state back to normal so subsequent objects aren't rotated.

One thing a subclassed listener might do is some custom GDI+ rendering. Because GPGraphics in _GDIPlus.VCX does a lot of the hard work for us, the Init method of SFReportListener instantiates a GPGraphics object into its custom oGDIGraphics property. GPGraphics needs a GDI+ handle to do its work, so the BeforeBand method calls GPGraphic's SetHandle method to set the handle to the value of the SharedGDIPlusGraphics property when the band being processed is the page header or title bands. However, there's another issue: the GDI+ handle changes on every page. So, BeforeBand makes sure that SharedGDIPlusGraphics is updated properly first.

```
lparameters tnBandObjCode, ;
  tnFRXRecNo
with This
  if inlist(tnBandObjCode, FRX_OBJCOD_PAGEHEADER, FRX_OBJCOD_TITLE)
    if not .IsSuccessor
      .SharedGDIPlusGraphics = .GDIPlusGraphics
    endif not .IsSuccessor
    .oGDIGraphics.SetHandle(.SharedGDIPlusGraphics)
  endif inlist(tnBandObjCode ...
  dodefault(tnBandObjCode, tnFRXRecNo)
endwith
```

A few other _ReportListener methods have successor issues as well. The DoStatus, EvaluateContents, and AdjustObjectSize methods of _ReportListener don't handle successors at all, so those methods in SFReportListener do.

GetReportObject returns an object for the specified record in the FRX. This makes it easier to examine information about any FRX object.

```
lparameters tnFRXRecno
local lnRecno, ;
  loObject
This.SetFRXDataSession()
lnRecno = recno()
go tnFRXRecno
scatter memo name loObject
go lnRecno
This.ResetDataSession()
return loObject
```

Because events like Render and EvaluateContents fire once for every record in the FRX and for every object that gets rendered (meaning they fire close to the number of objects in the FRX times the number of records in the data set being reported on), you should minimize the amount of work done in these methods. For example, if you store a directive in the USER memo that tells a listener how to process a report object, any code that parses this memo will be called many times, even though it's really only needed once. (You can access the USER memo for an object in a report from the Other page of the properties dialog for that object in the Report Designer.) So, SFReportListener has a custom array property called aRecords that can contain any information you need about the records in the FRX.

To support this concept, the BeforeReport event dimensions aRecords to the number of records in the FRX and calls the ProcessFRXRecord method (abstract in this class) for each record in the FRX. In a subclass, you can override ProcessFRXRecord to update aRecords with any information you deem necessary.

```
with This

* Switch to the FRX datasession, dimension aRecords to as many records as
* there are in the FRX, then go through each record in the FRX in case we need
* to gather information about it. Switch back to our datasession.

  .SetFRXDataSession()
  if alen(.aRecords, 2) > 0
    dimension .aRecords[reccount(), alen(.aRecords, 2)]
  else
    dimension .aRecords[reccount()]
  endif alen(.aRecords, 2) > 0
  scan
    .ProcessFRXRecord()
  endscan
  .ResetDataSession()

* Do the usual behavior.

  dodefault()
endwith
```

SFReportListener also has code in the OutputPage method. Because this method is called with a particular page number, and a successor won't necessarily know what page that is, the code in this method stores the passed page number to a custom nOutputPageNo property that other listeners can use because their property is updated by SetSuccessorDynamicProperties.

The Developer Download files for this chapter, available at
***www.hentzenwerke.com**, include SFReportListener.VCX. Because*
SFReportListener is a subclass of _ReportListener, and it's likely the path to
_ReportListener on your system is different than the one built into the class,
be sure to open SFReportListener in the Class Designer, locate
_ReportListener.VCX in the FFC directory when prompted, and save the
class to update the path to the parent class on your system. Also, note that
one of the include files, SFReporting.H, includes \Program Files\Microsoft
Visual FoxPro 9\FFC\FoxPro_Reporting.h. If you install these samples on a
different drive than where VFP is installed, or if VFP is installed in a different
directory than \Program Files\Microsoft Visual FoxPro 9, be sure to change
the #INCLUDE statement in SFReporting.H to point to the correct path, and
then rebuild Samples.PJX with the "recompile all files" option checked.

Report directives

SFReportListenerDirective is a subclass of SFReportListener. Its purpose is to support directives in the USER memo that tell the listener how to process a report object. An example of a directive is *:LISTENER ROTATE = -45, which tells the listener to rotate this object 45 degrees counter-clockwise. Because USER might be used for a variety of purposes, directives supported by SFReportListenerDirective must start with *:LISTENER (those of you who used GENSCRNX in the FoxPro 2.x days will recognize this type of directive).

Different directives handle different objects. They don't necessarily have to be subclasses of ReportListener (some of the examples you will see later are based on Custom) if they simply change properties of the object being rendered. Because you may use multiple directives for the same object, SFReportListenerDirective maintains a collection of directive handlers and calls the appropriate one as necessary.

The Init method creates the collection of directive handlers and fills it with several commonly used handlers. You can add additional handlers in a subclass or after the class is instantiated by adding to the collection (note that the keyword used for the collection must be upper-case). (In this code and other code in this class, ccDIRECTIVE_* are constants defined in SFReportListener.H.)

```
with This
  .oDirectiveHandlers = createobject('Collection')
  loHandler = newobject('SFDynamicForeColorDirective', 'SFReportListener.vcx')
  .oDirectiveHandlers.Add(loHandler, ccDIRECTIVE_FORECOLOR)
  loHandler = newobject('SFDynamicBackColorDirective', 'SFReportListener.vcx')
  .oDirectiveHandlers.Add(loHandler, ccDIRECTIVE_BACKCOLOR)
  loHandler = newobject('SFDynamicStyleDirective', 'SFReportListener.vcx')
  .oDirectiveHandlers.Add(loHandler, ccDIRECTIVE_STYLE)
  loHandler = newobject('SFDynamicAlphaDirective', 'SFReportListener.vcx')
  .oDirectiveHandlers.Add(loHandler, ccDIRECTIVE_ALPHA)
endwith
```

ProcessFRXRecord, called from the Init method of SFReportListener, parses the USER memo of the current FRX record, looking for *:LISTENER directives. Any it finds are checked for validity by seeing whether a handler for it exists in the oDirectiveHandlers collection; if so, the directive is added to a collection object stored in the aRecords element for the report object.

```
local laLines[1], ;
  lnLines, ;
  lnI, ;
  lcLine, ;
  lnPos, ;
  lcClause, ;
  lcExpr
  loHandler, ;
  loDirective
with This

* Process any lines in the User memo.

  lnLines = alines(laLines, USER)
  for lnI = 1 to lnLines
    lcLine = alltrim(laLines[lnI])

* If we found a listener directive and it's one we support, add it and the
* specified expression to our collection (create the collection the first time
* it's needed).

    if upper(left(lcLine, 10)) = ccDIRECTIVE_LISTENER
      lcLine   = substr(lcLine, 12)
      lnPos    = at('=', lcLine)
      lcClause = alltrim(left(lcLine, lnPos - 1))
      lcExpr   = alltrim(substr(lcLine, lnPos + 1))
      try
        loHandler   = .oDirectiveHandlers.Item(upper(lcClause))
        lcExpr      = loHandler.ProcessExpression(lcExpr)
        loDirective = createobject('Empty')
        addproperty(loDirective, 'DirectiveHandler', lcClause)
        addproperty(loDirective, 'Expression',       lcExpr)

* Create a collection of all directives this record has.

        if vartype(.aRecords[recno()]) <> 'O'
          .aRecords[recno()] = createobject('Collection')
        endif vartype(.aRecords[recno()]) <> 'O'
        .aRecords[recno()].Add(loDirective)
      catch
      endtry
    endif upper(left(lcLine, 10)) = ccDIRECTIVE_LISTENER
  next lnI
endwith
```

The EvaluateContents method checks to see if the element for the current FRX record in aRecords contains a collection of directives for this report object (since there may be more than one directive for a given object). If so, each item in the collection contains the name of a directive handler object in the oDirectiveHandlers collection and the directive argument (for example, if the directive is *:LISTENER ROTATE = -45, this argument would be "-45"). EvaluateContents calls the HandleDirective method of each handler in the collection, passing it the properties object passed in to EvaluateContents and the directive argument. Here's the code for EvaluateContents:

```
lparameters tnFRXRecno, ;
  toObjProperties
local loDirective, ;
  loHandler
with This
  if vartype(.aRecords[tnFRXRecno]) = 'O'
    for each loDirective in .aRecords[tnFRXRecno]
      loHandler = .oDirectiveHandlers.Item(loDirective.DirectiveHandler)
      loHandler.HandleDirective(This, loDirective.Expression, ;
        toObjProperties)
    next loDirective
  endif vartype(.aRecords[tnFRXRecno]) = 'O'
endwith
dodefault(tnFRXRecno, toObjProperties)
```

Directive handlers

SFReportDirective is an abstract class for subclassing directive handlers from. It's a subclass of Custom with just two abstract methods: HandleDirective, called from the EvaluateContents method of SFReportListenerDirective to handle the directive, and ProcessExpression, called from the ProcessFRXRecord method of SFReportListenerDirective to convert the directive argument from text into a format the handler can use.

SFDynamicStyleDirective is a directive handler that changes the font style (that is, whether it's normal, bold, italics, or underlined) for a report object based on a dynamically evaluated expression for every record in the report's data set. Specify the directive in the USER memo of a report object using the following syntax:

```
*:LISTENER STYLE = StyleExpression
```

where StyleExpression is an expression that evaluates to the desired style.

One complication: styles are stored in an FRX as numeric values. So to make it easier to specify styles, SFDynamicStyleDirective allows you to use #NORMAL#, #BOLD#, #ITALIC#, #STRIKETHRU#, and #UNDERLINE# to specify the style. These values are additive, so #BOLD# + #ITALIC# would give bold italicized text. The ProcessExpression method takes care of converting the style text into the appropriate numeric values (the FRX_FONTSTYLE_* constants represent the numeric values for the different styles).

```
lparameters tcExpression
local lcExpression
lcExpression = strtran(tcExpression, '#NORMAL#', ;
  transform(FRX_FONTSTYLE_NORMAL))
lcExpression = strtran(lcExpression, '#BOLD#', ;
  transform(FRX_FONTSTYLE_BOLD))
lcExpression = strtran(lcExpression, '#ITALIC#', ;
  transform(FRX_FONTSTYLE_ITALIC))
lcExpression = strtran(lcExpression, '#UNDERLINE#', ;
  transform(FRX_FONTSTYLE_UNDERLINED))
lcExpression = strtran(lcExpression, '#STRIKETHRU#', ;
  transform(FRX_FONTSTYLE_STRIKETHROUGH))
return lcExpression
```

Here's an example of a directive (taken from the SHIPVIA field in TestDynamicFormatting.FRX) that displays a report object in bold under some conditions and normal under others:

```
*:LISTENER STYLE = iif(SHIPVIA = 3, #BOLD#, #NORMAL#)
```

The HandleDirective method evaluates the expression. If the expression is valid, it sets the FontStyle property of the properties object to the desired style and sets Reload to .T. so the report engine knows the report object has changed.

```
lparameters toListener, ;
  tcExpression, ;
  toObjProperties
local lnStyle
lnStyle = evaluate(tcExpression)
if vartype(lnStyle) = 'N'
  toObjProperties.FontStyle = lnStyle
  toObjProperties.Reload    = .T.
endif vartype(lnStyle) = 'N'
```

SFDynamicAlphaDirective is very similar to SFDynamicStyleDirective, but it sets the PenAlpha property of the report object to the specified value. Specify the directive using the following syntax:

```
*:LISTENER ALPHA = AlphaExpression
```

SFDynamicColorDirective is also very similar to SFDynamicStyleDirective, but it deals with the color of the report object instead of its font style. As with styles, colors must be specified as RGB values, so SFDynamicColorDirective supports colors to be specified as text, such as #RED#, #BLUE#, and #YELLOW#. Specify the directive using the following syntax:

```
*:LISTENER FORECOLOR = ColorExpression
*:LISTENER BACKCOLOR = ColorExpression
```

where ColorExpression is an expression that evaluates to the desired color.

The code in the HandleDirective method is similar to the SFDynamicStyleDirective, but it calls SetColor rather than setting the FontStyle property. SetColor is abstract in this class and it's implemented in two subclasses of SFDynamicColorDirective: SFDynamicBackColorDirective and SFDynamicForeColorDirective. Here's the code from SFDynamicBackColorDirective to show how the color is set:

```
lparameters toObjProperties, ;
  tnColor
with toObjProperties
  .FillRed   = bitand(tnColor, 0x0000FF)
  .FillGreen = bitrshift(bitand(tnColor, 0x00FF00), 8)
  .FillBlue  = bitrshift(bitand(tnColor, 0xFF0000), 16)
endwith
```

The code in the ProcessExpression method of SFDynamicColorDirective is also very similar to the SFDynamicStyleDirective; it converts the color text into the appropriate RGB values.

TestDynamicFormatting.FRX shows how these two directive handlers (and SFReportListenerDirective) work. It prints records from the sample Northwind Orders table that comes with VFP. The SHIPPEDDATE field has the following in USER:

```
*:LISTENER FORECOLOR = iif(SHIPPEDDATE > ORDERDATE + 10, #RED#, #BLACK#)
```

This tells the listener to display this field in red if the date the item was shipped is more than 10 days after it was ordered or black if not. The SHIPVIA field displays in bold if the shipping method is 3 or normal if not, as discussed earlier. This field uses the following expression to display the desired value:

```
icase(SHIPVIA = 1, 'Fedex', SHIPVIA = 2, 'UPS', SHIPVIA = 3, 'Mail')
```

The following code (taken from TestDynamicFormatting.PRG) shows how to run this report with SFReportListenerDirective as its listener. **Figure 1** shows the results.

```
use _samples + 'Northwind\orders'
loListener = newobject('SFReportListenerDirective', ;
  'SFReportListener.vcx')
report form TestDynamicFormatting.FRX preview object loListener next 20
```

SFTranslateDirective allows you to create multi-lingual reports by specifying that certain fields be translated. Its Init method opens a STRINGS table that contains a record for each string with a column for each language. HandleDirective looks up each word in the text in the field being rendered in STRINGS and finds the appropriate translation from the column for the desired language. (It assumes a global variable called gcLanguage contains the language to use for the report; you could, of course, substitute any other mechanism you wish.) If the text is different, it's written to the Text property of the properties object and Reload is set to .T. so the report engine will use the new string.

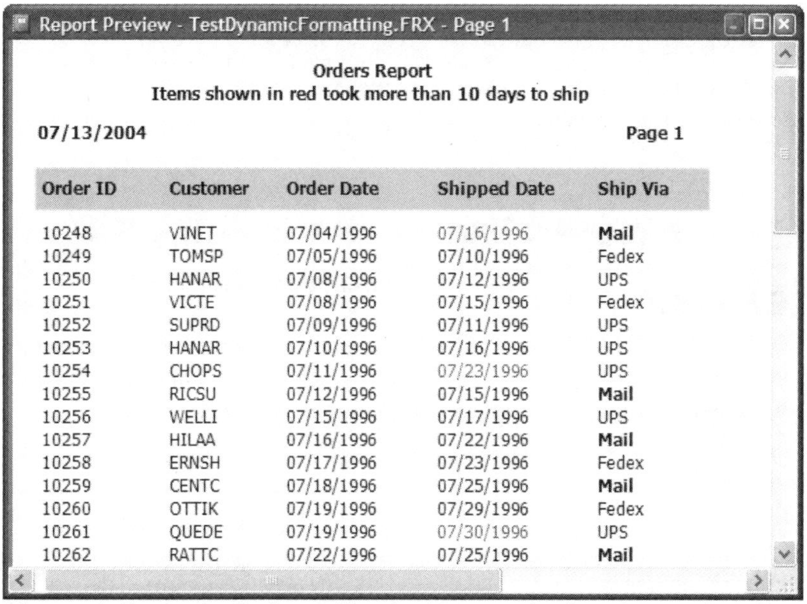

Figure 1. *Dynamically formatting text is easy to do using custom ReportListener classes such as SFReportListenerDirective.*

```
lparameters toListener, ;
  tcExpression, ;
  toObjProperties
local lcText, ;
  lcNewText, ;
  lnI, ;
  lcWord
store toObjProperties.Text to lcText, lcNewText
for lnI = 1 to getwordcount(lcText)
  lcWord = getwordnum(lcText, lnI)
  if seek(upper(lcWord), 'STRINGS', 'ENGLISH')
    lcNewText = strtran(lcNewText, lcWord, trim(evaluate('STRINGS.' + ;
      gcLanguage)))
  endif seek(upper(lcWord) ...
next lnI
if not lcNewText == toObjProperties.Text
  toObjProperties.Text   = lcNewText
  toObjProperties.Reload = .T.
endif not lcNewText == toObjProperties.Text
```

To use this listener, simply place *:LISTENER TRANSLATE in the USER memo of any field objects you want translated and set gcLanguage to the desired language. Note that because EvaluateContents is only called for field objects, you have to use them instead of label objects. TestTranslate.PRG shows how to add SFTranslateDirective to the collection of directive handlers recognized by SFReportListenerDirective. This sample uses Pig Latin for fun. **Figure 2** shows what the report looks like when it's run.

```
use _samples + 'Northwind\customers'
loListener = newobject('SFReportListenerDirective', 'SFReportListener.vcx')
loHandler  = newobject('SFTranslateDirective',       'SFReportListener.vcx')
loListener.oDirectiveHandlers.Add(loHandler, 'TRANSLATE')
gcLanguage = 'PigLatin'
report form TestTranslate.FRX preview object loListener
```

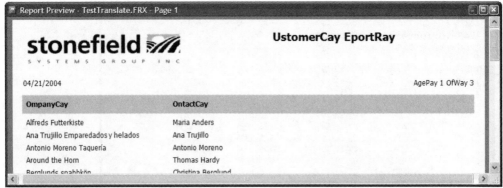

***Figure 2**. You can dynamically change the text of field objects, such as creating multi-lingual reports.*

SFRotateDirective is another directive handler, but it's based on SFReportListener rather than SFReportDirective because it doesn't just change the properties of the report object via the properties object. Instead, it overrides the Render method to rotate the report object.

To specify a report object be rotated, put a directive in the USER memo using the following syntax:

```
*:LISTENER ROTATE = AngleExpression
```

where AngleExpression is an expression that evaluates to the angle to rotate to (clockwise angles are specified as positive values, counter-clockwise angles as negative).

The BeforeRender method, called just before an object is rendered, starts by checking whether a rotation angle was specified for the report object. (The code in ProcessFRXRecord does that. We won't look at the code in that method; it's similar to, albeit simpler, than the SFReportListenerDirective.) If a rotation angle was specified, BeforeRender uses methods of the oGDIGraphics object to save the current GDI+ state and change the drawing angle for the object, and uses DODEFAULT() to do the normal behavior, which is to call the BeforeRender method of any successors.

```
lparameters tnFRXRecno, ;
  tnLeft, ;
  tnTop, ;
  tnWidth, ;
  tnHeight, ;
  tnObjectContinuationType, ;
  tcContentsToBeRendered, ;
  tnGDIPlusImage
```

```
local lnAngle, ;
  lnState
with This

* If we're supposed to rotate this object, do so.

  lnAngle = evaluate(evl(.aRecords[tnFRXRecno], '0'))
  if lnAngle <> 0

* Save the current state of the graphics handle.

    .oGDIGraphics.Save(@lnState)
    .nState = lnState

* Move the 0,0 point to where we'd like it to be so when we rotate,
* we're rotating around the appropriate point.

    .oGDIGraphics.TranslateTransform(tnLeft, tnTop)

* Change the angle at which the draw will occur.

    .oGDIGraphics.RotateTransform(lnAngle)

* Restore the 0,0 point.

    .oGDIGraphics.TranslateTransform(-tnLeft, -tnTop)
  endif lnAngle <> 0

* Do the usual behavior.

  dodefault(tnFRXRecno, tnLeft, tnTop, tnWidth, tnHeight, ;
    tnObjectContinuationType, tcContentsToBeRendered, tnGDIPlusImage)
endwith
```

AfterRender restores the GDI+ state so subsequent objects render properly. Just for fun, try commenting out the code in this method and run a report. The results are cool but completely impractical.

```
with This
  if .nState <> 0
    .oGDIGraphics.Restore(.nState)
    .nState = 0
  endif .nState <> 0

* Do the usual behavior.

  dodefault()
endwith
```

TestRotate.FRX is a sample report that show how this works. The column headings for the date fields have rotate directives so the date fields can be placed closer together. The following code (taken from TestRotate.PRG) shows how to run this report with SFRotateDirective as its listener. The results are shown in **Figure 3**.

```
use _samples + 'Northwind\orders'
loListener = newobject('SFRotateDirective', 'SFReportListener.vcx')
report form TestRotate.FRX preview object loListener next 20
```

Order Id	Customer	Order Date	Required Date	Shipped Date
10248	VINET	07/04/1996	08/01/1996	07/16/1996
10249	TOMSP	07/05/1996	08/16/1996	07/10/1996
10250	HANAR	07/08/1996	08/05/1996	07/12/1996
10251	VICTE	07/08/1996	08/05/1996	07/15/1996
10252	SUPRD	07/09/1996	08/06/1996	07/11/1996
10253	HANAR	07/10/1996	07/24/1996	07/16/1996
10254	CHOPS	07/11/1996	08/08/1996	07/23/1996
10255	RICSU	07/12/1996	08/09/1996	07/15/1996
10256	WELLI	07/15/1996	08/12/1996	07/17/1996
10257	HILAA	07/16/1996	08/13/1996	07/22/1996
10258	ERNSH	07/17/1996	08/14/1996	07/23/1996
10259	CENTC	07/18/1996	08/15/1996	07/25/1996
10260	OTTIK	07/19/1996	08/16/1996	07/29/1996
10261	QUEDE	07/19/1996	08/16/1996	07/30/1996
10262	RATTC	07/22/1996	08/19/1996	07/25/1996
10263	ERNSH	07/23/1996	08/20/1996	07/31/1996
10264	FOLKO	07/24/1996	08/21/1996	08/23/1996

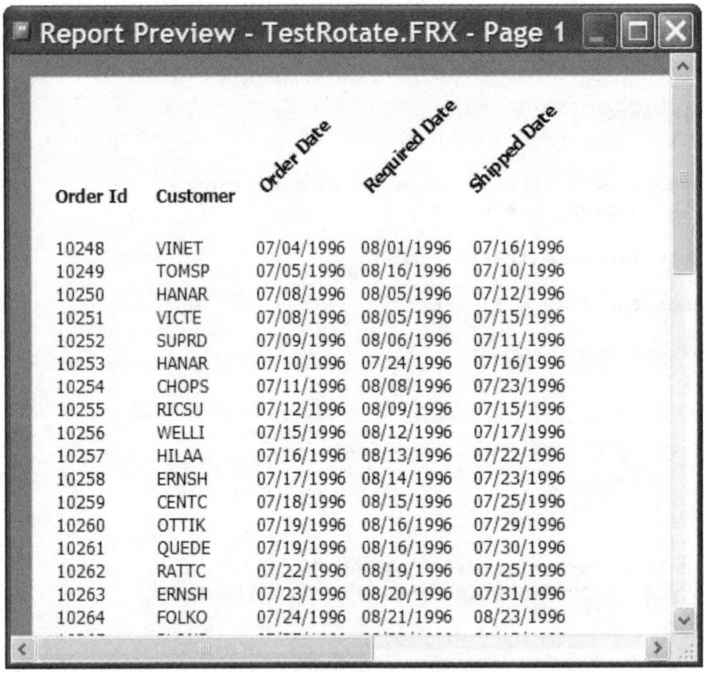

***Figure 3**. Text can be rotated dynamically by changing the way it's rendered.*

*The Developer Download files for this chapter, available at **www.hentzenwerke.com**, include SFReportListener.VCX, TestDynamicFormatting.PRG, TestTranslate.PRG, Strings.DBF, TestRotate.PRG, TestDynamicFormatting.FRX, TestRotate.FRX, and TestTranslate.FRX. Run the PRG files to see how the report directive classes discussed in this section work.*

SFReportListenerGraphic

The OutputPage method of ReportListener supports outputting pages to graphics files. SFReportListenerGraphic, a subclass of SFReportListener, makes it easier to do this. It has two custom properties: cFileName that is set to the name of the file to create, and nFileType that is either set to the number representing the file type or left at 0, in which case SFReportListenerGraphic will set it to the proper value based on the extension of the filename in cFileName.

If ListenerType is 2 ("page-at-a-time" mode with no output, the default for this class), OutputPage is automatically called after each page is rendered. In that case, OutputPage will handle outputting to the specified file. If ListenerType is 3 ("all-pages-at-once" mode with no output), pages are only output when OutputPage is specifically called, so AfterReport goes through the rendered pages and calls OutputPage for each one. Notice that if a multi-page TIFF file is specified, the first page must be output as a single-page TIFF file, and then subsequent pages are appended to it by outputting them as a multi-page TIFF file. Here's the code from AfterReport; OutputPage is similar but slightly simpler. (In this code, LISTENER_* are constants defined in FoxPro_Reporting.H, which is referenced by SFReporting.H, which itself is referenced by SFReportListener.H, the include file for this class.)

```
local lcBaseName, ;
  lcExt, ;
  lnI, ;
  lcFileName
with This
  dodefault()
  if .ListenerType = LISTENER_TYPE_ALLPGS
    if .nFileType = 0
      .GetGraphicsType()
    endif .nFileType = 0
    lcBaseName = addbs(justpath(.cFileName)) + juststem(.cFileName)
    lcExt      = justext(.cFileName)
    for lnI = 1 to .SharedOutputPageCount
      do case
        case .nFileType <> LISTENER_DEVICE_TYPE_MTIF
          lcFileName = forceext(lcBaseName + padl(lnI, 3, '0'), lcExt)
          .OutputPage(lnI, lcFileName, .nFileType)
        case not file(.cFileName)
          .OutputPage(lnI, .cFileName, LISTENER_DEVICE_TYPE_TIF)
        otherwise
          .OutputPage(lnI, .cFileName, .nFileType)
      endcase
      .DoStatus(strtran(strtran(ccSTR_PAGE_X_OF_Y, ccMSG_INSERT1, ;
        transform(lnI)), ccMSG_INSERT2, ;
        transform(.SharedOutputPageCount)))
    next lnI
    .ClearStatus()
  endif .ListenerType = LISTENER_TYPE_ALLPGS
endwith
```

SFReportListenerGraphic also has a ShowFile method to display the file using the Windows API ShellExecute function, which uses the registered application for the file type.

TestGraphicOutput.PRG shows how SFReportListenerGraphic works. It combines the effects of multiple listeners to render the report properly (this uses the same TestDynamicFormatting.FRX you saw earlier) and output to graphics files.

```
use _samples + 'Northwind\orders'
loListener = newobject('SFReportListenerGraphic', 'SFReportListener.vcx')
loListener.cFileName = fullpath('TestReport.gif')
loListener.Successor = newobject('SFReportListenerDirective', ;
  'SFReportListener.vcx')
report form TestDynamicFormatting.FRX object loListener range 1, 6
loListener.ShowFile(1)
```

The Developer Download files for this chapter, available at
www.hentzenwerke.com, *include SFReportListener.VCX,*
TestGraphicOutput.PRG, and TestDynamicFormatting.FRX.

Custom rendering

The combination of the Render method and GDI+ functions provides the ability to render just about anything you wish in place of an object. For example, a common request is to output charts on a report without relying on General fields and ActiveX controls. The report shown in **Figure 4** is an example of such a report. The chart shows sales by product category as a column graph. When viewed in the Report Designer, however, all you see is a rectangle where the chart should go.

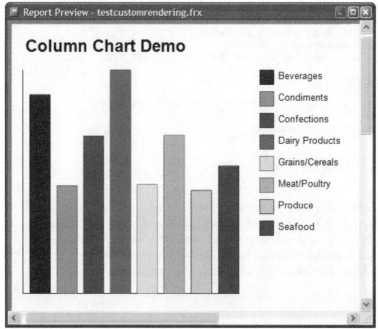

Figure 4. Using GDI+ functions, you can render shapes as anything you wish.

TestCustomRendering.PRG, which runs the TestCustomRendering.FRX report, uses the SFColumnChartListener class to replace the rectangle with a chart. The code for this class isn't shown here for space reasons. However, as an example, the following code is taken from the DrawColumnChart method, which is called from the BeforeRender method when the rectangle is about to be rendered. As you can see, this code makes extensive use of the classes in the FFC's _GDIPlus.VCX, discussed in the "_GDIPlus.VCX" section of this chapter. This code uses several properties of the class:

- aValues is a two-dimensional array of values to graph. Column 1 contains the names of the product categories and column 2 contains the total sales for each category.

- aColumnColors is an array containing the color to use for each column.

- nSpacing is the space between the columns.

- cLegendFontName and nLegendFontSize are the font name and size to use for the legend.

- nLegendSpacing is the space between the chart and its legend.

- nLegendBoxSize is the size of a box in the legend, nLegendBoxSpacing is the spacing between the boxes, and nLegendTextSpacing is the spacing between a box and its associated text.

```
lparameters tnLeft, tnTop, tnWidth, tnHeight
local lnMax, ;
  lnColumns, ;
  lnI, ;
  lnColumnWidth, ;
  loColumnBrush, ;
  loPen, ;
  loFont, ;
  loStringFormat, ;
  loPoint, ;
  loTextBrush, ;
  lnColors, ;
  lnColor, ;
  lnLeft, ;
  lnHeight, ;
  lnTop
with This

* Figure out the highest value and the width of each column.

  lnMax      = 0
  lnColumns = alen(.aValues, 1)
  for lnI = 1 to lnColumns
    lnMax = max(lnMax, .aValues[lnI, 2])
  next lnI
  lnColumnWidth = (tnWidth - (lnColumns * .nSpacing))/lnColumns

* Create _GDIPlus objects we'll need for drawing.

  loColumnBrush  = newobject('GPSolidBrush',  home() + 'ffc\_GDIPlus.vcx')
  loPen          = newobject('GPPen',          home() + 'ffc\_GDIPlus.vcx')
```

```
loFont          = newobject('GPFont',         home() + 'ffc\_GDIPlus.vcx')
loStringFormat = newobject('GPStringFormat', home() + 'ffc\_GDIPlus.vcx')
loPoint         = newobject('GPPoint',        home() + 'ffc\_GDIPlus.vcx')
loTextBrush     = newobject('GPSolidBrush',   home() + 'ffc\_GDIPlus.vcx')
loPen.Create(.CreateColor(0))  && Black
loFont.Create(.cLegendFontName, .nLegendFontSize, ;
   GDIPLUS_FontStyle_Regular, GDIPLUS_Unit_Point)

* Draw the border for the column chart.

.oGDIGraphics.DrawLine(loPen, tnLeft, tnTop, tnLeft, ;
   tnTop + tnHeight)
.oGDIGraphics.DrawLine(loPen, tnLeft, tnTop + tnHeight, ;
   tnLeft + tnWidth, tnTop + tnHeight)

* Draw the column.

lnColors = alen(.aColumnColors)
for lnI = 1 to lnColumns
   lnColor = .aColumnColors[(lnI - 1) % lnColors + 1]
   loColumnBrush.Create(lnColor)
   lnLeft   = tnLeft + lnI * .nSpacing + (lnI - 1) * lnColumnWidth
   lnHeight = cast(tnHeight/lnMax * .aValues[lnI, 2] as Numeric(7, 2))
   lnTop    = tnTop + tnHeight - lnHeight
   .oGDIGraphics.DrawRectangle(loPen, lnLeft, lnTop, ;
      lnColumnWidth, lnHeight)
   .oGDIGraphics.FillRectangle(loColumnBrush, lnLeft, lnTop, ;
      lnColumnWidth, lnHeight)

* Draw the legend for the column.

   lnLeft = tnLeft + tnWidth + .nLegendSpacing
   lnTop  = tnTop + (lnI - 1) * (.nLegendBoxSize + .nLegendBoxSpacing)
   .oGDIGraphics.DrawRectangle(loPen, lnLeft, lnTop, ;
      .nLegendBoxSize, .nLegendBoxSize)
   .oGDIGraphics.FillRectangle(loColumnBrush, lnLeft, lnTop, ;
      .nLegendBoxSize, .nLegendBoxSize)
   lnLeft = lnLeft + .nLegendBoxSize + .nLegendTextSpacing
   loPoint.Create(lnLeft, lnTop)
   loTextBrush.Create(.CreateColor(0))  && Black
   .oGDIGraphics.DrawStringA(.aValues[lnI, 1], loFont, loPoint, ;
      loStringFormat, loTextBrush)
   next lnI
endwith
```

The Developer Download files for this chapter, available at
www.hentzenwerke.com, *include TestCustomRendering.PRG,*
TestCustomRendering.FRX, and SFReportListener.VCX.

Previewing reports

As discussed in Chapter 5, "Enhancements in the Reporting System," VFP 9 sports a new preview window for reports. A new system variable, _REPORTPREVIEW, specifies the name of a VFP application used as a "factory" to create the preview window. (A factory is an object that doesn't provide the functionality required by a client object, but instead creates another object that provides this functionality.) By default, the variable points to ReportPreview.APP in the VFP home directory, but you could substitute your own application if you wish to. The ability to use a VFP application as the preview window provides a lot more control over the appearance and behavior of previewing than in earlier versions.

When you preview a report, by default the PreviewContainer property of the listener used for the report is null. In that case, the reporting engine calls the application pointed to by _REPORTPREVIEW, which instantiates a VFP form to use as the preview window. A reference to the form is stored in PreviewContainer. If PreviewContainer isn't null, the reporting engine doesn't bother calling the preview factory application.

Because the preview window is simply a VFP form, you can customize its appearance by setting the appropriate properties. To create an instance of the preview window prior to running a report, pass ReportPreview.APP a variable; it will instantiate the preview window class into that variable. You can then set properties of the form as necessary and store the variable to the PreviewContainer property of the listener for the report.

For example, the following code (taken from CustomizePreview.PRG) displays a preview window with a custom caption and without a toolbar, using 2-up pages displayed at 75% (zoom level 4) starting at page 4:

```
local loPreview, ;
  loListener
do (_ReportPreview) with loPreview
with loPreview
  .CurrentPage      = 4
  .ToolbarIsVisible = .F.
  .CanvasCount      = 2
  .ZoomLevel        = 4
  .Width            = _screen.Width - 20
  .Caption          = 'Chapter 7 Preview Window'
endwith
loListener = newobject('SFReportListenerDirective', 'SFReportListener.vcx')
loListener.PreviewContainer = loPreview
use _samples + 'Northwind\orders'
report form TestDynamicFormatting object loListener preview
```

 *The Developer Download files for this chapter, available at **www.hentzenwerke.com**, include CustomizePreview.PRG, SFReportListener.VCX, and TestDynamicFormatting.FRX.*

A common question on VFP forums such as the Universal Thread is "how do I remove the print button from the VFP preview toolbar?" In earlier versions, you had to create a custom resource file, customize the preview toolbar to remove the print button, and use the custom resource file in your application. In VFP 9, you simply set the Visible property of the print button in the toolbar to .F. However, there are a couple of minor complications:

- The PreviewContainer property of the listener doesn't point to the preview form but to a proxy object for the form; that is, it references an object that acts as an intermediary between the listener and the preview form. The proxy object has an oForm property that references the actual preview form. The preview form has a Toolbar property that contains a reference to the Toolbar, so set the Visible property of cmdPrint in loListener.PreviewContainer.oForm.Toolbar to .F. to hide the print button.

- The preview window also has a shortcut menu with a print function. The shortcut menu is populated in the InvokeContextMenu method of the preview window, so you might think that removing the print function from the menu requires subclassing the preview form class and overriding this method. Fortunately, the VFP team thought of this, and provided a hook mechanism to allow you to change the menu. This hook is implemented via an object stored in the ExtensionHandler property. If that property contains an object, InvokeContextMenu calls the object's AddBarsToMenu method after populating the shortcut menu. So, you can create a custom object with an AddBarsToMenu method that removes the print bar and store a reference to that object in the ExtensionHandler property (call SetExtensionHandler to do that). Such a custom object must also have a few other methods because if ExtensionHandler references an object, other methods will also use this object. See the code below for an example of such a class.

The following code, taken from NoPrintButton.PRG, shows how to handle this:

```
use _samples + 'Northwind\orders'
loListener = newobject('SFReportListenerDirective', 'SFReportListener.vcx')
report form TestDynamicFormatting.FRX preview object loListener next 20 nowait
loExtension = createobject('ExtensionHandler')
loListener.PreviewContainer.SetExtensionHandler(loExtension)
loListener.PreviewContainer.oForm.Toolbar.cmdPrint.Visible = .F.

define class ExtensionHandler as Custom
  function AddBarsToMenu(tcMenu, tnNextBar)
    release bar 12 of &tcMenu
  endfunc

  function Release
    if type('This.PreviewForm') = 'O'
      This.PreviewForm.ExtensionHandler = .NULL.
      This.PreviewForm = .NULL.
    endif type('This.PreviewForm') = 'O'
  endfunc

  function Show(tnStyle)
  endfunc

  function Paint
  endfunc

  function HandleKeyPress(tnKeyCode, tnShiftAltCtrl)
  endfunc
enddefine
```

The Developer Download files for this chapter, available at **www.hentzenwerke.com**, *include NoPrintButton.PRG, SFReportListener.VCX, and TestDynamicFormatting.FRX.*

You don't have to use the preview form class defined in ReportPreview.APP to preview a report. SFPreviewForm.SCX (shown in **Figure 5**) acts as both a report manager and preview window at the same time. Select a report from the list and click the Preview button to preview the report in the form. The Next and Previous buttons display the next and previous pages in the report.

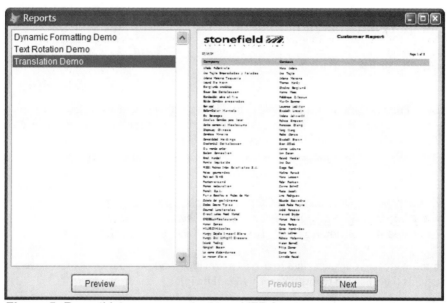

Figure 5. *ReportListener can output to a VFP form so you can create custom preview windows.*

Here's the key code from the form's PreviewReport method, called from the Click method of the Preview button:

```
with Thisform
  .oListener = createobject('ReportListener')
  .oListener.ListenerType = LISTENER_TYPE_ALLPGS
  report form (lcReport) object .oListener
  .oListener.OutputPage(1, .oPreviewContainer, LISTENER_DEVICE_TYPE_CTL)
endwith
```

Because its ListenerType property is set to 3, the ReportListener renders the pages in "all-pages-at-once" mode, but doesn't perform any output. Once the rendering is done, the form calls the listener's OutputPage method, instructing it to output page 1 to the oPreviewContainer shape. (LISTENER_DEVICE_TYPE_CTL is a constant that evaluates to

2, the value used by OutputPage to specify a VFP control.) OutputPage doesn't actually output a page to the shape; instead, it uses the size and position of the shape as the location for the output.

Another important method is Paint. The code in this method redisplays the current page whenever the form is redrawn. Without this code, things that cause the form to be redrawn, such as resizing the form, result in the preview disappearing because the shape is redrawn. This code is wrapped in a TRY structure because the form may be painted before the listener has finished rendering the first page.

```
with This
  if vartype(.oListener) = 'O'
    try
      .oListener.OutputPage(.nCurrentPage, .oPreviewContainer, ;
        LISTENER_DEVICE_TYPE_CTL)
    catch
    endtry
  endif vartype(.oListener) = 'O'
endwith
```

Note that SFPreviewForm is just a simple demo. It doesn't handle many of the issues the new VFP 9 preview window does, such as printing from preview or multiple pages at once. Also, since PreviewReport just uses a base class listener, there's no dynamic formatting, text rotation, or other effects. You could, of course, add these features yourself if you wish.

 The Developer Download files for this chapter, available at ***www.hentzenwerke.com****, include SFPreviewForm.SCX, TestDynamicFormatting.FRX, TestRotate.FRX, and TestTranslate.FRX.*

If you want to create your own class to use as a preview window, your class must have a couple of methods (because the report listener will call them):

- SetReport: this method should accept an object reference to the report listener, and store it somewhere. In order to preview the report, the preview form must call methods of the listener, especially OutputPage, so it needs a reference to the listener. When the report is done, the listener will call SetReport a second time, passing it .NULL. so the reference can be removed. Otherwise, with the listener and the preview form having references to each other, the objects can't be destroyed. (Note that SFPreviewForm.SCX doesn't have this method because it's not being called from the report engine as a preview window but drives the previewing process.)

- Show: this method should accept the same parameter as the Show method of a form, which indicates whether the form is modal or not.

When the preview form is closed, it should call the OnPreviewClose method of the listener to ensure things are properly cleaned up.

The NewPreview class (in NewPreview.VCX) is a very simple example. It's just a base class form with a shape named oPreviewContainer and a custom property named oListener. The SetReport method has the following code:

```
lparameters toListener
This.oListener = toListener
```

The Paint method displays the first page of the report:

```
if vartype(This.oListener) = 'O'
  This.oListener.OutputPage(1, This.oPreviewContainer, 2)
endif vartype(This.oListener) = 'O'
```

The QueryUnload method tells the report listener to clean up:

```
if vartype(This.oListener) = 'O'
  This.oListener.OnPreviewClose()
endif vartype(This.oListener) = 'O'
```

That's it! Here's some code (NewPreview.PRG) that uses this class as the preview form
for a report:

```
local loPreview, ;
  loListener
loPreview  = newobject('NewPreview', 'NewPreview.vcx')
loListener = createobject('ReportListener')
loListener.ListenerType    = 1
loListener.PreviewContainer = loPreview
use _samples + 'Northwind\orders'
report form TestDynamicFormatting object loListener
```

Of course, this preview window has almost no functionality; it only displays the first page
of the report. To create your own customized preview window with complete functionality,
you may want to subclass the FRXPreviewProxy and FRXPreviewForm classes in
ReportPreview.APP (the source code is in the Tools\XSource\VFPSource\ReportPreview
subdirectory of the VFP home directory after you unzip Tools\XSource\XSource.ZIP) and add
the additional behavior you require.

 The Developer Download files for this chapter, available at
www.hentzenwerke.com, include NewPreview.VCX,
NewPreview.PRG, and TestDynamicFormatting.FRX.

New SYS() functions
There are a couple of new SYS() functions in VFP 9 related to report listeners.

SYS(2024) returns "Y" if the current report was canceled before completion or "N" if
there is no current report or the report finished normally. SYS(2024) is reset to "N" after the
UnloadReport event fires, so you can't use this value from code that executes a REPORT or
LABEL command. It's typically used in methods of a report listener to take different action
based on whether the report completed or not.

SYS(2040) indicates the status of a report. It returns "0" if there is no current report, "1"
if the report is being previewed, and "2" if it's being output to a file or printer. This can be

used, for example, in the Print When expression of a report object to conditionally output the object based on whether the report is being printed or previewed.

Summary

Microsoft has done an incredible job of opening up the VFP reporting engine, both at design-time and run-time. By passing report events to ReportListener objects, they allow you to react to these events to do just about anything you wish, from providing custom feedback to users to providing different types of output, to dynamically changing the way objects are rendered. We look forward to seeing the type of things the VFP community does with these new features.

Updates and corrections for this chapter can be found on Hentzenwerke's website, **www.hentzenwerke.com**. Click "Catalog" and navigate to the page for this book.

Chapter 8
SQL Changes

After leaving the SQL portion of VFP virtually unchanged for a long time, Microsoft began to introduce additional features and increased compliance with the ANSI-92 standard with VFP 8. VFP 9 continues that process, offering additional functionality for SELECT, INSERT, UPDATE, and DELETE, as well as a number of other improvements.

VFP's SQL sublanguage lets you manipulate data without worrying about record pointers or work areas. VFP 9 includes a number of enhancements to this part of the language. Many of the limits related to queries have been removed, the use of subqueries has been expanded, and the UPDATE and DELETE commands accept join conditions to specify the records to modify or remove. VFP 9 also offers some performance improvements, an easier way to test performance, and the ability to query against a buffered table.

VFP 9 has no limits

The most basic change to queries in VFP 9 is the elimination of a number of restrictions. In earlier versions, for example, the total number of joins and subqueries in a single query was limited to nine; in VFP 9, there's no limit. **Table 1** shows the limits related to queries removed or raised in VFP 9.

Table 1. SQL queries were limited in a number of ways in earlier versions of Visual FoxPro. Many of those limits were lifted in VFP 9.

Description	Limit in VFP 8 (and earlier)	Limit in VFP 9
Total number of joins and subqueries	9	No limit
Number of UNIONs	9	No limit
Number of tables and aliases referenced	30	No limit
Number of items listed in IN clause	24	Based on SYS(3055) setting
Nesting level for subqueries	1	No limit

For everyday queries, most developers never run into these limits, but each of them can pose problems in certain situations.

Lots of tables

With fully normalized data, the old limits on joins, as well as those on the number of tables and aliases referenced, can make it difficult to pull together all the information for a particular entity. For example, consider the Northwind database that comes with VFP 8 and 9. Collecting all the data related to each order, including customer information, shipper information, supplier information and so forth, involves 11 tables. **Listing 1** shows such a query.

The Developer Downloads for this chapter, available from
www.hentzenwerke.com, *include the query in Listing 1 as*
ManyTables.PRG.

Listing 1. *Flattening a normalized database can involve many joins and tables.*

```
SELECT ProductName, CategoryName, OrderDate, ;
      Customers.CompanyName AS CustomerName, ;
      OrderDetails.Quantity, ;
      OrderDetails.UnitPrice, ;
      Suppliers.CompanyName AS SupplierName, ;
      Employees.LastName, Employees.FirstName, ;
      Territories.TerritoryDescription, ;
      Region.RegionDescription, ;
      Shippers.CompanyName AS ShipperName;
  FROM Orders ;
    LEFT JOIN Customers ;
      ON Orders.CustomerID = Customers.CustomerID ;
    LEFT JOIN OrderDetails ;
      ON Orders.OrderID = OrderDetails.OrderID ;
    LEFT JOIN Products ;
      ON OrderDetails.ProductID = Products.ProductID ;
    LEFT JOIN Categories ;
      ON Products.CategoryID = Categories.CategoryID ;
    LEFT JOIN Suppliers ;
      ON Products.SupplierID = Suppliers.SupplierID ;
    LEFT JOIN Shippers ;
      ON Orders.ShipVia = Shippers.ShipperID ;
    LEFT JOIN Employees ;
      ON Orders.EmployeeID = Employees.EmployeeID ;
    LEFT JOIN EmployeeTerritories ;
      ON Employees.EmployeeID = EmployeeTerritories.EmployeeID ;
    LEFT JOIN Territories ;
      ON EmployeeTerritories.TerritoryID = Territories.TerritoryID ;
    LEFT JOIN Region ;
      ON Territories.RegionID = Region.RegionID ;
  ORDER BY Products.ProductID, Orders.OrderDate ;
  INTO CURSOR Unfolded
```

This query lists 11 different aliases and performs 10 joins; VFP 8 and earlier versions can't run it because it generates error 1805, "SQL: Too many subqueries." VFP 9 executes it without a problem. (While this particular example is a little contrived, flattening a normalized database is a common problem and can involve many, many joins.)

Nearly unlimited IN list

In earlier versions of VFP, the IN (list of items) operator was limited to 24 items in the list. While VFP 9 doesn't entirely remove the limit, it does give you control over it through the SYS(3055) function. Even without manipulating SYS(3055), the limit is significantly higher than in earlier versions. In our tests, we could include 154 items before we had to raise SYS(3055).

> *The IN operator can be used both to filter based on a list of items and to filter based on subquery results. The change here affects only the use of IN with a specific list of items.*

When you control the query yourself, the limit on the IN clause isn't generally a problem. You can usually find another approach to avoid a large IN clause. One solution is to store the list of values to a cursor and do a join with that cursor. For example, this query:

```
SELECT cFirst, cLast ;
   FROM Person ;
   WHERE UPPER(cLast) IN ("BLACK", "BROWN", "GREEN", "SILVER", "WHITE")
```

could be replaced with:

```
CREATE CURSOR Names (cName C(25))
INSERT INTO Names VALUES ("BLACK")
INSERT INTO Names VALUES ("BROWN")
INSERT INTO Names VALUES ("GREEN")
INSERT INTO Names VALUES ("SILVER")
INSERT INTO Names VALUES ("WHITE")

SELECT cFirst, cLast ;
   FROM Names ;
     JOIN Person ;
       ON UPPER(cLast) = RTRIM(cName)
```

However, you don't always have the chance to write this kind of code. In particular, other applications that access VFP data through OLE DB may generate queries that use the IN clause and offer no chance to code around it.

SYS(3055) was added in VFP 6 to solve a problem in updating views. It controls the allocation of space for evaluating FOR and WHERE clauses. The default value is 320, and it can be increased in increments of 8. In our tests, each increase of 8 in the SYS(3055) value allowed 4 more items in the list for IN.

Nested Subqueries

The ability to use subqueries (a query within a query) makes it possible to get some results with a single query that would otherwise require multiple queries. Perhaps the most common query involving a subquery is finding all the records in one table that are not in another. For example, this query (using the TasTrade database that comes with VFP) gets a list of companies from the Customer table that placed no orders:

```
SELECT Company_Name ;
   FROM Customer ;
   WHERE Customer_ID NOT IN ;
     (SELECT Customer_ID FROM Orders) ;
   INTO CURSOR NoSales
```

Another common use for a subquery is to perform aggregation and then allow the main query to retrieve additional information about the aggregate results. For example, you can use a subquery to get a list of the products included in each customer's most recent order, as in

Listing 2. The subquery in this example is *correlated*, meaning it uses a field from a table not listed in the subquery itself, only in the main query. In the example, OrdLast.Customer_ID is used in the WHERE clause of the subquery, but OrdLast is an alias for Orders defined in the main query.

The Developer Downloads for this chapter, available from www.hentzenwerke.com, include the query in Listing 2 as CustProducts.PRG and the query in Listing 3 as ProductFirstNotLast.PRG.

Listing 2. The subquery here finds each customer's most recent order, and then uses those results to get the list of products included in that order.

```
SELECT CustLast.Customer_ID, Product_ID ;
   FROM Order_Line_Items OLILast;
     JOIN Orders OrdLast;
       ON OLILast.Order_ID = OrdLast.Order_ID ;
     JOIN Customer CustLast;
       ON OrdLast.Customer_ID = ;
          CustLast.Customer_ID ;
   WHERE OrdLast.Order_Date = ;
     (SELECT MAX(Order_Date) ;
        FROM Orders Ord ;
        WHERE OrdLast.Customer_ID = ;
              Ord.Customer_ID ) ;
   INTO CURSOR CustProducts
```

In VFP 8 and earlier, subqueries cannot be nested. That is, the WHERE clause of a subquery can't use another subquery. VFP 9 allows nested subqueries, increasing the number of questions you can answer with a single query.

Suppose you want to find out what products a company included in its first order, but not its most recent. While you could use the cursor created in **Listing 2** in another query, in VFP 9, you can do the whole job with a single query, shown in **Listing 3**.

Listing 3. Nesting subqueries lets you solve more problems with a single query rather than a series of queries.

```
SELECT Customer.Company_Name, Product_ID ;
  FROM Order_Line_Items ;
    JOIN Orders ;
      ON Order_Line_Items.Order_ID = Orders.Order_ID ;
    JOIN Customer ;
      ON Orders.Customer_ID = Customer.Customer_ID ;
    WHERE Orders.Order_Date = ;
      (SELECT MIN(Order_Date) ;
         FROM Orders Ord ;
          WHERE Orders.Customer_ID=Ord.Customer_ID );
      AND Product_ID NOT IN ;
       (SELECT Product_ID ;
          FROM Order_Line_Items OLILast;
            JOIN Orders OrdLast;
              ON OLILast.Order_ID = OrdLast.Order_ID ;
            JOIN Customer CustLast;
              ON OrdLast.Customer_ID = ;
```

```
           CustLast.Customer_ID ;
   WHERE OrdLast.Order_Date = ;
     (SELECT MAX(Order_Date) ;
        FROM Orders Ord ;
        WHERE OrdLast.Customer_ID = ;
             Ord.Customer_ID ) );
INTO CURSOR FirstNotLast
```

More flexible subqueries

The previous section looked at one way subqueries have improved in VFP 9. In fact, the VFP team did a lot of work with subqueries for this version. In VFP 8 and earlier, subqueries could be used only in the WHERE clause of a SQL command, that is, only in filtering data. In addition to removing the limit on nesting, VFP 9 allows you to use subqueries in the field list and the FROM clause of a query and in the SET clause of the SQL UPDATE command. VFP 9 also allows the GROUP BY clause in correlated subqueries (subqueries that refer to one or more fields from tables in the main query, like the subquery in **Listing 2**). Finally, VFP 9 allows you to use the TOP clause in subqueries, as long as those subqueries are not correlated.

Derived tables—Subqueries in the FROM clause

The result of a subquery in the FROM clause is called a *derived table*. One use for a derived table is retrieving additional data when you use an aggregate function.

Continuing to use the TasTrade database that comes with VFP, consider the problem of finding out about each customer's most recent order. If all you want is the customer id and the order date, it's easy:

```
SELECT Customer_ID, MAX(Order_Date) ;
  FROM Orders ;
  GROUP BY 1 ;
  INTO CURSOR MostRecentOrder
```

This query is simple and works in every version of VFP. Suppose, though, you want not just the customer id, but additional information about the order, such as the company name, the contact person for the company, and the name of the shipper. Prior to VFP 9, you need to use a correlated subquery, two queries in sequence, or a very ugly subquery. **Listing 4** shows the solution using a correlated subquery, **Listing 5** shows the two queries in sequence technique, and **Listing 6** shows the ugly subquery approach. What makes the subquery in **Listing 6** so ugly is the need to combine the customer id and the most recent date into a single field for comparison.

 The queries shown in Listing 4, Listing 5, and Listing 6 are included in the Developer Downloads for this chapter, available from **www.hentzenwerke.com**, *as MostRecentCorrelated.PRG, MostRecentTwoQueries.PRG, and MostRecentSubquery, respectively.*

Listing 4. *Finding data associated with an aggregate is one reason to use a correlated subquery.*

```
SELECT Orders.Order_ID, Customer.Company_Name as Cust_Name, ;
```

```
        Shippers.Company_Name AS Ship_Name, Orders.Order_Date ;
  FROM Orders ;
    JOIN Customer ;
      ON Orders.Customer_ID = Customer.Customer_ID ;
    JOIN Shippers ;
      ON Orders.Shipper_ID = shippers.Shipper_ID ;
  WHERE Orders.Order_Date = ;
    (SELECT MAX(Order_Date) ;
        FROM Orders Ord WHERE Orders.Customer_ID=Ord.Customer_ID );
  ORDER BY Cust_Name ;
  INTO CURSOR MostRecentOrders
```

Listing 5. *Another way to find the data associated with an aggregate result is to use two queries in sequence. The first query does the grouping, and then the second query joins with that result.*

```
SELECT Customer_ID, MAX(Order_Date) as Order_Date ;
  FROM Orders ;
  GROUP BY 1 ;
  INTO CURSOR RecentOrder

SELECT Orders.Order_ID, Customer.Company_Name as Cust_Name, ;
      Shippers.Company_Name AS Ship_Name, Orders.Order_Date ;
  FROM Orders ;
    JOIN RecentOrder ;
      ON Orders.Customer_ID = RecentOrder.Customer_ID ;
      AND Orders.Order_Date = RecentOrder.Order_Date ;
    JOIN Customer ;
      ON Orders.Customer_ID = Customer.Customer_ID ;
    JOIN Shippers ;
      ON Orders.Shipper_ID = shippers.Shipper_ID ;
  ORDER BY Cust_Name ;
  INTO CURSOR MostRecentOrders
```

Listing 6. *Yet another way to find data associated with an aggregate result is to use a subquery in the WHERE clause. The resulting query is hard to maintain because of the strange expression used to match data to the subquery result.*

```
SELECT Orders.Order_ID, Customer.Company_Name as Cust_Name, ;
      Shippers.Company_Name AS Ship_Name, Orders.Order_Date ;
  FROM Orders ;
    JOIN Customer ;
      ON Orders.Customer_ID = Customer.Customer_ID ;
    JOIN Shippers ;
      ON Orders.Shipper_ID = shippers.Shipper_ID ;
  WHERE Orders.Customer_ID + DTOS(Orders.Order_Date) IN ;
    (SELECT Customer_ID + DTOS(MAX(Order_Date)) ;
        FROM Orders GROUP BY Customer_ID );
  ORDER BY Cust_Name ;
  INTO CURSOR MostRecentOrders
```

VFP 9 gives you a better alternative. You can perform the subquery on the fly right in the join clause. Putting the subquery into the join clause means it doesn't have to be correlated; in some cases, that means it will run faster. The query in **Listing 7** uses this approach. Here, the subquery has moved into the JOIN clause, and doesn't need to combine the customer id and most recent date. Instead, the ON portion of the JOIN compares the two fields separately, much like the two query solution in **Listing 5**.

 *The query in Listing 7 is included in the Developer Downloads for this chapter, available from **www.hentzenwerke.com**, as MostRecentOrderDetails.PRG.*

Listing 7. This query uses a subquery in the FROM clause (a derived table) to solve the problem of finding data associated with aggregates.

```
SELECT Orders.Order_ID, Customer.Company_Name as Cust_Name, ;
       Shippers.Company_Name AS Ship_Name, Orders.Order_Date ;
   FROM Orders ;
     JOIN (SELECT Customer_ID, MAX(Order_Date) as Order_Date ;
       FROM Orders CheckOrderDate ;
       GROUP BY 1) RecentOrder ;
       ON Orders.Customer_ID = RecentOrder.Customer_ID ;
       AND Orders.Order_Date = RecentOrder.Order_Date ;
     JOIN Customer ;
       ON Orders.Customer_ID = Customer.Customer_ID ;
     JOIN Shippers ;
       ON Orders.Shipper_ID = shippers.Shipper_ID ;
   ORDER BY Cust_Name ;
   INTO CURSOR MostRecentOrders
```

Be aware that a subquery in the FROM clause can't be correlated, which means it may not refer to fields of tables used in the main query, only to fields of the tables it lists. This is because all subqueries in the FROM clause are computed before the joins are performed, thus it's not yet clear what records are in the result.

Computing fields with a subquery

In addition to supporting derived tables, VFP 9 lets you put subqueries in the field list of a query. That is, you can use a subquery to compute a field to appear in the result. A subquery used this way must return a single field and no more than a single record. If there are no records in the result for a particular record, that field is assigned the null value.

Why would you do this? Why not include the expression in the main query and add any necessary tables? As with derived tables, this approach is handy when grouping is involved. Suppose you want to find the total value of the orders placed for each customer in a particular year. Along with that, you want a great deal of customer information, including the address, phone number, and fax number.

Clearly to compute the total value of orders for a customer, you need to group data from Order_Line_Items by customer. You can extract multiple fields from Customer along the way as long as you add them to the GROUP BY clause. (Prior to VFP 8, you could include additional fields, even without putting them in the GROUP BY clause. In VFP 8, you can do so by issuing SET ENGINEBEHAVIOR 70.) **Listing 8** shows a query that retrieves the customer id, company name, address, phone, and fax information along with the total value of that customer's orders.

*The query in Listing 8 is included in the Developer Downloads for this chapter, available from **www.hentzenwerke.com**, as CustomerTotalGrouped.PRG.*

Listing 8. *In a query aggregating a field or fields of a child table, you can add fields from a parent table as long as you add them to the GROUP BY clause. Don't forget to define nYear before running this query.*

```
SELECT Customer.Customer_ID, Customer.Company_Name, ;
       Customer.Address, Customer.City, Customer.Region, ;
       Customer.Postal_Code, Customer.Phone, Customer.Fax, ;
       SUM(quantity*unit_price) AS yTotal ;
FROM Customer ;
  LEFT JOIN Orders ;
    JOIN Order_Line_Items;
      ON Orders.Order_ID = Order_Line_Items.Order_ID ;
    ON Customer.Customer_ID = Orders.Customer_ID ;
    AND BETWEEN(Order_Date,DATE(m.nYear,1,1),DATE(m.nYear,12,31)) ;
  GROUP BY 1, 2, 3, 4, 5, 6, 7, 8;
INTO CURSOR CustomerTotal
```

However, adding so many fields to the GROUP BY clause slows the query down. One alternative that works in this situation is to remove the fields from the GROUP BY clause and wrap them in MAX() or MIN(). As with grouping, because these fields are the same for all records in the group, using MAX() or MIN() doesn't change the results. This version, shown in **Listing 9**, is somewhat faster than listing all the fields in the GROUP BY clause.

*The query in Listing 9 is included as CustomerTotalMax.PRG in the Developer Downloads for this chapter, available from **www.hentzenwerke.com**.*

Listing 9. *Another approach to retrieving parent data in a grouped query is to wrap the extra fields in MAX() or MIN(). Again, don't forget to define nYear before running this query.*

```
SELECT Customer.Customer_ID, MAX(Customer.Company_Name), ;
       MAX(Customer.Address), MAX(Customer.City), MAX(Customer.Region), ;
       MAX(Customer.Postal_Code), MAX(Customer.Phone), MAX(Customer.Fax), ;
       SUM(quantity*unit_price) AS yTotal ;
FROM Customer ;
  LEFT JOIN Orders ;
    JOIN Order_Line_Items;
      ON Orders.Order_ID = Order_Line_Items.Order_ID ;
    ON Customer.Customer_ID = Orders.Customer_ID ;
    AND BETWEEN(Order_Date,DATE(m.nYear,1,1),DATE(m.nYear,12,31)) ;
  GROUP BY 1;
  INTO CURSOR CustomerTotal
```

However, the ability to use a subquery in the field list provides an even simpler and more efficient solution to this problem. You can compute the total value of the orders in a subquery, allowing the main query to refer only to the parent table. Not only do you eliminate the extra fields in GROUP BY and the extra calls to aggregate functions, but you can also eliminate the outer join. **Listing 10** shows the query.

 *The query in Listing 10 is included in the Developer Downloads for this chapter, available from **www.hentzenwerke.com**, as CustomerTotal.PRG.*

Listing 10. *Using a subquery in the field list simplifies the problem of showing additional fields from the parent table when data is aggregated based on a child table. Be sure to give nYear a value before running this query.*

```
SELECT Customer.Customer_ID, Customer.Company_Name, ;
       Customer.Address, Customer.City, Customer.Region, ;
       Customer.Postal_Code, Customer.Phone, Customer.Fax, ;
       (SELECT SUM(quantity*unit_price) ;
          FROM Orders ;
            JOIN Order_Line_Items;
              ON Orders.Order_ID = Order_Line_Items.Order_ID ;
          WHERE BETWEEN(Order_Date,DATE(m.nYear,1,1),DATE(m.nYear,12,31)) ;
            AND Customer.Customer_ID=Orders.Customer_ID ) as yTotal ;
   FROM Customer ;
   INTO CURSOR CustomerTotal
```

In our tests, using the queries shown, the subquery version (**Listing 10**) was about 12% faster than the version with calls to MAX() (**Listing 9**), which in turn was about 12% faster than listing all the parent fields in the GROUP BY clause (**Listing 8**). The more fields from the parent in the field list, the greater the advantage of the subquery version.

Computing replacements in UPDATE

The third new place you can use subqueries is the SET clause of the UPDATE command. That is, you can use a subquery to compute the value to which a field is to be set. However, when you use this approach, the UPDATE command cannot include a subquery in the WHERE clause. In addition, you're limited to a single subquery in the SET clause, so you can't use this approach to compute the values of multiple fields.

For this example, imagine that you have a data warehouse (SalesByProduct) for TasTrade data that tells you how many of each product were sold and the dollar amount of those sales. It's designed to hold data for a single month and you want to update it at the end of the month.

To update the data, use the following UPDATE commands. Set nMonth and nYear to the month and year of the data you're collecting before running the code in **Listing 11**. ("Correlated Updates," later in this chapter, provides a better solution to this problem.)

*Code to create the data warehouse as a cursor is included in the Developer Downloads for this chapter, available from **www.hentzenwerke.com**, as CreateWarehouse.PRG. The code in Listing 11 is SubqueryInSet.PRG.*

Listing 11. *You can use a subquery in the SET portion of the SQL UPDATE command to calculate the new field values on the fly.*

```
UPDATE SalesByProduct ;
  SET TotalSales = (;
    SELECT NVL(SUM(quantity*unit_price),$0) ;
      FROM Order_Line_Items ;
        JOIN Orders ;
          ON Order_Line_Items.Order_ID = Orders.Order_ID ;
        WHERE MONTH(Order_Date) = nMonth AND YEAR(Order_Date) = nYear;
          AND Order_Line_Items.Product_ID = SalesByProduct.Product_ID)

UPDATE SalesByProduct ;
  SET UnitsSold = (;
    SELECT CAST(NVL(SUM(quantity),0) AS N(12)) ;
      FROM Order_Line_Items ;
        JOIN Orders ;
          ON Order_Line_Items.Order_ID = Orders.Order_ID ;
        WHERE MONTH(Order_Date) = nMonth AND YEAR(Order_Date) = nYear;
          AND Order_Line_Items.Product_ID = SalesByProduct.Product_ID)
```

The second UPDATE in the example uses the new CAST() function that lets you change data types on the fly. See Chapter 14, "Language Improvements," for details.

Correlated subqueries and grouping

A correlated subquery is one that refers to one or more fields of the main query, generally in the subquery's WHERE clause. VFP 8 prohibits the GROUP BY clause in correlated subqueries. Because correlation can give you the same effect as grouping in many cases (see **Listing 4**, for example), you may not have run into this limit.

But there are a few situations where the ability to use GROUP BY in a correlated subquery makes it easier to get the desired results. Fortunately, VFP 9 permits grouping in a correlated subquery.

For example, consider the case where you want a list of customers who placed at least one order totaling more than a specified value and had that order shipped somewhere other than their address of record. (You might be checking into suspicious transactions.) In VFP 8 and earlier, extracting this information requires two queries in sequence: the first collects information about orders over the specified amount, while the second compares the shipping address of those records to the customer address and extracts customer information. **Listing 12** shows one way to do this, with the threshold value set to $4000.

*The code in **Listing 12** is included in the Developer Downloads for this chapter, available from **www.hentzenwerke.com**, as SuspiciousTwoQueries.PRG. The query in Listing 13 is called SuspiciousOrders.PRG.*

Listing 12. *In VFP 8 and earlier, it takes two queries to get a list of large orders shipped somewhere other than their home office, along with customer information.*

```
SELECT Orders.Customer_ID, Orders.Ship_to_Address, ;
       Orders.Order_ID, Orders.Order_Date ;
  FROM Orders ;
    JOIN Order_line_items ;
      ON Orders.Order_ID=Order_Line_Items.Order_ID ;
  GROUP BY 1, 2, 3, 4 ;
  HAVING SUM(Quantity*Unit_Price)> 4000 ;
  INTO CURSOR BigOrders

SELECT Company_Name, Order_ID, Order_Date ;
  FROM Customer ;
    JOIN BigOrders ;
      ON Customer.Customer_ID = BigOrders.Customer_ID ;
  WHERE BigOrders.Ship_to_Address <> Customer.Address ;
  INTO CURSOR Suspicions
```

In VFP 9, the ability to group in correlated subqueries means you can find this result with one, more readable query. **Listing 13** shows the one-query version.

Listing 13. *Using GROUP BY in a correlated subquery in VFP makes it possible to find customers with suspicious orders in a single query.*

```
SELECT Company_Name, Ord.Order_ID, Ord.Order_Date ;
  FROM Customer ;
    JOIN Orders Ord;
      ON Customer.Customer_ID = Ord.Customer_ID ;
  WHERE Ord.Order_ID in (;
    SELECT Orders.Order_ID;
    FROM Orders ;
      JOIN Order_Line_Items ;
        ON Orders.Order_ID=Order_Line_Items.Order_ID ;
        AND Orders.Customer_ID=Customer.Customer_ID ;
        AND Orders.Ship_to_Address <> Customer.Address ;
    GROUP BY Orders.Order_ID ;
    HAVING SUM(Quantity*Unit_Price)> 4000 ) ;
  INTO CURSOR Suspicions
```

As with a number of other situations where a single query replaces two queries, the version in Listing 13 is faster than the one in Listing 12.

Using TOP n in subqueries

The TOP n clause of SELECT lets you return only the first n records (or first n% of the records) of the result set. While the MIN() and MAX() functions let you choose the single smallest or largest value in a given field, TOP n lets you choose multiple items. You can use it to see things like the 10 most recent orders or the 30 most expensive products. For example, this query finds the 10% of products with the fewest overall sales.

```
SELECT TOP 10 PERCENT Product_ID, ;
      SUM(Quantity) AS nSales ;
   FROM Order_Line_Items ;
   GROUP BY Product_ID ;
   ORDER BY nSales ;
   INTO CURSOR LowSales
```

In VFP 8 and earlier, you can't use the TOP n clause in subqueries. VFP 9 changes that, permitting TOP n in subqueries unless the subquery is correlated. When you use TOP n in a subquery, you must include an ORDER BY clause in that subquery.

Imagine that you're considering discontinuing the items extracted by the query above (the lowest-selling items). You might want to contact customers who have purchased those items to make sure it won't be a problem for them. The query in **Listing 14** uses the previous query as a subquery to create that list of customers.

 *The code in Listing 14 is included in the Developer Downloads for this chapter, available from **www.hentzenwerke.com**, as Discontinue.PRG.*

Listing 14. *The subquery here finds the lowest-selling 10% of products. The main query uses that information to get a list of customers who purchased those products.*

```
SELECT DISTINCT Company_Name, English_Name ;
   FROM Customer ;
     JOIN Orders ;
       ON Customer.Customer_ID = Orders.Customer_ID ;
     JOIN Order_Line_Items ;
       ON Orders.Order_ID = Order_Line_Items.Order_ID ;
     JOIN ( ;
      SELECT TOP 10 PERCENT Product_ID, ;
            SUM(Quantity) AS nSales ;
        FROM Order_Line_Items ;
        GROUP BY Product_ID ;
        ORDER BY nSales );
        AS LowSales ;
      ON Order_Line_Items.Product_ID = ;
        LowSales.Product_ID ;
     JOIN Products ;
       ON LowSales.Product_ID = Products.Product_ID ;
   ORDER BY English_Name, Company_Name ;
   INTO CURSOR BoughtLowSellers
```

Correlated updates

In addition to supporting subqueries in the SET clause, the SQL UPDATE command in VFP 9 has a new FROM clause that allows you to draw the update data from another table. This gives what you might call *correlated updates*.

The example in Listing 11 has one serious drawback. You have to use a separate UPDATE command for each field you want to change. Using the FROM clause, you can achieve the same result with a query followed by an UPDATE command. The code in **Listing**

15 computes the new values, stores them in a cursor, and then references that cursor in the UPDATE command.

 The code in Listing 15 is included in the Developer Downloads for this chapter, available from www.hentzenwerke.com, as CorrelatedUpdate.PRG. The code in Listing 16 is CorrelatedUpdateSubquery.PRG in the Developer Downloads.

Listing 15. *The new FROM clause in SQL UPDATE lets you draw replacement values from another table.*

```
SELECT Order_Line_Items.Product_ID, ;
       SUM(Quantity*Order_Line_Items.Unit_Price) as TotalSales, ;
       SUM(Quantity) AS UnitsSold ;
  FROM Order_Line_Items ;
    JOIN Orders ;
      ON Order_Line_Items.Order_ID = Orders.Order_ID ;
      AND MONTH(Order_Date) = nMonth AND YEAR(Order_Date) = nYear ;
  GROUP BY 1 ;
  INTO CURSOR MonthlySales

UPDATE SalesByProduct ;
   SET SalesByProduct.TotalSales = NVL(MonthlySales.TotalSales, $0), ;
       SalesByProduct.UnitsSold = NVL(MonthlySales.UnitsSold, 0) ;
  FROM SalesByProduct ;
    LEFT JOIN MonthlySales ;
      ON SalesByProduct.Product_ID = MonthlySales.Product_ID
```

Along with specifying that the values come from another table, you can actually perform joins in the FROM clause to put together the list of values. In Listing 15, the outer join ensures that the records for products not sold in the specified month are set to 0.

In fact, the FROM clause of UPDATE supports subqueries (derived tables), so you can do this entire operation in a single UPDATE command, as shown in **Listing 16**.

Listing 16. *Instead of running a query ahead of time to compute the results, you can use a derived table in the FROM clause of an UPDATE command.*

```
UPDATE SalesByProduct ;
   SET SalesByProduct.TotalSales = NVL(MonthlySales.TotalSales, $0), ;
       SalesByProduct.UnitsSold = NVL(MonthlySales.UnitsSold, 0) ;
  FROM SalesByProduct ;
    LEFT JOIN (;
      SELECT Order_Line_Items.Product_ID, ;
             SUM(Quantity*Order_Line_Items.Unit_Price) as TotalSales, ;
             SUM(Quantity) AS UnitsSold ;
        FROM Order_Line_Items ;
          JOIN Orders ;
            ON Order_Line_Items.Order_ID = Orders.Order_ID ;
            AND (MONTH(Order_Date) = nMonth AND YEAR(Order_Date) = nYear) ;
        GROUP BY 1) AS MonthlySales ;
      ON SalesByProduct.Product_ID = MonthlySales.Product_ID
```

Correlated DELETEs

In VFP 8 and earlier, the SQL DELETE command lets you list only one table. While you can use subqueries in the WHERE clause, deleting records based on information in other tables can be tricky. VFP 9 allows you to list multiple tables in a DELETE's FROM clause, joining them according to the usual rules. This provides a much cleaner way to perform *correlated deletion*, deletion from one table based on data in one or more other tables.

The syntax for a correlated DELETE is a little confusing. If the FROM clause of DELETE contains more than one table, you must specify the target table for the deletion between DELETE and FROM:

```
DELETE [Target] FROM Table1 [JOIN Table2 …]
```

Use the local alias of the target table between DELETE and FROM. This may be the name of the table, but if you assign a local alias to the table in the FROM clause, use that instead. (Note that the same rules apply for UPDATE, when the table being updated is also included in the FROM clause, as in Listing 16.)

The TasTrade database doesn't lend itself to an example of this sort of deletion; it's designed with the assumption that records are marked inactive rather than deleted. Assume, though, you have Products and Suppliers tables like those in TasTrade, with the primary key of Supplier used as a foreign key in Products. Suppose there's a problem getting products from Australia and you decide to eliminate from your product list all products that come from suppliers in Australia. To perform this deletion in VFP 8, you use a subquery as in **Listing 17**. In VFP 9, you can use a JOIN condition instead. **Listing 18** shows a DELETE command to remove those products from the Products table.

 The code in Listing 17 is included as DeleteProductSubquery.PRG, while Listing 18 is included as DeleteProduct.PRG in the Developer Downloads for this chapter. Both programs include code to create and populate the tables.

Listing 17. In VFP 8 and earlier, deleting from one table based on data in another requires a subquery.

```
DELETE FROM Products ;
    WHERE Supplier_ID IN ( ;
      SELECT Supplier_ID ;
        FROM Supplier ;
          WHERE UPPER(Supplier.Country) = "AUSTRALIA" )
```

Listing 18. The DELETE command now supports multiple tables in the FROM clause. The join conditions determine which records are deleted.

```
DELETE Products ;
  FROM Products ;
    JOIN Supplier ;
      ON Products.Supplier_ID = Supplier.Supplier_ID ;
      WHERE UPPER(Supplier.Country) = "AUSTRALIA"
```

A more perfect UNION

The UNION clause of SELECT lets you combine the results of several queries into a single result set. In VFP 8, the rules for UNION were loosened, making the clause easier to use. VFP 9 offers two more improvements to UNION and one restriction.

Use names in ORDER BY with UNION

In earlier versions of VFP, when you use the UNION clause to combine multiple queries into a single result, the ORDER BY clause can list only the positions of the fields in the field list. You can't refer to fields by name, even if the field has the same name in every query in the UNION. This makes such queries hard to read and hard to maintain, because the ORDER BY list must be corrected if the field list changes.

In VFP 9, you can use field names in the ORDER BY clause of a UNIONed query. The field names you use are the ones in the result set. Be aware that when the names of corresponding fields in the UNION are different, the result draws the field name from the last query in the UNION. (A better approach than depending on the order of the queries is to use the AS clause to ensure corresponding fields have the same name in each query in the UNION.)

Listing 19 is a simple example that uses this capability. Even with this straightforward query, using the field names increases readability considerably.

 *The query in Listing 19 is included in the Developer Downloads for this chapter, available from **www.hentzenwerke.com**, as AllCompanies.PRG.*

Listing 19. Field names in ORDER BY—VFP 9 allows you to use the field names of the result set in the ORDER BY clause of a UNIONed query.

```
SELECT Company_Name, Address, City, Region, Postal_Code, Country ;
  FROM Customer ;
UNION ;
SELECT Company_Name, Address, City, Region, Postal_Code, Country ;
  FROM Supplier ;
ORDER BY Country, City ;
INTO CURSOR AllCompanies
```

Insert data from UNIONed result

VFP 8 introduced the ability to populate a table or cursor directly from a query result with the addition of the INSERT INTO … SELECT syntax. This made it possible to compute results and add them in a single step.

VFP 9 adds another capability to that syntax: the query used can include the UNION clause. This means you can consolidate data and add it to a table or cursor in one step.

For example, suppose you have a data warehouse for TasTrade, containing the annual sales for each employee by product as well as an annual total for each employee. (Note that this is a different data warehouse than the one described in "Computing Replacements in UPDATE," earlier in this chapter.)

You can compute the sales for each product by each employee in a specified year with a single query; similarly, you can compute the totals for each employee for a year with one query. However, collecting both the product-specific and the total data requires either two queries or a query involving a UNION. If you want to add a year's worth of data to the warehouse, you can do it with the INSERT in **Listing 20**.

 The command in Listing 20 is included in this chapter's Developer Downloads, available from **www.hentzenwerke.com***, as WarehouseUnion.PRG. The program includes code to create the warehouse. (Here, it's a cursor; in production code, of course, you'd use a table.)*

Listing 20. VFP 8 added the ability to INSERT directly from a query result; VFP 9 extends it to queries involving a UNION. Be sure to assign a value to the variable nYear before running this example.

```
INSERT INTO Warehouse ;
SELECT CrossProd.Product_ID, ;
       CrossProd.Employee_ID, ;
       m.nYear as nYear, ;
       NVL(nUnitsSold, 0), ;
       NVL(nTotalSales, $0) ;
   FROM (SELECT Employee.Employee_ID, ;
                Products.Product_ID ;
      FROM Employee, Products) AS CrossProd ;
     LEFT JOIN ( ;
     SELECT Product_ID, Employee_ID, ;
            SUM(Quantity) AS nUnitsSold, ;
            SUM(Quantity * Unit_Price) AS nTotalSales ;
        FROM Orders ;
          JOIN Order_Line_Items ;
            ON Orders.Order_ID = ;
               Order_Line_Items.Order_ID ;
          WHERE YEAR(Order_Date) = m.nYear ;
          GROUP BY Product_ID, Employee_ID ) ;
          AS AnnualSales ;
        ON CrossProd.Employee_ID = ;
           AnnualSales.Employee_ID ;
        AND CrossProd.Product_ID = AnnualSales.Product_ID ;
UNION ;
SELECT "Total" AS Product_ID, Employee.Employee_ID, ;
       m.nYear AS nYear, ;
       CAST(NVL(SUM(Quantity),0) as N(12)) ;
          AS nUnitsSold, ;
       NVL(SUM(Quantity * Unit_Price), $0) ;
          AS nTotalSales ;
   FROM Orders ;
     JOIN Order_Line_Items ;
```

```
      ON Orders.Order_ID = Order_Line_Items.Order_ID ;
      AND YEAR(Order_Date) = m.nYear ;
    RIGHT JOIN Employee ;
      ON Orders.Employee_ID = Employee.Employee_ID ;
  GROUP BY Employee.Employee_ID ;
ORDER BY 2, 1
```

No parentheses with UNION

Although it wasn't really syntactically correct, earlier versions of VFP didn't object if queries in a UNION were enclosed in parentheses. In VFP 9, a single query in a UNION can be surrounded by parentheses, but putting parentheses around multiple queries in a UNION raises a new error, error 2196. **Listing 21** shows a query that works in VFP 8, but fails in VFP 9, due to the new rule.

 *The query in Listing 21 is included in the Developer Downloads for this chapter, available from **www.hentzenwerke.com**, as UnionParens.PRG. When you run it in VFP 9, it generates an error.*

Listing 21. *Putting parentheses around multiple queries in a UNION raises a new error.*

```
SELECT Company_Name, Address, City, Region, Postal_Code, Country ;
  FROM Customer ;
UNION ;
(SELECT Company_Name, Address, City, Region, Postal_Code, Country ;
   FROM Supplier ;
UNION ;
SELECT Company_Name, "", "", "", "", "" FROM Shippers )
```

According to the Fox team, using parentheses around multiple UNIONs can cause incorrect results.

Combining DISTINCT and ORDER BY

VFP allows you to order query results by any field from the source tables; fields in the ORDER BY list don't have to be in the field list. In VFP 9, this is no longer true for queries that use SELECT DISTINCT. For example, this query executes in VFP 8, but it raises error 1808 ("SQL: ORDER BY clause is invalid.") in VFP 9:

```
SELECT Distinct Customer_ID;
  FROM Orders ;
  ORDER BY Order_Date
```

This behavior is affected by SET ENGINEBEHAVIOR. (See "Turn off new behavior" later in this chapter.)

Optimization changes

VFP 9 includes several changes to improve the performance of your queries, as well as a new function that makes testing optimization easier.

Fully optimize LIKE with "%"

The LIKE operator lets you compare strings. If a condition in a SQL command includes cField LIKE cString, the specified field is compared to the specified character string on a character by character basis. Unlike the = operator, if cString is shorter than cField, the two do not match, unless a wildcard character is used. The LIKE operator supports two wildcard characters—use "_" to represent a single unknown character and "%" to represent 0 or more unknown characters. For example, you can find all the customers in TasTrade whose names begin with the letter "P" using this query:

```
SELECT Customer_ID, Company_Name ;
   FROM Customer ;
   WHERE UPPER(Company_Name) LIKE "P%" ;
   INTO CURSOR PCompanies
```

Earlier versions of VFP could not fully optimize that query. LIKE "string%" expressions could only be partially optimized. VFP 9 fully optimizes such expressions. (Full optimization applies only when the % wildcard is at the end of the character string.)

Our tests showed mixed results regarding the effect of this optimization. For many queries, versions using LIKE and = were equally fast in both VFP 8 and VFP 9. However, in one situation, the case when VFP takes a shortcut and simply filters the original table, optimization of LIKE made a significant difference. VFP takes this shortcut with any query that involves a single table, has no calculated fields, and is fully optimizable. Filtering the source table rather than creating an actual file on disk saves considerable time. Optimization of LIKE means the VFP engine can take this approach with some additional queries. (You can turn off this shortcut by including the NOFILTER clause in the query.)

Better speed for TOP n

When you use the TOP n or TOP n PERCENT clause to return only a subset of the records that otherwise match the query conditions, VFP has to figure out which records are at the top of the list. When you specify the TOP n of a large set, that process can take considerable time. VFP 9 improves performance in that situation.

In our tests, we didn't see a difference until we worked with a very large table. Choosing the TOP 20 out of a table of nearly 75,000 records showed no difference. When we looked for the TOP 20 in a table of over a million records, however, VFP 9 finished in about one-third the time of VFP 8.

Along with making TOP n calculations faster, the behavior of TOP n queries has changed slightly. In earlier versions of VFP, a query with a TOP n clause could return more than n records due to ties in the data. VFP 9 never returns more than the exact number of records specified by the TOP n clause. (See "Turning off new behavior" later in this chapter for the exception to this rule.) When there are ties, it appears VFP chooses records in physical order from the group with the same value.

These changes are among those affected by the new SET ENGINEBEHAVIOR TO 90 setting. See "Turn off new behavior" later in this chapter for details.

Improved performance with OR

In earlier versions, when a query used the OR operator to combine conditions involving different tables, the result couldn't always be optimized. Changes to the VFP 9 SQL engine mean that such conditions should be optimized if the individual conditions are optimizable.

In our testing, not every query using OR with conditions based on different tables showed improvement, but we were able to see the difference in some cases. For example, this query (using the Northwind data) ran nearly four times as fast in VFP 9:

```
SELECT Orders.OrderId, ProductId ;
   FROM Orders ;
     JOIN OrderDetails ;
       ON Orders.OrderId=OrderDetails.OrderId  ;
 WHERE ;
   (Orders.OrderDate=DATE(1997,9,1) AND OrderDetails.Quantity>2) ;
   OR ;
   (Orders.OrderDate=DATE(1997,9,2) AND OrderDetails.Quantity>3) ;
 INTO CURSOR Result
```

You may also see some improvements where OR is used with subqueries.

Filtering and temporary indexes

When you join two tables in a query, VFP picks an index tag to match up corresponding records. If the fields in question aren't indexed, or the existing tag won't help much (for example, when the join involves a small table and a much larger table, and there's only a tag for the smaller table), the engine creates an index on the fly. In the output from SYS(3054), the join shows as "using temp index."

VFP 9 speeds up queries that build a temporary index and have a non-optimizable filter on the same table (the one for which the index is built). The effect is most noticeable with large tables and in cases where the non-optimizable filter eliminates many records. We suspect that the engine is filtering before building the temporary index, which speeds up both building the index and using it.

In our tests, none of the sample tables that come with VFP were large enough to see this effect. We were able to demonstrate the improvement using a table with about 75,000 records. Our test query joined the table to itself on an unindexed field, using a filter condition that selected only about 250 records. In VFP 9, the query took under a second. In VFP 8, the same query took almost 50 seconds.

Correlating faster

You may never run into another area where performance has been improved. If you have a query with a correlated subquery, and the query also includes a filter on the table from the main query that's used in the subquery, VFP 9 performs measurably better than VFP 8.

We tested with the following query using data from TasTrade and found VFP 9 about four times as fast:

```
SELECT Orders.Order_ID, Customer.Company_Name as Cust_Name, ;
       Shippers.Company_Name AS Ship_Name, Orders.Order_Date ;
  FROM Orders ;
    JOIN Customer ;
      ON Orders.Customer_ID = Customer.Customer_ID ;
```

```
    JOIN Shippers ;
      ON Orders.Shipper_ID = shippers.Shipper_ID ;
  WHERE Orders.Discount>0 AND ;
    Orders.Order_Date = (SELECT MAX(Order_Date) ;
       FROM Orders Ord ;
       WHERE Orders.Customer_ID=Ord.Customer_ID );
  ORDER BY Cust_Name ;
  INTO CURSOR MostRecentOrders
```

Logging optimization results

The SYS(3054) function was introduced in VFP 5. It gives you information about how FoxPro is optimizing a query. It's been improved several times and now offers a great deal of data about the optimization process. However, it's still hard to use SYS(3054) to gather information about query performance through an entire program or application.

Enter SYS(3092). This new function lets you direct SYS(3054) output to a log file. By itself, SYS(3054) can send output only to the active window or a variable. With SYS(3092), you can collect data about a whole series of queries and examine it at your leisure.

The syntax is:

```
cLogFile = SYS(3092 [, cFileName [, lAdditive ] ] )
```

The cFileName parameter specifies the name (including path) of the log file. Use lAdditive to specify whether an existing file is overwritten. The default is to overwrite an existing file.

To turn off logging and make the log file available for reading, pass the empty string as the cFileName parameter.

The function returns the name of the active log file. Note that the new log file is set before the value is returned, so to save the name of an old log file before changing it, you must call the function once with no parameters, and then call it again, passing the new value.

When you turn on logging with SYS(3092), the output from SYS(3054) is still echoed to the active window or stored to a specified variable.

Once you establish a log file with SYS(3092), use SYS(3054) as you normally would and run the queries you want to test. When you're done testing, reset SYS(3054) and then issue SYS(3092, "") to stop logging. You can then examine the log file to see your optimization results.

The information in the log file is most useful if you pass either 2 or 12 as the second parameter to SYS(3054). Added in VFP 7, those settings include the query itself in the output before reporting on optimization.

SELECT from buffered tables

Since VFP 3, FoxPro developers have been frustrated by the behavior of SELECT with buffering. When a buffered table is used in a query, VFP uses the actual table on disk, not the open buffered version. This means query results don't reflect uncommitted changes to the data.

This behavior follows naturally from the normal behavior of queries. In general, whether a table is open or not, when it's listed in the FROM clause of a query, the VFP engine opens it again in a new work area.

In some situations, it would be really handy to be able to pull data from a buffered table with a query. In VFP 8 and earlier, you have to turn to Xbase commands (such as CALCULATE) instead.

VFP 9 gives you the option of looking at the buffered data. Add the new WITH (Buffering=.T.) clause to a query and it uses an available buffer rather than the table on disk. **Listing 22** shows a query that counts the number of customers in each country using buffered data.

Listing 22. You can query buffered data using the new WITH (Buffering=.T.) clause.

```
SELECT Country, CNT(*) ;
   FROM Customer WITH (Buffering = .T.) ;
   GROUP BY Country ;
   INTO CURSOR BufferedCount
```

 *The Developer Downloads for this chapter, available from **www.hentzenwerke.com**, include QueryWithBuffering.PRG, which demonstrates the effect of the WITH clause.*

The WITH clause applies to a single table. If the query lists multiple tables for which you want to use buffered data, include a WITH statement for each.

One big warning. If you're using row buffering, the query commits the changes to the current row. This actually makes sense as the query moves the record pointer in the buffered table. In earlier versions, where queries operated against the data on disk, the record pointer in the buffer didn't move, but when you query the buffer itself, the record pointer does move.

You can also control the behavior of queries with buffered tables globally. The new SET SQLBUFFERING command lets you specify whether queries draw from disk or from buffers by default. The WITH (Buffering = lExpr) clause overrides the current setting for a particular table and query. SET SQLBUFFERING is scoped to the data session. Use SET("SQLBUFFERING") to query the current setting.

Turn off new behavior

The significant changes to VFP's SQL engine introduced in VFP 8 caused problems for some existing applications. Rather than force developers to change working code or be stuck in VFP 7, the Fox team added the SET ENGINEBEHAVIOR command, which allows you to turn off the VFP 8 changes. While it's not a good idea to use it all the time, the command provides a flexible solution for existing applications.

Most of the changes to the SQL engine in VFP 9 are unlikely to cause compatibility problems. However, there are a few items that may be an issue for some applications, so the Fox team added a new setting to SET ENGINEBEHAVIOR.

As noted in "Better speed for TOP n" earlier in the chapter, in VFP 9, a TOP n query now returns exactly n records; in the case of ties, it may discard some of the tied results.

When a query includes one of the aggregate functions (CNT(), SUM(), AVG(), MIN() or MAX()), but has no GROUP BY clause, VFP 9 always returns a single record. If no records meet the join and filter conditions, the result record has the null value for all fields. In earlier versions, such a query returned an empty result.

Finally, all fields listed in the ORDER BY clause of a query using SELECT DISTINCT must be included in the field list of the query.

To turn off these behaviors, SET ENGINEBEHAVIOR to 80 or 70. The default is SET ENGINEBEHAVIOR 90, which enables the new behaviors.

The bottom line

Many of the SQL changes in VFP 9 increase compatibility with the SQL-92 standard. They also provide more tools for manipulating your data as needed. While some of the changes aren't likely to have a strong impact on your day-to-day work, you will probably find that others come in handy over and over. The ability to extract some data with a single query, where previously two queries were needed, not only tends to speed up the code, but also makes it easier to define views for those tasks.

Although we are already finding many uses for derived tables, we suspect our favorite SQL change may well turn out to be SYS(3092), which turns on logging of optimization results.

Updates and corrections for this chapter can be found on Hentzenwerke's website, **www.hentzenwerke.com**. Click "Catalog" and navigate to the page for this book.

Chapter 9
New Data and Index Types

It's been a while since VFP had any new data or index types. VFP 9 adds three new data types and a new index type. The new data types make it easier to work with other database engines that already support these data types. The new binary index improves Rushmore optimization for logical conditions such as DELETED().

VFP 3 added several new data types to the product—Double, Currency, Integer, and DateTime—and two new index types, Candidate and Primary. However, since then, the only change to data types was the addition of the auto-incrementing Integer field in VFP 8, which isn't really a new data type.

Because some other database engines, such as SQL Server, support a wider range of data types, VFP has to map from those data types to its own smaller set. Sometimes, the mapping isn't perfect. VFP 9 helps with this problem by adding three new data types.

Varchar

The first new data type is Varchar. Varchar isn't really a new data type; it's essentially Character but not padded with spaces. The single character abbreviation for Varchar is "V."

> *Because the DBF structure hasn't changed significantly (although the new data types have some impact on the structure; see the "How the new data types affect DBF files" section later in this chapter), Varchar fields are actually stored as fixed length fields. However, when you access a Varchar field, the value appears to be trimmed rather than padded with spaces to the length of the field.*

Here's an example, taken from TestVarchar.PRG, which creates a cursor with a Varchar field and shows how it differs from Character:

```
create cursor Test (CField C(20), VField V(20))
insert into Test values ('Fox Rocks',    'Fox Rocks')
insert into Test values ('Fox Rocks   ', 'Fox Rocks   ')
go top
? len(CField), len(VField)     && displays 20 and 9
skip
? len(CField), len(VField)     && displays 20 and 12
```

Notice that the second record includes the three spaces specified in the Varchar field, since spaces specifically included in the value stored in the field are considered significant.

Varchar was added to VFP 9 to provide better support for other databases, including SQL Server, that support this data type. For example, in VFP 8, if you create a remote view from a SQL Server table containing Varchar fields, and then use TABLEUPDATE() to write changes back to SQL Server, the Varchar fields in the updated records are padded with spaces because those spaces exist in the VFP 8 view. Doing the same thing in VFP 9 gives the desired results: the Varchar fields are not padded with spaces.

TestVarcharWithSQLServer.PRG demonstrates this. It opens a view in the Test database based on the Customers table in the SQL Server Northwind sample database. The CompanyName field is defined in that table as nvarchar, but the view defines it as Character. Updating the table forces the spaces padding the field into the database. Changing the data type of that field in the view to Varchar and updating the table again removes the extra spaces.

```
* Connect to the SQL Server Northwind database. Change the connection string as
* necessary.

lnHandle = sqlstringconnect('driver=SQL Server;server=(local);' + ;
  'Database=Northwind;trusted_connection=yes;')
if lnHandle < 1
  return
endif lnHandle < 1

* Open the sample database.

open database Test

* Ensure the CompanyName field in the CustomerView view is Character, then open
* the view and display the contents of CompanyName in the first record.

dbsetprop('CustomerView.CompanyName', 'Field', 'DataType', 'C(40)')
use CustomerView connstring (lnHandle)
messagebox('CompanyName in the first record is ' + CompanyName + ;
  ', which is ' + transform(len(CompanyName)) + ' characters.')

* Update the record and save it.

replace CompanyName with trim(CompanyName)
tableupdate()
use

* Now do it again with CompanyName defined as Varchar. Show that the first
* record has extra spaces because of the change we just saved.

dbsetprop('CustomerView.CompanyName', 'Field', 'DataType', 'V(40)')
use CustomerView connstring (lnHandle)
messagebox('CompanyName in the first record is ' + CompanyName + ;
  ', which is ' + transform(len(CompanyName)) + ' characters.')

* Update the record and save it.

replace CompanyName with trim(CompanyName)
tableupdate()
requery()
messagebox('CompanyName in the first record is ' + CompanyName + ;
  ', which is ' + transform(len(CompanyName)) + ' characters.')

* Clean up and exit.

sqldisconnect(lnHandle)
close databases all
```

Of course, just because Varchar was added to support other databases doesn't mean you can't use it in native VFP tables. However, note that using Varchar makes a table inaccessible in earlier versions of VFP; see the "How the new data types affect DBF files" section later in this chapter for details.

Here are some details about Varchar:

- Varchar can be used the same way Character can: you can index on it (the index keys are padded with spaces to the length of the field, because index keys must be a fixed length), it accepts null values, and Varchar fields have a limit of 254 characters in a table or cursor.

- Like Character fields, you can define a field in the Table Designer as Varchar (Binary), which is the same thing as specifying NOCPTRANS in a CREATE TABLE/CURSOR command: no code page translation is done on that field.

- TYPE() and VARTYPE() return "C" for Varchar fields and Varchar values stored to memory variables. This is because Varchar isn't really a different data type but just a different way of dealing with character values. DISPLAY/LIST STRUCTURE and AFIELDS() do indicate "Varchar" and "V," respectively, for Varchar fields.

- Varchar has priority over Character when they are mixed. For example:

```
select CField + VField as NewField from Test into cursor Test2
display structure     && NewField is Varchar
```

- LIKE expressions with trailing spaces in the value are only partially Rushmore optimizable:

```
index on VField    tag VField
index on deleted() tag Deleted
sys(3054, 12)
select * from Test where VField like 'Fox Rocks%' into cursor Test2
          && displays full optimization
? _tally    && displays 2
select * from Test where VField like 'Fox Rocks %' into cursor Test2
          && displays partial optimization
? _tally    && displays 1
```

- By default, text boxes pad values with spaces to the maximum width of the field. To suppress that behavior, add "F" to the Format property of the Textbox. You should also set MaxLength to the width of the field to ensure the user can enter the maximum number of characters if necessary. To see an example of this, run TestVarcharInTextbox.SCX, type something like "test" in both text boxes, and click on the Results button. Because the second text box has "F" in its Format property, its content is trimmed while the content of the first one is not.

The Developer Download files for this chapter, available at
www.hentzenwerke.com, *include TestVarchar.PRG,*
TestVarcharWithSQLServer.PRG, Test.DBC, and
TestVarcharInTextbox.SCX. Change the connection string in the
first line of code of TestVarcharWithSQLServer.PRG as necessary
to connect to the Northwind database on your SQL Server.

Varbinary

Varbinary really is a new data type: it contains binary values. Like Varchar, Varbinary fields are not padded to the maximum size of the field. Microsoft added Varbinary to VFP 9 for the same reason it added Varchar: better support of other databases. However, they can also be used for binary values such as timestamps or GUIDs in native VFP tables. The single character abbreviation for Varbinary is "Q."

Values are stored into Varbinary fields using a new notation: 0h (a zero followed by the letter "h") followed by a series of hexadecimal bytes. The value is not enclosed in quotes. Here's an example, taken from TestVarbinary.PRG, which shows the use of Varbinary:

```
create cursor Test (Field1 Q(20))
insert into Test values (0h466F7820526F636B73)
   && the binary representation of the string "Fox Rocks"
? vartype(Field1)    && displays "Q"
? len(Field1)        && displays 9
? Field1             && displays 0h466F7820526F636B73
```

Here are some details about Varbinary:

- Varbinary has similar features to Varchar: you can index on it (the index keys are padded with binary zeros to the length of the field, because index keys must be a fixed length), it accepts null values, and Varbinary fields have a limit of 254 characters in a table or cursor.

- One difference between Varbinary and Varchar is MACHINE is the only collate sequence allowed for indexes on Varbinary fields; using any other sequence results in an "invalid collation sequence" error.

- Another difference is the SQL LIKE operator and the LIKE(), LIKEC(), BINTOC(), and CTOBIN() functions aren't permitted on Varbinary values.

- You can SEEK() on the binary or character representation of a Varbinary field. For example, SEEK 0h466F7820526F636B73 and SEEK 'Fox Rocks' will both find the same record.

- No code page translation is performed on Varbinary fields, so there is no Varbinary (Binary) choice in the Table Designer and NOCPTRANS isn't required in a CREATE TABLE/CURSOR command.

> Although their names are similar, Varchar (Binary) is not the same as Varbinary. The former holds non-padded character values that are not code page translated while the latter holds binary data.

- TYPE() and VARTYPE() return "Q" for Varbinary fields and Varbinary values stored to memory variables.

- The data type of the result of concatenating Varbinary and Character (or Varchar) values is the first value. For example, continuing with the previous sample code:

```
? "It's true that " + Field1   && displays "It's true that Fox Rocks"
? Field1 + " tonight"          && displays 0h466F7820526F636B7320746F6E69676874
```

You can use this behavior to convert between Character and Varbinary. The first line of the following code converts Varbinary to Character while the second converts Character to Varbinary.

```
? '' + 0h466F7820526F636B73      && displays "Fox Rocks"
? substr(0h00 + "Fox Rocks", 2)  && displays 0h466F7820526F636B73
```

Of course, you can also use the new CAST() function discussed in Chapter 14, "Language Improvements," to convert between Character and Varbinary.

- As with Character, comparing Varbinary values is sensitive to the setting of EXACT. SET EXACT ON means the values are compared byte-for-byte, the shorter of the two expressions is zero-padded to the length of the longer, and trailing zeros are ignored. SET EXACT OFF means the comparison stops at the end of the expression on the right side. Use == for an exact comparison, including binary zeros.

- Comparison between Varbinary and Character or Varchar values depends on the order of the values. If the Varbinary value is on the left side of the comparison operator, trailing binary zeros are ignored in the Varbinary value but trailing spaces in the Character value are significant. If the Varbinary value is on the right, trailing spaces are ignored in the Character value, but trailing binary zeros in the Varbinary value are significant. For example, continuing with the previous sample code:

```
? Field1 = 'Fox Rocks'           && displays .T.
? Field1 + 0h00 = 'Fox Rocks'    && displays .T.
? Field1 = 'Fox Rocks '          && displays .F.
? 'Fox Rocks' = Field1           && displays .T.
? 'Fox Rocks ' = Field1          && displays .T.
? 'Fox Rocks' = Field1 + 0h00    && displays .F.
```

- Adding "F" to the Format property of a Textbox bound to a Varbinary field prevents the value entered by the user from being padded with binary zeros. You can also use

"H" in InputMask to prevent non-hexadecimal characters from being entered in the specified position.

- The TRIM() functions—TRIM(), RTRIM(), LTRIM(), and ALLTRIM()—remove leading and/or trailing zeros from Varbinary values.

- ALINES() removes trailing binary zeros when .T. or 1 is specified for the third parameter. Also, if the parse characters aren't specified, ALINES() breaks lines at 0h0A values (line feed in hexadecimal).

- TRANSFORM() returns the character representation of binary values without the 0h. For example, TRANSFORM(0hA0A1A2) returns "A0A1A2."

- ISBLANK() and EMPTY() return .T. when the field is empty or contains only binary zeros.

- With the exception of BITLSHIFT() and BITRSHIFT(), the BIT functions support Varbinary values. All of the values passed to BITAND(), BITOR(), and BITXOR() must be Varbinary values if any of them are. BITCLEAR(), BITNOT(), and BITSET() have new nStartBit and nBitCount parameters that indicate the range of bits the operation applies to. Leaving these parameters out means the operation applies to all bits, while specifying only nStartBit means the operation applies to the specified bit only.

 The Developer Download files for this chapter, available at **www.hentzenwerke.com**, *include TestVarbinary.PRG.*

Blob

Blob is like a cross between Memo and Varbinary: it stores binary data in an FPT file. As with the other data types, Microsoft added Blob to VFP 9 to provide better support for other databases. However, as you'll soon see, they have great uses even with native VFP tables. The single character abbreviation for Blob is "W."

Here are some details about Blob:

- Blob has similar features to Memo: you can't index on it, it accepts null values, and Blob fields have a limit of 2 GB of data in a table or cursor (of course, the total size of FPT files is still 2 GB). In a BROWSE window or grid, a Blob field appears as "blob" if it's empty or "Blob" if not.

- You can use an edit box or MODIFY MEMO to display the contents of a Blob field. The binary data displays as hexadecimal values without the leading 0h. However, the contents are read-only. The values in Blob fields must be modified programmatically, such as with REPLACE or GATHER.

- As with Varbinary, no code page translation is performed on Blob fields.

- TYPE() and VARTYPE() return "Q," not "W" as you may expect, for Blob fields and Blob values stored to memory variables. DISPLAY/LIST STRUCTURE and AFIELDS() do indicate "Blob" and "W," respectively, for Blob fields.

- TRIM(), RTRIM(), LTRIM(), ALLTRIM(), ALINES(), TRANSFORM(), ISBLANK(), and EMPTY() work the same as they do with Varbinary fields.

- The SQL LIKE operator, LIKE(), LIKEC(), BINTOC(), CTOBIN(), and APPEND FROM don't support Blob fields.

- Blob fields can be a replacement for General fields that contain images. General fields suffer from many problems: hard to use, hard to update, huge size, and so forth. Instead of storing images in a General field, which requires a file association to an ActiveX server, store them in a Blob field. They're easier to update; rather than APPEND GENERAL, you can use something like the following to pull an image into a Blob field:

```
replace Picture with filetostr('BobJones.gif') in Employees
```

To display an image stored in a Blob field on a form, simply set the new PictureVal property of an Image control to the contents of the Blob field:

```
Thisform.imgEmployee.PictureVal = Employees.Picture
```

To see a demo of this, run BlobDemo.SCX. It provides a simple picture viewer form. Its Load method creates a cursor of images using the following code:

```
create cursor TEST (FIELD1 Blob)
insert into TEST values (filetostr(home() + 'FOX.BMP'))
insert into TEST values (filetostr(home() + 'WIZARDS\BANDRPT.BMP'))
insert into TEST values (filetostr(home() + 'WIZARDS\WIZFLAX.BMP'))
insert into TEST values (filetostr(home() + 'WIZARDS\WIZSTONE.BMP'))
insert into TEST values (filetostr(home() + 'WIZARDS\FOXQSTRT.BMP'))
go top
```

The Next and Previous buttons set the PictureVal property of the image on the form to FIELD1 in the cursor.

 The Developer Download files for this chapter, available at ***www.hentzenwerke.com***, *include BlobDemo.SCX.*

Specifying the data type of variable length values

In previous versions of VFP, using an expression in a SQL SELECT statement that results in variable length data has one of two consequences: the values are padded with spaces rather than trimmed and/or the values are truncated to the length of the value in the first record in the result.

Here's an example, taken from TestVarcharMapping.PRG, which shows both of these issues:

```
select trim(FirstName) + ' ' + trim(LastName) as FullName ;
  from Employees ;
  into cursor Test
clear
scan
  ? FullName, len(FullName)
endscan
use

* Do it using a function to show that the fields are sized to the value for the
* first record.

select GetFullName(FirstName, LastName) as FullName ;
  from Employees ;
  into cursor Test
scan
  ? FullName, len(FullName)
endscan

function GetFullName(tcFirstName, tcLastName)
return trim(tcFirstName) + ' ' + trim(tcLastName)
```

The first loop shows all records in the result set are padded to 31 characters even though the expression in the SQL SELECT statement trimmed the fields. The second loop shows all records are truncated at 13 characters because that's the length of the result of the expression for the first record; VFP uses this value as the template for the cursor structure.

It's unlikely you want either of these behaviors. In the first case, although you requested trimmed values, the results are not trimmed. In the second case, data is actually lost because the field isn't wide enough to contain the proper value for each record.

Fortunately, VFP 9 has an easy solution to the first problem: the new SET VARCHARMAPPING command. The VARCHARMAPPING setting, which is off by default, determines whether the values in a result set are Character or Varchar when expressions returning variable length values are used. The VARCHARMAPPING setting is scoped to the current data session. You can also specify this setting in CONFIG.FPW by adding VARCHARMAPPING = ON or VARCHARMAPPING = OFF.

Running the code shown earlier with SET VARCHARMAPPING ON shows the values in each record in the first loop are variable length. However, the second loop still shows truncated values. That's because VFP still uses the length of the value in the first record as the size of the field in the cursor when a user-defined function is called. Fortunately, a slight change to the SQL SELECT statement takes care of that. The new CAST() function is discussed in more detail in Chapter 14, "Language Improvements."

```
select cast(GetFullName(FirstName, LastName) as V(31)) as FullName ;
  from Employees ;
  into cursor Test
```

The Developer Download files for this chapter, available at **www.hentzenwerke.com**, *include TestVarcharMapping.PRG.*

In CursorAdapter and XMLAdapter objects, you can control the mapping of Varchar results to Varchar fields with their new MapVarchar property. Set this property to .T. to use Varchar (for results less than 255 bytes) or Memo (for results more than 255 bytes) fields or .F. to use Character or Memo. Similarly, setting the new MapBinary property to .T. maps binary values to Varbinary or Blob fields. Both of these properties default to .F. for backward compatibility reasons.

You can also control mapping in SQL passthrough. CURSORSETPROP('MapVarchar') specifies whether Varchar values from ODBC data sources map to Varchar (when the setting is .T.) or Character (the setting is .F.) fields. CURSORSETPROP('MapBinary') controls the mapping of binary values to Varbinary or Blob fields. Note that these settings can only be set at the "session" level; meaning you must pass 0 as the third parameter for CURSORSETPROP(). These settings are read-only for SQL passthrough cursors and invalid for VFP tables. TestMapVarchar.PRG demonstrates the use of the MapVarchar setting.

```
* Connect to the SQL Server Northwind database. Change the connection string as
* necessary.

lnHandle = sqlstringconnect('driver=SQL Server;server=(local);' + ;
  'Database=Northwind;trusted_connection=yes;')
if lnHandle < 1
  return
endif lnHandle < 1

* Get data from the Customers table with MapVarchar .F.

cursorsetprop('MapVarchar', .F., 0)
sqlexec(lnHandle, 'select * from Customers')
messagebox('CompanyName in the first record is ' + CompanyName + ;
  ', which is ' + transform(len(CompanyName)) + ' characters.')
use

* Do it again with MapVarchar .T.

cursorsetprop('MapVarchar', .T., 0)
sqlexec(lnHandle, 'select * from Customers')
messagebox('CompanyName in the first record is ' + CompanyName + ;
  ', which is ' + transform(len(CompanyName)) + ' characters.')
use

* Clean up and exit.

sqldisconnect(lnHandle)
close databases all
```

The Developer Download files for this chapter, available at
www.hentzenwerke.com, include TestMapVarchar.PRG. Change the
connection string in the first line of code as necessary to connect to the
Northwind database on your SQL Server.

How the new data types affect DBF files

You may be interested to know how VFP 9 implements these new data types in a table. The DBF structure doesn't allow for variable length fields, so Varchar and Varbinary fields actually are padded with spaces in the DBF file. Therefore, Microsoft had to come up with a mechanism to track the length of the contents for Varchar and Varbinary fields so the proper trimmed value can be returned when requested. Here's how it works:

- All versions of VFP add a hidden field called _NullFlags to a DBF if any of the fields can accept null values. This field contains bit values that indicate whether a particular field in a given record contains a null. For example, if the first nullable field in a record contains null, bit 0 is set to 1. If the second nullable field contains a non-null value, bit 1 is 0. Because there are eight bits in a byte, _NullFlags has a width of the number of nullable fields divided by 8.

- In VFP 9, _NullFlags serves double-duty: bits also indicate whether the values in Varchar and Varbinary fields fill the fields. If a bit contains 0, the length of the value in a field equals the field size (the field is full). If the bit contains 1, the length of the value is less than the field size, in which case the field is padded with spaces as necessary and the last byte contains the field size. For example, a 10-byte Varchar field containing "AB" actually contains "AB" followed by seven spaces and CHR(2) (2 represents the size of the value) and the bit for the field in _NullsFlags is 1.

- If a field is both nullable and Varchar or Varbinary, two bits are used to represent a field. The lower bit represents the "full" status and the higher bit represents the null status. For example, a nullable 10-byte Varchar field containing "AB" is represented by 01 in _NullFlags (0 means not null, 1 means not full-size) while a null value in the same field is represented by 11 (null and not full-size).

Here's an example that shows the various values of _NullFlags for nullable Character (Field3), non-nullable Varchar (Field2), and nullable Varchar fields (Field4). Bit 0 represents the "full" status for Field2, bit 1 contains the null status for Field3, bit 2 contains the "full" status for Field4, and bit 3 contains the null status for Field4. This example uses the HexEdit utility that comes with VFP to show the binary contents of the DBF file. Scroll to address 000001C0 to see the contents of the seven records in the table.

```
create table TestVarchar (Field1 C(1), Field2 V(1), Field3 C(1) null, ;
  Field4 V(1) null)
insert into TestVarchar values ('A', 'A', 'A', 'A')
  && Record 20 41 41 41 41, _NullFlags 00000000 = 00
insert into TestVarchar values ('A', '', 'A', 'A')
  && Record 20 41 00 41 41, _NullFlags 00000001 = 01
```

```
insert into TestVarchar values ('A', 'A', 'A', '')
  && Record 20 41 41 41 00, _NullFlags 00000100 = 04
insert into TestVarchar values ('A', 'A', .NULL., 'A')
  && Record 20 41 41 20 41, _NullFlags 00000010 = 02
insert into TestVarchar values ('A', 'A', 'A', .NULL.)
  && Record 20 41 41 41 00, _NullFlags 00001100 = 0C
insert into TestVarchar values ('A', 'A', .NULL., .NULL.)
  && Record 20 41 41 20 00, _NullFlags 00001110 = 0E
insert into TestVarchar values ('A', '', .NULL., .NULL.)
  && Record 20 41 00 20 00, _NullFlags 00001111 = 0F
use
do home() + 'Tools\HexEdit\HexEdit' with 'TestVarchar.dbf'
```

(In the comments in the code, the initial 20 in the record, a space character, indicates the record is not deleted. 41 is the letter "A," 00 indicates the length of the value in a Varchar field is 0 bytes because the field is either empty or null, and 20 in a Character field is a space, indicating the field is empty or null.)

 The Developer Download files for this chapter, available at ***www.hentzenwerke.com***, *include ShowDBFStructure.PRG.*

Blob fields don't affect the DBF structure as they are stored in an FPT file using the same organization as normal Memo fields.

One other DBF change: if a table contains any of the new data types, the first byte, which indicates the type of table, contains 0x32 (50 decimal). (You can retrieve this value using SYS(2029).) As a result, you cannot open the table in earlier versions of VFP or with the VFP ODBC driver.

Binary indexes

VFP developers often create an index on the DELETED() function. This tag helps with Rushmore optimization because VFP doesn't have to hit the disk to determine whether records are deleted; it simply looks in the index, which is likely cached in memory. (However, under certain conditions, this index can actually slow down VFP. For information, see an article by Chris Probst in the May 1999 issue of FoxPro Advisor. There are also several topics on this issue on the FoxPro Wiki; **http://fox.wikis.com**)

Because indexes on DELETED() and other logical expressions contain only one of two possible values (.T. or .F.), Microsoft discovered they could change the way such an index is stored in the CDX file, resulting in much smaller and faster indexes. Thus, VFP 9 sports a new index type: binary.

To create a binary index, add the BINARY keyword to the INDEX command. For example:

```
index on DELETED() tag DELETED binary
```

Here are some details about binary indexes:

- Binary indexes can be an order of magnitude smaller, and therefore significantly faster, than normal indexes. TestBinaryIndex.PRG creates a sample table with normal and binary indexes on DELETED(). The binary index is more than 90% smaller than the normal one.

- The only use for binary indexes is Rushmore optimization. You cannot SEEK on them, nor can you SET ORDER to them.

- The logical expression must never evaluate to a null value, neither when the index is created nor in later use of the table, or you'll get an error.

- You cannot use the FOR, ASCENDING, DESCENDING, UNIQUE, or CANDIDATE clauses in the INDEX command and cannot create an IDX index file when creating a binary index.

- According to the VFP help (the "Visual FoxPro Index Types" topic), VFP may create the Rushmore optimization bitmap faster or slower for a binary index, depending on whether the number of records returned is more or less than 3% of the total number of records. However, this threshold depends on several factors, including the total number of records. As is often the case, you need to test this under real-world conditions to determine the impact binary indexes will have on your queries. Another VFP help topic, "Indexes Based on Deleted Records," has additional information about what VFP can optimize under various conditions.

 The Developer Download files for this chapter, available at **www.hentzenwerke.com**, *include TestBinaryIndex.PRG.*

Summary

The new data types added to VFP 9 make it easier than ever to work with non-native databases such as SQL Server, but also prove useful when used in native tables. Blob fields are especially useful if you currently store images in General fields. Binary indexes can improve the performance of your SQL SELECT statements beyond VFP's already blinding speed.

Updates and corrections for this chapter can be found on Hentzenwerke's website, **www.hentzenwerke.com**. Click "Catalog" and navigate to the page for this book.

Chapter 10
Managing XML

VFP 9 again improves the usability of XML in VFP applications by enhancing the XMLAdapter classes as well as XML functions. The enhancements center on nested XML, multiple language, and better XPATH support. VFP 9 applications can now produce and consume a wider range of XML documents.

Extensible Markup Language (XML) is slowly but surely becoming a standard for data transmission and is supported in most Microsoft applications. VFP has had XML capabilities since version 7 when the XMLTOCURSOR(), XMLUPDATEGRAM(), and CURSORTOXML() functions were added. VFP 8 introduced the XMLAdapter classes (including XMLTable and XMLField) to overcome the limitations of the existing functions. The XMLAdapter classes in VFP 8 work fairly well, but still have some limitations. For one, the XMLAdapter is fairly picky about the schemas it can understand. Also, there is no easy way to create nested or hierarchical XML. The only way to do so is manually creating the document using something like text merge. VFP 9 lifts many of the XML limitations imposed in VFP 8 and earlier.

Creating nested XML

One of the most useful enhancements in VFP 9 is the improved ability for the XMLAdapter to read and write hierarchical XML. Under VFP 8, the XMLAdapter can not create nested XML using the ToXML method nor can it always parse nested data into multiple tables using ToCursor or ChangesToCursor. VFP 9 lifts this limitation.

The most straightforward way to get VFP data into the XMLAdapter is to use the AddTableToSchema method. This method loads the data from an open VFP cursor into the adapter. In VFP 8, you could load several tables into the adapter, but each table appeared at the same level in the XML document. For example, the code in **Listing 1** produces the results in **Figure 1.**

 *The program Old_AddTableToSchema.PRG is included with the Developer Download files, available at **www.hentzenwerke.com**, for this chapter.*

***Listing 1**. Creating an XML document from more than one table without nesting.*

```
LOCAL ;
    loXMLAdapter AS XMLAdapter

CLOSE DATABASES ALL
OPEN DATABASE (HOME() + [samples\northwind\northwind])
USE Categories IN 0
USE Products IN 0

loXMLAdapter = CREATEOBJECT([XMLAdapter])
```

```
WITH loXMLAdapter
    .XMLSchemaLocation = [Old_AddTableToSchema.xsd]
    .AddTableSchema([Categories])
    .AddTableSchema([Products])
    .ToXML([Old_AddTableToSchema.xml], [], .T.)
    MODIFY FILE Old_AddTableToSchema.xml
ENDWITH

loXMLAdapter = .NULL.
```

```
<?xml version="1.0" encoding="Windows-1252" standalone="yes" ?>
- <VFPDataSet xmlns:xsi="http://www.w3.org/2001/XMLSchema-instance"
    xsi:noNamespaceSchemaLocation="C:\DOCUMENTS AND SETTINGS\TMF\MY
    DOCUMENTS\BOOKS\WN9\SOURCECODE\CH10\Old_AddTableToSchema.XSD">
  + <Categories>
  + <Categories>
  + <Categories>
  + <Categories>
  + <Categories>
  + <Categories>
  + <Categories>
  - <Categories>
      <categoryid>8</categoryid>
      <categoryname>Seafood</categoryname>
      <description>Seaweed and fish</description>
    </Categories>
  - <Products>
      <productid>1</productid>
      <productname>Chai</productname>
      <supplierid>1</supplierid>
      <categoryid>1</categoryid>
      <quantityperunit>10 boxes x 20 bags</quantityperunit>
      <unitprice>18.0000</unitprice>
      <unitsinstock>39</unitsinstock>
      <unitsonorder>0</unitsonorder>
      <reorderlevel>10</reorderlevel>
      <discontinued>false</discontinued>
    </Products>
  + <Products>
  + <Products>
  + <Products>
  + <Products>
  + <Products>
  + <Products>
  + <Products>
  + <Products>
```

Figure 1. The Old_AddTableToSchema.XML document is displayed in Internet Explorer for easier viewing. It shows multiple tables in a single XML document. Notice there is no nesting.

The nested XML in Figure 2 is easily generated by the XMLAdapter using the new properties and methods added in VFP 9.

```
<?xml version="1.0" encoding="Windows-1252" standalone="yes" ?>
- <VFPDataSet xmlns:xsi="http://www.w3.org/2001/XMLSchema-instance"
    xsi:noNamespaceSchemaLocation="C:\DOCUMENTS AND SETTINGS\TMF\MY
    DOCUMENTS\BOOKS\WN9\SOURCECODE\CH10\AddTableToSchema_Nest.xsd">
  - <Categories>
      <categoryid>1</categoryid>
      <categoryname>Beverages</categoryname>
      <description>Soft drinks, coffees, teas, beers, and ales</description>
    - <Products>
        <productid>1</productid>
        <productname>Chai</productname>
        <supplierid>1</supplierid>
        <categoryid>1</categoryid>
        <quantityperunit>10 boxes x 20 bags</quantityperunit>
        <unitprice>18.0000</unitprice>
        <unitsinstock>39</unitsinstock>
        <unitsonorder>0</unitsonorder>
        <reorderlevel>10</reorderlevel>
        <discontinued>false</discontinued>
      </Products>
    - <Products>
        <productid>2</productid>
        <productname>Chang</productname>
        <supplierid>1</supplierid>
        <categoryid>1</categoryid>
        <quantityperunit>24 - 12 oz bottles</quantityperunit>
        <unitprice>19.0000</unitprice>
        <unitsinstock>17</unitsinstock>
        <unitsonorder>40</unitsonorder>
        <reorderlevel>25</reorderlevel>
        <discontinued>false</discontinued>
      </Products>
    - <Products>
        <productid>24</productid>
        <productname>Guaran  Fant stica</productname>
        <supplierid>10</supplierid>
        <categoryid>1</categoryid>
```

Figure 2. Multiple tables in a single XML document with nesting.

RespectNesting

A new property RespectNesting was added to the XMLAdapter to control the default nesting behavior. This property controls the nesting behavior as tables are added to the schema as well as how the XML is generated. In order to nest tables in the XMLAdapter, a relation must exist using SET RELATION.

If the RespectNesting property is .T. when tables are added to the schema, they are added in a nested format. If the property is still true when the XML document is created using ToXML, the resulting document contains nested XML. Therefore, the code in **Listing 2** produces the XML document displayed in Figure 2.

*The program AddTableToSchema.PRG is included with the Developer Download files, available at **www.hentzenwerke.com**, for this chapter.*

Listing 2*. Creating a nested XML document.*

```
LOCAL ;
     loXMLAdapter

CLOSE DATABASES ALL
OPEN DATABASE (HOME() + [samples\northwind\northwind])
USE Categories IN 0
USE Products IN 0 ORDER CategoryID
SELECT Categories
SET RELATION TO CategoryId INTO Products ADDITIVE

loXMLAdapter = CREATEOBJECT([XMLAdapter])

WITH loXMLAdapter AS XMLAdapter
     .XMLSchemaLocation = [AddTableToSchema_Nest.xsd]
     .RespectNesting = .T.
     .AddTableSchema([Categories])
     .AddTableSchema([Products])
     .ToXML([AddTableToSchema_Nest.xml], [], .T.)
     MODIFY FILE AddTableToSchema_Nest.xml
ENDWITH

loXMLAdapter = .NULL.
```

If RespectNesting is set to .F. prior to calling ToXML, the XML document is created without nesting the table data. This is the same behavior seen in Visual FoxPro 8. In addition, if RespectNesting is .F. when the tables are added, the tables are not added in a nested structure unless .T. is passed to AddTableToSchema as the last parameter.

lAutoNest

An eighth argument, lAutoNest, was added to the AddTableToSchema method to support hierarchical XML. Like RespectNesting, this argument controls which tables are nested as the schema is added to the XMLAdapter. If this argument is .T., the table is nested according to the relations involving the table. If .F. is passed, the table is not nested. If no value is passed, the RespectNesting property of XMLAdapter controls nesting. In all cases, a relation must exist between the two tables for nesting to occur. The XML shown in Figure 2 can also be generated using the code in **Listing 3**.

 *The program AnotherAddTableToSchema.PRG is included with the Developer Download files, available at **www.hentzenwerke.com**, for this chapter.*

Listing 3*. Another way to create a nested XML document.*

```
LOCAL ;
     loXMLAdapter

CLOSE DATABASES ALL
OPEN DATABASE (HOME() + [samples\northwind\northwind])
USE Categories IN 0
USE Products IN 0 ORDER CategoryID
```

```
SELECT Categories
SET RELATION TO CategoryId INTO Products ADDITIVE

loXMLAdapter = CREATEOBJECT([XMLAdapter])

WITH loXMLAdapter AS XMLAdapter
    .XMLSchemaLocation = []
    .RespectNesting = .F.
    .AddTableSchema([Categories])
    .AddTableSchema([Products],,,,,,,,.T.)
    .RespectNesting = .T.
    .ToXML([AnotherAddTableToSchema_Nest.xml], [], .T.)
    MODIFY FILE AnotherAddTableToSchema_Nest.xml
ENDWITH

loXMLAdapter = .NULL.
```

While it seems the easiest way to create hierarchical XML is to set the RespectNesting property of the XMLAdapter class before adding any tables, it is an all or nothing solution. The lAutoNest parameter gives you some flexibility in determining which tables are nested and which ones are not.

New errors

VFP 9 has two new error numbers to handle situations where hierarchical XML cannot be generated. Error 2178, "There is no relation to the nested table <table name>," occurs if you call ToXML when the tables in the XMLAdapter are nested, the RespectNesting property is .T., and no relation exists between the data.

The second error, 2179 ("Nested XML format is incompatible with 'Changes Only' mode"), occurs when the tables are nested, RespectNesting is .T., and the lChangesOnly parameter passed to the ToXML method has a value of .T. The XMLAdapter class does not support nested changes.

XMLTable enhancements

The XMLTable class was also enhanced to support hierarchical XML. It has three new read-only properties, shown in **Table 1,** to indicate how tables are nested.

Table 1. New XMLTable properties.

Property	Description
NestedInto	An object reference to the parent of a table if the table is nested. If the table is not nested, .NULL. is returned.
NextSiblingTable	An object reference to the next sibling table if the table is nested and there is a sibling. If the table is not nested or there is no sibling, .NULL. is returned.
FirstNestedTable	An object reference to the first nested table if there are nested tables. If there is no nested table, .NULL. is returned.

Along with the three new properties, two new methods were added for more flexibility. The Nest method manually nests one table object inside another. The syntax for this method is:

```
XMLTable.Nest( oXMLTable [ , oAfterXMLTable | nAfterIndex ])
```

XMLTable is a reference to the outer table and oXMLTable is an object reference to the table that should be nested. The second parameter is used to control the location where oXMLTable is nested. oAfterXMLTable is an object reference to the table that should come before oXMLTable in the hierarchy. nAfterIndex is used to determine location by number rather than object reference. If an index or table object is not specified, the new table is inserted as the last table in the nesting order. **Table 2** shows the possible values for nAfterIndex.

When using the Nest method, tables do not need to be related. However, in order to create hierarchical XML based on the nested tables the relations must be set before calling the ToXML method.

Table 2. Possible values for the nAfterIndex parameter on the Nest method.

Value	Meaning
0	Nest the table first in the nesting order.
-1	Nest the table last in the nesting order.
Valid index position	Nest the table after the table at the specified position.
Invalid index position	Nest the table last in the nesting order.

When nesting tables, the tables must be associated with the same XMLAdapter and they cannot be nested recursively. A new error, 2177, "Inner and outer XMLTable objects are not associated with the same XMLAdapter object," occurs if you try to nest tables from two different XMLAdapter objects. The error, 2187, "Recursive XMLTable nesting is not allowed," occurs if you try to nest XMLTable objects into themselves or nested child XMLTable objects.

The second new method, UnNest, removes an XMLTable from being nested. The syntax is as follows:

```
XMLTable.UnNest()
```

The two examples in **Listing 4** and **Listing 5** show how to use the properties and methods of the XMLTable class. The first example, ManualNest, shows how to use the Nest method to manually nest tables after the schema is added to the adapter. The second example, ShowNextSibling, shows how to use the NextSibling property to step through all of the children of a parent table. The FirstNestedTable property provides an object reference to the first nested table and the NextSibling property is used to reference all other nested tables.

 *The programs ManualNest.PRG and ShowNextSibling.PRG are included with the Developer Download files, available at **www.hentzenwerke.com**, for this chapter.*

Listing 4. _Manually nesting tables in the XMLAdapter._

```
* ManualNest.PRG
LOCAL ;
     loXMLAdapter AS XMLAdapter, ;
     loOrders AS XMLTable, ;
     loDetails AS XMLTable, ;
     loProducts AS XMLTable, ;
     loEmployees AS XMLTable

CLOSE DATABASES ALL
OPEN DATABASE (HOME() + [samples\northwind\northwind])
USE Orders IN 0
USE OrderDetails IN 0 ORDER OrderId
USE Products IN 0 ORDER ProductId
USE Employees IN 0 ORDER EmployeeId
SELECT Orders
SET RELATION TO OrderID INTO OrderDetails ADDITIVE
SET RELATION TO EmployeeId INTO Employees ADDITIVE
SELECT OrderDetails
SET RELATION TO ProductId INTO Products ADDITIVE

loXMLAdapter = CREATEOBJECT([XMLAdapter])

WITH loXMLAdapter AS XMLAdapter
     .RespectNesting = .F.
     .XMLSchemaLocation = []
     .AddTableSchema([Orders])
     .AddTableSchema([OrderDetails])
     .AddTableSchema([Products])
     .AddTableSchema([Employees])
     loOrders = .Tables(1)
     loDetails = .Tables(2)
     loProducts = .Tables(3)
     loEmployees = .Tables(4)

     loOrders.Nest(loDetails)
     loOrders.Nest(loEmployees)
     loDetails.Nest(loProducts)
     ? [The first relation from Orders is: ] + loOrders.FirstNestedTable.Alias
     ? [The Employee table is nested into:] + loEmployees.NestedInto.Alias
ENDWITH

loXMLAdapter = .NULL.
```

Listing 5. _Using the FirstNestedTable and NextSiblingTable properties to step through the hierarchy._

```
*ShowNextSibling.PRG
LOCAL ;
     loXMLAdapter AS XMLAdapter, ;
     loOrders as XMLTable, ;
     loNextTable AS XMLTable, ;
     lnI as Integer

CLOSE DATABASES ALL
OPEN DATABASE (HOME() + [samples\northwind\northwind])
USE Orders IN 0
```

```
USE Customers IN 0 ORDER CustomerId
USE OrderDetails IN 0 ORDER OrderId
USE Shippers IN 0 ORDER ShipperId
USE Employees IN 0 ORDER EmployeeId
SELECT Orders
SET RELATION TO CustomerId INTO Customers ADDITIVE
SET RELATION TO OrderID INTO OrderDetails ADDITIVE
SET RELATION TO ShipVia INTO Shippers ADDITIVE
SET RELATION TO EmployeeId INTO Employees ADDITIVE

loXMLAdapter = CREATEOBJECT("XMLAdapter")

WITH loXMLAdapter AS XMLAdapter
    .RespectNesting = .T.
    .AddTableSchema([Orders])
    .AddTableSchema([Customers])
    .AddTableSchema([OrderDetails])
    .AddTableSchema([Shippers])
    .AddTableSchema([Employees])
    loOrders = .Tables(1)
    lnI = 1
    loNextTable = loOrders.FirstNestedTable

    DO WHILE NOT ISNULL(loNextTable)
        ? [The cursor: ] + loNextTable.Alias + ;
            [ is nested in Orders at Level ] + TRANSFORM(lnI)
        lnI = lnI + 1
        loNextTable = loNextTable.NextSiblingTable
    ENDDO

ENDWITH

loXMLAdapter = .NULL.
```

Consuming nested XML

So far, the examples show how to create nested XML. However, the new features of
XMLAdapter apply when reading XML documents as well. The LoadXML method now
populates the new nesting properties as the document is loaded. Take for example the XML
in **Listing 6**.

Listing 6. *Nested XML.*

```
<SalesOrder>
   <Order>
      <OrderId>6715</OrderId>
      <Description>An Order for some things.</Description>
      <OrderDetail>
         <OrderDetailId>5240</OrderDetailId>
         <OrderId>6715</OrderId>
         <Category>2</Category>
         <Remark>4/10/2003 12:05:14 PM</Remark>
      </OrderDetail>
      <OrderDetail>
         <OrderDetailId>5241</OrderDetailId>
         <OrderId>6715</OrderId>
         <Category>4</Category>
         <Remark>4/10/2003 12:05:14 PM</Remark>
```

```
      </OrderDetail>
      <OrderDetail>
         <OrderDetailId>5242</OrderDetailId>
         <OrderId>6715</OrderId>
         <Category>1</Category>
         <Remark>4/10/2003 12:05:14 PM</Remark>
      </OrderDetail>
   </Order>
</SalesOrder>
```

To save space the schema was removed from this document. However, with a valid schema, the following program loads both the Order and OrderDetails tables into the Tables collection of the XMLAdapter and sets the nesting properties correctly. In VFP 8 the tables collection is populated correctly, but there is no data to indicate that the tables are nested. The code in **Listing 7** displays alias names for both tables (Order and OrderDetail) and shows that OrderDetail is nested into Orders.

 *The program ConsumeNested.PRG is included with the Developer Download files, available at **www.hentzenwerke.com**, for this chapter.*

Listing 7. *With VFP 9, the XML is parsed and the table collection is populated, but the nesting properties are also set so the hierarchy can be read from the VFP side.*

```
LOCAL ;
     loAdapter AS XMLAdapter

loAdapter = CREATEOBJECT([XMLAdapter])
WITH loAdapter AS XMLAdapter
     .RespectNesting = .T.

     IF .LoadXML([orders.xml], .T.)
          ? [The number of tables read is: ] + TRANSFORM(.Tables.Count)
          ? [The first table is: ] + .Tables(1).Alias
          ? [The second table is: ] + .Tables(2).Alias
          ? [The first table is nested into ] + .Tables(1).NestedInto.Alias
     ENDIF

ENDWITH

loAdapter = .NULL.
```

XPath expressions for XML documents
XPath is a language used, mainly by Extensible Stylesheet Language (XSLT), for extracting portions of an XML document. The language is similar to the old DOS syntax used to navigate directory structures. For example the syntax ..\ refers to an XML node one above the currently selected node. The XMLAdapter class in VFP 9 has new XPath features to help manage large, complex XML documents. Some very good, basic XPath tutorial information is available at **http://www.zvon.org/xxl/XPathTutorial/General/examples.html** if you want more information on XPath.

XMLNameIsXPath

The XPath features added to the XMLAdapter take the form of three properties. The most notable property is the XMLNameIsXPath property. This property allows you to specify an XPath reference as the name for an XMLAdapter element because the XMLNameIsXPath property applies to XMLAdapter, XMLTable, and XMLField. The following example, **Listing 8**, uses an XML document called CategoriesAndProducts.XML.

Listing 8. *Creating a "virtual" field using the XMLAdapter.*

```
* CarryOverData.prg
LOCAL ;
    loXMLAdapter, ;
    loXMLTable, ;
    loXMLField

CLOSE DATABASES all
CLEAR

loXMLAdapter = CREATEOBJECT([XMLAdapter])
loXMLAdapter.LoadXML([CategoriesAndProducts.XML],.T.)

* This code createa a new XMLField object with an XPath reference
* as the name. It will cause a "virtual" field containing the
* category name to be added to the products table when it is
* rendered to a cursor.
loXMLField = CREATEOBJECT([XMLField])
loXMLField.XMLNameIsXPath = .T.
loXMLField.XMLName = STRCONV([parent::Categories/categoryname], 5)
loXMLField.Alias = [CategoryName]
loXMLField.DataType = [C]
loXMLField.MaxLength = 15
loXMLTable = loXMLAdapter.Tables(STRCONV([Products],5))
loXMLTable.Fields.Add(loXMLField, loXMLField.XMLName)

FOR EACH loXMLTable IN loXMLAdapter.Tables
    loXMLTable.ToCursor()
NEXT

SELECT Products
BROWSE
```

Figure 3 displays the results produced by the program code in **Listing 8**. Notice the Category name in the BROWSE window. This data comes from the nested table in the XML document.

Productid	Productname	Supplierid	Categoryid	Categoryname	Quantityperunit	Unitprice	Units
1	Chai	1	1	Beverages	10 boxes x 20 bags	18.0000	39
2	Chang	1	1	Beverages	24 - 12 oz bottles	19.0000	17
24	Guaran Fant stica	10	1	Beverages	12 - 355 ml cans	4.5000	20
39	Chartreuse verte	18	1	Beverages	750 cc per bottle	18.0000	69
43	Ipoh Coffee	20	1	Beverages	16 - 500 g tins	46.0000	17
3	Aniseed Syrup	1	2	Condiments	12 - 550 ml bottles	10.0000	13
4	Chef Anton's Cajun Seasoning	2	2	Condiments	48 - 6 oz jars	22.0000	53
5	Chef Anton's Gumbo Mix	2	2	Condiments	36 boxes	21.3500	0
16	Pavlova	7	3	Confections	32 - 500 g boxes	17.4500	29
19	Teatime Chocolate Biscuits	8	3	Confections	10 boxes x 12 pieces	9.2000	25
20	Sir Rodney's Marmalade	8	3	Confections	30 gift boxes	81.0000	40
21	Sir Rodney's Scones	8	3	Confections	24 pkgs. x 4 pieces	10.0000	3
25	NuNuCa Nuá-Nougat-Creme	11	3	Confections	20 - 450 g glasses	14.0000	76
11	Queso Cabrales	5	4	Dairy Products	1 kg pkg.	21.0000	22
12	Queso Manchego La Pastora	5	4	Dairy Products	10 - 500 g pkgs.	38.0000	86
22	Gustaf's Knäckebröd	9	5	Grains/Cereals	24 - 500 g pkgs.	21.0000	104
9	Mishi Kobe Niku	4	6	Meat/Poultry	18 - 500 g pkgs.	97.0000	29
17	Alice Mutton	7	6	Meat/Poultry	20 - 1 kg tins	39.0000	0
29	Thüringer Rostbratwurst	12	6	Meat/Poultry	50 bags x 30 sausgs.	123.7900	0

Figure 3. *The program in Listing 8. Creating a "virtual" field using the XMLAdapter.*

The program code in **Listing 9** shows how to use XPath to filter out records that don't match a certain condition. The results are displayed in **Figure 4**.

Listing 9. *Use XPath to filter out only products with a supplierid >10.*

```
* FilterXML.prg
LOCAL ;
    loXMLAdapter, ;
    loXMLTable

CLOSE DATABASES all
CLEAR

loXMLAdapter = CREATEOBJECT([XMLAdapter])
loXMLAdapter.LoadXML([CategoriesAndProducts.XML], .T.)

* Filter so only products with a supplier id > 10 appear

* Get a reference to the products table.
loXMLTable = loXMLAdapter.Tables(STRCONV([Products],5))

* Remove the products data.
loXMLAdapter.Tables.Remove(STRCONV([Products],5))
loXMLTable.XMLNameIsXPath = .T.

* Set the XMLName property of the old products table to an XPath expression.
loXMLTable.XMLName = STRCONV([Categories/Products[supplierid>=10]], 5)

* Add the table back to the adapter.
loXMLAdapter.Tables.Add(loXMLTable, loXMLTable.XMLName)

FOR EACH loXMLTable IN loXMLAdapter.Tables
    loXMLTable.ToCursor()
NEXT

SELECT Products
BROWSE
```

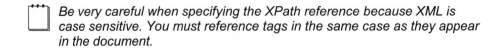

Figure 4. *The results after running the code in Listing 9.*

 Be very careful when specifying the XPath reference because XML is case sensitive. You must reference tags in the same case as they appear in the document.

The files CategoriesAndProducts.XML, CarryOverData.PRG, and FilterXML.PRG are included with the Developer Download files, available at **www.hentzenwerke.com**, *for this chapter.*

SelectionNamespaces

This property allows you to specify a custom namespace (prefix) for XPath expressions when loading XML documents. This property only applies to the XMLAdapter class and corresponds to the SelectionNamespaces property of the XML DOM. For more information see the MSDN documentation on MSXML4 at
http://msdn.microsoft.com/library/default.asp?url=/library/en-us/xmlsdk/html/xmpro2nd_selectionnamespaces.asp

DeclareXMLPrefix

This new logical property of the XMLAdapter and XMLTable determines if the XMLAdapter should declare an XML Prefix when parsing XML. If the XMLPrefix or XMLNamespace properties are empty, this property is ignored as there is no prefix/namespace to declare. If the RespectNesting property of an XMLAdapter object is true, this property applies to the XMLAdapter and all children (XMLTables) in the document. This is similar to the SelectionNamespaces property. However, SelectionNamespaces applies to **all** parsing operations, not just the current nesting scheme.

More new errors

The new XPATH support in the XMLAdapter is mainly for reading complex XML documents into VFP cursors. For this reason, several new errors numbers were added. **Table 3** shows the new error numbers and what they mean.

Table 3. *New error numbers related to XPATH support in XMLAdapter.*

Error Number	Description
2180	This error applies when XMLAdapter.XMLNameIsXPath is true. The property is not supported when creating XML, so the error is raised when the ToXML Method is called and the XMLName is not empty. The error also occurs when calling ApplyDiffGram, ChangesToCursor, or ToCursor and IsDiffGram is also .T.
2181	This error applies when XMLTable.XMLNameIsXPath is true and ToXML, ApplyDiffGram, or ChangesToCursor are called. This is different from error 2180, which applies to the XMLAdapter and this error applies to XMLTable.
2182	This error occurs when XMLNameIsXPath is true and the XMLName property contains a value that is not a legal XPath reference.

Non-Dataset XSD schema support

In VFP 8, when an XML document with an XSD schema is loaded into an XMLAdapter, the tables collection is only populated if the schema is in the ADO.NET DataSet format. If not, the XML is loaded, but the tables collection is not populated.

In VFP 9, the XMLAdapter class now supports XSD schemas in other formats. The schema shown in **Listing 10** is a standard, but non-ADO.NET DataSet, XSD schema. This schema was derived from an example schema found at **www.xml.com**.

 *The files Library.XSD, Books.XML, and NoDatasetXSD.PRG are included with the Developer Download files, available at **www.hentzenwerke.com**, for this chapter.*

Listing 10. *Library.XSD is a standard XSD schema not in the ADO.NET DataSet format.*

```
<?xml version="1.0" encoding="utf-8"?>
<xs:schema xmlns:xs="http://www.w3.org/2001/XMLSchema">
 <xs:element name="book">
  <xs:complexType>
   <xs:sequence>
    <xs:element name="title" type="xs:string"/>
    <xs:element name="author" type="xs:string"/>
    <xs:element name="character" minOccurs="0" maxOccurs="unbounded">
     <xs:complexType>
      <xs:sequence>
       <xs:element name="name" type="xs:string"/>
       <xs:element name="friend-of" type="xs:string" minOccurs="0"
```

```
maxOccurs="unbounded"/>
      <xs:element name="since" type="xs:date"/>
      <xs:element name="qualification" type="xs:string"/>
    </xs:sequence>
   </xs:complexType>
  </xs:element>
 </xs:sequence>
 <xs:attribute name="isbn" type="xs:string"/>
 </xs:complexType>
</xs:element>
</xs:schema>
```

The XML document, Books.XML, that references this schema is shown in **Listing 11.** This XML document was also derived from an example found at **www.xml.com**.

Listing 11. Books.XML references the schema in Listing 10

```
<?xml version="1.0" encoding="utf-8" ?>
<book isbn="0836217462" xmlns:xsi="http://www.w3.org/2001/XMLSchema-instance"
xsi:noNamespaceSchemaLocation="library.xsd">
 <title>Being a Dog Is a Full-Time Job</title>
 <author>Charles M. Schulz</author>
 <character>
   <name>Snoopy</name>
   <friend-of>Peppermint Patty</friend-of>
   <since>1950-10-04</since>
   <qualification>extroverted beagle</qualification>
 </character>
 <character>
   <name>Peppermint Patty</name>
   <since>1966-08-22</since>
   <qualification>bold, brash and tomboyish</qualification>
 </character>
</book>
```

If you run the following program in both VFP 8 and 9, you will see the difference in the number of tables in the collection. In VFP 8 the number is zero and in VFP 9 it is two.

Listing 12. NoDatasetXSD.PRG loads an XML document that uses a non-ADO.NET DataSet schema.

```
LOCAL ;
    loAdapter AS XMLAdapter

loAdapter = CREATEOBJECT([XMLAdapter])

WITH loAdapter

    IF .LoadXML([books.XML], .T.)
        ? [The number of tables in the tables collection is: ] + ;
            TRANSFORM(.Tables.Count)
    ENDIF

ENDWITH
```

In addition, if the RespectNesting property of the XMLAdapter is .T. when the XML is loaded, the tables are nested according to the XML schema.

When XML with a non-Dataset schema is loaded, the XMLName and XMLPrefix properties are left empty. These properties are populated when using a Dataset based schema.

Multi-language support

XMLAdapter is enhanced for VFP 9 to provide better language support when generating and parsing XML documents.

Three methods that read XML data into VFP cursors, ToCursor, ApplyDiffGram, and ChangesToCursor, are enhanced to include a new nCodePage parameter. This parameter represents the code page number to use when the VFP cursor is created. This parameter, if passed a non-zero value, always controls the code page of the newly created cursor.

The XMLAdapter, XMLTable, and XMLField classes are also enhanced to include a CodePage property. This property controls how the cursor is created and/or how field data is populated. Set this property to a valid code page number or an error occurs.

A new property, UseCodePage, was also added to the XMLAdapter class. This property controls the encoding of data when XML is generated as well as the creation of cursors if the code page parameter is not passed.

Let's start with how these features work when a cursor is created. If the code page parameter is not passed to the ToCursor, ApplyDiffGram, or ChangesToCursor methods, the CodePage property of the XMLTable class dictates the code page for the cursor. If the XMLTable.CodePage property is zero, the XMLAdapter.CodePage is used. All of this happens only when the UseCodePage property is true. If UseCodePage is false, the cursor is created just as it was in VFP 8 using the default code page.

Once a cursor is created and field data is being written, the XMLField object's CodePage determines the code page translation for the actual data. If the CodePage property of the field object is zero, the code page of the cursor applies.

Things are a little different when creating XML. The UseCodePage property controls the generation of the XML and works in conjunction with the RespectCursorCP and UTF8Encoded properties. **Table 4** shows the difference in behaviors.

Table 4. Behaviors associated with UseCodePage, RespectCursorCP, and UTF8Encoded.

UseCodePage	RespectCursorCP	UTF8Encoded	Behavior
.T.	.T.	.T.	UTF-8 is used as the encoding for the XML document. Character data is translated using the cursor's code page or XMLField.CodePage if it is greater than zero. Unicode data is translated using UTF-8.

UseCodePage	RespectCursorCP	UTF8Encoded	Behavior
.T.	.T.	.F.	Cursor's code page is used for the XML document encoding. Character data is not translated. Unicode data is translated using the cursor's code page. If an XMLField CodePage is greater than zero, but does not match the cursor's code page, an error occurs.
.T.	.F.	.T.	UTF-8 is used as the encoding for the XML document. Character data is translated using the current code page. Fields with NOCPTRANS are not translated. Unicode data is translated using UTF-8.
.T.	.F.	.F.	Windows-1252 is used for XML document (root node) Character data is translated using the current code page. Fields with NOCPTRANS are not translated. Unicode data is translated using code page 1252.
.F.	.T.	.T.	UTF-8 is used as the encoding for the XML document. Character data is translated using the current code page. Fields marked as NOCPTRANS are translated to UTF-8 using the code page specified by SYS(3005). Unicode data is translated using UTF-8.
.F.	.T.	.F.	Cursor's code page is used for the XML document encoding. Character data is not translated. Unicode data is translated using the cursor's code page.

UseCodePage	RespectCursorCP	UTF8Encoded	Behavior
.F.	.F.	.T.	UTF-8 is used as the encoding for the XML document. Character data is translated using the current code page. Fields with NOCPTRANS are not translated. Unicode data is translated using UTF-8.
.F.	.F.	.F.	Windows-1252 is used for XML document Character data is translated using the current code page. Fields with NOCPTRANS are not translated. Unicode data is translated using code page 1252.

> *See the Help Topic "Code Pages Supported by Visual FoxPro" in the VFP Help File for a list of valid code page numbers.*

In addition to multi-language support in the XMLAdapter class, this support is also available with the following functions using the nFlag parameter.

- XMLTOCURSOR()
- CURSORTOXML()
- XMLUPDATEGRAM()

A new flag value of 32768 indicates that a code page should be used. This is similar to setting the UseCodePage property of the XMLAdapter class to .T. and respects the flag values for RespectCursorCP (16) and UTF8Encoded (32) as seen in **Table 4**. If VFP is unable to determine the code page when using the 32768 flag, the error message "Unable to infer cursor's code page from XML document" displays. The error number for this error is 2185.

Data type support

XMLAdapter has two new properties to support the mapping of remote data to the new data types in VFP 9. **Table 5** lists these properties. Please see Chapter 9, "New Data and Index Types," for more information on the new data types and possible values for these properties.

Table 5*. New XMLAdapter data type conversion properties.*

Property	Description
MapBinary	Specifies how binary data from the remote data source is mapped to VFP data types. Setting the property to .T. means the VarBinary data returned from a remote database is mapped to the new VarBinary data type unless the value is longer than 254 in which case it is mapped to the new Blob data type. Setting the property to .F. (the default) mimics the existing FoxPro behavior and maps VarBinary data values to Character data types unless the value is longer than 254. In this case, the data is mapped to a memo or general field.
MapVarChar	Specifies how Varchar data from the remote data source is mapped to VFP data types. Setting the value to .T. results in VarChar values returned from a remote database stored as VarChar on the FoxPro side. Setting the value to .F. results in VarChar data mapping to character data types. The default value is .F.

In addition to XMLAdapter support for the new data types, an existing function, TTOC(), is enhanced to better support XML data. TTOC() has the following syntax:

```
TTOC(tExpression [, 1 | 2 | 3])
```

VFP 9 adds a new value of 3 for the second argument to this function. This value tells TTOC() to return the character string in a valid XML data format. The format is yyyy-mm-ddThh:mm:ss. The return value is always 19 characters regardless of SET CENTURY and SET SECONDS.

For example:

```
ltTime = DATETIME()
? TTOC(ltTime, 3)      && Returns 2004-06-25T14:35:46
```

Summary

As the XML standards continue to evolve, we see each version of VFP step up support for the current standard. Since XML support was added in VFP 7, the number and type of documents that cannot be handled with a VFP class or function have become fewer and fewer. Version 9 further narrows the gap.

Updates and corrections for this chapter can be found on Hentzenwerke's website, **www.hentzenwerke.com**. Click "Catalog" and navigate to the page for this book.

Chapter 11
Working With Remote Data

VFP 9 adds a number of features to the CursorAdapter to make it work better with remote databases. In addition, enhancements to SQL Pass-Through, ADO, and the OLE DB provider give you improved control when accessing remote data.

Since the transition from FoxPro to Visual FoxPro, VFP has provided easy access to remote data using remote views and SQL Pass-Through. VFP 7 introduced the OLE DB provider to extend VFP's capabilities as a remote data provider. VFP 8 introduced the CursorAdapter which gave us a unified, object-oriented means to access both local and remote data.

VFP 9 adds several new features to the CursorAdapter to improve remote data access, such as auto-refresh of identity and default values, timestamp support, conflict checking, and delayed memo fetching. The OLE DB provider can now return results from stored procedures, making it much more useful as a remote data provider. Finally, a number of minor SQL enhancements make it easier to handle connection management and delayed fetching of remote data.

SQL Pass-Through enhancements

VFP's SQL Pass-Through functions have been enhanced to give new options when disconnecting from a remote database, and to provide more information on the results of remote operations.

Temporarily disconnecting from a database

One of the first rules you learn about accessing remote databases is to limit the number of connections. Each active connection to a back-end database consumes resources on the server, and the total number of concurrent connections may be limited by licensing. On the other hand, continually closing and reopening connections requires extra coding and takes time.

VFP 8 introduced two changes to help minimize the number of connections you need. SQLCONNECT() can use an existing shared connection, and you can open a remote view using an existing shared connection by specifying a statement handle in place of the cConnectionName parameter. In our applications, we normally open a single shared connection based on the user's login information, and use that connection for the duration of the application.

However, there are situations where you may need to open additional connections for short periods of time. For example, you may need to retrieve data periodically from a different database, or execute an occasional long-running query in the background using a separate connection. In the past, you needed to reissue SQLCONNECT() or SQLSTRINGCONNECT() each time you wanted to reconnect to the remote data source, receiving a new statement handle on each reconnection.

The new SQLIDLEDISCONNECT() function temporarily disconnects from the remote database, but preserves the VFP statement handle and original connection parameters. The syntax is:

```
SQLIDLEDISCONNECT( nStatementHandle )
```

If your application attempts to use the statement handle again, VFP automatically reconnects to the remote database using the original connection parameters. If the connection cannot be reestablished, error 1526 ("Connectivity error") occurs. As a result, you can reuse the connection at any time without worrying about whether it is still active, and without reissuing SQLCONNECT() or SQLSTRINGCONNECT().

Note that the parameter passed to SQLIDLEDISCONNECT() is a statement handle. Beginning in VFP 8, SQL functions use statement handles rather than connection handles. A connection handle represents a unique connection to a database engine. If the connection is marked shareable, it can be used by multiple statement handles within an application. SQLIDLEDISCONNECT() disconnects the statement handle, but does not release the connection to the database server until all its statement handles have been released. After calling SQLIDLEDISCONNECT(), you can use SQLGETPROP() to determine whether the connection has been released. The ODBChstmt property is 0 if the statement handle has been disconnected; the ODBChdbc property is 0 if the connection to the back end has been released. (See "Determining what connections are open" later in this chapter for a way to determine which statement handles share a given connection.)

SQLIDLEDISCONNECT() returns 1 if successful, or -1 if it cannot disconnect. You cannot disconnect a connection if it is busy executing a query or if it is in manual transaction mode.

Here's an example that demonstrates how two shared connections become idle, and then automatically reconnect to the database. It displays the statement and connection handle for each connection at each stage. A third non-shareable connection is opened midway through that grabs the connection handle originally assigned to the first two connections. The idle connections then get a new connection handle when they reconnect. This demonstrates how, once all statement handles on a connection become idle, the physical connection to the database (represented by the connection handle) is dropped.

```
CLOSE DATABASES ALL
SET TALK OFF
CLEAR

LOCAL lcDir, lcDbc, lcConnStr, lnConn1, lnConn2, lnConn3, ;
  lnHandles, laHandles[1], n

*-- Connect to Tastrade sample database using ODBC.
lcDir = HOME(2) + "tastrade\data\"
lcDbc = lcDir + "tastrade.dbc"
IF ! FILE(lcDbc)
  MESSAGEBOX("The VFP sample database Tastrade.dbc cannot be found in " ;
  + lcDir, 16, "Sorry, I need to use the Tastrade sample database.")
  RETURN
ENDIF
```

```
*-- Open first connection to Tastrade database, mark sharable
lcConnStr = [Driver={Microsoft Visual FoxPro Driver};UID=;PWD=;SourceDB=] + ;
   lcDbc + [;SourceType=DBC;Exclusive=No;BackgroundFetch=No;Collate=Machine;]
lnConn1 = SQLSTRINGCONNECT(lcConnStr, .T.)
IF lnConn1 < 1
  MESSAGEBOX("Could not connect to Tastrade.dbc. Reason: " + MESSAGE(), ;
     16, "Sorry, could not connect")
  RETURN
ENDIF

*-- Open second statement handle on same connection
lnConn2 = SQLCONNECT(lnConn1)
IF lnConn2 < 1
  MESSAGEBOX("Could not connect to Tastrade.dbc. Reason: " + MESSAGE(), ;
     16, "Sorry, could not connect")
  SQLDISCONNECT(lnConn1)
  RETURN
ENDIF
DO showhandles WITH "Opened 2 connections", lnConn1, lnConn2

*-- Idle the second statement handle
SQLIDLEDISCONNECT(lnConn2)
DO showhandles WITH "Connection 2 idled", lnConn1, lnConn2

*-- Idle the first statement handle
SQLIDLEDISCONNECT(lnConn1)
DO showhandles WITH "Connection 1 idled", lnConn1, lnConn2

*-- Open another connection handle to the database. This is
* done to demonstrate that reconnecting an idle connection
* may create a new connection handle to the database.
lnConn3 = SQLSTRINGCONNECT(lcConnStr)
? "Connection 3 was assigned ODBC connection " ;
  + TRANSFORM(SQLGETPROP(lnConn3,"ODBChdbc"))
?

*-- Execute a query on idle statement handle 2
SQLEXEC(lnConn2, "SELECT * FROM customer")
DO showhandles WITH "Executed query on connection 2", lnConn1, lnConn2

*-- Execute a query on idle statement handle 1
SQLEXEC(lnConn1, "SELECT * FROM customer")
DO showhandles WITH "Executed query on connection 1", lnConn1, lnConn2

*-- Use new ASQLHANDLES() function to close open connections
lnHandles = ASQLHANDLES(laHandles)
FOR N = 1 TO lnHandles
  SQLDISCONNECT(laHandles[n])
NEXT
RETURN

***********************************************
PROCEDURE showhandles(tcMsg, tnConn1, tnConn2)
***********************************************
LOCAL lnCHnd1, lnCHnd2, lnSHnd1, lnSHnd2
```

```
*-- Get Connection handle for each connection
lnCHnd1 = SQLGETPROP(tnConn1,"ODBChdbc")
lnCHnd2 = SQLGETPROP(tnConn2,"ODBChdbc")
*-- Get Statement handle for each connection
lnSHnd1 = SQLGETPROP(tnConn1,"ODBChstmt")
lnSHnd2 = SQLGETPROP(tnConn2,"ODBChstmt")
? tcMsg
? "Connection 1: ODBC connection = " + TRANSFORM(lnCHnd1) ;
  + ", ODBC statement = " + TRANSFORM(lnSHnd1)
? "Connection 2: ODBC connection = " + TRANSFORM(lnCHnd2) ;
  + ", ODBC statement = " + TRANSFORM(lnSHnd2)
?
RETURN
```

 The Developer Download files for this chapter, available at ***www.hentzenwerke.com****, include this code in SqlIdleDisconnect.PRG.*

You will see the following results (the numbers will differ on your system, but the basic results should be the same):

```
Opened 2 connections
Connection 1: ODBC connection = 29562256, ODBC statement = 29564872
Connection 2: ODBC connection = 29562256, ODBC statement = 29567904

Connection 2 idled
Connection 1: ODBC connection = 29562256, ODBC statement = 29564872
Connection 2: ODBC connection = 29562256, ODBC statement = 0

Connection 1 idled
Connection 1: ODBC connection = 0, ODBC statement = 0
Connection 2: ODBC connection = 0, ODBC statement = 0

Connection 3 was assigned Connection handle 29562256

Executed query on connection 2
Connection 1: ODBC connection = 29568920, ODBC statement = 0
Connection 2: ODBC connection = 29568920, ODBC statement = 29564800

Executed query on connection 1
Connection 1: ODBC connection = 29568920, ODBC statement = 29571312
Connection 2: ODBC connection = 29568920, ODBC statement = 29564800
```

Rollback on disconnection
VFP 9 gives you control over handling manual transactions when a connection is disconnected. The standard syntax for starting a manual SQL transaction in VFP is:

```
SQLSETPROP(lnConn, "Transactions", 2)
```

The transaction remains in effect until SQLCOMMIT() or SQLROLLBACK() is issued. In previous versions of VFP, if the connection terminates unexpectedly before you issue one of these commands, the transaction is automatically committed. This can happen if there is a pending transaction and you call SQLDISCONNECT(), quit the app, or the app crashes.

In VFP 9, SQLSETPROP() and DBSETPROP() now include a DisconnectRollback property. (Use SQLSETPROP() to change the setting for an active connection and DBSETPROP() to change the default setting for a named connection in a database.) If DisconnectRollback is set to .T., any pending manual transaction on that connection is rolled back automatically if the connection terminates unexpectedly. If DisconnectRollback is .F. (the default), the transaction is automatically committed, as in previous versions. If a connection is shared, automatic rollback does not occur until the last statment handle associated with the connection is disconnected.

Get count of records affected by SQL Pass-Through

SQLEXEC() and SQLMORERESULTS() have a new optional parameter that provides more information on the number of records affected by a SQL command. The syntax is:

```
SQLEXEC( nStatementHandle [, cSQLCommand [, cCursorName [, aCountInfo ] ] ] )
SQLMORERESULTS( nStatementHandle [, cCursorName [, aCountInfo ] ] )
```

aCountInfo is the name of an array to populate with row count information. If the array doesn't exist, it's created. The array contains one row for each SQL command you issue that doesn't return a record set, and one row for each record set returned. The contents of each row depend on what happened. **Table 1** shows the possible values.

Table 1. *aCountInfo results. The array contains one row for each SQL command that does not return a result set and one row for each result set returned. These are the possible values for each row.*

Result	Column 1	Column 2
Command succeeded and does not return a result set (e.g., INSERT, UPDATE)	Empty string	Number of records affected, or -1 if not available
Command failed	"0"	-1
Command returned a result set	Cursor name	Number of records affected, or -1 if not available

If you execute a command that returns multiple result sets and the BatchMode property of the connection is .T., the array contains one row for each result set. If BatchMode is .F., each call to SQLMORERESULTS() replaces the previous contents of the array with a single row describing the new result set.

Here are a couple of ways to use the aCountInfo parameter to simplify your code. In the past, to determine the number of rows affected by an Insert, Update, or Delete command on a remote table, you needed to follow it immediately with a second command to retrieve the number of rows affected (assuming the backend supports a rowcount function). Here's an example of how to do this in SQL Server:

```
SQLEXEC(lnConn, "UPDATE products SET price = price * 1.05 where price < 10")
SQLEXEC(lnConn, "SELECT @@rowcount AS nchanged", "tmpCount")
```

Using aCountInfo makes it unnecessary to execute this secondary query to get the count:

```
SQLEXEC(lnConn, "UPDATE products SET price = price * 1.05 where price < 10",
aRowsUpdated)
```

Second, when a command is executed in batch mode and returns multiple result sets, VFP automatically creates the cursor name for result set 2 and above by adding "1", "2", etc. to the name of the first cursor. With aCountInfo, you can get a list of the cursor names without needing to guess at them.

Here is an example that shows several of the possible results for aCountInfo:

```
CLOSE DATABASES ALL
SET TALK OFF
CLEAR

LOCAL lcDir, lcDbc, lcConnStr, lnConn, laCount[1], ;
 lnRes, lcCmd

lcDir = HOME(2) + "tastrade\data\"
lcDbc = lcDir + "tastrade.dbc"
IF ! FILE(lcDbc)
  MESSAGEBOX("The VFP sample database Tastrade.dbc cannot be found in " ;
    + lcDir, 16, "Sorry, I need the Tastrade sample database.")
  RETURN
ENDIF

lcConnStr = [Driver={Microsoft Visual FoxPro Driver};UID=;PWD=;SourceDB=] + ;
  lcDbc + [;SourceType=DBC;Exclusive=No;BackgroundFetch=No;Collate=Machine;]
lnConn = SQLSTRINGCONNECT(lcConnStr)
IF lnConn < 1
  MESSAGEBOX("Could not connect to Tastrade.dbc. Reason: " + MESSAGE(), ;
    16, "Sorry, could not connect")
  RETURN
ENDIF

*-- Query returns 2 result sets
? "Two queries returning 2 result sets:"
TEXT TO lcCmd NOSHOW
SELECT * FROM customer WHERE country = 'USA';SELECT * FROM customer WHERE
country = 'Mexico'
ENDTEXT
lnRes = SQLEXEC(lnConn, lcCmd, "tmpCust", laCount)
DISPLAY MEMORY LIKE laCount
IF lnRes < 1
  ? "Error in query: " + MESSAGE()
ENDIF
?

*-- One query updates records, second query returns results
? "(1) Update records for some customers, (2) Query returns customers in UK:"
CLOSE TABLES ALL
TEXT TO lcCmd NOSHOW
UPDATE customer SET min_order_amt = min_order_amt + .01 WHERE min_order_amt <=
100;SELECT * FROM customer WHERE country = 'UK'
ENDTEXT
lnRes = SQLEXEC(lnConn, lcCmd, "tmpCust", laCount)
DISPLAY MEMORY LIKE laCount
IF lnRes < 1
  ? "Error in query: " + MESSAGE()
ENDIF
```

```
?

*-- Query is successful but did not update any records
? "Attempt to update records but do not return a result set, no records are
updated:"
CLOSE TABLES ALL
TEXT TO lcCmd NOSHOW
UPDATE customer SET min_order_amt = 1000 WHERE country = 'LalaLand'
ENDTEXT
lnRes = SQLEXEC(lnConn, lcCmd, "tmpCust", laCount)
DISPLAY MEMORY LIKE laCount
IF lnRes < 1
   ? "Error in query: " + MESSAGE()
ENDIF
?

*-- Query failed; no column named 'countryname'
? "Query fails due to erroneous column name:"
CLOSE TABLES ALL
TEXT TO lcCmd NOSHOW
SELECT * FROM customer WHERE countryname = 'UK'
ENDTEXT
lnRes = SQLEXEC(lnConn, lcCmd, "tmpCust", laCount)
DISPLAY MEMORY LIKE laCount

SQLDISCONNECT(lnConn)
```

 The Developer Download files for this chapter, available at **www.hentzenwerke.com**, *include this code in ACountInfo_vfp.PRG. They also include ACountInfo_sql.PRG, which uses the SQL Server Northwind database and demonstrates how the ACountInfo parameter is affected by asynchronous queries.*

Other SQL enhancements

VFP 9 adds new functionality to handle progressive fetching, delayed memo fetching, Unicode mapping, and connection management. While you may never have needed the first three features, the last one is something we have been wanting for a long time.

Detecting delayed memo fetching

If a remote view includes large memo fields, it can take a long time to return the results. To work around this, VFP has always supported delayed memo fetching. DBSETPROP() and DBGETPROP() include a FetchMemo property that invokes delayed memo fetching when set to .F. (The setting has no effect on local views.) In addition, the Advanced Options dialog in the View Designer has a Fetch Memo checkbox you can uncheck to turn on delayed memo fetching.

When delayed memo fetching is in effect, the contents of memo fields are not retrieved initially with the view results. Instead, VFP only retrieves the contents of a memo field for a given row the first time it is needed, such as for display in a form, in a memo edit window, or for use in an expression or command. The tradeoff is a small delay each time the memo field is first needed for a given row, versus a long delay when the view is initially queried if delayed memo fetching is off. Also, delayed memo fetching avoids retrieving the contents of memo fields never actually used by the application.

In VFP 8 and previous versions, when delayed memo fetching is in effect, there is no way to determine whether a memo field in a given record has been retrieved yet. Even a simple reference such as LEN("notes") causes the memo field's contents to be fetched. VFP 9 introduces a new function to give you this information. The syntax is:

```
ISMEMOFETCHED( cFieldName | nFieldNumber [, nWorkArea | cTableAlias ] )
```

ISMEMOFETCHED() returns .T. if the specified memo field in the current record of the cursor has been retrieved, .F. if it has not. If the cursor is at BOF() or EOF(), it returns .NULL. Calling ISMEMOFETCHED() does not cause the memo field to be fetched, so it can be used safely to determine whether a delay may occur before you try to access the memo field's contents. We haven't come up with a practical use for this yet; usually you either need the contents of the memo field or you don't. It's probably a case of the VFP team exposing previously internal functionality, but there's a good chance someone else will find it useful.

Monitoring fetch progress

CURSORGETPROP() has two new properties to help monitor the fetch status of an ODBC or ADO-based cursor. RecordsFetched returns the number of records fetched into the result cursor so far. FetchIsComplete returns .T. if the fetch is complete, .F. if it is still in progress. If you attempt to retrieve these properties for a local view or table, you get an error 1467 ("Property is invalid for local cursors").

There are several situations where these properties are useful. The first is when progressive fetching is in effect for a remote view. This happens when the view's FetchSize is less than the total number of records to be returned, and FetchAsNeeded is .F. In that case, VFP retrieves FetchSize number of records into the cursor, returns control to the application, and continues to retrieve the remaining records in the background. Previously, there was no straightforward way to know for sure whether progressive fetching was still in progress, or if all records had been retrieved. Now, you can check the value of FetchIsComplete; it continues to return .F. until all records have been retrieved.

Another situation is when fetch-on-demand is in effect for a remote view. This is done by setting the cursor's FetchAsNeeded property to .T. In this case, VFP does not employ progressive fetching in the background after retrieving the initial batch of records. Instead, it waits until the user or application attempts to access a record not yet retrieved into the cursor, such as when the user scrolls down in a grid. When that happens, VFP retrieves as many additional records from the back end as needed, in increments of FetchSize. Previously, there was no way to know whether all records had been returned. Evaluating RECCOUNT() in any way at all, such as in an expression like

```
IF RECNO() = RECCOUNT()
```

would cause VFP to immediately retrieve all records matching the query to determine the final RECCOUNT(), the same as if you issued GO BOTTOM. The new RecordsFetched property returns the number of records fetched so far, without triggering the retrieval of any additional records.

If a query is issued in asynchronous mode using SQLEXEC(), VFP retrieves a number of records equal to the current SQLGETPROP() FetchSize setting, and then stops. To retrieve the remaining records, you must keep repeating the SQLEXEC() command until it returns 1, indicating all records have been returned. The new RecordsFetched and FetchIsComplete properties can be used to determine whether there are additional records to retrieve. While useful, they are not essential here, because SQLEXEC() returns a value indicating whether the query is complete, and RECCOUNT() can be used on the cursor without forcing the retrieval of all records.

Finally, if you appended records to the local cursor, RecordsFetched still returns the original number of records retrieved from the remote database, where RECCOUNT() returns the current number of records in the cursor including appended records.

There are a couple of things to be aware of when using these new properties. If the MaxRecords property of the cursor is set to a positive value, and that value is less than the number of records matching the query, the fetch will stop once the cursor contains MaxRecords records. In that case, FetchIsComplete will return .T., even though the full query would have returned additional records. Also, if SET ESCAPE is ON, the user can press ESCAPE at any time to cancel the query. The cursor will contain the number of records fetched up to that point, and FetchIsComplete will be .T. even though the query was cut short. As far as we can tell, there is no way to determine whether the fetch was cut short by the user pressing ESCAPE.

Map remote Unicode data to ANSI in memo fields

The new SYS(987, lExpr) function determines whether remote Unicode data is mapped to ANSI in memo fields. If lExpr is .T., Unicode data is mapped to ANSI when retrieved into a memo field by SQL Pass-Through, remote views, and CursorAdapters. If lExpr is .F. (the default and the VFP 8 behavior), the memo field contains Unicode data.

Some SQL databases provide data types to store Unicode data, such as SQL Server's nChar and nVarchar data types. In Unicode data, every character is stored as two bytes (Unicode is not the same thing as double-byte characters, which VFP has always supported). By default, VFP retrieves each byte into a memo field as a separate character, producing odd-looking results. For example, assume a SQL Server table Unicodetest has a field named Notes, defined as nVarchar(1000), and you execute this code:

```
SQLEXEC(lnConn, "update unicodetest set notes = 'It looks like this' where
testid = 1")
SQLEXEC(lnConn, "select notes from unicodetest where testid = 1", "tmpResults")
MODIFY MEMO tmpResults.notes
```

The results are shown in **Figure 1**. The square boxes are CHR(0), which is the second byte of each two-byte Unicode character. If you execute SYS(987, .T.) prior to the query, the memo field will contain the ANSI string "It looks like this" instead.

Figure 1. *Remote Unicode data retrieved into a memo field. The square boxes are CHR(0), the second byte of each Unicode character. Use SYS(987, .T.) to convert the Unicode data to ANSI when it is retrieved.*

If you call SYS(987) without the lExpr parameter, it returns the current setting. Once a cursor is opened, changing the SYS(987) setting does not affect future fetches by that cursor. This setting is global to all data sessions.

Determining what connections are open

The new ASQLHANDLES() function provides an often-requested means to determine what statement handles are active. The syntax is:

```
ASQLHANDLES( ArrayName [, nStatementHandle ] )
```

This populates a one-dimensional array with a list of all active SQL statement handles, and returns the number of handles in use. If the array does not exist it is created; if it exists it is redimensioned appropriately. The optional nStatementHandle parameter allows you to supply an existing statement handle. In this case, the array is populated with a list of statement handles that share the same connection handle, including nStatementHandle itself.

This is a welcome addition, because prior versions of VFP don't provide any way to determine what handles are active, or the number of the highest handle in use. You probably have written cleanup code like this to make sure all connections are closed:

```
FOR n = 1 TO 200   && Hopefully high enough
    TRY
        SQLDISCONNECT(n)
    CATCH
    ENDTRY
NEXT
```

ASQLHANDLES() provides a more precise and much faster solution:

```
lnHandles = SQLHANDLES(laHnd)
FOR n = 1 TO lnHandles
    SQLDISCONNECT(laHnd[n])
NEXT
```

ADO enhancements

Prior to VFP 8, many if not most VFP developers avoided using ADO as a data access method, because it required a good deal of coding and because it did not fit into the VFP cursor model. The introduction of the CursorAdapter in VFP 8 made it possible to access ADO data directly using an updatable cursor. VFP 9 provides two more improvements when using ADO.

ADO bookmark support

CURSORGETPROP() supports a new ADOBookmark property that returns the ADO bookmark for the current record in an ADO-based cursor. An ADO bookmark uniquely identifies a single row in a recordset, much like the RECNO() function in a FoxPro cursor. The recordset can be positioned to a specific row by setting its Bookmark property to a previously obtained bookmark. This is particularly useful when saving the current position, executing a Find, and then returning to the previous position:

```
loBookmark = loRs.Bookmark
loRs.Find("country = 'Burkina Faso'")
IF loRs.EOF
   loRs.Bookmark = loBookmark
ENDIF
```

So why would you need to know the ADO bookmark for a record in a cursor if the cursor has its own RECNO() property? When a CursorAdapter uses an ADO recordset as its DataSource, moving the record pointer in the cursor does not move the row pointer in the recordset. If you need to access the row in the recordset that corresponds to the current record in the cursor, the ADOBookmark property provides a convenient way to do this:

```
loBookmark = CURSORGETPROP("ADOBookmark")
loRS.Bookmark = loBookmark
```

Not all databases support bookmarks, and they are usually supported only for keyset, static, and client-side cursors. To determine whether a recordset supports bookmarks, query its Supports method:

```
llBookmarks = loRS.Supports(adBookmark)   && adBookmark = 8192
```

If you call CURSORGETPROP("ADOBookmark") and the recordset does not support bookmarks, you get error 2188 ("Cursor doesn't support ADOBookmark property"). Calling it for a local cursor gives you error 1467 ("Property is invalid for local cursors").

Cancel ADO fetch

You can cancel a lengthy query in a CursorAdapter by pressing Escape, provided you SET ESCAPE ON prior to calling CursorFill or CursorRefresh. In VFP 8, this works for ODBC, XML and Native data sources, but not for ADO. If the DataSourceType is ADO, you must wait until the fetch process is complete, or else take drastic steps like releasing the CursorAdapter in order to cancel a runaway query.

In VFP 9, pressing Escape works with the ADO DataSourceType as well. Although this is a welcome change, you will find pressing Escape may not stop the query right away. That's because there are actually two steps involved in fetching data into a CursorAdapter through ADO. First, VFP tells ADO to execute the query, which brings the data into the ADO recordset. Then VFP converts the data in the recordset into a cursor. You can tell the second step has begun when the cursor name and record count appear on the status bar, if it is turned on. If you press Escape during the first step, the process will not stop until that step is complete, which is usually the longer of the two steps. If you press Escape while the second

ADO-to-cursor step is underway, the fetch stops as soon as the current batch of records (determined by the cursor's BatchSize property) has been retrieved from the recordset.

Allowing the user to cancel the CursorAdapter's fetch is a great idea in development mode, but may not be such a good idea in an application. There appears to be no way to determine whether CursorFill or CursorRefresh completed normally or were cut short by the user pressing Escape. As a result, you have no way to determine whether the result set contains all records matching the query.

The CursorAdapter Builder adds code to the Init method of the CursorAdapter to set the recordset's CursorLocation to 3 (adUseClient). In most cases you can reduce the time needed to open the recordset by changing the CursorLocation to 2 (adUseServer). Not all databases support server-based cursors.

CursorAdapter changes

Prior to VFP 8, we had several powerful technologies for accessing local and remote data: local views, remote views, SQL Pass-Through, ADO recordsets, and XML. Unfortunately, each had a different syntax, and only ADO provided an object-oriented interface. When the CursorAdapter was introduced in VFP 8, it provided a consistent object-oriented interface for accessing data, no matter what the source.

As exciting as it was, the CursorAdapter had some limitations when accessing remote data. If the remote database used identity columns or default values, it was necessary to add custom code to retrieve their values after an Insert. Conflict checking worked automatically if you let VFP generate the insert and update commands, but not if you overrode them. Conflict checking via timestamp fields did not work at all. VFP 9 removes all these limitations and provides several other improvements that make CursorAdapters work more smoothly with remote data.

Conflict checking

If you don't override a CursorAdapter's update or delete commands, the WhereType setting determines how VFP enforces conflict checking. The settings, shown in **Table 2**, are the same as for a remote view.

Table 2. WhereType settings for CursorAdapters and remote views.

Value	Foxpro.H constant	When an update conflict occurs
1	DB_KEY	If a key field has been changed in the local cursor
2	DB_KEYANDUPDATABLE	If any of the fields marked as updatable have been changed in the remote table
3	DB_KEYANDMODIFIED	If any of the fields changed in the local cursor have been changed in the remote table
4	DB_KEYANDTIMESTAMP	If the timestamp in the remote table has changed

VFP constructs the WHERE clause of the auto-generated update or delete statement in a way that ensures the update will succeed only if the WhereType conditions are met. (For a full explanation, see the topic "Managing Updates by Using Views" in Help.)

In a CursorAdapter, you can override the auto-generated commands either by entering your own commands in the UpdateCmd and DeleteCmd properties, or by overriding the

BeforeUpdate and BeforeDelete methods and changing the cUpdateInsertCmd or cDeleteCmd parameters. Once you do this, the WhereType setting is irrelevant, because VFP no longer auto-generates the update and delete commands.

It's unlikely you'll go through the tedious process of creating a WHERE clause that handles all four WhereType conditions. As a substitute, two new properties, ConflictCheckType and ConflictCheckCmd, have been added to simplify this task. (Note that these were new to VFP 8 SP1, not VFP 9.) They are ignored unless you override the auto-generated update or delete commands and set ConflictCheckType to a value other than zero. The five possible settings are shown in **Table 3**.

Table 3. *The possible values for the ConflictCheckType property. Note that, even though the values 1-4 are used, these do not have the same meanings as the corresponding WhereType values.*

ConflictCheckType	Description
0	Do not perform conflict checks.
1	If no records are updated or deleted, generate an error 1585 ("Update conflict...").
2	Verify that no more than one record is affected by an update or delete command. If more than one record is affected, generate error 1495 ('The key defined by the KeyField property for table "*alias*" is not unique.')
3	1 + 2. In other words, make sure one and only one record is affected by the update or delete command.
4	Appends any custom command specified in the ConflictCheckCmd property to the end of the command in the UpdateCmd or DeleteCmd properties.

To understand how these settings work, suppose you override UpdateCmd with this:

```
UPDATE customer SET custname=?cursor1.custname WHERE custid=
   ?cursor1.custid AND custname=?OLDVAL('custname','cursor1')
```

This is similar to the auto-generated code VFP produces with WhereType=3, assuming only the Custname field changed. It succeeds only if VFP finds a record in the remote data source with the same key value in Custid and the previous value of Custname. If another user changed Custname for this same record in the meantime, no records will match and the update fails. Without conflict checking, the update fails, but you do not know it. With ConflictCheckType set to 1, VFP generates a 1585 error because no records are updated in the remote data source.

Now consider the case where you override the Delete command with this:

```
DELETE FROM orders WHERE orderid=?cursor1.orderid
```

The choice of ConflictCheckType depends on how you want to handle two possibilities: another user deleted the order in the meantime, or more than one order has the same Orderid by accident. With ConflictCheckType=1, if another user already deleted the order, you get an error and the update fails. However, if more than one order has the same Orderid, the update succeeds and all matching orders are deleted. With ConflictCheckType=2, you don't get an error if another user already deleted the order, but you get an error if more than one order has this Orderid. With ConflictCheckType=3, you get an error in either case.

There are a couple situations where conflict checking may not give you the results you expect. First, the UpdateCmd and DeleteCmd properties can contain more than one command. In this case, conflict checking is only based on the number of records affected by the last command.

Also, if the CursorAdapter's BatchUpdateCount is set to a number greater than 1 (the default), ConflictCheckType settings of 1, 2, and 3 are ignored. When BatchUpdateCount is set to the default of 1 and table buffering is in effect, VFP sends a separate SQL command to the remote data source for each updated or deleted record in the cursor. If BatchUpdateCount is set to a number greater than 1, VFP concatenates multiple update or delete commands into a single string, separated by semicolons. The string is sent to the remote data source as a single SQL command, in order to increase efficiency. In this case, there is no way to know the number of records affected by each individual command in the concatenated string, so conflict checks based on the number of records affected do not work.

The Advanced Update Properties dialog of the CursorAdapter Builder has a new Conflict page (see **Figure 2**) that lets you select the ConflictCheckType and, optionally, enter a ConflictCheckCmd if the ConflictCheckType is set to 4.

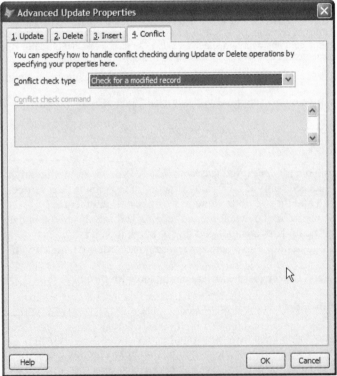

Figure 2. The CursorAdapter Builder has a new Conflict page that lets you select the value for the ConflictCheckType property and, optionally, enter the ConflictCheckCmd when ConflictCheckType is set to 4, "Check based on a custom command."

Auto-refresh

When a record is inserted or updated in a remote database, the remote database may change the contents of one or more columns based on autoincrement values, default values, or the results of triggers. When a CursorAdapter sends an insert or update command to a remote database, it only receives back a result code and/or error message. As a result, the CursorAdapter is not aware of changes made by the remote database, and the VFP cursor will not reflect those new values. In VFP 8, one workaround was to add code to the CursorAdapter AfterUpdate or AfterInsert methods to retrieve the new values and insert them into the cursor (this example assumes the DataSourceType is ODBC):

```
* Retrieve autoincrement value from SQL Server after an insert
SQLEXEC(this.Datasource, "select @@identity as keyval", "tmpKey")
REPLACE custid WITH tmpKey.keyval in (this.alias)
```

VFP 9 introduces six new CursorAdapter properties to automate this process. InsertCmdRefreshFieldList is a comma-delimited list of fields in the cursor that are refreshed automatically with values from the remote database when an insert is performed. InsertCmdRefreshKeyFieldList is the name of the key field used to query for these values. Immediately after a successful insert, VFP automatically queries the remote database for a record matching the key values in InsertCmdRefreshKeyFieldList and uses the results to refresh the cursor fields specified in InsertCmdRefreshFieldList.

In many cases those two properties are sufficient, but in other situations you must supply the command VFP uses for this query. The most common example is when the key field in the remote table is an Autoincrement column. In this case, VFP cannot perform an automatic auto-refresh query after the insert, because it does not know the key value the remote database just generated and inserted. Instead, you must supply a SQL command in the InsertCmdRefreshCmd property VFP can use to retrieve values from the new record. For example, assume a SQL Server table has an Autoincrement primary key column Custid and supplies a default value for the Dateadded column. The following property settings enable VFP to retrieve the new values for Custid and Dateadded after a successful insert:

```
.InsertCmdRefreshFieldList = "custid,dateadded"
.InsertCmdRefreshCmd="select custid,dateadded from customer where custid =
@@IDENTITY"
```

An experienced SQL Server developer might question why @@IDENTITY is used to retrieve the new Autoincrement value rather than SCOPE_IDENTITY(). Usually, SCOPE_IDENTITY() is indeed the better choice because of a limitation of @@IDENTITY. The @@IDENTITY function returns the last Autoincrement value generated on the current connection. If the table you are inserting a record into has a trigger that inserts a record in a second table, and the second table also has an Autoincrement column, @@IDENTITY will return the Autoincrement value from the second table, which is not what you want. The SCOPE_IDENTITY() function returns the last Autoincrement value from the "scope" of your command, which by definition does not include the actions of the trigger. Unfortunately, the SQL Server ODBC driver executes parameterized inserts using the sp_executesql stored procedure. Once this stored procedure is completed, its "scope" is gone, and SCOPE_IDENTITY() returns NULL rather than the Autoincrement value from the insert.

Because @@IDENTITY simply returns the last Autoincrement value on the connection, it works in an auto-refresh command.

The properties UpdateCmdRefreshFieldList, UpdateCmdRefreshKeyFieldList, and UpdateCmdRefreshCmd serve the same purpose for updates. Usually when performing an update, VFP already knows the key value, so a separate UpdateCmdRefreshCmd is not needed. One case where it is useful is for a database designed to only be accessed by stored procedures. You need to supply a stored procedure call in UpdateCmdRefreshCmd to return the values needed to refresh the cursor.

The CursorAdapter Builder has a new Refresh button on the Auto-Update page that brings up a Refresh Properties dialog (see **Figure 3**). The Refresh After Insert page allows you to enter the InsertCmdRefreshCmd and to select fields for the InsertCmdRefreshFieldList and the InsertCmdRefreshKeyFieldList. The Refresh After Update page allows you to enter the UpdateCmdRefreshCmd and to select fields for the UpdateCmdRefreshFieldList and the UpdateCmdRefreshKeyFieldList.

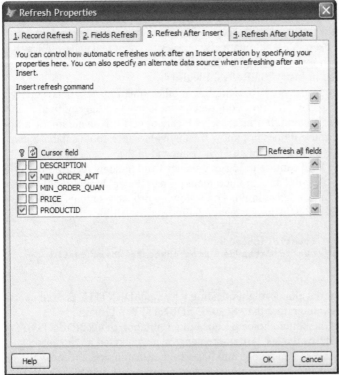

Figure 3. *The CursorAdapter Builder has a new Refresh Properties dialog that lets you set values for the auto-refresh properties, using pages 3 and 4. This dialog is accessed by clicking the Refresh button on the Auto-Update page.*

*The Developer Download files for this chapter, available at
www.hentzenwerke.com, include four forms, a database, and a readme file
that demonstrate how auto-refresh works. Autorefresh_sql.SCX,
Autorefresh_connect.SCX, and Autorefresh_add.SCX create a new table in
the SQL Server Northwind database and use that. Autorefresh_vfp.SCX and
Autorefresh_add.SCX use two tables, Autorefresh.DBF and Nextid.DBF, in
the Autorefresh.DBC database. The file Readme_autorefresh_sql.TXT
explains how the SQL demo works and what permissions may be required.*

Timestamp support

When you create a remote view with the WhereType property set to 4 (Key and timestamp),
VFP automatically determines which field in the remote table is timestamp-compatible and
saves this information in the view definition. When a record in the view is changed and
updated, VFP compares the value of the timestamp column in the cursor to the value of the
timestamp column in the remote database. If they are different, error 1585 ("Update
conflict...") results.

In VFP 8, the CursorAdapter allows you to set WhereType to 4, but does not have the
capability to determine which column in the remote table was a timestamp. As a result,
WhereType=4 does not work in CursorAdapters in VFP 8.

The new TimeStampFieldList property allows you to specify which field in the cursor is
considered a timestamp for conflict checking when WhereType is 4. If you set WhereType to
4, but do not supply a TimeStampFieldList value, conflict checking is not performed. The
timestamp field name must also be included in the UpdateNameList.

The RefreshTimeStamp property can be used to indicate which timestamp fields are
refreshed automatically when performing an insert or update. This has the same effect as
including these fields in the InsertCmdRefreshFieldList and UpdateCmdRefreshFieldList, and
is not necessary if you have done so.

The CursorAdapter Builder has a new **Timestamp fields** textbox on the Auto-Update
page that allows you to set the TimeStampFieldList property. It also has a **Refresh
timestamp** checkbox on the Fields Refresh page of the new Refresh Properties dialog (see
Figure 3) that allows you to set the RefreshTimeStamp property.

On-demand record refresh

A RecordRefresh method has been added to the CursorAdapter to perform the same function
REFRESH() performs for views. The syntax is:

```
.RecordRefresh( [ nRecords ] [, nRecordOffset ] )
```

The nRecords parameter specifies the number of records to refresh, in physical order. If it
is omitted, only the current record is refreshed. The nRecordOffset parameter specifies the
number of records prior to the current record where the refresh begins. If it is 0 or omitted,
refresh begins with the current record. For example, if you pass (2,3) for the parameters, two
records are refreshed, beginning with the 3rd record prior to the current record. If you pass
(3,0), three records are refreshed beginning with the current record.

The return value is the number of records refreshed. If no records are refreshed but there
is no error, 0 is returned. If there is an error, RecordRefresh returns -1 less the number of

records successfully refreshed. For example, if 3 records are refreshed before the error occurs, -4 is returned; if no records are refreshed but there is an error, -1 is returned.

If you inserted records into a cursor with table buffering on, but did not update them via TABLEUPDATE(), they are ignored and not counted in the return value. If you modified a record, the buffered changes are preserved and only the CURVAL() values are refreshed. If the target record in the cursor cannot be located in the local or remote table(s), it is marked Deleted. This is based on the assumption the record must have been deleted from the remote table after it was retrieved into the cursor. In view of this, it is important to make sure you specify a valid KeyFieldList before calling RecordRefresh, to avoid accidentally deleting records.

The RefreshIgnoreFieldList property is a comma-delimited list of fields to ignore when refreshing. BeforeRecordRefresh(nRecords, nRecordOffset) receives the same two parameters passed to RecordRefresh. If it fails or returns .F., RecordRefresh isn't executed. AfterRecordRefresh(nRecords, nRecordOffset, nRefreshed) receives the two parameters passed to RecordRefresh, plus a third parameter nRefreshed that is the return value from RecordRefresh.

The RefreshCmd property allows you specify an alternative to the automatically generated refresh command. The command must return a single record with fields in the same order as those in the cursor, excluding any fields in the RefreshIgnoreFieldList. RefreshCmdDataSourceType and RefreshCmdDataSource allow you to specify an alternative data source type and command for the RefreshCmd. RefreshAlias contains the name of the read-only cursor opened temporarily by VFP during a RecordRefresh to hold the data retrieved from the data source.

Here's an example using the SQL Server Northwind database. It creates a CursorAdapter and sets the properties needed for RecordRefresh, opens a connection to the database, and fills the cursor. It then changes the company name in the remote database and calls RecordRefresh to refresh five records in the cursor.

```
PUBLIC goCA
LOCAL lcConnStr, lnConn
*-- You may need to adjust the Server name:
lcConnStr = "driver={sql server};server=(local);database=northwind;" ;
  + "Trusted_Connection=yes;"

goCA = CREATEOBJECT("CursorAdapter")
WITH goCA
  .ALIAS = [cursor1]
  .DATASOURCETYPE = [ODBC]
  .SELECTCMD = [select CustomerID, CompanyName, Country, Fax,] ;
    + [Phone from Customers]
  .CURSORSCHEMA = [CustomerID C(5), CompanyName C(40), Country C(15),] ;
    + [ Fax C(24), Phone C(24)]
  .KEYFIELDLIST = [CustomerID]
  .TABLES = [Customers]
  .UPDATABLEFIELDLIST = [CustomerID, CompanyName, Country, Fax, Phone]
  .UPDATENAMELIST = [CustomerID Customers.CustomerID, CompanyName ] ;
    + [Customers.CompanyName, Country Customers.Country, Fax Customers.Fax,] ;
    + [Phone Customers.Phone]
  .USECURSORSCHEMA = .T.
  .SENDUPDATES = .F.
  .REFRESHCMD = [select CompanyName, UPPER(Country), Fax, Phone from ] ;
    +[Customers where CustomerID = ?EVAL(this.RefreshAlias + ".CustomerID")]
```

```
   .REFRESHCMDDATASOURCETYPE = [ODBC]
   .REFRESHIGNOREFIELDLIST = [CustomerID]
ENDWITH

*--   Open a shared connection to the database
CLEAR
? "Attempting to connect to the SQL Server Northwind database"
lnConn = SQLSTRINGCONNECT(lcConnStr, .T.)
IF goCA.DATASOURCE < 1
  MESSAGEBOX(MESSAGE())
  RELEASE goCA
  RETURN
ENDIF
*--   Set the DataSource and the RefreshCmdDataSource to this connection
goCA.DATASOURCE = lnConn
goCA.RefreshCmdDataSource = lnConn
*--   Fill the cursor and browse it
IF ! goCA.CURSORFILL()
  MESSAGEBOX(MESSAGE())
  RELEASE goCA
  RETURN
ENDIF
SELECT cursor1
BROWSE NOWAIT

*--   Put "*" on the end of each company's name in the remote database.
SQLEXEC(lnConn, "UPDATE customers SET CompanyName = " ;
  + "LEFT(RTRIM(CompanyName)+'*',40)")

*--   Move to record 10 and call RefreshRecord to refresh
*   the current record and the 4 previous records
GO 10
MESSAGEBOX("Press OK to see the refreshed CompanyName for rows 6-10", ;
  48, "About to refresh")
goCA.RECORDREFRESH(5,4)

*--   Remove the "*" from each customer
SQLEXEC(lnConn, "UPDATE customers SET CompanyName = " ;
  + "REPLACE(CompanyName, '*', '')")
SQLDISCONNECT(lnConn)
```

There are several things to note in this example. The RefreshIgnoreFieldList includes CustomerID because it's the primary key and cannot change on an existing record, so there is no reason to retrieve it. As a result, CustomerID is not included in the RefreshCmd, whose field list must match the field list in the SelectCmd in order, excluding any fields in the RefreshIgnoreFieldList Property. The RefreshCmd selects UPPER(Country) so we can see it works; in most cases you would not want to do this. It isn't really necessary to set the RefreshCmd here, because the CursorAdapter would accomplish the same thing by default. The RefreshCmdDataSourceType and RefreshCmdDataSource properties are shown for illustration purposes, but do not have to be specified if they are the same as the DataSourceType and DataSource.

The Developer Download files for this chapter, available at
www.hentzenwerke.com, include this code as RecordRefresh_Sql.PRG.
They also include a companion program, RecordRefresh_Vfp.PRG, that
uses the VFP Tastrade database and does not require SQL Server.

The CursorAdapter Builder's new Refresh Properties dialog (see Figure 3) provides a place to set these record refresh properties. The Record Refresh page allows you to enter the RefreshCmd, to select the RefreshCmdDataSourceType, and to specify the RefreshCmdDataSource. The Fields Refresh page allows you to select fields for the RefreshIgnoreFieldList. Be aware that the fields you pick on this page are the ignored fields, not the refreshed fields.

In VFP 8, calling REFRESH() on a cursor opened by a CursorAdapter not only does not work, but generates an error. This is because the CursorAdapter does not set certain properties of the cursor such as Tables, KeyFieldList, and UpdatableFieldList needed for the REFRESH() function. In VFP 9, this is fixed; if REFRESH() is called for a cursor opened by a CursorAdapter, VFP actually calls the RecordRefresh method of the CursorAdapter instead.

Set default values for CursorFill

The CursorFill method of the CursorAdapter includes the parameters lUseCursorSchema and lNoData, which are .F. by default. In VFP 8, if you want to change either of these to .T. you must override the CursorFill method. This is particularly annoying in the case of lNoData that you often need to override as follows:

```
LPARAMETERS luseCursorSchema, lNoData, nOptions, Source
RETURN DODEFAULT(luseCursorSchema, .T., nOptions, Source)
```

VFP 9 adds two new properties to CursorAdapter, UseCursorSchema and NoData. These are used as the default values for the CursorFill parameters lUseCursorSchema and lNoData, so you no longer need to override that method to change this behavior. If you do pass values for the lUseCursorSchema and lNoData parameters when you call CursorFill, the UseCursorSchema and NoData properties are ignored.

The CursorAdapter Builder has a new checkbox in the Schema section of the Data Access page, Use CursorSchema when filling cursor, to set the UseCursorSchema property. The Data fetching section of the same page has a new checkbox, Initially open with no data, to set the value of the NoData property.

Delayed memo fetch

In VFP 8, delayed memo fetching did not work in CursorAdapters. If the FetchMemo property was set to .F., the cursor was retrieved without the memo contents as expected. However, if you attempted to access the memo field, you received an error 1491 ("No update tables are specified. Use the Tables property of the cursor."). VFP 9 fixes this and the contents of the memo field are retrieved as soon as you attempt to access it.

In addition, VFP 9 provides a way for you to override delayed memo fetching. DelayedMemoFetch(cMemoName) is a protected method called when you try to access the contents of a memo, general, or blob field not fetched yet. If you override this method, your code must return text for VFP to put into the memo field in the cursor. In the case of a blob field, DelayedMemoFetch must return blob data rather than text by using the CAST() function:

```
RETURN CAST(DODEFAULT(cFieldName) as W)
```

You might need to override delayed memo fetching to format or clean up the memo data before displaying it in VFP, to retrieve the contents from an alternate source, or if a stored procedure must be called to retrieve it. The FetchMemoDataSourceType and FetchMemoDataSource properties allow you to specify an alternative data source for DelayedMemoFetch.

When DelayedMemoFetch is called, a copy of the local cursor is opened temporarily, positioned on the current record. The name of this temporary cursor is found in the RefreshAlias property. The cursor referenced by RefreshAlias contains the original values of each field; the cursor referenced by Alias contains buffered changes. Neither of these cursors contain the actual contents of the memo field yet.

Because DelayedMemoFetch is a protected method, it can not be called from outside the class. In fact, it is not meant to be called directly at all. Calling it from another method in the class generates an error 2077 ("Operation is not allowed for CursorAdapter at this time.").

The FetchMemoCmdList property provides another way to override delayed memo fetching. It is a comma-delimited list containing memo field names and the corresponding commands to retrieve the memo field contents. The commands must be placed in angle brackets. For example:

```
.FetchMemoCmdList = "notes <select notes from customer where custid =
    ?EVAL(this.refreshalias + '.custid')>, followup <select followup from
    customer where custid = ?EVAL(this.refreshalias + '.custid')>"
```

FetchMemoCmdList is ignored if the FetchMemoDataSourceType is ADO.

The CursorAdapter Builder has a new Memo button in the Data fetching section of the Data Access page. This brings up a Memo Fetching Properties dialog (see **Figure 4**) that allows you to enter values for the FetchMemoCmdList, FetchMemoDataSourceType, and FetchMemoDataSource.

Disable automatic transactions

By default, the CursorAdapter tells ODBC and ADO to manage transactions automatically during Insert, Update, and Delete operations. In VFP 8, if you turn on manual transactions for a CursorAdapter's cursor, VFP still tells ADO or ODBC to use automatic transaction handling as well.

VFP 9 adds a UseTransactions property to the CursorAdapter. When .T. (the default), VFP tells ADO and ODBC to use automatic transaction handling, as in VFP 8. When .F., automatic transaction handling is disabled, allowing you to use manual transactions without any undesired interaction with automatic transactions. The Auto-Update page of the CursorAdapter Builder has a new Use transactions checkbox to set the UseTransactions property.

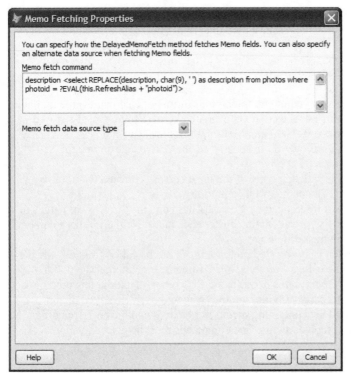

Figure 4. The CursorAdapter Builder has a new Memo Fetching Properties dialog that lets you set values for FetchMemoCmdList, FetchMemoDataSourceType, and FetchMemoDataSource. This dialog is accessed by clicking the Memo button on the Data Access page.

Specify code page for XML data

The CursorAdapter Flags property now supports a value of 32768. The Flags property only applies when the DataSourceType property is "XML," and is passed when constructing an XML UpdateGram. The 32768 value indicates a code page should be used. For more information on the effect of this setting, see the "Multi-language support" section in Chapter 10, "Managing XML."

CHECK constraints and default values for all data sources

The CursorSchema property of a CursorAdapter defines the structure of its cursor. While you may primarily think of a cursor's schema as defining field names and data types, the CREATE CURSOR command also supports CHECK constraints (field and record validation rules) and default values. Although it was undocumented, in VFP 8, you could include CHECK constraints and default values in the CursorSchema property:

```
loCursorAdapter.CursorSchema = "CUSTID I, NAME C(40) CHECK !EMPTY(name)
ERROR 'You must enter the customer name', STREET C(40), POBOX C(40),
CITY C(25), STATE C(2) DEFAULT 'CO', ZIP C(9), CHECK ! (EMPTY(street)
and EMPTY(pobox)) ERROR 'You must enter either a street or PO Box'"
```

However, these CHECK constraints and default values were only enforced if the DataSourceType was "XML." VFP 9 enforces constraints and default values for all four data source types (Native, ODBC, ADO, and XML).

If you create CHECK constraints or default values in the local or remote table, the CursorAdapter Builder does not automatically add them to the CursorSchema when you click the Build button on the Schema section of the Data Access page. You must edit the CursorSchema property and add them manually, or set them programmatically before calling CursorFill. Note that any NULL constraints you add to the CursorSchema are ignored, and the NULL constraints from the actual local or remote table are used instead.

MapBinary and MapVarchar

The MapBinary and MapVarchar properties determine whether certain ADO and ODBC data types map by default to the new VFP 9 Blob, Varbinary, and Varchar types in CursorAdapters. **Table 4** shows the default mapping behavior for the MapBinary property setting and **Table 5** shows the default mapping behavior for the MapVarchar property setting.

These two properties are ignored if UseCursorSchema is set to .T. or if the lUseCursorSchema parameter passed to CursorFill is .T.; in that case the type conversion defined in CursorSchema is used. The CursorAdapter Builder has two new checkboxes on the Data Access page, Map Varchar and Map Binary, to set these properties. However, the CursorAdapter Builder itself ignores these property settings and builds the CursorSchema as if both were set to .F. The SET VARCHARMAPPING setting is ignored by CursorAdapters.

Table 4. Effect of the MapBinary property setting on default mapping of remote data types to VFP data types in CursorAdapters.

Data source	Remote data type	MapBinary = .T.	MapBinary = .F.
ODBC	SQL_LONGVARBINARY	Blob	Memo (binary)
ODBC	SQL_BINARY (precision <= 254)	Varbinary	Memo (binary)
ODBC	SQL_BINARY (precision > 254)	Blob	Memo (binary)
ODBC	SQL_VARBINARY (precision <= 254)	Varbinary	Memo (binary)
ODBC	SQL_VARBINARY (precision > 254)	Blob	Memo (binary)
ADO	adVarBinary (precision <= 254)	Varbinary	Memo (binary)
ADO	adVarBinary (precision > 254)	Blob	Memo (binary)
ADO	adBinary (precision <= 254)	Varbinary	Memo (binary)
ADO	adBinary (precision > 254)	Blob	Memo (binary)

Table 5. Effect of the MapVarchar property setting on default mapping of remote data types to VFP data types in CursorAdapters.

Data source	Remote data type	MapVarchar = .T.	MapVarchar = .F.
ODBC	SQL_WVARCHAR (precision <= 254)	Varchar	Character
ODBC	SQL_WVARCHAR (precision > 254)	Memo	Memo
ADO	adVarChar (precision <= 254)	Varchar	Character
ADO	adVarChar (precision > 254)	Memo	Memo

Logical data type conversions

VFP 9 allows greater flexibility when mapping between remote data types and the VFP Logical data type in CursorAdapters and remote views. Previously, you could only map the remote data type Bit to a VFP Logical field. This caused problems if the remote database did not support the Bit data type (like Oracle), or if the database designer chose to store logical data as 1 and 0 in an integer or numeric column.

In VFP 9, you can map the ODBC and ADO data types listed in **Table 6** to the VFP Logical data type. Numeric and decimal types can be mapped to VFP Logical only if the scale is zero.

Table 6. ODBC and ADO data types that can be mapped to the VFP logical data type in VFP 9.

ODBC data types	ADO data types
SQL_TINYINT	adSingle
SQL_SMALLINT	adTinyInt
SQL_INTEGER	adSmallInt
SQL_BIGINT	adInteger
SQL_DECIMAL	adBigInt
SQL_NUMERIC	adUnsignedTinyInt
	adUnsignedSmallInt
	adDecimal
	adNumeric

When VFP retrieves data from the remote data source, it considers 0 to be .F. and all other values to be .T. When updates are sent to the remote database, the conversion is backend specific as determined by the ODBC driver, although in most cases .F. is mapped to 0 and .T. to 1.

Increased size of property values

In VFP 9, the Property Sheet can accept up to 8,191 characters for a property value; previously this limit was 255 (see the "Specifying property values" section in Chapter 2, "Controlling the Properties Window"). The previous limit caused problems with CursorAdapters, because many of the properties need to be more than 255 characters. To work around this, in VFP 8 the CursorAdapter Builder inserted code into the Init method to set the values of certain properties programatically (the 255 character limit only applied when setting property values in the Property Sheet). Unfortunately, the CursorAdapter Builder did not do this in the case of CursorSchema. As a result, if you tried to close the Builder with a large number of fields selected, you received the error message "The CursorSchema property must be no longer than 255 characters."

With the Property Sheet limit increased substantially, you no longer receive the CursorSchema error message. In addition, the CursorAdapter Builder now sets the values of most properties directly in the Property Sheet rather than inserting code into the Init method.

VFP OLE DB enhancements

The VFP OLE DB provider was introduced in VFP 7 because Microsoft was shifting emphasis from ODBC to OLE DB as its primary data access model. It has become much more important since then, because Microsoft has made it clear the VFP ODBC provider will not be updated to handle new database features introduced in VFP 7, 8, and 9 such as database events and Autoincrement, Varchar, Binary, and Blob fields. If your database contains any of these newer features, attempting to access it via ODBC will produce the error "File was created in a later version of Visual FoxPro than the current version."

Fortunately, the VFP OLE DB provider has been updated in both VFP 8 and 9 to handle all these new features, making it the preferred means to provide other applications access to your databases. In addition, VFP 9 introduces a few other improvements that make the OLE DB provider even more powerful.

XML support

The VFP 9 OLE DB provider now supports the CURSORTOXML(), XMLTOCURSOR(), and XMLUPDATEGRAM() functions, with one limitation. In an application, the _VFP.VFPXMLProgID property can be set to the name of a COM component that overrides the internal functionality for these functions. The OLE DB provider does not support the _VFP system variable, so there is no way to override the internal functions.

EXECSCRIPT() support

The EXECSCRIPT() function is now supported in the VFP OLE DB provider, but of course generates an error if you attempt to execute lines of code not allowed in the provider. For a complete list of these, see the Help topic "Unsupported Visual FoxPro Commands and Functions in OLE DB Provider."

Return ADO recordset from a stored procedure

In VFP 7 and 8, the OLE DB provider could only return an ADO recordset to another application based on a SQL command passed in from that application. While another application could call a stored procedure in your VFP database, the stored procedure could not return the results in the form of a recordset. Instead, it returned an ADO recordset with a single row containing a single column named Return_value. That column contained whatever scalar value the stored procedure returned via a RETURN statement, or True if the stored procedure did not contain an explicit return value. The most common use of stored procedures in SQL databases is to return result sets, so this seriously limited the usefulness of VFP stored procedures when called from OLE DB enabled applications

The VFP 9 OLE DB provider includes a major enhancement, the ability to return ADO recordsets from stored procedures. The new SETRESULTSET(nWorkArea | cTableAlias) function allows you to mark an open cursor in a stored procedure as a result set. If the stored procedure is called using the VFP OLE DB provider, the marked cursor is returned in the form of an ADO recordset. If SETRESULTSET() is called more than once during a stored procedure, each time it is called it returns the work area number of the previously marked cursor, and then marks the new cursor as the result set. Only one cursor can be marked as the result set at a time, which means a VFP stored procedure can only return a single recordset.

Calling SETRESULTSET() with an invalid alias produces an error 11 ("Function argument value, type, or count is invalid"). Calling it with an empty work area number does not produce an error. If no cursor is marked, or if the marked cursor is closed before the stored procedure ends, a recordset with one row and one column named Return_value is returned, similar to the pre-VFP 9 behavior. If the stored procedure is called directly from VFP, marking of result sets is ignored.

CLEARRESULTSET() clears the marked cursor and returns its work area. If no cursor is currently marked, it returns 0. GETRESULTSET() returns the work area number of the marked cursor, or 0 if no cursor is currently marked as the result set. All three functions are scoped to the current DataSession.

 The Developer Download files for this chapter, available at ***www.hentzenwerke.com****, include a form (Recordset.SCX) and a database (Recordset.DBC) that demonstrates how to return an ADO recordset from a VFP stored procedure. The Help button on the form explains how it works.*

Summary
In VFP 8, the CursorAdapter had a few missing features that made it difficult to use in certain situations. VFP 9 not only fixes those problems, but it also gives the CursorAdapter additional features that now make it the ideal method for remote data access in VFP. The other new remote data features in VFP 9 are icing on the cake for the best data-centric language there is.

Updates and corrections for this chapter can be found on Hentzenwerke's website, **www.hentzenwerke.com**. Click "Catalog" and navigate to the page for this book.

Chapter 12
Other Data Changes

VFP has the fastest database engine of all desktop application databases. As Microsoft enhances other areas of the product, it makes sense they would also enhance the database engine. This chapter outlines some miscellaneous data changes included in VFP 9.

Transaction support

One major enhancement in VFP 9 is the support of transactions for free tables and cursors (created with CREATE CURSOR). Two new functions were added for this purpose, MAKETRANSACTABLE() and ISTRANSACTABLE(). MAKETRANSACTABLE() accepts a work area number or alias as a parameter and returns a logical value indicating whether transactions are supported for the table or cursor. Once transactions are turned on, use BEGIN TRANSACTION, END TRANSACTION, and ROLLBACK to manage the transactions for the free table or cursor in the same way they work with DBC-bound tables and views.

MAKETRANSACTABLE() turns on transactions for all aliases of a table in the current data session. If the table or cursor is open in another data session when MAKETRANSACTABLE() is executed, the error 2191, "File is in use in another data session," occurs. Therefore, transactions must be enabled the first time a table or cursor is opened if it is to be opened in multiple data sessions. Once transactions are activated for a table, all subsequent calls to MAKETRANSACTABLE() does not generate an error, but it will not do anything because transactions are already enabled.

Transactions on free tables and cursors are only supported when using row buffering. If the table or cursor is table buffered when issuing MAKETRANSACTABLE(), the error 1579, "Command cannot be issued on a table with cursors in table buffering mode," occurs.

There is no way to turn off transactions for free tables or cursors once activated without closing the table in all data sessions where it is open. The program code in **Listing 3** (in the "AUSED()" section) might be helpful in doing this.

The ISTRANSACTABLE() function returns a logical value indicating whether or not the alias supports transactions. Pass the work area number or alias to this function. This function works for all open aliases, not just free tables. It always returns .T. for tables contained in a database container.

These new functions are supported through the VFP OLEDB provider in addition to the VFP development environment and runtime.

BLANKing data

The BLANK command is used to clear out the data in some or all fields in the currently selected record. This command has been enhanced to allow for resetting fields to their default value as specified in the database container rather than to an empty value. Two new optional arguments have been added for this feature, DEFAULT and AUTOINC. The new syntax for this command is:

```
BLANK [FIELDS FieldList] [DEFAULT [AUTOINC]] [Scope] [FOR lExpression1]

   [WHILE lExpression2] [NOOPTIMIZE] [IN nWorkArea | cTableAlias]
```

The DEFAULT clause indicates the fields should be initialized to the default value defined in the DBC. It applies to the fields list in the FieldList argument or all fields if the FieldList argument is absent. The DEFAULT clause alone will not reset autoincrementing fields to their default value. In order to reset autoincrementing the AUTOINC clause must be included in addition to the DEFAULT clause. This forces autoincrementing fields to be initialized to the next available value. **Listing 1** below shows an example using the new clauses on the BLANK command.

 *The Developer Download files, available at **www.hentzenwerke.com**, include the database, Chapter12.dbc, table Names.dbf, and program BlankExample.PRG.*

***Listing 1**. Blank fields and reset generated fields to their Default value.*

```
SET MULTILOCKS ON
USE Names
INSERT INTO Names ;
     (cName) ;
VALUES ;
     ([Tom])

INSERT INTO Names ;
     (cName, dAdded) ;
VALUES ;
     ([Mary], DATE(2004,12,31))

BROWSE
BLANK DEFAULT AUTOINC
BROWSE
```

Because the autoincrementing fields must lock the table header, SET MULTILOCKS must be on if the table is opened SHARED. If SET MULTILOCKS is OFF, error 2183, "Operation requires that SET MULTILOCKS is set to ON," is thrown. In addition, the DEFAULT clause can be used without the AUTOINC clause, but AUTOINC requires DEFAULT.

The last generated value

VFP 8 introduced autoincrementing fields. However, if you work with local views or remote views of VFP tables, there is no way to know the last value generated until the data is saved and the view requeried. VFP 9 includes a new function, GETAUTOINCVALUE(), to return the last value generated for an autoincrement field. The syntax for this new function is:

```
GETAUTOINCVALUE( [ nDataSessionNumber | 0 ] )
```

You can pass a data session number to the function if the incremented value is in a different data session from the current one. If no value is passed, the current data session is assumed. Passing a value of zero returns the last incremented value within the currently executing program, procedure, method, or function rather than the data session. **Listing 2** demonstrates using the new GETAUTOINCVALUE() function.

 The program GetLastValue.PRG and supporting files are included with the Developer Download files for this chapter, available at ***www.hentzenwerke.com****.*

Listing 2*. Use GetAutoIncValue to retrieve the last value generated for a parent view in order to populate the foreign key for a child view.*

```
LOCAL ;
    liParentId AS Integer, ;
    llEndTrans AS Boolean

llEndTrans = .F.
CLOSE ALL
SET MULTILOCKS ON
OPEN DATABASE Chapter12
USE NamesView NODATA
CURSORSETPROP("Buffering", 3)
SELECT 0
USE ChildView NODATA
CURSORSETPROP("Buffering", 5)
INSERT INTO NamesView ;
    (cName) ;
VALUES ;
    ([Dee])

INSERT INTO ChildView ;
    (cChildName) ;
VALUES ;
    ([Tiffani])

INSERT INTO ChildView ;
    (cChildName) ;
VALUES ;
    ([Erika])

BEGIN TRANSACTION

IF TABLEUPDATE(0,.F.,"NamesView")
    liParentId = GETAUTOINCVALUE()

    IF NOT ISNULL(liParentId)
        REPLACE ALL iParentId WITH liParentId IN ChildView
        llEndTrans = TABLEUPDATE(1, .F., "ChildView")
    ENDIF

ENDIF

IF llEndTrans
    END TRANSACTION
```

```
ELSE
     ROLLBACK
ENDIF

SELECT NAMES
BROWSE
SELECT Children
BROWSE
```

REFRESHing your data

The SET REFRESH command controls how often VFP data stored in buffers is updated based on the physical data. It does so in two ways. First, it controls how often a BROWSE, EDIT, or CHANGE window is updated with current data. Secondly, it controls how often the local workstation buffers are updated with current data changes. Prior to VFP 9, the number of seconds ranged from 0 to 3600 but could only be whole numbers. VFP 9 changes this limitation for the second clause on the SET REFRESH command, the one that controls buffer updates. This value can now range between .001 and 3600 seconds and does not have to be a whole number. In addition, use -1 to specify always reading data from disk and never buffered. Keep in mind that a lower setting can reduce the overall performance of the application.

Because the SET REFRESH clauses changed, the VFP development environment has also changed to support this new clause.

Figure 1 shows the Data page of the Options dialog. You will notice the **Table refresh interval** setting now allows fractional values.

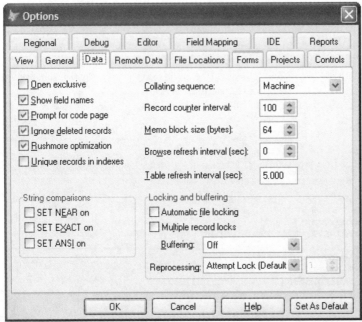

Figure 1. Table refresh interval, specified in seconds, now supports decimal values.

In addition to the changes to SET REFRESH, the CURSORSETPROP() function now includes a Refresh property. This property allows you to establish different refresh settings for each open cursor or for all newly opened cursors within a data session. The syntax for CURSORSETPROP() is:

```
CURSORSETPROP( cProperty [, eExpression ] [, cTableAlias | nWorkArea ] )
```

If the work area parameter is passed, the function changes the refresh value just for the specified cursor. If the last parameter is 0, the refresh rate for the existing cursors in the data session do not change, but all newly opened cursors use the new refresh rate.

The default value for the Refresh property is -2. This value indicates the cursor should refresh at the rate specified by the SET REFRESH command. Similarly, if SET REFRESH is 0, the refresh setting of CURSORSETPROP() is disregarded. This is because SET REFRESH TO 0 indicates the data in the buffers is always used and not updated by the physical data.

Flushing your data

The FLUSH command has been enhanced for VFP 9. Prior to this version of VFP, the FLUSH command had no clauses. When FLUSH was issued, VFP would flush the buffers at the next convenient time. Now, there are two clauses on the FLUSH command.

```
FLUSH [ [ IN nWorkArea | cTableAlias ] | [ cFileSpec ] ] [ FORCE ]
```

The first clause specifies the work area or alias for the cursor to be flushed. Additionally, this clause can be the name of an individual file to flush, such as an index (CDX file). It can also include files open with low-level file functions.

The second clause FORCE passes the flush call to the Windows FlushFileBuffers() function in order to have the flush happen at once. Temporary files and ReadOnly files are not flushed using this option because there cannot be local changes to these files.

If no clauses are included on the command, VFP flushes the contents of all tables, memos, and indexes in the current data session as soon as possible.

The FFLUSH() function also has a new parameter.

```
FFLUSH( nFileHandle [, lForce ] )
```

Passing .T. for the lForce parameter tells VFP to flush the file immediately using the Windows API. This is the same behavior as the FORCE option on the FLUSH command.

AUSED()

AUSED() is improved for VFP 9. An optional third parameter was added to specify the array only include rows for aliases of a specified table or view.

Before the addition of the cTableName parameter, the current datasession was assumed when the nDataSessionNumber parameter was omitted. In order to specify the current datasession and also specify the cTableName parameter, pass .NULL. for the nDataSessionNumber parameter.

The new syntax for AUSED() is:

```
AUSED( ArrayName [, nDataSessionNumber [, cTableName ] ] )
```

The new parameter, cTableName, can be in one of several formats:

- DBC!Table
- DBC!View
- Path\DatabaseName!TableName
- Path\DatabaseName!ViewName
- Table – In the current DBC
- View – In the current DBC
- Table (with Path if necessary)

This parameter could prove useful when you need to close all open instances of a table so the table can be opened EXCLUSIVE for another purpose such as pack or reindex. The program in **Listing 3** shows an example using this new parameter.

 *The program Ex_Aused.PRG is included with the Developer Download files for this chapter, available at **www.hentzenwerke.com**.*

Listing 3. *Using the AUSED() function to close all instances of the Customer table in all data sessions.*

```
LOCAL ;
    lnSessions AS Integer, ;
    laSessions[1], ;
    lnI AS Integer, ;
    lnCursors AS Integer, ;
    laCursors[1], ;
    lnJ

lnSessions = ASESSIONS(laSessions)

FOR lnI = 1 TO lnSessions
    SET DATASESSION TO (laSessions[lnI])

    lnCursors = AUSED(laCursors, lnI, "Customer")

    FOR lnJ = 1 TO lnCursors
        USE IN (laCursors[lnJ, 1])
    ENDFOR

ENDFOR
```

Production code would require a little more testing to insure there are no changes pending before closing the table.

SET TABLEPROMPT

Many Visual FoxPro commands such as SQL – SELECT require a table be open or at least in the current Path. If the table is not available, the Open File Dialog is displayed so the user can select the table. This is not always desirable in an application, so a new SET command, SET TABLEPROMPT, was added to control the display of the Open File Dialog. The valid values are On or Off.

If SET TABLEPROMPT is ON, the open file dialog will display. If SET TABLEPROMPT is OFF, it will not display. SET("TABLEPROMPT") can be used to determine the current setting of SET TABLEPROMPT.

> *Care should be taken when using SET TABLEPROMPT ON in COM server applications as it could place the server in a modal wait state. SET TABLEPROMPT should probably be set to OFF or SYS(2335) used to establish unattended server mode for the application.*

SET("REPROCESS")

The SET REPROCESS command specifies how many times or for how long a record lock is attempted. Prior to VFP 9, you could determine the numeric value for SET REPROCESS using the SET() function, but not the type, attempts, or time. VFP 9 adds two new parameter values to SET("REPROCESS"). Passing 2 for the second parameter returns the type of REPROCESS for the current data session. Passing 3 returns the setting type for the system data session. The function returns 0 when the setting type is attempts and 1 when the setting type is seconds. The following code illustrates these new parameter values.

```
SET REPROCESS TO 10
? SET("REPROCESS")            && Returns 10 which is the value.
? SET("REPROCESS", 2)         && Returns 0 which is the type.
SET REPROCESS TO 10 SECONDS
? SET("REPROCESS", 2)         && Returns 1 which is the type.
```

Data conversion

Several enhancements have been made in VFP 9 to assist in data conversion issues. The first change is to the ALTER TABLE command. This command now correctly converts memo data to character data. In VFP 8, the ALTER TABLE command does not convert memo data to character data at all, resulting in loss of all data. Similarly, memo data values are correctly converted to character data when making structure changes using the Table Designer. If the character field is not defined large enough to store all of the data in the memo field, the extra characters are truncated when the data is converted.

In VFP 8, the BINTOC() and CTOBIN() functions are used to convert integer values to binary character values and vice versa. These functions are extremely useful for numeric indexes because the character representation can be smaller and faster. Due to user requests, these two functions have been enhanced to support more than just integer values. For VFP 9, all numeric data types are supported. For more information on the changes to BINTOC() and CTOBIN(), see Chapter 14 "Language Improvements." The example in **Listing 4** shows how you might use BINTOC()when indexing and SEEKING values.

The program Ex_Bintoc.PRG is included with the Developer Download files for this chapter, available at **www.hentzenwerke.com**.

Listing 4. *An indexing example using BINTOC()*

```
CREATE TABLE indextest (iId I AUTOINC, nQTY N(5, 2), yAmount Y)
INDEX ON BINTOC(iId) TAG Id
INDEX ON BINTOC(nQty, 8) TAG Qty
INDEX ON BINTOC(yAmount, 8) TAG Amount

INSERT INTO IndexTest ;
    (nQty, ;
    yAmount ) ;
VALUES ;
    (10.2, ;
    $299.95)

? SEEK(1, "IndexTest", "Id")          && Generates an error.
? SEEK(BINTOC(1), "IndexTest", "Id")           && Returns .T.

? SEEK(10.2, "IndexTest", "Qty")           && Generates an error.
? SEEK(BINTOC(10.2, 8), "IndexTest", "QTY")           && Returns .T.

? SEEK(299.95,"IndexTest", "Amount")           && Generates an error.
? SEEK(BINTOC($299.95, 8), "IndexTest", "Amount")           && Returns .T
```

With many options available now when indexing numeric data, Microsoft has the following recommendations when using BINTOC() for index expressions:
1. When the index should be 8 bytes, use 8 as the parameter rather than "B".
2. Only use 4 when the 4 byte index expression is being generated from an integer data type. Otherwise, "F" should be used for floating point types.

International issues

An nCodePage clause has been added to the CREATE TABLE and CREATE CURSOR commands. This allows the code page to be programmatically specified as the cursor or table is created. Prior to this enhancement, the code page was established when a table or cursor was created based on the currently active codepage, which can only be specified through the CODEPAGE = setting in the Configuration file (Config.FPW). Therefore, creating multiple tables using different code pages was very cumbersome before now. In VFP 9, code like the following can be used.

```
CREATE CURSOR Fees CODEPAGE = 1251 (cName C(10), yAmount Y)
```

The VFP Help file has a complete listing of the supported code pages. If an invalid code page number is specified, error 1914, "Code page number is invalid," is generated.

Long type name support

When referring to VFP data types, only single character references were supported before VFP 9. In an attempt to make the VFP data language consistent with other languages, VFP 9 introduces long type name support. The long name for each data type is the one you see in the **Type** combobox found in the Table Designer. The following now support the full data type name along with the single character reference:

- ALTER TABLE
- CREATE CURSOR
- CREATE TABLE
- CREATE FROM
- CAST()
- CursorSchema Property of CursorAdapter
- Datatype property of XML Field

For example:

```
CREATE CURSOR TempCursor ;
    (cName Character(30), ;
    iId Integer, ;
    yAmount Currency)
```

In addition, Character, Numeric, and Integer field types support a third notation; Char, Num, and Int respectively.

If the long name supplied is not valid, VFP uses just the first letter as the field type. If the first letter is not a valid field data type, the error "Function argument value, type or count is invalid" occurs.

The example below generates an error because Alphabetic and A are not valid field data types.

```
CREATE CURSOR TempCursor ;
  (cName Alphabetic(30), ;
  iId Integer, ;
  yAmount Currency)
```

This example does not generate an error; however, the yAmount field is created as a memo field because Money is not a valid data type.

```
CREATE CURSOR TempCursor ;
  (cName Character(30), ;
  iId Integer, ;
  yAmount Money)
```

Behavior changes

Microsoft has always done a terrific job of making VFP backward compatible. Applications written in prior versions of VFP should run in the next release without change. However, upon occasion some changes could cause existing applications to break. This section lists two behaviors that may cause your VFP 8 or earlier applications to no longer work as expected.

TABLEREVERT()

The behavior of TABLEREVERT() was changed in VFP 8 SP1. It prohibits the use of TABLEREVERT() while TABLEUPDATE() is in progress and when a CursorAdapter class is being used. The code in **Listing 5** works under VFP 8 and no longer works under after VFP 8 SP1:

*The program, No_TableRevert.PRG is included with the Developer Download files for this chapter, available at **www.hentzenwerke.com**.*

Listing 5: *This program would not generate an error under VFP8, but will generate an error when using VFP8 SP1 or later.*

```
loAdapter = CREATEOBJECT('MyAdapter')
loAdapter.CursorFill()
BROWSE    && Just to make sure we have a cursor.
INSERT INTO Names_CA ;
  (cName) ;
VALUES ;
  ([Fred])

? TABLEUPDATE(1)

DEFINE CLASS MyAdapter AS CursorAdapter
BufferModeOverride = 5
CursorSchema = [IID I, CNAME C(30), DADDED D]
DataSourceType = [Native]
SelectCmd = [select iId, cName, dAdded from Names]
Tables = [Names]
Alias = [Names_CA]
BreakOnError = .T.

FUNCTION BeforeInsert
  LPARAMETERS cFldState, lForce, nUpdateType, cUpdateInsertCmd, cDeleteCmd
  TABLEREVERT(.T.)
  RETURN DODEFAULT(cFldState, lForce, nUpdateType, cUpdateInsertCmd, cDeleteCmd)
ENDFUNC

ENDDEFINE
```

Indexes

VFP has never supported variable length indexes. Indexes are always padded to the maximum length as defined by field sizes and the index expression. In some cases, the length of the index could change from session to session, such as with date and datetime values converted to strings. If SET CENTURY is ON, the value is longer than if SET CENTURY is OFF. The program in **Listing 6** outlines an example of this.

*The program, NewIndexBehavior.PRG is included with the Developer Download files for this chapter, available at **www.hentzenwerke.com**.*

Listing 6. *This program would not generate an error under VFP version 8 and earlier, but does generate an error in VFP9.*

```
SET CENTURY OFF
DELETE FILE AppSecurity.dbc
DELETE FILE AppSecurity.dct
DELETE FILE AppSecurity.dcx
DELETE FILE Applogin.dbf
DELETE FILE Applogin.cdx

CREATE DATABASE AppSecurity

CREATE TABLE AppLogin ;
   (cUserId C(30), ;
   tLoggedIn T DEFAULT DATETIME(), ;
   tLoggedOut T)

INDEX ON UPPER(cUserId) + TTOC(tLoggedIn) TAG UniqueKey

INSERT INTO AppLogin ;
      (cUserId) ;
VALUES ;
      ([TMF])

INSERT INTO AppLogin ;
      (cUserId) ;
VALUES ;
      ([TEG])

SET CENTURY ON

INSERT INTO AppLogin ;
      (cUserId) ;
VALUES ;
      ([DH])

USE IN AppLogin
CLOSE DATABASES ALL
```

Under VFP 8, this program runs without error. Under VFP 9, the last INSERT INTO stops with error 2199, "Error building key for index <index file name> tag <tag name>," and the data is not saved.

In this particular example, the problem is corrected by passing 1 as the second parameter to TTOC() so the function returns a value usable in an index. In other situations, the index expression needs to be changed to one that will not return different size values, depending on the system configuration.

Summary

Many times it's the little things that make our programming lives much easier. Once again, the VFP team has done a great job of adding data-related enhancements that make our applications easier to program, perform better, and fit better in many different environments.

Updates and corrections for this chapter can be found on Hentzenwerke's website, **www.hentzenwerke.com**. Click "Catalog" and navigate to the page for this book.

Chapter 13
Forms and Controls

While some VFP applications do most of their work behind the scenes, forms are still the principal way for an application to communicate with users. VFP 9 offers a variety of ways to make forms more attractive and easier to use.

The bottom line in writing applications is providing some functionality. While some applications do that invisibly, most include at least some interaction with users. To those users, the application's interface *is* the application. So anything that helps you provide an easier to use, more attractive user interface makes the people you write code for happier.

VFP 9 includes many changes aimed at the user interface. They range from significant new capabilities to minor tweaks. In this chapter, the changes are organized based on what piece of the interface they impact.

Controlling forms

Two major changes in VFP 9 affect forms as whole. First, VFP forms can now be docked. Second, a new property of controls makes it much easier to cope when a form is resized.

Docking user forms

VFP 7 introduced docking to the product, making a number of the IDE windows dockable, including the Command Window, the Property Sheet, and the View window. VFP 8 improved docking of those windows, providing programmatic control over docking and making docking persistent between sessions.

VFP 9 ups the ante significantly, making user-defined forms dockable. This change means you can put dockable forms into your applications, and all the developer tools written in VFP code (like the Class Browser, the Toolbox, and so on) can be docked. (Only the Toolbox is configured as dockable out of the box, but you can modify the others to be dockable.)

Forms have three new properties and two new methods to support docking. The properties are shown in **Table 1**. The methods are Dock, which docks and undocks the form, and GetDockState, which lets you check on the status of a form.

Table 1. Forms have three new properties to support docking; two of them are the same properties as for toolbars.

Property	Meaning
DockPosition	Indicates the current docking status of the form. Read-only.
Dockable	Specifies whether the form can be docked.
Docked	Indicates whether the form is currently docked. Read-only.

In order to dock a form, it must support docking, as specified by the Dockable property. The property takes three values, shown in **Table 2**. You can change the property at run-time, for example, to let users decide whether or not a particular form is docked.

Table 2. A form can support docking or not. If it supports docking, at any given time, it's either dockable or not.

Dockable setting	Meaning
0	The form cannot be docked (does not support docking).
1	The form supports docking and is dockable now.
2	The form supports docking, but is not dockable now.

As with IDE windows, when a form is dockable (Dockable is set to 1 or 2), its context menu includes a **Dockable** item. When that item is checked, Dockable is set to 1; when it's unchecked, Dockable is set to 2.

Turning on docking support for a form (that is, setting Dockable to 1 or 2) affects quite a few other properties. The complete list is included in the Help topic for the Dockable property. Most immediately apparent is that HalfHeightCaption is set to .T., which changes the appearance of the title bar. **Figure 1** shows the impact of Dockable on the title bar. Setting Dockable to 1 or 2 in the Property Sheet makes the form visible before code in the Init method executes, instead of waiting for the Show method. If you have code to manipulate the form in the Init method, you may want to set Dockable in the Show method instead of in the Property Sheet. In addition, when a form supports docking, the settings of MaxHeight, MaxWidth, MinHeight, and MinWidth are ignored and BorderStyle is set to 3-Sizable; this means the user has free reign over the size and shape of your form, so make sure it behaves appropriately.

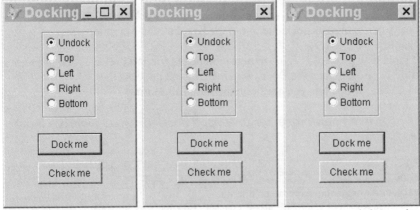

Figure 1. The setting of Dockable affects many properties and determines the appearance of the title bar. The three forms here have Dockable set to 0, 1, and 2, from left to right.

Once a form supports docking and has docking turned on (Dockable=1), you can dock it interactively or programmatically.

Interactive docking of user forms works like docking of IDE forms—just drag the form to the border where you want to dock it. User forms can be docked with other user forms as well. Again, you use the same approach as with IDE forms. To tab dock two forms, drag the title bar of one onto the title bar of the other. To link dock two forms, drag one over the other until the outline of the dragged form changes to indicate docking. Interactive undocking of user forms is the same as for IDE windows, as well. In all cases except tab docking, drag the title of the form you want to undock. For tab docked forms, drag the tab of the form you want to undock. Of course, unchecking Dockable in the context menu of the form's title bar immediately undocks the form. Use the Dock method to dock forms programmatically. A new parameter has been added to this method to support docking one form with another. The new syntax is:

```
Form.Dock( nPosition [, oForm ] )
```

The values for nPosition are shown in **Table 3**. oForm is an object reference to another form. When you include an oForm parameter, the two forms are either tab-docked or link-docked, depending on the value of nPosition.

Table 3. *The nPosition parameter of the Dock method determines how the form is docked.*

nPosition	Meaning
-1	Undock the form
0	Dock the form at the top.
1	Dock the form at the left.
2	Dock the form at the right.
3	Dock the form at the bottom.
4	Tab dock the form with the specified form.

Interactively, you can dock user forms with any dockable windows, whether they are VFP forms, VFP tools written in VFP (like the Toolbox or Class Browser), or IDE windows (like the Command Window). Programmatically, though, you can dock user forms only with other VFP forms, including those for tools written in VFP. You can't dock user forms with built-in windows programmatically.

Of course, once you can dock windows, you need a way to check whether they're docked and, if so, to what. The new GetDockState method fills an array with information about the docking state of the form.

GetDockState accepts a single parameter: the name of an existing array. If the form is dockable (Dockable = 1), the array is sized appropriately and filled with data; in that case, the method returns .T. If the form is not dockable (Dockable = 0 or 2), the array is unchanged and the method returns .F.

> The parameter to GetDockState is unusual. You have to either pass the name of the array as a string, or pass the array by reference.

The array GetDockState creates has six columns. **Table 4** shows the columns and their meanings. Although GetDockState is closely related to the ADockState() function, it never returns more than one row.

Table 4. *The GetDockState method tells you about the docking status of a dockable form. It populates an array with these columns.*

Column	Contents
1	Caption of the form that called the method. (Note that Help says this is the name of the form.)
2	1 if the form is docked. 2 if the form is not docked.
3	Docking position, using the values shown in **Table 3**.
4	Caption of the form or window to which the form is docked.
5	Object reference to the form that called the method,
6	Object reference to the form to which the calling form is docked. If the form is docked to an IDE window, the empty string.

> GetDockState shares a confusing behavior with ADockState(). When forms or windows are tab-docked or link-docked, the first form or window in the group (the leftmost or top) shows as docked (column 2 = 1), but has −1 in the third column and columns 4 and 6 contain the empty string.

Anchoring controls

Ever since FoxPro gained resizable windows, developers have been struggling with the question of how to handle form content when a window is resized. Should controls be resized? moved? left alone? How do we know what the user was trying to do by resizing the window?

Over the years, many solutions have been proposed. What they all have in common (except for those recommending you don't let users resize forms) is that they involve a lot of code, often requiring code for every control as well as the form itself. (You can find one solution in the FoxPro Foundation classes, as _resizable in the _controls.vcx class library.)

VFP 9 makes all that code obsolete by adding the Anchor property to all visible controls. Anchor lets you specify what happens to a control when the control's container is resized. The control can move, change size, or both, and the horizontal and vertical directions are controlled independently.

When a user resizes a form, you may not want all the controls to do the same thing. For example, if a form gets both wider and taller, a textbox should probably get wider, but an editbox should get larger in both directions. Any controls under such an editbox need to move down, but controls above the editbox may want to stay where they are. The Anchor property lets you consider all the possibilities and set up your forms to behave in the way you think users will find most natural.

Anchor is an additive property; you choose the values you want and add them together to form a single value. Because the number of possibilities is large enough to make specifying this value difficult, VFP 9 includes a tool (discussed in "The Anchor Editor" later in this chapter) to help you.

Anchoring takes place with respect to the four borders of the control's container. For each, there are three options:

- the control is anchored absolutely to that border, meaning the distance between the specified edge of the control and that border remains constant;

- the control is anchored relatively to that border, meaning the distance between the specified edge of the control and that border is changed to maintain the ratio of that distance to the form's size in that direction;

- the control is not anchored to that border, meaning a change to that border doesn't affect the size and position of the control.

Rather than anchoring to each border, you can specify that the center of the control is anchored relative to the borders, either horizontally or vertically, but the control itself doesn't change size. This is a good choice for controls that should move in order to remain in a particular part of a form, such as buttons that should always be in the lower right corner.

Table 5 shows the values you can add together for Anchor. Note that some of these values are mutually incompatible. The Help topic for Anchor lists the incompatibilities.

Table 5. To specify the Anchor property, add the values you want together.

Value	Name	Meaning
0	Top Left	Anchors the control to the top and left borders of its container, keeping the distance constant. This is the old, default behavior of controls.
1	Top Absolute	Anchors the control to the top border of its container, keeping the distance constant.
2	Left Absolute	Anchors the control to the left border of its container, keeping the distance constant.
4	Bottom Absolute	Anchors the control to the bottom border of its container, keeping the distance constant.
8	Right Absolute	Anchors the control to the right border of its container, keeping the distance constant.
16	Top Relative	Anchors the control to the top border of its container, keeping the distance relative to the original distance.
32	Left Relative	Anchors the control to the left border of its container, keeping the distance relative to the original distance.
64	Bottom Relative	Anchors the control to the bottom border of its container, keeping the distance relative to the original distance.
128	Right Relative	Anchors the control to the right border of its container, keeping the distance relative to the original distance.
256	Horizontal Fixed Size	Anchors the center of the control to the left and right borders of its container, keeping the control's width constant.
512	Vertical Fixed Size	Anchors the center of the control to the top and bottom borders of its container, keeping the control's height constant.

Consider the form shown in **Figure 2**. The original form is shown on the left and the resized form on the right. When this form is resized, the size of the labels remains unchanged, the textboxes change size horizontally only, the editbox changes both horizontally and vertically, and the buttons remain centered horizontally. All the controls below the editbox move appropriately as the editbox changes size. **Table 6** shows the settings used for the controls in this form.

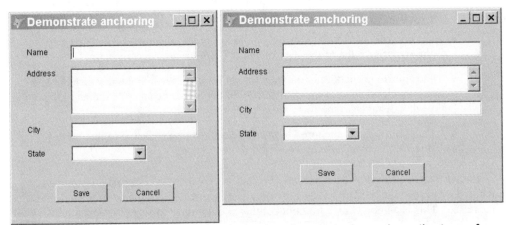

Figure 2. When a form is resized, the behavior of controls depends on the type of control and the control's position on the form. With Anchor, you can specify the behavior of each control separately.

Table 6. The form in *Figure 2* demonstrates a number of useful combinations for Anchor.

Control	Anchor	Meaning
lblName (Name label) lblAddress (Address label)	0	Anchor absolutely to top left corner. Don't move or resize.
txtName (Name textbox)	10	Anchor absolutely to left and right sides, so resize horizontally.
edtAddress (Address editbox)	15	Anchor absolutely to all four borders. Resize both horizontally and vertically.
lblCity (City label) lblState (State label) cboState (State combobox)	4	Anchor absolutely to bottom border. Move vertically.
txtCity (City textbox)	14	Anchor absolutely to left, right, and bottom borders. Resize horizontally and move vertically.
cmdSave (Save button)	132	Anchor absolutely to bottom border and relatively to right border. Move horizontally to keep relative to original position. Move vertically.
cmdCancel (Cancel button)	36	Anchor absolutely to bottom border and relatively to left border. Move horizontally to keep relative to original position. Move vertically.

*The form in **Figure 2** is included in the Developer Downloads for this chapter, available from **www.hentzenwerke.com**, as Anchoring.SCX. The Downloads also include States.DBF, which is used by the form.*

VFP's anchoring computations are based on the position of the control at the time the Anchor property is set. (No doubt what's going on internally is that when Anchor is set, the Left, Top, Height, and Width properties for the control are stored somewhere.) Subsequent changes in code to the control's position or size are ignored when resizing and repositioning due to resizing of the control's container. To reset the base position for a control, set its Anchor property to 0, and then reset it to the desired value.

You may have noticed that setting Anchor to 3 seems to offer the same behavior as leaving the default Anchor value of 0. The difference is that with Anchor set to 3, subsequent changes to the control's position or size are ignored when resizing, but with Anchor set to 0 they are not.

 *The Developer Downloads for this chapter, available from **www.hentzenwerke.com**, include Anchor0vs3.SCX, a form that demonstrates the difference between Anchor=0 and Anchor=3. Click the Right or Down button on the form, and then resize the form. Watch the button marked 3 jump back to its original position, while the button marked 0 stays put.*

The Anchor Editor
Figuring out the right value for Anchor for each control on a form could get tedious fast. To make it simpler, the VFP team included a property editor (see Chapter 2, "Controlling the Properties Window") for Anchor. This tool, called the Anchor Editor, lets you set Anchor visually; it's shown in **Figure 3**. To use the Anchor Editor, click the Anchor property in the Property Sheet, and then click the ellipsis (…) button next to the textbox where you type values, as shown in **Figure 4**.

The Anchor Editor offers three ways to specify the setting you want. The diagram on the left lets you click or use the keyboard to set each of the four directions. Click between the parallel lines (called the "anchor bars") or type the specified letter to toggle the setting for that border among no anchoring, absolute anchoring, and relative anchoring. As the setting changes, the diagram does as well. Black indicates relative anchoring, gray indicates absolute anchoring, and no color (the background color) indicates no anchoring.

The two checkboxes let you choose the two fixed size settings (512 and 256, respectively).

The dropdown list offers common combinations; the list of choices changes based on the control's base class. For example, for a textbox, it includes "Resize width," "Move horizontally," and "Move vertically," but for an editbox, the list includes "Resize height and width," "Resize width," and "Resize height." The list always includes "No anchoring" as a choice.

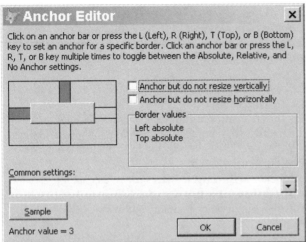

Figure 3. *The Anchor Editor lets you specify the Anchor property visually. It offers several ways to specify the desired setting.*

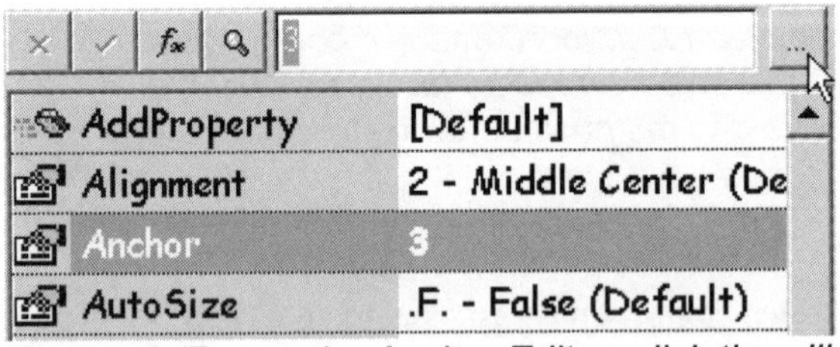

Figure 4. *To use the Anchor Editor, click the ellipsis button when the Anchor property is selected.*

In addition to shading the anchor bars, the Anchor Editor shows the current settings in two ways. The **Border values** box lists the current settings for each border for which anchoring is set. Also, the current numeric value is shown as the bottom left of the dialog.

The Anchor Editor also lets you examine the consequences of your current choices. Click the Sample button and a test form (titled "Anchor test form") opens. It contains a control of the appropriate type (even using the Caption of your cóntrol) with its Anchor property set as currently specified in the Anchor Editor. Resize the form to see how the control behaves. The sample form is modal, so you have to close it to make changes.

When you close the Anchor Editor by clicking OK, the calculated value is saved to the Anchor property.

> The Anchor Editor can work with multiple objects at once. If you select multiple controls, choose the Anchor property, and click the ellipsis button, the anchor settings you choose are applied to all of the selected controls. Be aware that when working with multiple controls, even several controls of the same base class, the dropdown for common settings is disabled.

Maximum form size

In VFP 8 and earlier, the Height and Width of a form were restricted to twice the screen resolution. VFP 9 raises the limit to 32,735 pixels for Height and 32,759 pixels for Width. We're not sure why anyone would want to create a form that big, but you no longer have to worry about the screen resolution in creating large forms.

Displaying graphical elements

While FoxPro has included graphical elements (shapes, lines) since VFP 3, their use has been fairly restricted. VFP 9 introduces a number of changes that give you more control over the graphical elements on a form, including rotation of labels, the ability to create and rotate complex shapes, better handling of separators in toolbars, and the ability for labels to take on theme characteristics.

Rotating labels

Labels in VFP 9 have a new Rotation property that lets you change their position. Rotation accepts an integer value between 0 and 360. (If you specify decimals, they're truncated.) Rotation takes place counter-clockwise. **Figure 5** shows a label rotated 45 degrees.

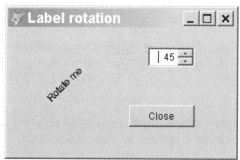

Figure 5. Rotate labels by specifying the new Rotation property. Note that rotating a label doesn't change the orientation of its Caption.

There are several caveats when rotating labels. First, be aware that the text rotates as a whole. Rotation doesn't provide a way to create vertical text with one letter under the next, for instance.

Second, you need to make the label large enough to contain the rotated text. In the form shown in **Figure 5**, the Height and Width of the label are both 100 pixels. (Think of the Height and Width properties as creating a "bounding box" for the label.)

Third, a number of properties are applied only when Rotation is 0. They include AutoSize, Alignment, and WordWrap. (See the Help for the Rotation property for the complete list.)

You might expect Rotation=0 to give the same results as Rotation=360. However, when Rotation is greater than 0, the caption is centered in its bounding box, and then rotated. With Rotation=0, the caption obeys the Alignment setting, which doesn't offer vertical position. As a result, the caption appears at the top of the bounding box.

*The form shown in **Figure 5** is included as Rotation.SCX in the Developer Downloads for this chapter, available at **www.hentzenwerke.com**.*

Creating and rotating complex shapes

VFP has always included Line and Shape controls. However, the shapes you can create with these controls has been limited. Not surprisingly, the Line control has been limited to straight lines, with the LineSlant property determining their orientation (NW-SE or SW-NE). Shapes have offered a few more options. Depending on the setting of the Curvature property, you could have anything from a rectangle or square to an ellipse or circle, including a full range of rounded rectangles. But if you wanted any other kind of shape, you had to build it yourself using multiple Line or Shape controls; specifying colors or fill patterns for the result was difficult, if possible at all.

VFP 9 changes that. You can now create any shape, providing you know how to specify its vertices. Both Line and Shape include a new PolyPoints property you can use to specify an array of points that determine the line or shape displayed.

The array must be in scope when you run the form. The easiest way to ensure that is to use a property of the form or control. Specify the name of the array as the value for PolyPoints.

If the array is in scope and contains data at design-time, the actual shape or line is shown in the Form or Class Designer. Unfortunately, this is never the case when you use a form or control property for the array. In that case, you see the boundaries for the shape.

PolyPoints can handle both one-dimensional and two-dimensional arrays. It simply looks at the elements in order, treating all the odd-numbered elements as x-coordinates and all the even-numbered elements as y-coordinates. That said, it's easiest if you use a two-column array. Then the first column provides the x-coordinates and the second column gives y-coordinates.

The values you specify in PolyPoints are percentages of the space occupied by the bounding box of the Line or Shape. To have the vertices appear, the values should range from 0 to 100. Unlike the usual Cartesian coordinate system, however, the point (0,0) specifies the upper left corner and the point (100,100) indicates the lower right corner of the bounding box. You can actually specify points outside the box; when you do so, lines within the bounding box appear, but the object is clipped by the bounding box.

Keep in mind that using percentages means the actual rendering of the shape or line changes when the Height or Width properties of the Shape or Line change.

We think the easiest way to take advantage of these new capabilities is to subclass the Line and Shape base classes (or your first level subclasses of them) and add the necessary array property. Set PolyPoints to point to that array property. Then, create all your complex shapes and lines by subclassing or instantiating these subclasses. We also recommend adding a SetPoints method called from the Init method to handle population of the array.

The Developer Downloads for this chapter, available from ***www.hentzenwerke.com***, *include Shapes.VCX, a class library containing Line and Shape subclasses that use the new capabilities. The library includes abstract Line and Shape classes with the necessary properties and method, and concrete subclasses of those classes.*

Figure 6 shows a form containing two Shape subclasses (the star and hexagon) and two Line subclasses (the W and teeth), as well as a label positioned over one of the shapes. The Resize button changes the height or width of each shape or line (the change is different for each—see the code for the details) to demonstrate the effect of Height and Width on the resulting shapes. **Figure 7** shows the form after clicking the Resize button twice. (Note that the Wow! label contains code that keeps it centered over the star.)

You can change the points for a polygon or polyline even after the object has been displayed. For your changes to take effect, however, you have to call the object's Refresh method.

Polylines offer an alternative to connecting all the points with straight lines. If you specify "S" or "s" for the LineSlant property (which until now has been limited to "\" and "/"), a Bezier curve is drawn instead. (A complete explanation of Bezier curves is beyond the scope of this book. Briefly, a Bezier curve is one method of approximately fitting a curve to a set of data points.) To use a Bezier curve, the number of points specified must be one more than a multiple of 3; the number of curves drawn is the multiplier of 3 used. That is, to have one curve, specify four points; for two curves, specify seven points; for three curves, ten, and so forth. If the number of points specified is not $3N+1$ (for some positive value of N), the polyline doesn't show up at all.

The right-hand polyline (the "teeth") in the form in Figure 6 and Figure 7 has 10 points specified. The checkbox beneath it toggles the LineSlant property between "\" and "S". **Figure 8** shows the form after checking the Bezier checkbox.

Lines and shapes with an array specified for PolyPoints can be rotated using the new Rotation property. **Figure 9** shows the form with all the lines and shapes (and the label) rotated 45 degrees.

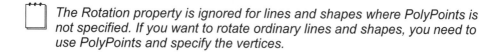 *The Rotation property is ignored for lines and shapes where PolyPoints is not specified. If you want to rotate ordinary lines and shapes, you need to use PolyPoints and specify the vertices.*

 The form in Figures 6, 7, 8, and 9 is included as UseShapes.SCX in the Developer Downloads for this chapter, available from ***www.hentzenwerke.com***.

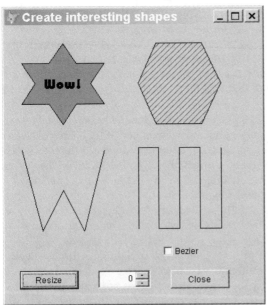

Figure 6. *The new PolyPoints property lets you create polygons and polylines using the Shape and Line classes.*

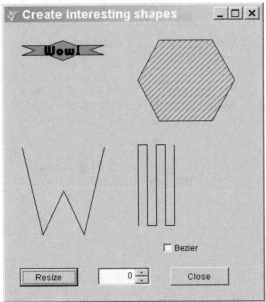

Figure 7. *The actual appearance of polygons and polylines depends on both the points specified and the Height and Width of the Shape or Line control.*

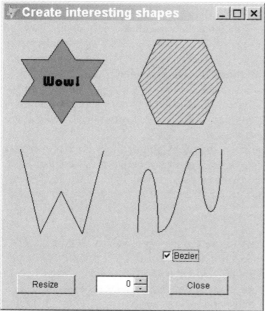

Figure 8. Specifying "S" for LineSlant causes a polyline to be displayed using Bezier curves.

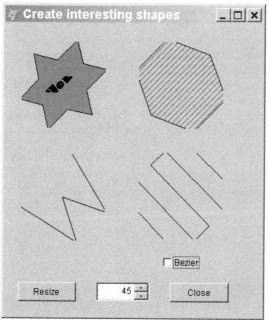

Figure 9. Rotate Polygons and polylines by changing the Rotation property. The "missing" sections of the polygons are caused by the shapes being clipped by their bounding boxes.

Managing toolbar separators

The Separator object is one of the simplest in VFP. Separators can appear only on toolbars and serve to divide the controls on toolbars into groups. VFP 9 gives you a little more control over separators.

Normally, a separator is just a space between controls. But when the Style property of a separator is set to 1, the separator displays as a line (as it does in VFP's own toolbars). Prior to VFP 9, however, if the toolbar was undocked and arranged so the separator should be a horizontal line, no line displayed. In VFP 9, regardless of the docking status of the toolbar and its orientation, a separator with Style=1 displays a line.

VFP 9 also adds the ability to turn separators on and off by adding the Visible property to the Separator class. In earlier versions, once you placed a separator between two controls, the space or line appeared unless you actually removed the separator from the toolbar. In VFP 9, you can set Visible to False to hide the separator and pull the controls together on either side.

Combining labels and themes

Windows XP's theme support added many complications to display issues in VFP; many of them were dealt with in VFP 8. VFP 9 offers a solution to one remaining problem.

When you put a label on a container object with gradient color (like a page of a pageframe), you normally want the gradient coloring to show behind the text of the label. You can make that happen by setting BackStyle to transparent. However, there are some situations where you really need an opaque label, but want it to use the same gradient background as its container. For example, if you have a shape on a page and you're using a label over the border of the shape (such as to label a group of controls), you usually want BackStyle to be opaque so the border of the shape doesn't show through the label.

VFP 8 offers two settings for the Style of a label: 0-Normal and 3-Themed. Neither of those settings handles the case described above well. With Style=0-Normal, the label uses a solid background rather than the gradient coloring of its container. Style=3-Themed uses gradient coloring, but changes the ForeColor of the label. To resolve this problem, VFP 9 offers a new Style setting for labels: 4-Themed Background Only. With this setting, the label uses the theme's gradient coloring in the background, but leaves the ForeColor of the label as you set it. **Figure 10** shows a form with three rectangles on a page of a pageframe. Each has a label overlaying the top border; each label shows one of the settings for Style.

 *The form in **Figure 10** is included in the Developer Downloads for this chapter, available from **www.hentzenwerke.com**, as ThemedLabels.SCX.*

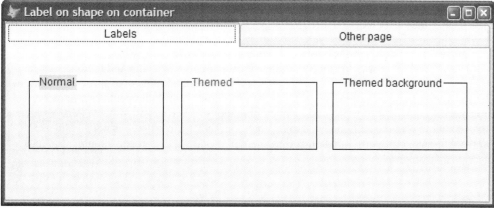

Figure 10. *The new setting for Style in labels lets you use labels over transparent containers and have the background look right.*

Dealing with pictures

Graphical images can serve a variety of purposes on forms. Each version of VFP has provided additional capabilities for using images, either by expanding the list of formats accepted or by offering more control over their display. VFP 9 continues this practice, with improvements in all the controls that can display pictures and text at the same time, as well as a new way to specify pictures for an Image control.

Controlling pictures and captions

VFP 8 added the PicturePosition property, allowing you to specify the relative position of an image and a text caption on command buttons, option buttons, and checkboxes. VFP 9 increases your control over the relationship between pictures and captions on these controls in several ways.

PicturePosition has a new value, 14, to indicate the Picture should be displayed and the Caption hidden. This is useful if you want to have a button or checkbox with only a picture, but also provide a hotkey. You can specify a caption with an appropriate hotkey, but set PicturePosition to 14 to hide the caption. (Of course, this means there's no visual cue to the user for the hotkey.) For checkboxes and option buttons, a PicturePosition setting of 14 is relevant only when the Style property is set to 1-Graphical.

Once PicturePosition gave us control over the relationship between the picture and the text, VFP developers noticed that wasn't enough. We wanted more control over the placement of the items in the control. The new PictureMargin and PictureSpacing properties address this issue.

PictureMargin specifies the number of pixels between the image and the border of the control. It's measured from the edge specified by the PicturePosition property. For example, if PicturePosition is 10 (image centered below the caption), PictureMargin controls the distance between the bottom of the control and the image.

PictureSpacing specifies the number of pixels between the image and the caption. As this property increases, the image stays in the position specified by PicturePosition and PictureMargin, and the text caption moves up, down, left, or right to provide the specified spacing. If PictureSpacing is large enough, the caption can disappear entirely.

PictureMargin and PictureSpacing are used only when PicturePosition is 11 or less. This makes sense because PicturePosition values of 12 or more specify that the picture is centered. As with the new PicturePosition value, PictureMargin and PictureSpacing are applied to checkboxes and option buttons only when Style is 1-Graphical.

There's one more way to control all this. Starting in VFP 9, command buttons support the Alignment property, which indicates how the text is positioned in its own space. In addition, checkboxes and option buttons support many more choices for Alignment. There are 9 possible values (0-2, 4-9) representing all combinations of vertical alignment (Top, Middle, or Bottom) with horizontal alignment (Left, Center, or Right). Note that 3 is not a valid setting for the Alignment property of command buttons; it's used for Automatic alignment in those controls that support it.

> *For option buttons and checkboxes, the setting of Alignment is ignored when Style=1-Graphical and WordWrap=.F. (See "Odds and Ends" later in the chapter for more on these controls and the WordWrap property.) This is to ensure compatibility with forms created in VFP 8.*

Figure 11 shows a form that lets you experiment with the different settings of PicturePosition, PictureMargin, PictureSpacing, and Alignment. It includes a command button, a checkbox, and a set of option buttons.

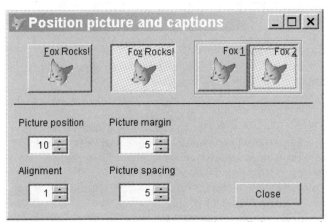

Figure 11. A whole group of properties collaborate to determine the positions of images and text on command buttons, option buttons, and checkboxes.

*The form in **Figure 11** is included as Pictures.SCX in the Developer Downloads for this chapter, available from **www.hentzenwerke.com**.*

Using GDI+ to specify images

VFP 8 added support for GDI+, a powerful graphics library. VFP 9 increases the ways you can take advantage of GDI+ in your applications. (One big way is in reports; see Chapter 7, "Customizing the Report Designer at Run time.")

Through VFP 8, the only way to specify the picture used in an Image control was by pointing at a graphics file. VFP 9 offers an alternative; the new PictureVal property lets you specify a string or object that represents an image.

Why would you want to do this? You might have pictures stored in a Memo or Blob field. Using the Picture property, you have to save the picture from the field into a file and refer to that file. With PictureVal, you can just refer to the field, saving the step of copying the file and cleaning up afterwards.

PictureVal accepts either a character string or an object reference. If you supply a character string, it should be the binary representation of an image. For example, you might use FileToStr() to convert a graphic file into a character string. You can also specify the name of a Memo or Blob field containing the binary representation of an image file. However, PictureVal does *not* support General fields; think of it as a way to avoid using General fields.

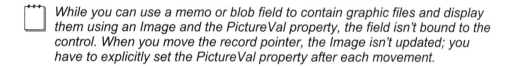 *While you can use a memo or blob field to contain graphic files and display them using an Image and the PictureVal property, the field isn't bound to the control. When you move the record pointer, the Image isn't updated; you have to explicitly set the PictureVal property after each movement.*

 *The Developer Downloads for this chapter, available from **www.hentzenwerke.com**, includes BlobDemo.SCX, a form that stores images in a blob field and displays them, letting you move through the cursor.*

If you supply an object reference, the object must conform to the IPicture interface; you can create such objects using the LoadPicture() function.

If you specify both Picture and PictureVal for an Image control, the PictureVal property is used.

Helping users

A key goal of any application that includes a user interface is to make it easy for users to enter the right data. Several VFP 9 features contribute to that goal. The most significant is support for auto-completion in textboxes. In addition, the InputMask and Format properties have some new values, and you have more control over movement of the cursor among controls.

Auto-complete text boxes

When a field is limited to a particular set of values, it's not unusual to use a combobox or listbox so the user can't enter anything else. But in some situations, while the user is likely to choose from among a small set of values most of the time, the actual list is unlimited, so a combo or list isn't the right choice. In other situations, the user is limited to one list, but will almost always choose from just a few values in that list. Consider an application for a doctor's office. Most patients are likely to come from a small geographic area, though occasionally a patient may come from much farther away. Choosing from a combo or list for fields like state, zip code, or area code in this situation is likely to be slower than just typing in the desired value. Defining a combo or list to specify the town would be difficult, but it's likely that most patients come from a handful of towns.

These are the situations for which auto-completion was created. This technique tracks a user's entries in a particular field. When the user returns to that field, she's offered a list of her most recent or most frequent entries. She can choose from the list or type something new. Internet Explorer is among the applications that supports auto-completion.

Figure 12 shows a form with a number of auto-complete textboxes. When you enter an auto-complete textbox, the list of choices appears. You can choose one with either the keyboard or the mouse, or you can start typing. As you type, the list narrows down to those items that match the characters you entered. If you type a new entry, it's added to the list. You can remove an item from the list by highlighting it and pressing the Delete key.

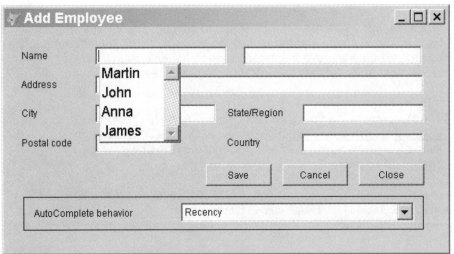

Figure 12. With auto-complete, a list of choices appears when you enter a textbox. Once you start typing, the list narrows down to those items that match what you entered so far.

Not surprisingly, auto-complete data is stored in a table. You can choose whether to put all auto-complete data in a single table, use separate tables for each application or even for each textbox that supports auto-complete within an application. By default, auto-complete data is stored in AutoComp.DBF in the directory specified by HOME(7) (the user application data directory). **Table 7** shows the required structure for the auto-complete table; VFP creates the table automatically when it's needed.

Table 7. The table that stores auto-complete data saves information that lets you organize the list in several different ways.

Field	Type	Purpose
Source	Character (20)	Identifies the textboxes that include this item in their auto-complete lists.
Data	Character (254)	The item to include in auto-complete lists.
Count	Integer	The number of times this item has been chosen.
Weight	Integer	A user-specified (or developer-specified) weight for this item to determine where it appears in the list.
Created	DateTime	The timestamp when this item was added.
Updated	DateTime	The timestamp when this item was last updated.
User	Memo	Available for user-specified data.

The auto-complete table supports several different ways of organizing the list of items. Those options are echoed in the AutoComplete property that turns this feature on. **Table 8** shows the values for AutoComplete. Not surprisingly, when AutoComplete is set to 2, 3, or 4, the list is sorted in descending order, based on the specified field. For AutoComplete values of 2 and 4, the Updated field is used to break ties. You can change the AutoComplete property at run time, so you can offer users the chance to control the order of these items. (The form in **Figure 12** does so, but in a production application, you're more likely to put this choice in an Options dialog.)

Table 8. Enabling auto-complete—the AutoComplete property controls auto-complete behavior for an individual textbox.

Value	Meaning
0	No auto-complete for this textbox.
1	Turn on auto-complete with the list in alphabetical order.
2	Turn on auto-complete with the list ordered by frequency of use (the Count field).
3	Turn on auto-complete with the list ordered by time of use (the Updated field).
4	Turn on auto-complete with a user-specified ordering of the list (the Weight field).

If every textbox in an application had its own list for auto-complete, the auto-complete table would grow far too large and, more importantly, users would become frustrated, as an item entered on one form fails to show up for the same field on another form. Fortunately, VFP's auto-complete feature is designed to avoid this problem. The new AutoCompSource property of textboxes lets you specify a category for the textbox, such as FirstName or City. All textboxes with the same value for AutoCompSource share a single list of items, based on the value of the Source field in the auto-complete table. (You have probably seen this behavior with websites where your name or email address appears in an Auto-complete list for a website you never used before.)

In practice, this means that for each application you build, you probably want to subclass your textbox class for each category, setting AutoCompSource appropriately. Then, use your subclasses to build forms with textboxes that share auto-complete data. Alternatively, if you already have a builder for textboxes, you could add AutoCompSource there. You could also use the Toolbox's Properties functionality to ensure AutoCompSource gets set for each textbox.

By default, there's a single auto-complete table. (As noted above, it's stored in the directory referenced by HOME(7).) However, you can choose to put the table wherever you want and even to use multiple tables. The AutoCompTable property of the _SCREEN object specifies the default location for the AutoComp table. Set it to specify something other than the default location. Be aware that data is saved to the auto-complete table as soon as the user leaves the control, whether or not the user actually saves the data to the underlying table.

    The auto-complete table must be an actual table. It can't be a cursor or view.

In addition, textboxes have a new AutoCompTable property that lets you specify where to find the table for that particular textbox. When the property is empty, the textbox uses the table specified by _SCREEN.AutoCompTable. When both are empty, the default table is used.

The Developer Downloads for this chapter, available from **www.hentzenwerke.com**, *include the form shown in* **Figure 12** *as EmployeeAdd.SCX. It has Auto-complete enabled for all the textboxes except for the address. There's no code behind the form for the auto-complete capabilities; a number of properties are set for the various textboxes. The form also includes a combobox that lets you change the auto-complete setting for the textboxes, so the lists appear in a different order.*

New formatting options
The InputMask and Format properties let you limit or modify user input to increase the chance of it being right. VFP 9 offers two new values for InputMask and enhances an old Format setting.

InputMask controls individual characters in an input string. It includes settings to force you to enter alphabetic characters ("A"), or to force characters to uppercase ("!"). But there's never been a way to combine the two, to permit only alphabetic characters and force some of them to uppercase. (The Format setting "!" forces the whole string to uppercase.) Use "U" for any character in the InputMask that must be alphabetic and uppercase. For example, you might specify "UAAAAAAAAAAAAAA" for a name field. Use "W" for a character that must be alphabetic and lowercase.

The "Z" setting for Format displays the field as blank if it's empty. (The "Z" presumably stands for "zero.") VFP 9 enhances this setting, so that if the value is an empty date, the control is shown as completely empty, except when it has focus. That is, with Format="Z" and Value={ / / }, a control shows the slashes only when it has focus; when another control has focus, the control is totally blank.

Controlling focus

The Valid event has its roots in ancient Xbase. It lets you determine whether the entry in a control is valid and thus, whether that control should be allowed to lose focus. The return value for Valid determines where focus lands next. Return .T. to continue normally; return .F. or 0 to keep focus on the control. Return a number other than 0 to move focus forward or backward in the tab order.

VFP 9 introduces a new option that's far less arcane. You can return an object reference to move focus to that object. What's most intriguing about this new option is that you can even return a reference to an object on another form.

For example, you might have code like this in the Valid of a textbox for specifying a company name:

```
IF EMPTY(This.Value)
   RETURN CompanyForm.txtCompanyName
ENDIF
```

If the user leaves the company name field blank, focus is placed on the company name field of a company form. (Of course, the company form must be available; however, you can actually issue DO FORM to run a form from the Valid, and then set focus to a control on that form. If the specified control doesn't exist, error 1734, "Property <name> is not found" fires. If the container object doesn't exist, error 13, "Alias is not found" fires. If you're navigating a multi-level containership hierarchy and specify an object that doesn't exist, error 1923, "Object <name> is not found" fires.)

Managing tooltips

VFP 9 includes several new features related to tooltips, the little help items that appear when you hover the mouse over a control. Two new functions, SYS(3007) and SYS(3009), are discussed in Chapter 14, "Language Improvements."

SYS(3008) controls whether tooltips appear for hyperlinks (the tip that says "CTRL + click to follow link" when the mouse pauses over a hyperlink); it returns the current setting as a character value. Use SYS(3008, 0) to disable them, SYS(3008, 1) to enable them, or SYS(3008) to simply determine the current setting without changing it. The setting of SYS(3008) doesn't change the actual behavior of the hyperlink, just the tooltip.

_ToolTipTimeOut specifies how long a ToolTip displays when the mouse pointer pauses over a control. Setting this system variable to -1 (the default value) indicates the normal Windows timeout is used. Setting it to 0 means a ToolTip displays until the mouse is moved. Use a value greater than 0 as the number of milliseconds to display the ToolTip.

Better combos and listboxes

Comboboxes and listboxes are extremely versatile controls, useful in a wide variety of situations. VFP 9 makes them even more so, adding support for collections as RowSource, and providing more control over their behavior.

Basing a combo or list on a collection

Collections are widely used in object-oriented programming to gather and process related items. Visual FoxPro supports both native collections (through the Collection baseclass) and

COM collections. In VFP 9, a collection, whether native or COM, can be used as the RowSource for a combobox or listbox.

To specify a collection as the RowSource, set RowSourceType to 10-Collection. For RowSource, specify the name of an object reference to the collection. You can also specify which properties of the objects in the collection display in the list. If you don't include one or more properties in the RowSource, the behavior of the list depends on the underlying type of the collection's elements. If they're scalar values (ordinary data), the value displays. For any item in the list that is an object, the string "(Object)" displays.

Figure 13 shows a form containing a listbox. The listbox displays the contents of VFP's Projects collection (which is a COM collection). RowSource for the listbox is set to "_VFP.Projects, Name"; specifying Name tells the list to show only the value of the Name property.

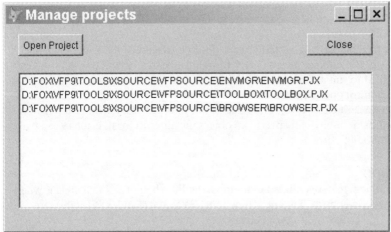

Figure 13. Lists and combos can now be based on the contents of a collection, including COM collections such as _VFP.Projects.

If you specify multiple properties for RowSource, they display in multiple columns. However, you must set ColumnCount appropriately.

 *The form shown in **Figure 13** is included as CollectionList.SCX in the Developer Downloads for this chapter, available from **www.Hentzenwerke.com**.*

Control the dropdown portion of a combo

The DropDown event of a combobox fires when the user clicks the down arrow to open the list. In VFP 8 and earlier, there's no way to prevent the dropdown portion from opening. In VFP 9, issuing the NODEFAULT command in the DropDown method keeps the list from opening up.

As with other methods, you can use code in DropDown to determine whether to issue NODEFAULT. For example, you might have a form-level property, lCanDrop, that determines whether or not the dropdown can open. In that case, you use code like:

```
IF NOT ThisForm.lCanDrop
   NODEFAULT
ENDIF
```

 *The Developer Downloads for this chapter, available at
www.hentzenwerke.com, include ComboDrop.SCX, a form that
demonstrates the ability to use NODEFAULT in the DropDown method.*

Controlling the scrollbar in listboxes

By default, a listbox always includes a vertical scrollbar. Most of the time, that's a good
choice, but sometimes you have a list that doesn't need one some of the time. VFP 9 lets you
decide whether such a list includes a scrollbar.

A new property, AutoHideScrollbar, lets you decide whether a listbox that doesn't need a
scrollbar has one. The default setting of 0 indicates the listbox should always have a scrollbar.
When AutoHideScrollbar is set to 1, a scrollbar displays only when some items on the list are
not shown. The listbox in **Figure 13** has AutoHideScrollbar set to 1, so the scrollbar doesn't
appear until the list is filled.

Click fires more in listboxes

The Click event in a listbox is a little unusual. Not only does it fire when you actually click an
item in the list, but it also fires (along with a bunch of other events) as you move through the
list with the arrow keys. However, in VFP 8 and earlier, other navigation keys don't fire Click,
even though they do fire the other events.

VFP 9 adds some logic to the situation by firing Click when the Home, End, PgUp, and
PgDn fires are used.

Mouse support

VFP 9 offers several improvements related to the mouse, including one unrelated to forms and
probably more useful for developers than for end-users.

Memo and field tips

In Browse windows and grids, memo fields show either "memo" (for empty fields) or "Memo"
(if there's data). Until VFP 9, the only way to see the actual data in the memo
field was to open a memo window. VFP 9 offers memo tips, a quick way to see memo
field contents.

Hover the mouse over a memo field in a Browse window or grid and a tip (like a tooltip)
appears, showing the contents of the field. What makes this feature really cool is that you
see the memo contents for the record the mouse is over, whether or not it's the selected record
in the Browse or grid. **Figure 14** shows a memo tip for the Notes field of the TasTrade
Employee table.

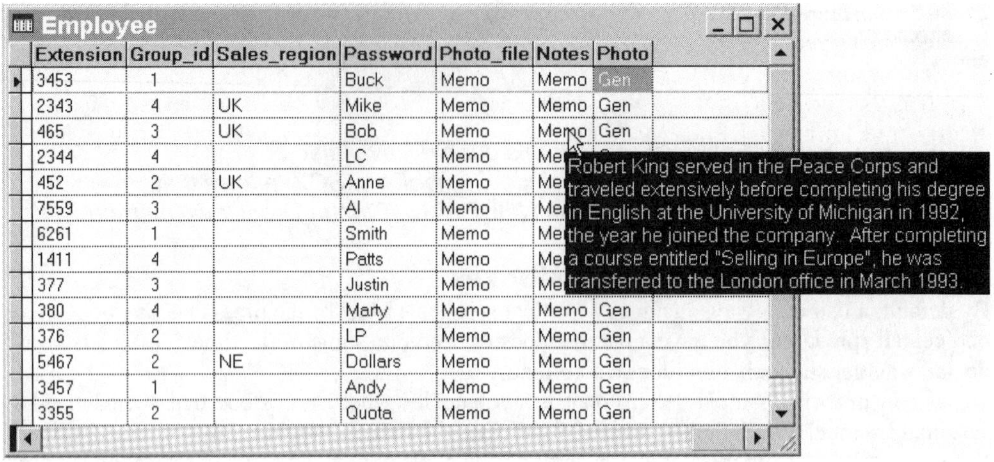

Figure 14. *Memo tips make it easy to see what's in a memo field.*

> For memo tips to work in grids, the form's ShowTips property must be set to True. To see memo tips in the VFP IDE, _Screen.ShowTips must be True.

Having tips for memo fields would be good enough, but the VFP team went farther. Tips are available for all fields wider than their columns. That is, if you have a Browse window or grid where some columns are not wide enough to display the entire contents of the field, you can hold the mouse over the field to see the entire value.

Controlling the mouse pointer in grids

The MousePointer and MouseIcon properties control the appearance of the mouse pointer. MousePointer lets you choose from among the familiar icons, such as the various sizers, the I-beam, and so forth. You can also set MousePointer to 99 to indicate that MouseIcon points to an icon file for a custom choice. In VFP 8 and earlier, the Column and Header objects don't include the MousePointer and MouseIcon properties; columns and headers use the same mouse pointer as the grid itself.

VFP 9 adds these properties to Column and Header, so each column and header in a grid can use a different pointer (though that's not likely to be a good choice from a user interface perspective). The first place you're likely to use these properties is in a grid where clicking the header sorts on that column. You can use MousePointer to indicate that effect.

As with many other items in a grid, your settings for MousePointer and MouseIcon propagate downward unless you specify otherwise. That is, if you leave MousePointer at the default 0 for a column, it uses the grid's setting. Similarly, if MousePointer is 0 for a header, it uses the setting for that column.

Determine accurate mouse position

The MROW() and MCOL() functions return the row and column, respectively, of the current mouse position. The return value is relative to the window where output is currently being sent. Most of the time, that's the active form. However, when a form's AllowOutput property (added in VFP 8) is True, the two are not the same. (In code terms, WOUTPUT() <>

_SCREEN.ActiveForm.) This is a problem when you want to position something, like a shortcut menu, relative to the mouse.

VFP 9 solves this problem with a new, optional parameter to MROW() and MCOL(). Pass 0 as the first parameter to specify that the mouse position should be computed relative to the active form, whether or not output is being sent there. For example, you might have code like this:

```
nRow = MROW(0)
nCol = MCOL(0)
This.ShortcutMenu(nRow, nCol)
```

Grid improvements

In addition to memo and field tips, described in the previous section, VFP 9 offers one major improvement and one change in functionality related to grids. The improvement means grids can be used in many situations where they were previously unworkable.

Optimize filtered grid performance

In earlier versions of VFP, filtered grids do not use Rushmore to optimize their display. As a result, a form with a grid on a large filtered table may be so slow to appear that the user thinks the application has frozen.

VFP 9 finally gives you the option to apply Rushmore in this situation. The new Optimize property tells a grid whether or not to use Rushmore. The default, False, keeps the old, slow behavior. Set Optimize to True to make filtered grids pay attention and appear instantly.

Why would you ever choose not to set Optimize to True? According to Help, there are some situations where the process of optimizing could affect your results. Optimization is performed not only when the grid is initially drawn, but when it's activated or its Refresh method fires. If the underlying data use row buffering (probably not a good choice with a grid, anyway), the optimization process may commit changes.

Our take is that we will set Optimize to True in our base classes and don't expect to ever turn it off.

ControlSource reset with RecordSource

Changing the RecordSource of a running grid is a risky proposition. It throws away any customization, such as changing the controls in the grid or sizing the columns. According to Help, VFP 9 adds one more thing to that list. When the RecordSource of a grid is changed, the ControlSource property of each column is set to the empty string. This prevents errors that might occur if the new RecordSource has different fields than the old one.

We see this behavior in VFP 9. That said, in our tests, we also see it with VFP 8 SP1 and VFP 7 SP1. Perhaps this is one of those situations where it didn't work under certain circumstances in earlier versions and now always works.

Odds and ends

This section looks at a few more changes that affect forms and controls, but aren't easily categorized.

WordWrap for checkboxes and option buttons

While the captions for most checkboxes and option buttons are brief, now and then, you need a longer caption. In VFP 8 and earlier, these controls don't support word wrap, so making long captions look good is difficult. VFP 9 adds the WordWrap property to CheckBox and OptionButton.

The control must be large enough to show the caption. You can either manually size it or set AutoSize to True. When WordWrap is True and you set AutoSize to True, the control leaves the Width as is and expands vertically to make room for the caption.

These two controls also have many additional choices for Alignment in VFP 9. When WordWrap is .T., the Alignment setting controls not only the position of the caption relative to the graphical portion of the control, but also the positioning of the wrapped text within the control. The form in **Figure 15** includes three checkboxes, all with WordWrap set to True, but using three (of the nine) different values for Alignment.

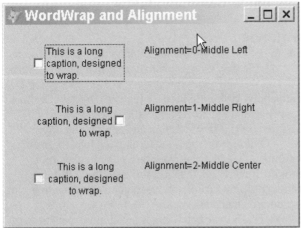

Figure 15. For word-wrapped checkboxes and option buttons, Alignment determines whether text appears on the left or right of the control and how the text is aligned within the control.

 *The form in **Figure 15** is included as Wrapped.SCX in the Developer Downloads for this chapter, available from **www.hentzenwerke.com**.*

No deletion in grid used as listbox

VFP 8 added several properties that make it easier to use a grid like a listbox, as a control for a user to choose one record. VFP 9 plugs one flaw in that scenario.

When you set the AllowCellSelection property to False, cells in the grid don't get focus. However, in VFP 8, a user can still click into the delete mark column and delete records from the grid. In VFP 9, when AllowCellSelection is False, clicks in that column are ignored.

Set index order in the data environment

VFP has always allowed you to specify the index order to use for tables in the Data Environment via the Order property. VFP 9 adds the ability to determine the direction of the index.

When you specify an index programmatically, using the SET ORDER command or the ORDER clause of the USE command, you can specify ascending or descending order. The new OrderDirection property gives you the same ability for tables opened in the Data Environment. OrderDirection has three values, shown in **Table 9**.

Table 9. *The OrderDirection property lets you specify whether an index is used in ascending or descending order.*

Value	Meaning
0	Use the order in which the index tag was created.
1	Use ascending order.
2	Use descending order.

You might be surprised to see three settings for this property. Ascending and descending are straightforward, but the default setting of 0 calls for explanation. VFP allows you to create indexes in either ascending or descending order; to create an index in descending order, add the DESCENDING keyword to the INDEX command. Setting OrderDirection to 0 indicates that the table should use the index in the direction it was created, whether ascending or descending.

More control over added properties and methods

The AddProperty and WriteMethod methods let you add properties and methods, respectively, to an object. AddProperty is available at design-time and run time, while WriteMethod is design-time only. VFP 9 adds the ability to specify at design-time whether a new property or method is public, protected, or hidden, as well as letting you provide a description for the new member. Two additional parameters, nVisibility and cDescription, are used for the new information.

The new syntax for AddProperty is:

```
oObject.AddProperty( cName [, eValue [, nVisibility [, cDescription ] ] ] )
```

The new syntax for WriteMethod is:

```
oObject.WriteMethod( cName, cCode [, lCreate [, nVisibility
                [, cDescription ] ] ] )
```

The nVisibility parameter has three possible values: 1-Public, 2-Protected, and 3-Hidden. cDescription accepts a string to serve as the member's description.

Not only can you use AddProperty and WriteMethod to add members with specified visibility and description, but you can also change the visibility or description of an existing property or method by passing a different value for nVisibility or cDescription. If you omit either parameter, an existing member keeps its current value for that attribute.

The bottom line

VFP 9 continues the pattern of making it easier for developers to create attractive, functional user interfaces. Improvements range from major, such as dockable forms, to minor, such as specifying direction for an index, but each contributes to a better result.

Updates and corrections for this chapter can be found on Hentzenwerke's website, **www.hentzenwerke.com**. Click "Catalog" and navigate to the page for this book.

Chapter 14
Language Improvements

Visual FoxPro's programming language is rich and powerful. But there's always room for improvement. Beyond the enhancements described in other chapters, VFP 9 includes a variety of changes in the language that can make your code faster to write, faster to run, and even allow you to do things you couldn't in earlier versions.

Some of the enhancements in the programming language in VFP 9 are discussed in other chapters, such as improvements in the SQL sub-language (Chapter 8, "SQL Changes") and enhancements in the SQL pass-through functions (Chapter 11, "Working with Remote Data"). However, a number of other changes make life easier for VFP developers. One big enhancement is support for Windows message events. Other smaller changes include improvements in some string functions.

Fewer limits

One of the design goals for VFP 9 was to eliminate or at least raise the limits of earlier versions. For example, arrays can now have more than 64K elements. Given VFP's powerful cursor engine, why would you ever need an array of more than 65,535 elements? There may be several valid reasons, but Rick Schummer ran into one himself: ADIR(). A client asked him to process a directory of images in some way. It turns out the directory had more than 14,000 images in it (why you'd do that is a valid question, but it wasn't Rick's choice). ADIR() creates an array with five columns, and 14,000 x 5 is more than 65,535, so his program bombed on the ADIR() statement. Fortunately, VFP 9 was in beta by this point, so he ran the program in that version without problems. You are limited by the amount of memory available or 2 GB, whichever is lower. Also, arrays containing objects are still limited to 64K elements because that's the maximum number of objects that can be created.

Procedure size limits have been removed. Previously, the compiled size of a procedure was limited to 64K. The limit now is just available memory. Again, in a powerful OOP system such as VFP, you have to wonder why someone would design a system that pushed these limits.

VFP 9 also lifts the former limit of 128 levels on the call stack. The new STACKSIZE setting in CONFIG.FPW allows you to set the maximum nesting level from 32 to 64,000. Once again, other than highly recursive code, we can't see why this was an issue for VFP developers, but perhaps it was an easy thing to do so the VFP team just went ahead with it.

Improved string handling

VFP has always had fast yet powerful string handling functions. VFP 9 improves some of these functions even further.

TRIM(), RTRIM(), LTRIM(), and ALLTRIM()

You can now specify what characters the TRIM functions—TRIM(), RTRIM(), LTRIM(), and ALLTRIM()—remove from a string. These functions accept new parameters: a numeric value indicating case-sensitivity (0 or omitted for case-sensitive, 1 for case-insensitive) and one or more characters to remove. For example, in the past, you might write code like the following to strip all white space (spaces, tabs, carriage returns, and line feeds) from the start and end of a string while preserving any occurrences in the middle:

```
do while inlist(left(lcString, 1), chr(13), chr(10), chr(9), ' ')
  lcString = substr(lcString, 2)
enddo
do while inlist(right(lcString, 1), chr(13), chr(10), chr(9), ' ')
  lcString = left(lcString, len(lcString) - 1)
enddo
```

In VFP 9, this simply becomes:

```
lcString = alltrim(lcString, 0, chr(13), chr(10), chr(9), ' ')
```

ALINES()

There are a couple of changes in ALINES(). First, the third parameter, which used to indicate whether the lines should be trimmed (.T.) or not (.F.), can now accept a numeric value. See **Table 1** for a list of the values, which are additive. The second change is if ALINES() is used on a Varbinary or Blob data, the resulting array contains Varbinary elements.

Table 1. *The values for the third parameter to ALINES().*

Value	Description
1	For character values, remove leading and trailing spaces from lines. For Varbinary and Blob values, remove trailing zeroes. This is the same as passing .T. (which you can still do for backward compatibility) in earlier versions.
2	Include the last element in the array even if it's empty.
4	Omit empty elements in the array.
8	Use case-insensitive parsing.
16	Include the parsing characters in the array.

Here's an example (taken from TestALines.PRG) that shows the differences between using 2 and 4 for the third parameter. There are four lines in the array with no parameter specified, five when 2 is used, and three when 4 is used.

```
text to lcText noshow
Hi
What's New

readers

endtext
lnLines0 = alines(laLines, lcText)
```

```
lnLines2 = alines(laLines, lcText, 2)
lnLines4 = alines(laLines, lcText, 4)
messagebox(transform(lnLines0) + ' lines with no parameter' + chr(13) + ;
    transform(lnLines2) + ' lines with "include last line" (2)' + chr(13) + ;
    transform(lnLines4) + ' lines with "no empty elements" (4)')
```

In the next example, also taken from TestALines.PRG, the elements only have the closing brackets when 16 is specified:

```
lcText = '<html><body>This is some text</body></html>'
lcMessage = ''
for lnI = 1 to alines(laLines, lcText, '>')
  lcMessage = lcMessage + laLines[lnI] + chr(13)
next lnI
messagebox('Without "include parsing characters" (16):' + chr(13) + chr(13) + ;
    lcMessage)
lcMessage = ''
for lnI = 1 to alines(laLines, lcText, 16, '>')
  lcMessage = lcMessage + laLines[lnI] + chr(13)
next lnI
messagebox('With "include parsing characters" (16):' + chr(13) + chr(13) + ;
    lcMessage)
```

 The Developer Download files for this chapter, available at **www.hentzenwerke.com**, *include TestALines.PRG.*

TEXT

The TEXT command has a new clause, FLAGS nValue, that customizes the behavior of the command. Specifying 1 for nValue suppresses output to the file specified in _TEXT. (_TEXT provides a way of performing text merge to a file opened with low-level file functions. See the sample code for an example.) Specifying 2 preserves blank lines preceding the text. These values are additive. Using 2 is especially helpful because without it, you have to manually add a blank line between outputs to avoid having the end of one output appear on the same line at the start of another. A common use for this is generating log files or HTML.

The following code (TestText.PRG) shows the effect of these values. The first message shows "This is test 1This is test 2" on one line and "This is test 3" on another line (it was preceded by a carriage return and line feed because 2 was included in the FLAGS value) and the second message shows that "This is test 3" was not sent to the output file because 1 was included in the value.

```
_text = fcreate('somefile.txt')
text to lcText noshow
This is test 1
endtext

text to lcText additive noshow
This is test 2
endtext
```

```
text to lcText additive noshow flags 3
This is test 3
endtext

fclose(_text)
messagebox('The contents of the string are:' + chr(13) + chr(13) + lcText)
messagebox('The contents of the file are:' + chr(13) + chr(13) + ;
  filetostr('somefile.txt'))
```

The PRETEXT clause of the TEXT command supports a new (additive) value: add 8 to eliminate linefeeds before each line.

The Developer Download files for this chapter, available at ***www.hentzenwerke.com****, include TestText.PRG.*

STREXTRACT()

VFP 9 supports a new value in the last parameter (the flags parameter) for STREXTRACT(): add 4 to include the delimiters in the return value. This is particularly handy when parsing HTML or XML, because previously you had to manually add the delimiters back to the expression. In the following example (TestStrExtract.PRG), the return value of the first STREXTRACT() doesn't include "<img " or ">" but the second one does.

```
text to lcText noshow
<html>
<body>
Here is a picture: <img src="SomeFile.GIF" width="150" height="200">
</body>
</html>
endtext

messagebox('Without "include delimiters" (4) flag:' + chr(13) + chr(13) + ;
  strextract(lcText, '<img ', '>', 1) + chr(13) + chr(13) + ;
  'With "include delimiters" (4) flag:' + chr(13) + chr(13) + ;
  strextract(lcText, '<img ', '>', 1, 4))
```

The Developer Download files for this chapter, available at ***www.hentzenwerke.com****, include TestStrExtract.PRG.*

Object-related functions

Developers who write design-time tools will like this new feature: passing 0 for the third parameter to NEWOBJECT() creates the specified object without firing any initialization code (that is, code in events such as Init, Load, Activate, and BeforeOpenTables). When the object is destroyed, no destructor code (such as in Destroy or Unload) is fired. This is typically needed when you want to examine the structure of a class using AMEMBERS() (which means you have to instantiate it), but don't want its normal behavior to occur. For example, suppose the following class exists in TestClass.PRG:

```
define class Noisy as Custom
  function Init
    messagebox('In init')
  endfunc
  function Destroy
    messagebox('In destroy')
  endfunc
enddefine
```

The following code won't display the message boxes from the Noisy class, only the one in this code:

```
loObject = newobject('Noisy', 'testclass.prg', 0)
messagebox('Noisy has ' + transform(amembers(laMembers, loObject, 1)) + ;
  ' members')
release loObject
```

AGETCLASS() and PEMSTATUS(, 0) (which tells you if the specified member was changed) now operate in the VFP run-time. Most developers don't need to use AGETCLASS() at run time, but some tool developers may. However, the change to PEMSTATUS(, 0) is important because one of the things it provides is the ability to tell whether a method has code in it or not.

Here's an example. Suppose you use the Chain of Responsibility error handling mechanism described in the error handling white paper available on the Technical Papers page of **http://www.stonefield.com**. This mechanism needs to determine if its container has any code in its Error method or not, because if it doesn't, passing the error to that method breaks the chain and improperly handles errors as a result. (An example of such a container is a base class Page in a PageFrame.) The following code uses PEMSTATUS(, 0) to determine whether it can safely pass the error to its container; if not, it continues to look up the containership hierarchy until it finds a container it can use.

```
loParent = This.Parent
do while vartype(loParent) = 'O'
  do case
    case pemstatus(loParent, 'Error', 0)
      exit
    case type('loParent.Parent') = 'O'
      loParent = loParent.Parent
    otherwise
      loParent = .NULL.
  endcase
enddo while vartype('loParent') = 'O'
if vartype(loParent) = 'O'
  loParent.Error(tnError, tcMethod, tnLine)
else
* handle the error ourselves since this is the end of the chain
endif vartype(loParent) = 'O'
```

In earlier versions of VFP, this code only works at run time if debug information is included in the EXE. In VFP 9, this works even if the debug info setting is off.

One other PEMSTATUS() change: PEMSTATUS(, 5) now returns .F. for hidden native properties. Visually subclassable objects, such as DataEnvironment, Relation, and CursorAdapter, inherit from an internal RECT class, so they have properties defined in that class, such as Visible, Top, Left, and so forth, that aren't applicable. VFP hides these properties in the Properties window and IntelliSense, and AMEMBERS() doesn't see them, but in earlier versions of VFP, PEMSTATUS(, 5) returns .T. The VFP 9 version now returns .F.

Microsoft added the Collection base class in VFP 8, and it's been a wonderful addition except for one peculiarity: if you add objects to a collection, the FOR EACH command returns COM objects rather than VFP objects. This causes problems with functions such as AMEMBERS() and COMPOBJ(), as TestForEach.PRG illustrates:

```
loCollection = createobject('Collection')
loCollection.Add(createobject('Custom'))
for each loObject in loCollection
  messagebox('The object has '+ transform(amembers(laMembers, loObject, 1)) + ;
    ' members as a COM object')
next loObject
for each loObject in loCollection foxobject
  messagebox('The object has '+ transform(amembers(laMembers, loObject, 1)) + ;
    ' members as a VFP object')
next loObject
```

The first message shows zero members for the object. That's obviously not right, but has to do with the fact that loObject isn't a VFP Custom object, but is recast as a COM object. The second message displays the correct value; because of the new FOXOBJECT keyword in the FOR EACH command, loObject is a real VFP object.

CLEAR CLASSLIB is enhanced in VFP 9 to implicitly do a CLEAR CLASS for each class within the specified class library.

You can no longer set the value of a class' property to an instantiated object when the property is defined. For example, the assignment to MyProperty in following code now gives a "statement is not valid in a class definition" error when you try to instantiate the class:

```
define class MyClass as Custom
  MyProperty = createobject('Custom')
enddefine
```

Perform the assignment to the property in the Init method of the class instead.

 *TestForEach.PRG is included in the Developer Download files for this chapter, available at **www.hentzenwerke.com**.*

Windows message events

Windows communicates events to applications by passing them messages. Although VFP exposes some of these messages through events in VFP objects, such as MouseDown and Click, many messages are not available to VFP developers. One common request is the ability to detect an application switch. For example, we're aware of a VFP application that hooks into GoldMine, a popular contact management system, displaying additional information about the current contact. If the user switches to GoldMine, moves to a different contact, and then switches back to the VFP application, it would be nice to refresh the display so it shows information about the new contact. Unfortunately, there was no direct way to do this in earlier versions of VFP; the application uses a timer to constantly check which contact is currently displayed in GoldMine.

VFP 9 extends the BINDEVENT() function added in VFP 8 to support Windows messages. The syntax for this use is:

```
bindevent(hWnd, nMessage, oEventHandler, cDelegate)
```

where hWnd is the Windows handle for the window that receives events, nMessage is the Windows message number, and oEventHandler and cDelegate are the object and method that fire when the message is received by the window. Unlike VFP events, only one handler can bind to a particular hWnd and nMessage combination. Specifying a second event handler object or delegate method causes the first binding to be replaced with the second. VFP doesn't check for valid hWnd or nMessage values; if either is invalid, nothing happens because the specified window can't receive the specified message.

For hWnd, you can specify _Screen.hWnd or _VFP.hWnd to trap messages sent to the application or a form's hWnd for those messages sent to the form. VFP controls don't have a Windows handle, but ActiveX controls do, so you also bind to them.

There are hundreds of Windows messages. Examples of such messages are: WM_POWERBROADCAST (0x0218), sent when a power event occurs such as low battery or switching to standby mode; WM_THEMECHANGED (0x031A), which indicates the Windows XP theme has changed; and WM_ACTIVATE (0x0006), raised when switching to or from an application. (Windows messages are usually referred to by a name starting with WM_.) Documentation for almost all Windows messages is available at **http://msdn.microsoft.com/library/en-us/winui/winui/windowsuserinterface/windowui.asp**. The values for the WM_ constants are in the WinUser.H file that's part of the Platform SDK, which you can download from **http://www.microsoft.com/msdownload/platformsdk/sdkupdate/**.

The event handler method must accept four parameters: hWnd, the handle for the window that received the message, nMessage, the Windows message number, and two Integer parameters, the contents of which vary depending on the Windows message (the documentation for each message describes the values of these parameters). The method must return an Integer, which contains a result value. One of the return values is BROADCAST_QUERY_DENY (0x424D5144, which represents the string "BMQD") that prevents the event from occurring.

If you want the message to be processed in the normal manner, which is something most event handlers should do, you have to call the VFP Windows message handler in the event handler method; this is sort of like using DODEFAULT() in VFP method code. The event handler method most likely returns the return value of the VFP Windows message handler. Here's an example of an event handler that does this (it does nothing else):

```
lparameters hWnd, ;
  Msg, ;
  wParam, ;
  lParam
local lnOldProc, ;
  lnResult
#define GWL_WNDPROC -4
declare integer GetWindowLong in Win32API ;
  integer hWnd, integer nIndex
declare integer CallWindowProc in Win32API ;
  integer lpPrevWndFunc, integer hWnd, integer Msg, integer wParam, ;
  integer lParam
lnOldProc = GetWindowLong(_screen.hWnd, GWL_WNDPROC)
lnResult  = CallWindowProc(lnOldProc, hWnd, Msg, wParam, lParam)
return lnResult
```

Of course, the event handler doesn't need to declare the Windows API functions or call GetWindowLong each time; you could put that code in the Init method of the class, storing the return value of GetWindowLong in a custom property, and then using that property in the call to CallWindowProc in the event handler. The next sample shows this.

To determine which messages are bound, use AEVENTS(ArrayName, 1). It fills the specified array with one row per binding and four columns, containing the values of the parameters passed to BINDEVENT().

You can unbind events using UNBINDEVENT(hWnd [, nMessage]). Omitting the second parameter unbinds all messages for the specified window. Pass only 0 to unbind all messages for all windows. Events are also automatically unbound the next time the message occurs after the event handling object is destroyed.

The VFP team added three SYS() functions related to Windows events in VFP 9. SYS(2325, wHandle) returns the wHandle (an internal VFP wrapper for hWnd) for the client window of the window whose wHandle is passed as a parameter. (A client window is a window inside a window; for example, _Screen is a client window of _VFP.) SYS(2326, nWnd) returns the wHandle for the window specified with hWnd. SYS(2327, wHandle) returns the hWnd for the window specified with wHandle. The documentation for these functions indicates they're for BINDEVENT() scenarios using the VFP·API Library Construction Kit. However, you can also use them to get the hWnd for the client window of a VFP IDE window. The FindIDEClientWindow method of the IDEWindowsEvents class in TestWinEventsForIDE.PRG shows an example using these functions.

TestWinEventsForIDE.PRG demonstrates event binding to VFP IDE windows. Set lcCaption to the caption of the IDE window you want to bind events to, run the program, and activate and deactivate the window, move it, resize it, and so forth. You should see Windows events echoed to the screen. When you finish, type RESUME and press Enter in the Command window to clean up. To test this with the client window of an IDE window, uncomment the indicated code. You can also bind to other events by adding BINDEVENT() statements to this code; use the constants in WinEvents.H for the values for the desired events.

> TestWinEventsForIDE.PRG only works with non-dockable IDE windows, so
> before you run this program, right-click in the title bar of the window you want
> to test and ensure Dockable is turned off.

```
#include WinEvents.H

lcCaption      = 'Command'
loEventHandler = createobject('IDEWindowsEvents')
lnhWnd         = loEventHandler.FindIDEWindow(lcCaption)
* Uncomment this code to receive events for the window's client window instead
*lnhWnd         = loEventHandler.FindIDEClientWindow(lcCaption)
if lnhWnd > 0
  bindevent(lnhWnd, WM_SETFOCUS,     loEventHandler, 'EventHandler')
  bindevent(lnhWnd, WM_KILLFOCUS,    loEventHandler, 'EventHandler')
  bindevent(lnhWnd, WM_MOVE,         loEventHandler, 'EventHandler')
  bindevent(lnhWnd, WM_SIZE,         loEventHandler, 'EventHandler')
  bindevent(lnhWnd, WM_MOUSEACTIVATE, loEventHandler, 'EventHandler')
  bindevent(lnhWnd, WM_KEYDOWN,      loEventHandler, 'EventHandler')
  bindevent(lnhWnd, WM_KEYUP,        loEventHandler, 'EventHandler')
  bindevent(lnhWnd, WM_CHAR,         loEventHandler, 'EventHandler')
  bindevent(lnhWnd, WM_DEADCHAR,     loEventHandler, 'EventHandler')
  bindevent(lnhWnd, WM_KEYLAST,      loEventHandler, 'EventHandler')
  clear
  suspend
  unbindevents(0)
  clear
else
  messagebox('The ' + lcCaption + ' window was not found.')
endif lnhWnd > 0

define class IDEWindowsEvents as Custom
  cCaption = ''
  nOldProc = 0

  function Init
    declare integer GetWindowLong in Win32API ;
      integer hWnd, integer nIndex
    declare integer CallWindowProc in Win32API ;
      integer lpPrevWndFunc, integer hWnd, integer Msg, integer wParam, ;
      integer lParam
    declare integer FindWindowEx in Win32API;
      integer, integer, string, string
    declare integer GetWindowText in Win32API ;
      integer, string @, integer
    This.nOldProc = GetWindowLong(_screen.hWnd, GWL_WNDPROC)
  endfunc

  function FindIDEWindow(tcCaption)
    local lnhWnd, ;
      lnhChild, ;
      lcCaption
    This.cCaption = tcCaption
    lnhWnd        = _screen.hWnd
    lnhChild      = 0
    do while .T.
      lnhChild = FindWindowEx(lnhWnd, lnhChild, 0, 0)
```

```
      if lnhChild = 0
        exit
      endif lnhChild = 0
      lcCaption = space(80)
      GetWindowText(lnhChild, @lcCaption, len(lcCaption))
      lcCaption = upper(left(lcCaption, at(chr(0), lcCaption) - 1))
      if lcCaption = upper(tcCaption)
        exit
      endif lcCaption = upper(tcCaption)
    enddo while .T.
    return lnhChild
  endfunc

  function FindIDEClientWindow(tcCaption)
    local lnhWnd, ;
      lnwHandle, ;
      lnwChild
    lnhWnd = This.FindIDEWindow(tcCaption)
    if lnhWnd > 0
      lnwHandle = sys(2326, lnhWnd)
      lnwChild  = sys(2325, lnwHandle)
      lnhWnd    = sys(2327, lnwChild)
    endif lnhWnd > 0
    return lnhWnd
  endfunc

  function EventHandler(hWnd, Msg, wParam, lParam)
    ? 'The ' + This.cCaption + ' window received event #' + transform(Msg)
    return CallWindowProc(This.nOldProc, hWnd, Msg, wParam, lParam)
  endfunc
enddefine
```

When you run TestWinEventsForIDE.PRG, you'll find not all events occur for all IDE or client windows. This is likely due to the way VFP implements windows, which is somewhat different from other Windows applications.

WindowsMessagesDemo.SCX is another example. It shows hooking into activate and deactivate events as well as certain Windows shell events, such as inserting or removing a CD or USB drive. The latter shows an interesting use of Windows events: the code registers _VFP to receive a subset of Windows shell events as a custom Windows event. The following code, taken from the Init method of this form, handles the necessary setup. Items in upper-case are constants defined in either WinEvents.H or ShellFileEvents.H. The call to SHChangeNotifyRegister tells Windows to register _VFP to receive disk events, media insertion and removal events, and drive addition and removal events using a custom message. This code then binds device change events and the custom message we just defined to the HandleEvents method of the form:

```
declare integer SHChangeNotifyRegister in shell32 ;
  integer hWnd, integer fSources, integer fEvents, integer wMsg, ;
  integer cEntries, string @SEntry

* Register us to receive certain shell events as a custom Windows event.

lcSEntry = replicate(chr(0), 8)
This.nShNotify = SHChangeNotifyRegister(_vfp.hWnd, SHCNE_DISKEVENTS, ;
  SHCNE_MEDIAINSERTED + SHCNE_MEDIAREMOVED + SHCNE_DRIVEADD + ;
```

```
SHCNE_DRIVEREMOVED, WM_USER_SHNOTIFY, 1, @lcSEntry)

* Bind to the Windows events we're interested in.

bindevent(_vfp.hWnd, WM_DEVICECHANGE,  This, 'HandleEvents')
bindevent(_vfp.hWnd, WM_USER_SHNOTIFY, This, 'HandleEvents')
```

> *The call to SHChangeNotifyRegister requires Windows XP. If you're using an earlier operating system, comment out the assignment statement for This.nSHNotify in the Init method of WindowsMessagesDemo.SCX.*

Support for Windows event binding is an incredible addition to VFP; it allows you to hook into just about anything that goes on in Windows. We expect to see many cool uses of this as the VFP community starts to learn about its capabilities.

> *The Developer Download files for this chapter, available at **www.hentzenwerke.com**, include TestWinEventsForIDE.PRG and WindowsMessagesDemo.SCX.*

Internationalization issues

FoxPro has had strong support for internationalization issues since FoxPro 2.x and the addition of code pages and collate sequences. VFP 9 adds additional support.

The fourth parameter for GETFONT() indicates what language script to display by default. In VFP 8, passing 0 means you want the Script combo box in the Font dialog disabled, while 1 means select Western by default. The problem is that unless you know the default language script setting for the user, what value should you pass for this parameter? In VFP 9, 0 now means Western and 1 means the user default script. As before, omit the parameter to disable the combo box.

There are three different mechanisms to indicate the character set for text: the code page, which is used for files such as tables, the FontCharSet property of various controls such as text boxes, and the locale ID, which applies to certain functions such as STRCONV(). Unfortunately, in earlier versions of VFP, there wasn't an easy way to convert between these different mechanisms. In VFP 9, STRCONV() accepts a locale ID, code page, or FontCharSet value for the third parameter (previously, only a locale ID was supported). A new fourth parameter indicates which type is used: 0 or omitted means locale ID, 1 means code page, and 2 means FontCharSet.

SET SYSMENU and DEFINE POPUP have new RTLJUSTIFY and LTRJUSTIFY clauses that tell VFP to justify the text in a right-to-left or left-to-right manner. These clauses are ignored unless Windows is configured to a Middle-Eastern locale. You can also set the justification for ToolTips using the new SYS(3009) function. SYS(3009, 1) specifies right-to-left and SYS(3009, 0) specifies left-to-right. This function returns the current value as a character.

There are three other internationalization changes. The new SYS(3101, [nCodePage]) function sets the code page used for character data translation in COM operations in the current datasession; it returns the current setting as a numeric value. SYS(3007, [nFontCharSet]) sets the language script used for ToolTips for controls; it returns the current value as a character. The FONT clause of the DEFINE MENU, DEFINE PAD, DEFINE POPUP, DEFINE BAR, DEFINE WINDOW, MODIFY WINDOW, and BROWSE commands can now accept a value for the language script to use; for example, BROWSE FONT Arial, 10, 161 specifies the Greek character set.

Other enhanced commands and functions

SET PATH
SET PATH has a new ADDITIVE clause that allows you to add to the existing VFP path. Formerly, you had to do something like:

```
lcCurrPath = set('PATH')
set path to &lcCurrPath, C:\MyNewDirectory
```

Now it's as simple as:

```
set path to 'C:\MyNewDirectory' additive
```

Note that quotes are required around the path even if there aren't any spaces in it when you use the ADDITIVE clause; if you omit them, the path becomes "C:\MyNewDirectory ADDITIVE." The size of the path has also increased from 1024 to 4095 characters.

TYPE()
The TYPE() function has a new parameter: specify 1 to determine if the variable is an array or collection; TYPE() returns "A" if it's an array, "C" if it's a collection, or "U" if neither. For example (TestType.PRG):

```
X = 1
dimension Y[1]
clear
? type('X', 1)          && displays "U"
? type('Y')             && displays "L", the data type for Y[1]
? type('Y', 1)          && displays "A"
loObject = createobject('Collection')
? type('loObject')      && displays "O"
? type('loObject', 1)   && displays "C"
```

 *The Developer Download files for this chapter, available at **www.hentzenwerke.com**, include TestType.PRG.*

INPUTBOX()

You can now specify what value to return if the user clicks Cancel or presses Esc in the dialog displayed by the INPUTBOX() function by specifying a value for the new sixth parameter. In previous versions of VFP, this function returns a blank string in this case. Here's an example that demonstrates this; the message displays "Cancel value" when you click the Cancel button or press Esc.

```
messagebox(inputbox('Click on cancel', 'Test inputbox()', 'Default value', 0, ;
   'Timeout value', 'Cancel value'))
```

SYS(1104), SYS(3056), and SYS(2019)

Three SYS() functions have been enhanced:

* SYS(1104), which purges cached memory, now supports an optional workarea or alias parameter. Specifying this tells VFP to purge the cache for the specified table or cursor.

* SYS(3056) can now write the settings of the Tools | Options dialog to the Registry if you use 2 as the optional parameter. This does the same thing as clicking the Set As Default button in that dialog.

* VFP 8 added the ability to specify an external configuration file by adding ALLOWEXTERNAL = ON to the configuration file built into an EXE. SYS(2019) returns the name of the internal configuration file if you specify 2 as the optional parameter. Specify 1 or omit the parameter to return the name of the external configuration file.

FFLUSH()

The FFLUSH() function, used to write out to disk changes to a file opened with low-level file functions, has a new second parameter. Pass .T. to force VFP to immediately write the file to disk. If you omit this parameter or pass .F., VFP writes the file when it gets a chance to.

SET DOHISTORY

Remember the SET DOHISTORY command? Okay, we don't either. It's a command that outputs lines of code as they execute. This was important in the days before Microsoft added the Trace window to FoxPro, but we haven't used it since. (Even the help topic for SET DOHISTORY states it's for backward compatibility only.) In VFP 9, the output now goes to the Debug Output window, if it's open, rather than to the current output device (such as _Screen or a printer if SET PRINT ON is used).

MROW() and MCOL()

You can now pass 0 to MROW() and MCOL() to return the position of the mouse pointer based on the active form. This prevents a problem using these functions under some conditions: they normally reference the form whose name is returned by WOUTPUT(), but WOUTPUT() doesn't return the name of the form when its AllowOutput property is .F.

EXECSCRIPT()

You can now pass parameters to code executed by EXECSCRIPT() by reference. For example, the following code, taken from TestExecScript.PRG, gives a "missing operand" error on the second EXECSCRIPT() statement in VFP 8 but runs properly in VFP 9:

```
text to lcCode noshow
lparameters tnValue
tnValue = tnValue + 1
endtext

x = 5
execscript(lcCode, x)
? x   && displays 5
execscript(lcCode, @x)
? x   && displays 6
```

The Developer Download files for this chapter, available at **www.hentzenwerke.com**, *include TestExecScript.PRG.*

SCATTER

The SCATTER command no longer allows the MEMVAR and NAME clauses to be specified at the same time, since that use is ambiguous. Earlier versions permit this, with the MEMVAR clause overriding NAME.

BINTOC() and CTOBIN()

These functions, which convert between numeric values and their binary character equivalents, are much more useful in VFP 9 because they've been enhanced to support more types of conversion. If you write code that does low-level manipulation of binary files, such as DBFs, or calls Windows API functions, you can replace many lines of code with single calls to BINTOC() and CTOBIN().

In earlier versions of VFP, the first parameter for BINTOC() is an integer value (the numeric value to convert to a binary string) and the second (which is optional; the default is 4) is the values 1, 2, or 4, indicating the length of the resulting string. VFP 9 supports a wider range of values for the first parameter and the second parameter can now accept character "flags" values.

Table 2 displays the possible values for the second parameter and the relationship they have with the first parameter. You can specify 1, 2, 4, or 8 as numeric or character values and "B," "F," "R," or "S" in upper or lower case. "R" and "S" can be combined with one of the other values (for example, "4RS") but the other values are mutually exclusive.

Table 2*. The values for second parameter for BINTOC().*

Value	Description
1	Creates a one-byte string. The first parameter must be an Integer between -128 and 127.
2	Creates a two-byte string. The first parameter must be an Integer between -32,768 and 32,767.
4	Creates a four-byte string. The first parameter must be an Integer between - 2,147,483,648 and 2,147,483,647. This is the default if the second parameter is omitted.
8	Creates an eight-byte string. The first parameter must be a Numeric, Float, Double, or Currency value.
B	Creates an eight-byte string from the Double value in the first parameter.
F	Creates a four-byte string from the Numeric or Float value in the first parameter.
R	Reverses the binary string so the least significant byte is in the first character and the most significant in the last character. This is the format normally used for binary values on Intel processors.
S	Prevents the sign bit from being toggled.

In earlier versions of VFP, CTOBIN() accepted just one parameter: the binary string to convert to a numeric value. In VFP 9, the optional second parameter specifies how to convert the string. See **Table 3** for the possible values. As with BINTOC(), you can specify 1, 2, 4, or 8 as numeric or character values and "N," "Y," "R," or "S" in upper or lower case. "R" and "S" can be combined with one of the other values but the other values are mutually exclusive.

Table 3*. The values for second parameter for CTOBIN().*

Value	Description
1	The first parameter is a one-byte Integer data type. This value doesn't have to be specified but can be for clarity.
2	The first parameter is a two-byte Integer data type. This value doesn't have to be specified but can be for clarity.
4	The first parameter is a four-byte Integer data type. This value doesn't have to be specified but can be for clarity.
8	The first parameter is an eight-byte expression.
B	The first parameter is an eight-byte Double data type. This is the default if the first parameter is eight bytes and the second parameter isn't specified.
N	The first parameter is a four- or eight-byte Numeric or Float data type.
Y	The first parameter is an eight-byte Currency data type. CTOBIN() returns a Currency value.
R	The first parameter has the least significant byte in the first character and the most significant in the last character.
S	The sign bit will not be treated as a sign bit.

Due to their limited conversion abilities, the most common use for these functions in earlier versions of VFP is to create smaller index keys. For example, Integers are eight-byte values but an index on BINTOC(MyIntegerField) takes only four bytes per key. The VFP 9 versions, however, are a lot more useful, especially since they can convert to and from the format for binary values used on Intel processors. This format is often used in binary files and Windows API functions.

An example of how BINTOC() and CTOBIN() can be used with Windows API functions is the _ComDlg class in _System.VCX in the FFC subdirectory of the VFP home directory.

This class provides a simple OOP interface to the Common Dialogs API functions, giving you more control over the appearance and behavior of the dialogs than the VFP GETFILE() and PUTFILE() functions. The DialogHandler method of _ComDlg has to deal with Windows structures, which can be represented in VFP as strings containing binary values. DialogHandler calls the IntegerToString method of this class to convert a numeric value into its binary equivalent, and then stores this value into the appropriate place in the string "structure." Here's the code for IntegerToString:

```
LPARAMETERS nInteger, nBytes
LOCAL cRetVal
IF pCount() < 2
  nBytes = 4
ENDIF
cRetVal = ""
FOR nCurByte = 1 to nBytes
  cRetVal = cRetVal + ;
    CHR(BITAND(BITRSHIFT(nInteger, 8 * (nCurByte -1) ), 255))
ENDFOR
RETURN cRetVal
```

In VFP 9, calls to this method can be replaced with either of the following statements, depending on the desired length of the result:

```
bintoc(nInteger, "2RS")
bintoc(nInteger, "4RS")
```

DialogHandler also calls the StringToInteger method in this class to convert binary values in the string "structure" back to numeric values; it does this to obtain the return values from the API functions. Here's the code for StringToInteger:

```
LPARAMETERS cPDWORD, nBytes
LOCAL nCurByte, nRetVal
IF PCOUNT() < 2
  nBytes = LEN(cPDWord)
ENDIF
nRetVal = 0
FOR nCurByte = 1 to nBytes
  nRetVal = nRetVal + ASC(SUBSTR(cPDWord, nCurByte, 1))*(256^(nCurByte-1))
ENDFOR
RETURN nRetVal
```

Calls to this method can be replaced with:

```
ctobin(cPDWord, 'RS')
```

Here are some other examples:

```
x = bintoc(10.789)
? ctobin(x)            && Returns 10
x = bintoc($23.45, 8)
? ctobin(x, 'Y')       && Returns 23.45
? ctobin(x, 'N')       && Returns 1.3142213770657E-286
? ctobin(x, 'B')       && Returns 0.0000000000000E+0
```

Other new commands and functions

ICASE()

ICASE(), which is an abbreviation for "Immediate CASE," is one of our favorite new functions. It's similar to IIF(), except it acts like a DO CASE structure rather than an IF structure. This function saves having to use nested IIF() calls when you need an expression that selects between more than two values. Field expressions in the Report Designer are a common use for this. For example, rather than:

```
iif(SHIPVIA = 1, 'Fedex', iif(SHIPVIA = 2, 'UPS', ;
  iif(SHIPVIA = 3, 'DHL', 'Mail')))
```

you can use:

```
icase(SHIPVIA = 1, 'Fedex', SHIPVIA = 2, 'UPS', SHIPVIA = 3, 'DHL', 'Mail')
```

Parameters go in pairs. The first of a pair is the expression to evaluate and the second is the value to return if the expression is .T. If the last parameter isn't one of a pair (that is, there's an odd number of parameters), it's considered to be the "otherwise" value, such as "Mail" in the preceding example. If you don't supply an "otherwise" value and none of the expressions evaluates to .T., ICASE() returns .NULL.

CAST()

CAST(), another of our favorite new functions, allows you to convert data from one type into another. Data type conversion must be within reason, of course; Date fields cannot be converted to Numeric and vice versa. See the VFP help topic for a conversion chart showing which types can be converted to other types.

The syntax for CAST() is:

```
CAST( uExpression AS DataType [ ( nFieldWidth [, nPrecision ] ) ]
  [ NULL | NOT NULL ] )
```

uExpression is the expression to convert and DataType is the data type to convert it to. You can specify DataType as a letter (for example, "T" for DateTime") or a name (as discussed in Chapter 12, "Other Data Changes," VFP 9 supports long names for data types, such as "Numeric"). As in the CREATE TABLE command, some data types require a field width and possibly precision. You can also indicate whether null values are allowed or not.

You can use CAST() anywhere you would use an expression, even in SQL SELECT statements. Here's a simple example that converts a DateTime field in a table into a Date value in a cursor:

```
select ORDERID, cast(ORDERDATE as Date) as ORDERDATE from ORDERS
```

CAST() can be used to force a SQL SELECT statement to create a field of the correct data type and size from an expression. For example, this SQL SELECT statement:

```
select UNITPRICE * QUANTITY as TOTAL, ;
  iif(UNITPRICE * QUANTITY >= 1000, 50, 0) as SHIPPING ;
  from ORDERDETAILS
```

works properly if the first record has a total amount of $1,000 or more, but not if the amount is less. That's because VFP uses the first record to determine the data type and size of the column. If the amount is less than $1,000, the expression returns 0, so the SHIPPING column will be N(1, 0). As a result, it isn't big enough for 50, and displays asterisks instead. A trick that helps with this is to specify the smallest number using a placeholder with the proper number of digits, such as 00. However, it may not work in every situation, such as when you call a user-defined function. It also can't help if you want a different data type than VFP thinks you need, such as Currency.

If you change the SQL SELECT statement to:

```
select UNITPRICE * QUANTITY as TOTAL, ;
  cast(iif(UNITPRICE * QUANTITY >= 1000, 50, 0) as Numeric(5, 2)) as SHIPPING ;
  from ORDERDETAILS
```

or even:

```
select UNITPRICE * QUANTITY as TOTAL, ;
  cast(iif(UNITPRICE * QUANTITY >= 1000, 50, 0) as Currency) as SHIPPING ;
  from ORDERDETAILS
```

the values in the first record are unimportant; SHIPPING will always be the desired data type and size.

See Chapter 8, "SQL Changes," for more examples using CAST().

 TestCast.PRG, which shows how CAST() works, is included in the Developer Download files for this chapter, available at **www.hentzenwerke.com**.

SYS(2910)

What would a new version of VFP be without new SYS() functions? In addition to those discussed earlier in this chapter, SYS(2910) allows you to determine or set the number of items that appear in IDE (Interactive Development Environment) list and combo boxes, such as IntelliSense, and in the new AutoComplete feature for text boxes (discussed in Chapter 13,

"Forms and Controls"). This corresponds to the List display count setting in the View page of the Tools | Options dialog. The range is 5 to 200; the default is 15. SYS(2910) by itself returns the current value as a character string.

Tablet PC support

There are two new features that provide better support for Tablet PCs. The ISPEN() function returns .T. if the last mouse event was a pen tap. A logical place to use this is in the Click method of a control if you want to perform different behavior for mouse clicks and pen taps. A new property of _Screen, DisplayOrientation, indicates the display orientation. The values for this property are shown in **Table 4**. Interestingly, this property is read-write; changing its value causes the display orientation to change as if you changed it from the Control Panel.

Table 4. The values for _Screen.DisplayOrientation.

Value	Description
0	Upright landscape
1	Upright portrait
2	Inverted landscape
3	Inverted portrait

Clearing error information

The new CLEAR ERROR command resets the internal error structures to the same state as if no error happened. This means AERROR() does not alter the specified array, the ERROR() function returns zero, MESSAGE() and MESSAGE(1) return an empty string, and SYS(2018) returns an empty string.

This command allows developers to control the reporting of errors more efficiently. Prior to Visual FoxPro 9, AERROR() would fill the passed array with the details of last error whether an error occurred within the code you were checking or not. Now you can CLEAR ERROR before executing code with a potential problem, then check the results with AERROR() to see if an error was triggered.

Microsoft warns in the Help file against using CLEAR ERROR inside structured error handling (TRY...CATCH...FINALLY) because the exception object might not be valid after CLEAR ERROR.

 The Developer Downloads for this chapter, available from **www.hentzenwerke.com**, *include a program called ClearErrorExample.PRG, which demonstrates how CLEAR ERROR works. Run this program in an older version of VFP and then in VFP 9 to see the difference with respect to the behavior of AERROR().*

Summary

The language enhancements in VFP 9 make it easier than ever before to deliver the kinds of powerful applications our users expect. Some of them make your code faster to write, faster to run, and more maintainable because you can write less code. Others allow you to do things you couldn't before, such as hooking into Windows events.

Updates and corrections for this chapter can be found on Hentzenwerke's website, **www.hentzenwerke.com**. Click "Catalog" and navigate to the page for this book.

Chapter 15
Setup and Deployment

Last, but not least, we address the setup and deployment issues with respect to the changes in Visual FoxPro 9.

Setup and deployment are not the first topics Visual FoxPro developers think about when they hear a new version of their favorite development tool is nearing release. Sure, developers realize new run-time files are inevitable and there could be new file dependencies for the run-time, so why an entire chapter dedicated to this topic? How about better support for Terminal Services? How about the ability to capture coverage logs during run-time? How about a brand new version of InstallShield Express Visual FoxPro Limited Edition? We address these topics and more in this chapter, so read on!

New run-time files

Applications updated and released after a Visual FoxPro version upgrade require all the new run-time files ship with your application. It is very important to keep the run-times synced with the development version of Visual FoxPro. So what files do you need to distribute?

> The Visual FoxPro Help file discusses the various run-time files in the "Visual FoxPro Run-Time Libraries" topic.

There are a few directories to check for new run-time files. Your directories could be different depending on the operating system and the directory structure where you installed Visual FoxPro. For Visual FoxPro 9 you have the following files:

- C:\Program Files\Common Files\Microsoft Shared\VFP\ contains the VFP9R.DLL (main run-time library) and VFP9T.DLL (multi-threaded run-time) files. The language resource files: VFP9RChs.DLL (Chinese, Simplified), VFP9RCht.DLL (Chinese, Traditional), VFP9RCsy.DLL (Czech), VFP9RDeu.DLL (German), VFP9REnu.DLL (English), VFP9REsn.DLL (Spanish), VFP9RFra.DLL (French), VFP9RKor.DLL (Korean), and VFP9RRus.DLL (Russian). Finally, FOXHHelp9.EXE and FOXHHelpPs9.DLL (HTML Help system run-times), and GdiPlus.DLL (graphics dependency file).

- C:\Program Files\Common Files\System\Ole DB\ contains VFPOleDb.DLL (Visual FoxPro OLE DB Provider).

- C:\Program Files\Common Files\Merge Modules\ contains the merge modules used by InstallShield Express and other install tools that leverage the Windows Installer technology. These files include VFP9RChs.MSM, VFP9RCht.MSM, VFP9RCsy.MSM, VFP9RDeu.MSM, VFP9REsn.MSM, VFP9RFra.MSM, VFP9RKor.MSM, VFP9RRus.MSM, VFP9Runtime.MSM, VFP9HtmlHelp.MSM, VFPOleDb.MSM, VFP_GdiPlus.MSM, and

VFP9RptApps.MSM. The merge modules are not directly distributed to the customers.

The Visual FoxPro 9 version of VFPOleDB.DLL/MSM overrides the same named files installed with VFP 7 and 8. Microsoft recommends distributing the latest version of this file, even if your applications are released with Visual FoxPro 7 or 8 run-times.

The Visual FoxPro 9 version of the GdiPlus.DLL and VFP_GdiPlus.MSM files install over the exact named files previously installed by Visual FoxPro 8. This means your Visual FoxPro 8 applications are distributed with the graphics library installed with Visual FoxPro 9. Microsoft notes the new version is completely backwards compatible and will not have a negative impact on your Visual FoxPro 8 releases.

New run-time dependencies

The Visual FoxPro 9 run-times have a new dependency, the Microsoft C Runtime Library 7.1 (MSVcR71.DLL). This replaces the dependency of Microsoft Visual C++ 7.0 Runtime in Visual FoxPro 7 and 8. The merge module for this file is C:\Program Files\Common Files\Merge Modules\VC_User_Crt71_Rtl_X86_---.MSM. If you are deploying this file without Windows Installer and the merge module, you should install this file in the WinSysDir folder (on Windows XP this would be the Windows System32 folder).

If you are using the new reporting functionality, you need to include ReportPreview.APP and ReportOutput.APP with your application unless you create your own preview code. You also need to distribute ReportBuilder.APP if you allow users to modify reports and want them to use the new dialogs. See Chapter 5, "Enhancements in the Reporting System," for details on these APP files. The Fox Team included a new merge module for easier deployment with Windows Installer tools. The merge module is C:\Program Files\Common Files\Merge Modules\VFP9RptApps.MSM and is called Microsoft Visual FoxPro 9 Report Applications.

Some developers feel releasing an APP file externally from the primary executable exposes a security risk because the APP can be replaced with rogue code to intercept report information. Fortunately, the source code for ReportBuilder.APP, ReportPreview.APP, and ReportOutput.APP comes with VFP (unzip XSource.ZIP in the Tools\XSource subdirectory of the VFP home directory). If you include this source code in your project, there is no need to distribute the APP files. Instead, add the following code to your main program, application object, or report object to set the Report Designer system variables to the main PRG of each of the APP files:

```
_REPORTPREVIEW = "FrxPreview.prg"
_REPORTOUTPUT  = "FrxOutput.prg"
_REPORTBUILDER = "FrxBuilder.prg"
EXTERNAL PROC  FrxBuilder
EXTERNAL PROC  FrxPreview, FrxOutput
```

The first time you build your project, the Project Manager prompts you to locate FrxBuilder.PRG, FrxPreview.PRG, and possibly one or two additional files, found in the ReportBuilder and ReportPreview folders under Tools\Xsource. It then adds all the necessary components normally compiled into the APP files to your project. Another approach includes setting the three Report Designer system variables in the application Config.FPW and include the EXTERNAL PROC in the main program.

If you are deploying run-time-based IntelliSense in your applications, you need to deploy FoxCode.APP, which uses FoxTools.FLL.

Minor operating system requirements change

Windows 2000 still supports developing applications with Visual FoxPro 9, but it now requires Service Pack 3 or later. Visual FoxPro 8 only requires Service Pack 2. You can create and distribute run-time applications for Windows 98, Windows Me, Windows 2000 Service Pack 3 or later, and Windows XP. Again, only the Service Pack for Windows 2000 changed in this version.

SET COVERAGE command available at run time

Have you ever had a customer call and ask why a certain feature is running slowly? You test it at your office with your test data and the code performs as expected. You have the client send you a backup copy of their data and the error logs. You install it and it still performs snappily. Frustrated, you confirm the configuration of the customer's computers and find out they are better machines than the one you are using to test on. So why is it running so darn slow? It sure would be nice if your client had a license of Visual FoxPro, but they don't. You could run a coverage log on the code in production to see what the problem is, but unfortunately, the SET COVERAGE command is one of those commands ignored at run-time. That is, ignored until Visual FoxPro 9!

The Coverage Profiler is an excellent tool to identify the bottlenecks in your application as well as what code is not executed. It allows Fox developers to be more efficient at problem solving in the development environment. The Coverage Profiler is not available at run-time, even with the addition of SET COVERAGE logging.

Getting back to the client with the slow performing feature in your application, you can now SET COVERAGE TO C:\temp\CoverageFile.TXT to start logging and SET COVERAGE TO to stop logging. Remember, just like in the development environment, these files can get large quickly. You might want to consider carefully placing the command to begin and stop logging. Your customers do not have the Visual FoxPro debugger to interactively control logging. Chances are very good you will need to send your client a build with strategically placed SET COVERAGE commands to turn logging on and off. The user runs the code and generates the logs. Another approach might include a combination of a local table and event binding strategy to start and stop the logging. After the logs are generated, the user compresses the files with WinZip or another compression tool and either e-mails the file or loads it to a FTP site where you can download it.

Unfortunately, nothing like this is free in our world. There is an issue with the logs recorded in the production environment. It shows the source code files in the log with a full path to the production directory where the EXE is loaded, plus the development directories to the source code file (as it is stored inside the application executable). If the source code is not in the directory tree directly below the project (like a common folder), the path is relative to the EXE folder. This means the coverage logs your clients send to you have paths different from the full source code path you have for your project. Here is an example. The first executable was run and logged in the project directory (see **Figure 1**). The second log was generated from a separate temporary "production" directory (see **Figure 2**).

What happens when your user sends you coverage logs with improper paths? You are prompted numerous times to locate each of the source code files recorded in the log entries when you start the Coverage Profiler. If your project code is anything like ours, you probably have numerous class libraries, programs, reports, and so forth scattered in various directories. You will spend time either locating the files, or ignoring the messages and not running the Coverage Profiler for the log. Is there any way around this? Sure, you can write a tool that preprocesses the coverage log and substitutes the production paths with the correct project source code path. Sound like fun? Sure, you are a Fox developer and quite accustomed to writing your own tools.

 *Included in the Developer Downloads for this chapter available from **www.hentzenwerke.com** is a form called CoverageLogPathFixer.scx/sct. This tool presents a user interface to help facilitate the path correction process between production and development directory structures.*

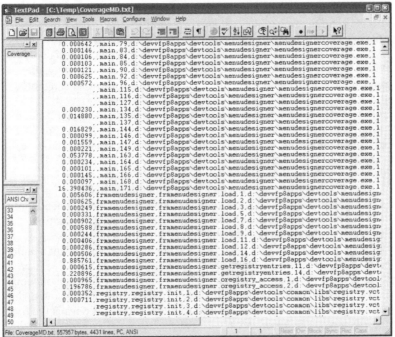

Figure 1. *The path collected in a coverage log run from the project root source directory records the proper path to the source code.*

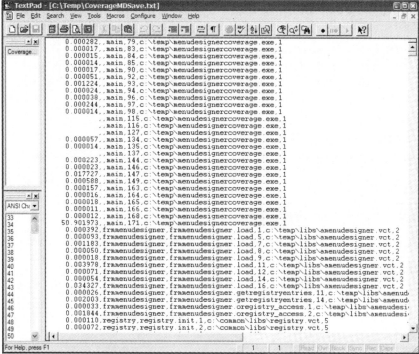

Figure 2. *The paths collected in a coverage log run from the production directory do not map to the source code.*

The Coverage Log Path Fixer (**Figure 3**) is very simplistic. Select the production coverage log file sent to you by your customer, either by entering the path and file name in the text box or by using the button to select the file name. Selecting the file triggers a few features:

- The tool creates a name for the fixed coverage log file by using the same name as the production log and adding "_fixed" to the end of the file name stem.

- It reads the production log file into a cursor.

- It enables the Edit Fix file button.

- It evaluates the cursor and presents the unique production paths in the second grid.

Select each of the unique production paths in the grid one-by-one. You can type in the development path or use the Select Directory button to the right of the grid to select the folder via the GETDIR() dialog. Each production path must have a development path assigned; if not a message displays when you try to fix the paths. The folders must exist. Once the directories are selected, press the Fix Paths button. If the file is created and the paths fixed, the Edit Fixed File button is enabled and the Fix Paths button is disabled. You can use the Edit Fixed File button to review the new file.

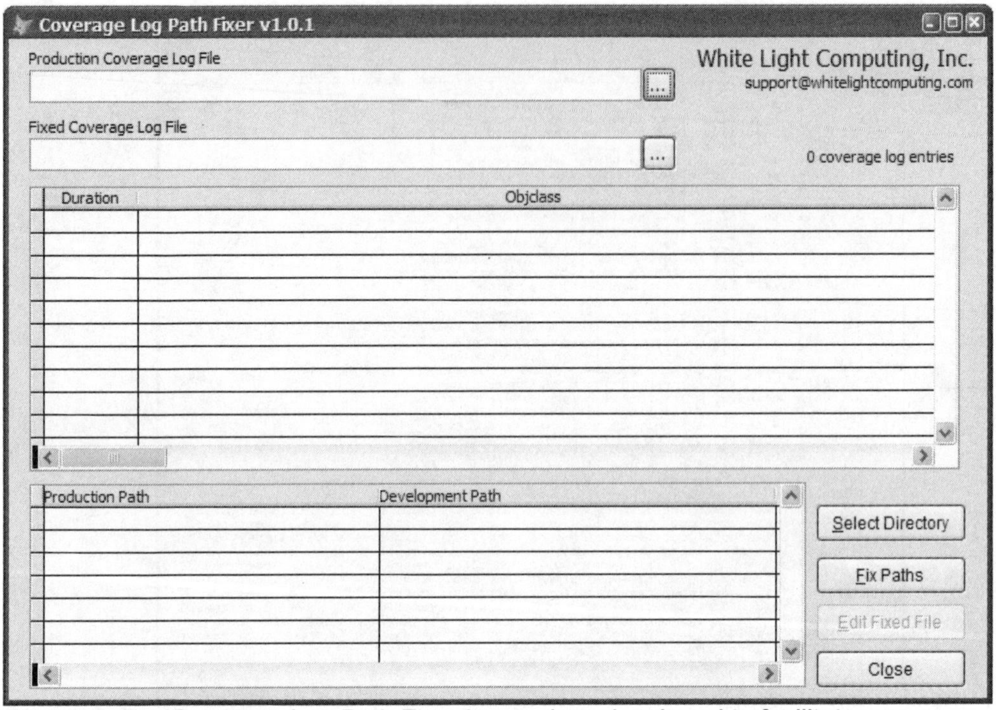

Figure 3. *The Coverage Log Path Fixer is a tool we developed to facilitate the correction of production paths to the source code paths on your development machine.*

Once the fixed file is created, start the Coverage Profiler to test the new file. The Coverage Profiler should open with the timings and coverage recorded in production, but it is compared to the source code on your development machine.

> *When you compare the coverage logs to the source code, you need to have the exact source code used to generate the production executable. Chances are, if you have an active client project, your source code has changes in the process of being readied for a future deployment. You need to archive the source code if you intend to use the coverage logging in production.*

Improved performance and support detecting Terminal Server

Visual FoxPro 9 automatically adds to each EXE support for running better in a Terminal Server session. The build process now includes the /TSAWARE flag as a new LINK command for your Visual FoxPro executable file. You do not have to do anything additional; this is automatically built into the executable each time you build the project into an EXE. This internal flag is used by the run-time loader to prevent the loading of unnecessary dynamic-link library (DLL) files, which impacts the performance of your applications.

If you read this chapter during the VFP 9 beta, you read about the use of EditBin.EXE to turn the /TSAWARE flag off if your application opens an INI file. This issue is no longer valid and there is no need to run EditBin.EXE for VFP 9.

You can view the change in the EXE only in a hex editor (**Figure 4**). We are not recommending this, but some developers might be curious about the change. Our research shows the /TSAWARE flag is at offset 14F (set to 0x8000).

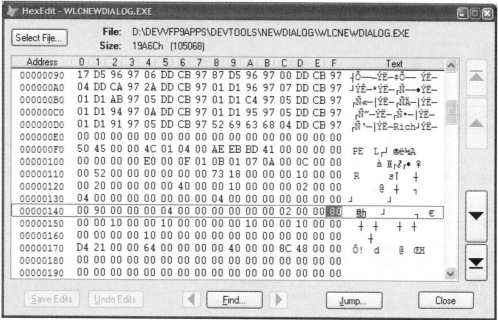

Figure 4. *You can use the HexEdit tool that ships with Visual FoxPro to view the /TSAWARE setting in the EXE you build.*

According to the Fox Team, you can use the .NET 2003 Visual C Link command to reveal the setting. The Terminal Server Aware setting is found under the Optional Header Values section. The command is run using the following syntax:

```
link /dump /headers WlcNewDialog.exe
```

Updated Dr. Watson error reporting to 2.0

Dr. Watson is the applet all users hate to see displayed (see **Figure 5**) as their program crashes and prepares to send some information to Microsoft. The applet has improved and is installed to capture errors when Visual FoxPro 9 crashes or when your application crashes with a "C5" or General Protection Fault (GPF) type error. The new and improved applet does a better job collecting important information Microsoft uses to find problem code in Visual FoxPro. Dr.

Watson 2.0 can also record your crashes when you are not connected to the Internet, and then report them back to Microsoft when you re-establish your connection.

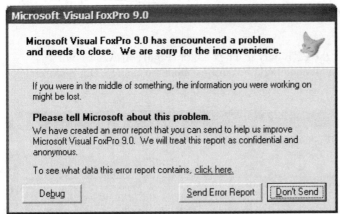

Figure 5. *Dr. Watson Error reporting provides some new features with respect to errors sent to Microsoft.*

The new Dr. Watson applet also lets you view the information sent to Microsoft. You access this information using the click here hyperlink. A dialog with the error signature and several paragraphs of privacy information displays (see **Figure 6**). This dialog has a View the contents of the error report hyperlink. Clicking the hyperlink displays the details of the error report (see **Figure 7**).

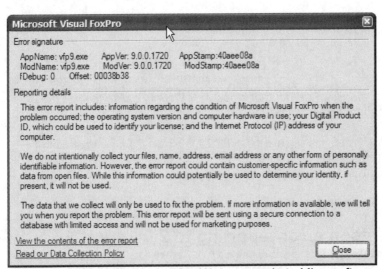

Figure 6. *The details of what Dr. Watson sends to Microsoft are prefixed with a privacy dialog (maybe Dr. Watson is an attorney).*

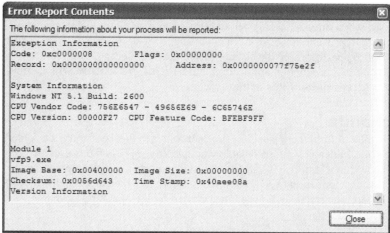

Figure 7. The Error Report Contents dialog is provided so you can review the information and verbose details sent to Microsoft for their review.

> If you read this chapter during the Visual FoxPro 9 beta, you read about non-critical errors being recorded in addition to the critical errors. This is not included in the shipping product.

If you think these error reports go into a bit bucket, fear not. The Product Support Services (PSS) team on the Fox Team reviews all the submissions looking for ways to improve the stability of Visual FoxPro.

New configuration settings

You have a new Config.FPW setting to help control the amount of memory dedicated to programs. The PROGCACHE is available to determine the amount of internal program cache Visual FoxPro applications, the development IDE, or a MTDLL COM Server allocate when they are started. When Visual FoxPro reaches the memory limits established by the setting, it flushes allocated memory to free memory.

PROGCACHE was created primarily for multithreaded DLL COM servers. MTDLL COM Servers often have many threads created on a single server and this configuration setting provides you better control of memory usage.

The setting is the number of pages of memory you want allocated. Each page is equivalent to 64K of memory. You can set the PROGCACHE from 1 to 65,000 (positive or negative) to designate how much memory is allocated. If you specify zero, no program cache is used and VFP uses dynamic memory allocation determined by the operating system. If you set the PROGCACHE to a negative number, VFP uses dynamic memory allocation, but is limited to the number of memory pages you specified. The default setting is 144 (over 9 megabytes) for single-threaded EXEs and the VFP IDE, and -2 (128 kilobytes) for a multi-threaded DLL. The VFP OLE DB Provider does not use this setting because it uses dynamic memory allocation.

It is possible that Visual FoxPro cannot free enough memory. In this case your error handler will be exercised when error 1202 is generated (Program is too large). You can adjust the PROGCACHE setting to prevent this error from occurring.

You can call SYS(3065) to determine the current PROGCACHE setting. This is not something you typically do in a production application, but CLEAR PROGRAM will attempt to clear unreferenced code regardless of this setting.

FoxRun.PIF change

The FoxRun.PIF file is moved from the Visual FoxPro root folder to the Tools\FoxRun folder. It should reside in the same folder as your executable when deployed. This file is used to control which operating system ComSpec is used by the RUN command. If you do not deploy a FoxRun.PIF file, and your application executes the RUN command, the current behavior of VFP is to use the command interpreter shell program specified by the operating system ComSpec environment variable.

> *You can determine the operating ComSpec setting by shelling out to the DOS command window, and typing in SET. This will list all the environment variables. You can also use the My Computer properties dialog. On the Advanced page is a button which displays the Environment Variables dialog (see **Figure 8**).*

Figure 8. In Windows XP you can review and set the ComSpec environment variable from the My Computer properties Advanced page.

> FoxRun.PIF is still configured to use Command.COM. This is different from the VFP 9 beta, in case you were testing your applications with beta code.

You should be aware of some differences when deciding which command interpreter you want to deploy with your applications. Command.COM is the single-threaded, 16-bit equivalent of MS-DOS embedded in Windows. On NT-based systems, Command.COM starts a basic DOS window in a "virtual DOS machine." The command line does not support long file names. This means you need to address the folders and file names with the 8.3 file naming standard. Folder names longer than eight characters require the tilde plus the number when you change folders using the change directory (CD) command. We have read you cannot run 32-bit applications from the Command.COM window; however, we have run a 32-bit application, like Excel on Windows XP. The difference is the command line is not available until the program is closed, demonstrating the single-threaded nature of Command.COM.

Cmd.EXE is the Windows 32-bit command interpreter, which launches the multi-threaded Windows NT command shell. You get long file names, an extended batch language, file and directory name completion, native command history, and access to NT services and security. Under Windows NT/2000, the command line is limited to 2047 characters. Under Windows XP, the command line is limited to 8191 characters.

One of the differences that might catch you off guard is the difference in the location of the temporary folder. If the application you are running uses the RUN command to look for a temporary file your application created in the temporary folder, the location could be different if you use Command.com as the interpreter in FoxRun.PIF.

InstallShield Express FoxPro Limited Edition

The version of InstallShield Express – Visual FoxPro Limited Edition (ISX LE) has been upgraded to version 5.0 from version 3.5 Service Pack 4 by InstallShield. This means an improved and enhanced interface, some additional features that may benefit your deployment packages, and the same limitations implemented in the version shipped with Visual FoxPro 8. The limited edition remains one major version behind the flagship InstallShield X Express offered directly from InstallShield (purchased by Macrovision).

Among the features still disabled in ISX LE are Custom Actions, Dynamic File Linking, Globalization, and File Dependency Scanning. Although you can get along without these and the other disabled features, you may wish you had them if you do a lot of setup development. Here is a list of the features disabled in ISX LE shipping with Visual FoxPro 9 compared to the full version of ISX v5.0.

- Support for Visual Studio .NET (this refers to the integration with Visual Studio .NET, not the deployment of the .NET framework)

- Billboards

- Custom Actions

- Dynamic File Linking

- Environment Variables

- Globalization

- Import and Export String Tables

- Objects

- Scanning Wizards

- Setup Files

- Text and Messages

- System Software Requirements (like Acrobat, Internet Explorer, MDAC)—this is a new limitation with ISX LE shipping with Visual FoxPro 9, as this feature was not available in the version shipped with Visual FoxPro 8.

- IIS Virtual Directories and Component Services—this is a new limitation with ISX LE shipping with Visual FoxPro 9, as this feature was not available in the version shipped with Visual FoxPro 8.

- Web Deployment

Installation

The first significant difference you may notice if you have a previous version of InstallShield Express (v4.0 or earlier, limited or not) installed is the fact it is still installed when you install ISX LE v5.0. Until this release, InstallShield automatically uninstalled previous versions and replaced them with the current version. This means you can continue using the older version with older installs until you choose to update the installation project.

> *One word of caution: if the full version of ISX v5.0 is already installed on your machine, installing ISX LE v5.0 will render the full version inoperable. It doesn't uninstall it, just changes the registry keys to point at ISX LE.*

When you installed the ISX LE shipped with Visual FoxPro 8, it removed the version you installed with Visual FoxPro 7 (or the full version purchased from InstallShield) and forced you to update the project files. In most cases this was not a problem, but as a developer approaching a deadline, you might not feel confident in releasing with new deployment software until you have a chance to test it. This is a significant advantage from our perspective.

Project Assistant

The second significant difference is the Project Assistant replaces the Project Wizard (**Figure 9**). Conceptually they are the same, assisting you with initial selections for your installation project, but the Project Assistant is better organized, includes a few more property settings, and is re-entrant.

There is no requirement to use the Project Assistant to create a new InstallShield project, but it can speed up the initial project selections in a sequence different than stepping through the choices in the Installation Designer (treeview of the steps processed in both version 3.5 and version 5.0). You answer a few questions, make a few selections, and the properties for the project fill in according to your choices.

If you do not like the Project Assistant you can remove it from the user interface by unselecting the menu item View | Project Assistant.

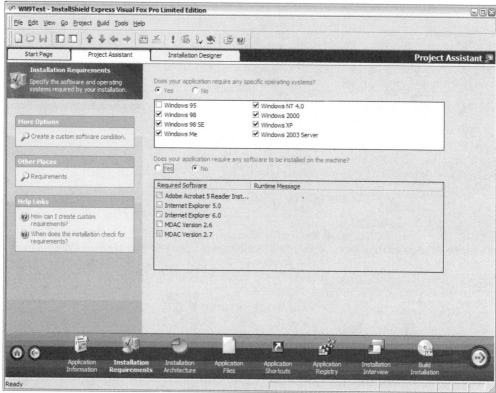

Figure 9. *The Project Assistant provides logical and rapid access to the common property settings for your InstallShield project.*

Once the Project Assistant is complete, you will find yourself going to the Installation Designer to make additional settings and customizing the installation package even further.

Redistributable Downloader

InstallShield has numerous merge modules available on their support Web site. All you have to do is go to the site (it is open even to developers who use other Windows Installer routines such as Wise for Windows Installer), pick the merge modules you want to use with ISX LE and install them after downloading. This version of InstallShield Express Limited Edition has a built-in wizard called the Redistributable Downloader (see **Figures 10** and **11**) that downloads and installs merge modules, third-party redistributables, and other files for you to use in your InstallShield Express Limited Edition projects.

The process is very straightforward. Start the wizard from the Tools | Redistributable Downloader menu. The first step is the introduction page, the second step is the merge module selection page, and the third page shows the progress of the download.

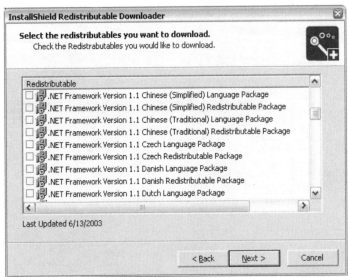

Figure 10. The second step of the InstallShield Redistributable Downloader wizard presents a list of merge modules you can download from the InstallShield Web site.

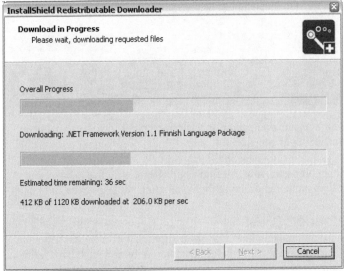

Figure 11. The third step of the InstallShield Redistributable Downloader wizard shows the progress of downloading the selected merge modules.

DemoShield Browser Wizard

The DemoShield Browser Wizard is, well, demo-ware. DemoShield is a separate product available for purchase from InstallShield assisting you in the creation of professional multimedia material you can include on the installation CD-ROM. This multimedia material can showcase your application, provide interactive demonstrations and simulations of the features (via animated screen shots), and provide additional contact information such as a link to your Web site. You can use the DemoShield Screen Capture Wizard to capture the screens, and then add in your own voiceovers describing the functionality as well as captions and callouts.

There is a 30-day evaluation of DemoShield included in the installation package. The wizard steps you through the entire process of creating the DemoShield database, but unless you purchase a separate license, it is not a good use of your time. More details on DemoShield are available at **http://www.installshield.com/ds/**.

Help

The new Help file merges the InstallShield Express and Windows Installer Help files into one file. Naturally, the information is updated to conform to the current feature set.

Product functionality changes

There are numerous enhancements between the limited edition shipped with Visual FoxPro 8 and 9. The following sections address only the changes. They do not describe in detail how to use the new features in the limited edition, only why you might find the functionality useful in your deployments.

Features

The Features functionality exposes the Key Name (read-only). This is the MSI Key used internally in the MSI database to represent the feature. If you select to purchase the full version of InstallShield Express, according to the documentation, the Key Name can be used in Custom Actions, but is read-only even in the full version.

Files

The Files destination folder pane has some new predefined folders in the list including [ALLUSERSPROFILE] and [USERPROFILE]. The InstallShield development team also removed the [COMMONFILES64FOLDER], [PROGRAMFILES64FOLDER], and [SYSTEM64FOLDER] predefined folders. If you used any of the removed destination folders, you need to verify that upgrading existing InstallShield project files converts the folders for any files you directed to these obsolete directories.

Redistributables

The Objects/Merge Modules step is renamed the Redistributables step. Two of the challenges Visual FoxPro developers face when assembling a deployment package are determining which merge modules to include in the package and locating the merge modules available. Prior to the new version, to determine the files included in a merge module you needed to use a product like the Orca MSI table editor from Microsoft, or some Microsoft Installer tool that could read the merge module and determine what was inside. ISE LE v5.0 provides a view inside the merge modules we think you will find very useful.

Dependencies and the list of files included in the merge module display in the Description pane (lower left pane to the right of the treeview – see **Figure 12**). This feature was introduced in the full version of InstallShield Express v4.0, but because Visual FoxPro developers did not get a limited edition of this version, it is new in version 5.0 of the limited edition. This is very useful for confirming a particular merge module includes the file(s) you want to install. The tool shows the Microsoft Visual FoxPro 9 Runtime Libraries merge module installs three

Visual FoxPro run-time files (see Figure 12) and is dependent on the Microsoft C Runtime Library 7.1 and GDI Plus Redist modules.

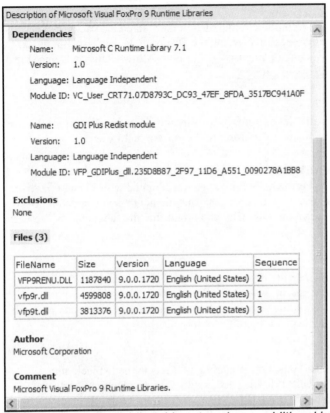

Figure 12. The Redistributables step shows additional information about the merge module including dependencies and what files are included for distribution when you select the module.

Earlier in the chapter (see "Redistributable Downloader") we covered the Redistributable Downloader and how you can download new or updated merge modules. The Redistributables feature helps developers locate merge modules available for download. The Redistributables view shows the list of merge modules; this list now shows different icons to indicate the status of merge modules and objects (see **Figure 13**). **Table 1** details the various settings.

Table 1. *The Redistributables view now shows icons in front of the merge module or object name. These icons have the following status.*

Icon	Status
	This object is installed on your computer
	This object is not installed, but is available for download.
	This object is installed on your computer, but is an old version. A new version is available for download.
	This merge module is installed on your computer.
	This merge module is not installed, but is available for download.
	This merge module is on your computer, but is an old version. A new version is available for download.

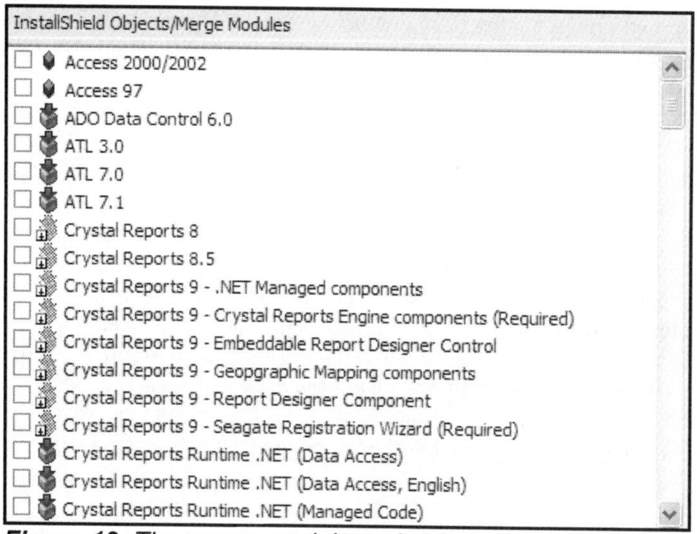

Figure 13. *The merge module and object status icons display in the InstallShield Objects/Merge Modules pane on the Redistributables page.*

The advantage for developers is two-fold: you can tell what merge modules/objects you do not have, but are available for download, and you can find out which modules/objects you do have, but are obsolete or out-of-date.

Shortcuts/Folders

The Shortcuts/Folders step has a new option to create an uninstall shortcut. This allows your users to uninstall the application without accessing the Windows Control Panel Add/Remove Programs applet. The new Uninstall Shortcut feature is not easy to find; it is only available on a shortcut menu when you select a folder in the shortcut treeview. You can set properties for the Description, Arguments to MsiExec.exe when running the uninstall, the Target (this is the uninstall program, defaulting to MsiExec.exe), Icon File and Icon Index, Run (normal, maximized, or minimized window), the Working Directory, a Hot Key, Comments, and which of your defined Features this shortcut is associated with (this is only available to change for Uninstall shortcuts, not regular or advertised shortcuts).

Cut/copy/paste options have been added to shortcut menus for custom folders and shortcuts.

ODBC Resources

InstallShield moved the ODBC attributes to the upper right pane, and Associated Features to the lower center pane. This is a purely cosmetic change. Additional attributes for the SQL Server and Visual FoxPro DSNs include Database destination, Permanent, and Driver Description. In general, reviewing other data sources, most have additional properties available in the new version of ISX LE.

Dialogs

The Setup Complete Success dialog found under the Dialogs step has a new option to Use Update Service User Interface. This functionality is off by default and can only be turned on if the Update Service feature is turned on under step five, Enable Automatic Updates. One note of caution: if you enable the update service, you disable the Show Launch Program and Show ReadMe options on this same dialog.

Enable Automatic Updates

If you are using the InstallShield Update Service, there is a new option where you can specify a self-hosting site via the Host property. If you are not familiar with the Automatic Updates functionality, it is a product and a service directly offered by InstallShield. It works on the same premise as Windows Update, automatically downloading and installing new versions of your applications. This service automates the entire update process from notifying your customers a new version of your application is available, all the way through the process of installation. This service eliminates the need for you to burn CD-ROMs and distribute them to the users, or instructing your customers to download and install the update from a Web site. The pricing for this service depends on the volume of customers downloading the updates. More information is available at **http://www.installshield.com/products/updateservice/**.

Requirements

InstallShield Express version 5 introduces Windows 2003 Server to the list of selectable operating systems required/supported for your deployment package.

One of the shortcomings of using one of the older versions of InstallShield Express is the operating system list is usually outdated. If you do not have a complete list of operating systems, you cannot use the Operating System Requirements feature to eliminate unsupported operating systems because doing so also eliminates newer operating systems.

In the case of ISX LE shipped with VFP 7, you quickly lost the ability to use this feature because Windows XP was not on the list. The version of ISX LE shipped with VFP 8 does not have Windows 2003 Server on the list of operating systems you can deploy your application on. Therefore, to really be current, you need to use InstallShield Express v5.0 (limited edition or full edition), or InstallShield X Express (only available as the full version). The other option is not to restrict installations based on the operating system the user has installed on the target computer.

Build Your Release

There are a couple of new features with respect to building the installation package: DemoShield file names, support for the .NET Framework, and a new way to review the log files generated by the build.

Each of the physical media builds (CD-ROM, DVD, or Custom) has a new property called Demo File Name. This feature is not available for diskette, Web deployments, or SingleImage releases. The Demo File Name allows you to specify a fully qualified path to a DemoShield Browser Database file (DBD extension). The DemoShield Browser Database can be created by selecting the DemoShield Browser Wizard option on the Project menu (described earlier in this chapter in the section called "DemoShield Browser Wizard.") This wizard steps you through the various selections necessary to build the DBD file and sets the Demo File Name property for the build.

The .NET Framework Location properties are new to this version of ISX LE. Visual FoxPro developers typically do not release the .NET framework with their deployment packages. The main reason this is included is because the Limited Edition is also distributed with Borland's Delphi, C++ Builder and C# Builder.

The log files generated by the build are available under the media type (see **Figure 14**) if you drill down in the Builds treeview to the Logs node. This feature was available in the previous version of ISX LE. The new feature with respect to the log is the availability of a hyperlink in the build output at the end of the listing, right after the counts for error and warning for the build. Click the hyperlink to open the log in the application associated to the TXT extension (by default, Notepad). This saves you from resizing the output pane in InstallShield Express, or the need to drill through the build treeview to get access to the current log.

Menus and toolbars

The menu has several minor changes to incorporate new features and expose existing functionality differently:

- The Project menu has a DemoShield Browser Wizard option, used to create a DemoShield Browser Database.

- The Build menu has Quick Build (not available in ISX LE) and Uninstall options.

- The Tools menu has Create Quick Patch (not available in ISX LE) and Redistributable Downloader options (see Figure 10).

- The Help menu has links to the InstallShield Support Web site, InstallShield Community (online help forums with peer-to-peer support), and InstallShield Home Page.

The main toolbar has a new button to run the Uninstall functionality.

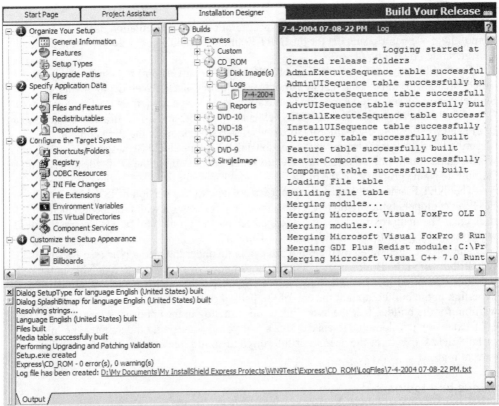

Figure 14. *A history of the build log files is in the treeview under the build type. The current log file is accessible through the hyperlink at the end of the build output.*

Tools Option dialog

The Tools Option dialog has new functionality as well as some removed functionality. The settings made on this dialog are general settings used for all installation projects.

The General page has a new option to stop the build process when the first error occurs. This is great for large projects when a build could take 10 minutes. Allowing it to stop when the error occurs could save several minutes per build when you first set up the project.

Merge Module locations have moved from the File Locations page to the new Merge Module Options page.

The all-new Preferences page has two options for you to configure: Uninstall before installing, and Reload last opened project on startup. It is not uncommon for a developer to work repeatedly with the same InstallShield Express project file, so selecting this option saves you time opening the project via the menu. The option is not new, just the location where you set it is new. Previously this was set on the Installshield Today page in version 3.5.

Merge Module search behavior options on the Merge Module Options page is a great feature. If you add a file to the project, ISX searches all the installed merge modules to see if the file is available in the merge module. You have options to define how ISX determines if it uses the merge module or the file you included:

- Matching files must have the same version

- Matching files must have the same destination

The all-new Quality page allows you to participate in an InstallShield survey. This is optional; you select whether you want to spend the time helping InstallShield improve their product.

The InstallShield developers removed the option to select when updates are processed (when launched or never) on the InstallShield Updates page.

The .NET page is completely new (.NET was not supported in the previous version). You use this page only if you leverage ISX LE for any .NET releases you make. This page has settings for the location of the .NET product files and the ability to determine how the .NET Scan at Build property is set. The all-new Files View page allows you to select the columns displayed on the Files view.

InstallShield X Express

As noted earlier in this chapter, the limited edition is one version behind the flagship InstallShield X Express product. If you find the limitations of the version included with Visual FoxPro a serious problem for your installation packages, you may want to consider getting the full version.

> *If you want to compare the features available in the ISX LE v5.0 and the full version of InstallShield X Express (Standard, Professional, and Premier), check out the information on the InstallShield Web site at:*
> **http://www.installshield.com/products/x/express/features/le_compare.asp**

Summary

The Fox Team at Microsoft and the InstallShield team have both added a number of features to make deployment and support of your applications easier. We think you will agree that the changes will save you time and give your installation setups a more professional and polished look.

Updates and corrections for this chapter can be found on Hentzenwerke's website, **www.hentzenwerke.com**. Click "Catalog" and navigate to the page for this book.

Index

Note that you can download the PDF file for this book from **www.hentzenwerke.com** (see the section "How to download files" at the beginning of this book). The PDF is completely searchable and provides additional keyword lookup capabilities not practical in an index.